LIVING FEMINISM

RESHAPING AUSTRALIAN INSTITUTIONS

Series editors: Geoffrey Brennan and Frances G. Castles, Research School of Social Sciences, Australian National University.

Published in association with the Research School of Social Sciences, Australian National University.

This program of publications arises from the School's initiative in sponsoring a fundamental rethinking of Australia's key institutions before the centenary of Federation in 2001.

Published in this program will be the work of scholars from the Australian National University and elsewhere who are researching and writing on the institutions of the nation. The scope of the program includes the institutions of public governance, intergovernmental relations, Aboriginal Australia, gender, population, the environment, the economy, business, the labour market, the welfare state, the city, education, the media, criminal justice and the Constitution.

Brian Galligan   *A Federal Republic*
Patrick Troy (ed.)   *Australian Cities*
Ian Marsh   *Beyond the Two Party System*
Elim Papadakis   *Environmental Politics and Institutional Change*

This book is dedicated to two generations of feminists: Edna, Julia and Lyndall. Edna Ryan was a political 'mother' to many Australian feminists. Lyndall has been unfailing in her intellectual and emotional generosity as a colleague, while also showing me the deft ways in which feminist academics can use their position and knowledge to work for feminist outcomes.

LIVING FEMINISM

THE IMPACT OF THE WOMEN'S MOVEMENT ON THREE GENERATIONS OF AUSTRALIAN WOMEN

CHILLA BULBECK

CAMBRIDGE UNIVERSITY PRESS

PUBLISHED BY THE PRESS SYNDICATE OF THE UNIVERSITY OF CAMBRIDGE
The Pitt Building, Trumpington Street, Cambridge CB2 1RP, United Kingdom

CAMBRIDGE UNIVERSITY PRESS
The Edinburgh Building, Cambridge CB2 2RU, United Kingdom
40 West 20th Street, New York, NY 10011-4211, USA
10 Stamford Road, Oakleigh, Melbourne 3166, Australia

© Cambridge University Press 1997

This book is in copyright. Subject to statutory exception
and to the provisions of relevant collective licensing agreements,
no reproduction of any part may take place without
the written permission of Cambridge University Press.

First published 1997

Printed in Australia by Print Synergy

Typeset in New Baskerville 10/12 pt

National Library of Australia Cataloguing in Publication data
Bulbeck, Chilla, 1951– .
Living feminism: the impact of the women's movement on
three generations of Australian women.
Bibliography.
Includes index.
ISBN 0 521 46042 5.
ISBN 0 521 45596 6 (pbk.).
1. Feminists – Australia – Interviews. 2. Women – Australia
– Interviews. 3. Feminism – Australia – History – 20th
century. 4. Women – Australia – Social conditions – 20th
century. I. Title.
305.420994

A catalogue record for this book is available from the British Library

ISBN 0 521 46042 5 hardback
ISBN 0 521 45596 6 paperback

Contents

List of Tables — viii
Preface — ix
List of Women Who Told their Biographies for the Book — xiii
Abbreviations — xxiii

Introduction — 1

Part One: Women's Lives Through A Feminist Lens — 19

1 Growing Up As Girls — 26
2 Training For Life — 46
3 Work — 69
4 Marriage and Motherhood — 95

Part Two: Present and Future Feminisms — 123

5 Finding Feminism — 128
6 Is Feminism a White Middle-class Movement? — 156
7 Beating the Backlash — 182

Conclusion — 210

Appendix 1 — 226
Appendix 2 — 229
Notes — 231
Bibliography — 248
Index — 276

Tables

3.1:	Women as percentage of total workforce in different occupational groups, 1911–1992	70
3.2:	Distribution of women across occupational groups, 1994	71
4.1:	Mean hours per week spent on childcare, housework, paid work	115
A1.1:	Life chances of three generations of Australian women	226
A1.2:	Life chances of the sixty women in the study	227

Preface

In 1993 Anne Summers wrote a letter addressed to 'women who were born since 1969', claiming that the world in which they came of age was 'almost unrecognisable' to women like herself, born a generation earlier. She reminded these 'daughters' that abortion was no longer illegal and dangerous, that married and pregnant women were no longer fired, that women were now entitled to the same wages as men, that women no longer went to university to find husbands, that more women could be seen in politics and management (Summers 1993:195). Thus, according to Summers, a revolution has occurred but those born after its effects had become commonplace are unaware of the revolution.

I envisaged this book as my own 'letter to the next generation', a celebration of the tidal wave of post-war feminism. From my own history, such a celebration seemed called for. I am an exceptionally lucky beneficiary of feminism. On the occasions when I have considered an abortion, I have always been in a jurisdiction which allowed it. My job depends on feminism, and I am an extremely highly paid woman, earning about four times the average income for women and about twice that of men. Marlene Goldsmith (1994:181) suggests women with 'Dr' in front of their names are taken more seriously; certainly I rarely interact with men who are other than respectful, at least superficially. Feminism has allowed me to refute the need for male emotional support and approval; I look to female friends rather than male lovers for my affirmation. Like many young women, I was 'date raped' during my university days although I did not define the experience as rape. While I was sexually assaulted four years ago while jogging, the other sustaining messages in my life allowed me to resist the assault and recover relatively speedily.

Born half-way through this century into the complacency of white middle-class Australia's post-war boom, I was given enough positive messages to notice the contradictory ones. As the eldest child in my family, I learned both to hand my dad a spanner as he fixed the car and to time a roast dinner following my mother's instructions. Although my parents expected all their children to complete university degrees and pursue interesting careers, my brother's household chores were limited to outside tasks. While university entrance was the expectation at the private girls' school I attended, we were to remain feminine as well as ambitious (see also Kaplan 1996:15). A school friend was not allowed to study three science subjects because it was 'unfeminine'; I was advised by a well-meaning teacher to curb my independence if I wanted boys to like me (she was probably right). Although anti-Vietnam war protests coloured my university days, I can remember reading Germaine Greer's *The Female Eunuch*, although I cannot remember who told me to read it or what I made of it. For me, women novelists like Lisa Alther and Fay Weldon offered a far more powerful message – that failed heterosexual relations were the fault of inadequate men and not their independent, clever, female protagonists. However, feminism's message did not reach me forcefully enough to prevent me from marrying in the hope that I would deflect the taunt: 'No wonder she's not married, she's so fat, she's so ugly'. But I knew enough about women's liberation to expect my husband to do half the housework, although he didn't. When we divorced, a scarce two years later, I had enough sense to keep the house which he agreed to in exchange for the car and a good deal of money.

Anne Summers and I share not only the same alma mater, but also a similar ethnic and class background. Australian feminism has long been criticised for solely serving the interests of white middle-class women, despite (or perhaps because of) the lack of research concerning changes in the lives and attitudes of women who did not 'make' women's liberation. My conviction that I would write a celebratory letter to the next generation has been undermined by the weight of testimony from women who do not share my privileged class and ethnic background. While some of the sixty women with whom I spoke share at least some of my privilege, I also spoke with women who are not white and middle-class, who did not make the women's movement, who live or have lived outside the capital cities, who are daughters facing today's harsher economic climate. In general, these women have struggled on far more fronts than I have.

These women told me about their experiences of education, work, marriage and motherhood; about discrimination and inequality; about early dreams sometimes lately realised. But more significantly, they spoke to me about how they have changed; how they redefined themselves and their relationships in the light of new opportunities, how they grappled with feminism and its vertiginous possibilities. They revealed how lives defined by nappies, economic necessity, or difficult marriages intersected with both the structural changes in women's opportunities for education, work, independent living and the new interpretations of those changes offered by feminism. This is not, then, another book about 'official' feminism, based on archives or interviews with those who made it happen, but a book about how 'ordinary' women grappled with the meanings of the women's movement in terms of their own lives.

This is a book about two years, and about eighty years, and about thousands of years. Most immediately, it is a book concerning how sixty women across three generations thought about their lives and feminism in 1994 and 1995 when I spoke to them. But in their reminiscences, women have understood the present in terms of life histories which stretch back for up to eighty years. These life histories, in turn, are embedded in a longer chain of women's activism, which feminists like to think is older than the coining of feminism as a term in the early nineteenth century, an activism which includes rebellious actions of women in Europe in the fifteenth century, in Arabia in the seventh century and India in the eighth century (Rowbotham 1992:8, 18–19). In Australia, it might be claimed that feminism is older than white colonisation, part of the dreamings of Indigenous Australian women who tell of matriarchs, both legendary and temporal.

Heartfelt thanks go to those women who opened their lives and their houses to me: Jan Anderson, Nadine Behan, Laila Bjornsson, Auriel Bloomfield, Noela Blackmore, Berenice Carrington, Kerry Charlton, Mayra Christiansen, Barbara Colledge, Del Douglas, Hanna Drewiecki, Margaret Ekeberg, Deanna Eriksen, Audrey Evans, Yasmin Evans, Sue Ferguson, Teresa Forest, Indrani Ganguly, Rachel Grahame, Fiorenza Jones, Glenn Keller, Therese Ngoc Le Dang, Margaret Lewins, Alison Main, Valerie Hall Mathews, Aileen Moreton-Robinson, Matina Mottee, Halina Netzel, Pat O'Hara, Gisela Possin, Yvonne Protheroe, Gladys Revelo, Lea Stevens, Shirley Su-Lan Huang, Amber Stanley, Rita Tomasella, Lita Vidal, Joan Whetton, Agnes Whiten, Mary Wilkins, Gerda Willemsen, Vera Woodward. And those who know who they are: Anna, Aquarius, Catherine, Claudia, Glenda, Grace, Helen, Jennifer, Lucinda, Martha, Melinda, Myra, Nikita, Phylis, Rosemary, Sage, Shona, Willow.

In particular, I would like to thank Halina Netzel, now sadly no longer with us, for offering me access to her superb network of women from different ethnic backgrounds in Brisbane; Aileen Moreton-Robinson for trusting me with introductions to Indigenous Australian relatives and friends; Angela Toppin (President of the Peninsula Branch of the Association of Women Educators) and Rosemary McBain (of FNQ Family Resource Services) for identifying contacts in Cairns; and Agnes

Whiten for suggesting further contacts with women active in ethnic women's affairs.

I thank Peter Mayer for alerting me to Anne Summers' and Collette Snowden's honours theses, and sending me copies of same; Jan Young for locating several New Zealand references; the Office of the Status of Women for sending me Riley-Smith's focus group analyses in 1992; Peter McDonald for his comments on the life chances data used to construct table A1.1; and Thelma Hunter for suggesting that I interview 'generations' of women rather than merely baby boomers. A substantial proportion of the research for, and draft preparation of, this book was undertaken in 1995 when I was a visiting fellow with the Reshaping Australian Institutions Project in the Research School of Social Sciences at the Australian National University. I would like to thank Carol Bacchi, Deborah Mitchell and John Braithwaite for their contributions towards establishing a gender strand within the Project, Frank Jones of the Sociology Department for welcoming me as a visitor and providing financial support for the transcription of some of the interview tapes. For tape transcription, I thank Beverley Bullpitt, Margaret Tyrie, Janice Mitchell, and Karen Yarrow. Finally, I would like to thank the anonymous reviewers for their constructive responses to earlier drafts and Phillipa McGuinness of Cambridge University Press for her enthusiasm and support for the project.

List of Women Who Told Their Biographies for the Book
(in alphabetical order within each generation)

The Grandmothers

Aquarius was born in 1927 in England, one of two children. Her parents were unskilled workers and Aquarius left school at the age of fourteen and has been a telephonist, factory worker, sales assistant, and bar worker. She emigrated to Australia with her first husband and her four children; she now lives with her third husband.

Barbara was born in 1925 in Woodley, England, one of a family of seven children. Her father leased a confectionery-cum-tobacconist shop and her mother was often unemployed. Barbara has worked as an assistant nurse and shop assistant. She has married three times and is now widowed. In 1992 she enrolled in a Bachelor of Arts course when she could not afford the materials needed for a fine arts course.

Fiorenza, born in 1930 in Milan, Italy, was an only child. Her father was an administrative clerk and her mother a 'modern woman'. Fiorenza emigrated to England where she met her husband; they moved to Africa and then Australia. She has raised four children, and completed a Diploma in Accounting, a Diploma in Community Work and a Bachelor of Arts (1991). She has worked in secretarial positions and is now a community development worker.

Glenn was born in 1922 in Tenterfield, New South Wales, to an orchardist family, one of two children. Her family background is English and Anglo-Australian. Although her teachers urged her to study medicine, Glenn became a qualified general nurse and later a geriatric nurse. After marriage and two children, Glenn worked in the family mixed business, returning to nursing when her husband died.

BIOGRAPHIES

Halina was born in the early 1920s to a wealthy Polish family, she had two siblings. When she and her husband emigrated to Australia after the Second World War, Halina worked in a factory, became an accredited interpreter and a tireless worker in the Brisbane community, including the presenter of programs on ethnic radio, 2EB. She passed away in 1996, leaving a husband and son.

Joan was born in 1917 in Adelaide to an Irish-Australian family; she has ten siblings. Her father was a cabinet maker and her mother a school teacher before she married. After clerical work during and after the war, Joan returned to university as a mature-age student, completing a social work diploma. She worked with Indigenous Australians in Darwin and New South Wales, her husband travelling with her to her work destinations. She is now widowed and has not had children.

Margaret was born in 1931 in Melbourne to a family of Celtic background, one of five children. Her father was in commerce. Margaret worked as a secretary and assistant, particularly in legal firms, in Melbourne, Papua New Guinea and Brisbane. She raised four children, is separated, and enrolled in a Bachelor of Arts course in 1993.

Matina was born in 1931 in Hobart to parents of Greek background, one of a family of six children. Her father ran a small business. After marrying and raising four children, Matina returned to paid work as an ethnic community worker and administrator. She has completed a Diploma in Community Organisations.

Myra, Anglo-Australian, was born in 1928 at Eden Hills on the fringes of Adelaide, and had a sister and a brother. Her father was a furniture maker and city shop owner. She left school at fourteen to become a shop assistant in the family shop. She married and raised four children, as well as working in the family shop.

Pat was born in 1925 in England, one of a family of three children. Because her family was poor she left school at the age of sixteen. She migrated to Australia with her first husband. After leaving him she ran a post office, worked in an import business and moved to Cairns with her third husband where she became active in the Women's Electoral Lobby and other women's groups. She has five children, including those in melded families.

Vera was born in 1914 in Atherton, Queensland, of Anglo-Australian background. She had three siblings. Her father owned a drapery business in which she worked after she completed her junior certificate. After the Second World War, during which she married and had a child, Vera co-managed the family cane farm, and was a partner and manager of a mixed business shop. She has long been active in community service in Cairns, especially the Girl Guides. She had four children, of whom three survive.

Yvonne, Anglo-Australian, was born in 1929 in Rockhampton, Queensland, in a family of two children. Her father was a saddler. She completed senior school year. She has two sons by her first marriage and a daughter by her second marriage, and between marriages worked as a senior clerk to support her family. She is active in the Queensland Country Women's Association and other community groups.

The Mothers

Agnes was born in 1942 in the Philippines. Her parents were public servants. Agnes completed a Bachelor of Engineering (Metallurgy) and worked as an engineer in the Philippines before meeting her husband and migrating to Australia. They have two sons. Agnes has been extensively involved in community work, has completed a Master of Science (Metallurgy) and a Bachelor of Arts (Japanese), and was the first Women's Advisor to the Catholic Archbishop of Brisbane in Queensland.

Alison was born in 1937 in Sydney, the only child of a couple with an Anglo-Australian background. Her father was a psychiatrist. Alison studied architecture when she left school, and worked as an architect for many years. She has no children but is now in a heterosexual partnership and has pursued a new career as an artist, following the completion of a master's degree in this field.

Amber was born in 1941 in Mullumbimby, New South Wales, to an Anglo-Australian family, one of three children. Her father left when the children were young and her mother worked in a number of small businesses in country towns. Amber married, gave birth to seven children (of whom four survive), and worked long hours on the family farms where she raised her children. Amber was finally able to return to study, choosing social work.

Anna was born in 1951 in Adelaide, one of two children. Her parents are post-war migrants from Latvia who ran a small business. After finishing her schooling, Anna completed a Bachelor of Economics degree and then a Master of Urban and Regional Planning degree. She worked as a town planner and public servant before marrying and working in the family business with her husband. They have two sons.

Audrey was born in 1933 in Longreach, Queensland, one in a family of ten children. Her mother was an Indigenous Australian foundling and her father worked in casual and unskilled labouring jobs. After leaving school Audrey worked in milk bars and a factory. Her family consists of four children, of whom **Yasmin** is her oldest daughter. Audrey has been married twice and is now widowed. She returned to study as a mature-age student, including enrolment in a masters degree.

Auriel was born in 1954 in Canberra. She is an Indigenous Australian, her father a temporary public servant (all his working life) and her mother a housewife. She has a brother, is married and has no children. After working as a typist and typist controller, Auriel completed a degree in comunications and has since been a senior public servant in a number of departments.

Catherine was born in 1947 in England, one of three children. Her parents were factory workers. She gained teaching qualifications after leaving school, married and had two sons. She returned to teaching soon after her first son was born and worked as a ministerial advisor before becoming a senior TAFE administrator.

Claudia was born of Anglo-Celtic Australian background in 1940 in Brisbane, one of two children. Her father was a radio technician. Claudia worked as a nurse's aide, researcher and bookkeeper before marrying and having seven children. She returned to mature-age study, divorced, completed a doctoral dissertation and became an academic.

Deanna was born in 1943 in Brisbane to an Anglo-Australian family, one of six daughters. Her father was a labourer. Deanna left school, completed a commercial course and worked as a book-keeper until she married. She had five children, returned to study and divorced. She has completed a degree and a Diploma of Education, hoping to return to her teenage dream of teaching.

Del was born in 1930 in the Philippines. Her father was an army engineer. Del has a Bachelor of Science in Elementary Education and a masters (incomplete), and worked as a teacher-librarian in Manila before migrating to Australia after her first husband died. She has five children. Del remarried in Australia but was unable to find work

BIOGRAPHIES

matching her qualifications and experience. She works in a voluntary capacity for the Filipino community in Brisbane.

Gerda was born in 1947 in Holland, one of a family of eight children. Her father was a paper maker. Gerda became a dress-maker before she married. She has had fourteen children, of whom thirteen survive.

Gisela was born in 1945 in Germany of Estonian background. She is an only child and her mother, working in hospital and hotel domestic work, raised Gisela on her own. After leaving high school, Gisela became a librarian. She married, had a son, and lived in Papua New Guinea for a time before divorcing. She later returned to study as a mature-age student to complete her Bachelor of Arts degree and professional diploma, working as a librarian since her divorce.

Glenda was born in 1949 in Maryborough, Queensland, to an Anglo-Australian family, one of three children. Her father was a council worker. She completed a Bachelor of Arts degree on leaving school, worked as a teacher and later completed a Bachelor of Laws degree and now has her own legal practice. She lives in a lesbian partnership with **Shona**.

Grace was born in 1943 in Townsville, Queensland, to an Anglo-Australian family, one of two children. Her father was an office worker. Grace married and raised two children while working as a teacher-aide librarian. She returned to study as a mature-age student, completing a Bachelor of Arts degree and a Graduate Diploma in Adult Vocational Education. She is now separated.

Hanna was born in the late 1940s in Poland, and completed an engineering degree after leaving school. After some setbacks she gained employment in Australia as an engineer. She is married and has two children.

Helen was born in 1945 in Dalby, Queensland, to an Anglo-Australian family, one of three children. She worked as a nurse, married a bank worker, and raised four children, including **Jennifer**. When the children were old enough, Helen worked in community health services and as an electoral officer before returning to study to complete a nursing degree.

Jan was born in 1943 in Atherton, Queensland, to an Anglo-Australian family, one of two children. Her father was a clerk and her mother a casual dress-making teacher. Jan completed her high school certificate, and worked as a stenographer/accounting machine operator prior to her marriage to a sugar-cane farmer. The couple have three children.

BIOGRAPHIES

Jane is the fictitious name of one of the mothers who asked that her true identity be disguised in relation to a discussion of reproductive choices.

Laila was born in 1945 in Norway. Her father was a gynaecologist and obstetrician, her mother a receptionist. Laila completed an art college degree, working as a receptionist and artist. She had three children before migrating with her husband to Australia, and has since had a further child. She is completing a Bachelor of Arts degree.

Lea was born in 1947 in Adelaide to an Anglo-Australian family, one of three children. She completed a Bachelor of Science degree and became a school principal, before entering parliament. She is married with two sons.

Lucinda was born in 1940 in Asia of European-background parents. She studied music and worked as a stenographer before marrying and having two children. She is now in her second marriage.

Marg was born in 1943 in Melbourne to an Anglo-Australian family, one of four children. Her father owned a dry-cleaning business. After completing high school, Marg did a commercial course and worked as a secretary prior to her marriage. She has two grown children, and returned to study as a mature-age student. She is now a senior public servant.

Martha, an Indigenous Australian, was born in the 1930s in south-east Queensland. She is married and gained a university degree as a mature-age student.

Mary was born in 1936 in Sydney to an Anglo-Australian family, one of three children. Her father owned a produce business which her mother took over when he died while the children were still young. Her mother also ran an SP bookmaking business. Mary married, moved to the country and had three children. She left her husband because of his alcoholism and returned to Sydney. She has completed a business course, and more recently, a welfare certificate. Mary is a community worker.

Noela was born in 1935 in Cairns, Queensland, to a family of Irish background, one of two children. Her father was a swimming pool manager and her mother the manager of the canteen at the pool. On finishing school Noela completed a degree and became a physical education teacher, joined the Sisters of Mercy where she taught, and later completed a Master of Arts in religious studies in the United States.

She left the Sisters and is now a senior co-ordinator in a Catholic girls' school.

Phylis was born in 1940 in Melbourne of Anglo- and Greek-background parents, one of two children. Her mother was a sex worker and her father a gambler and pimp. Phylis left school at thirteen and worked in a number of unskilled jobs before marrying. She had four children before leaving her husband. She returned to mature-age study and is now enrolled in a doctoral dissertation.

Rachel, of Anglo-Australian background, born in 1939 in Inverell, Queensland, is one of a family of five daughters. Her father was a country doctor. Rachel completed a Bachelor of Arts in politics, married and had three children, returning to the workforce as a teacher when the children were old enough. Rachel enrolled in a Master of Literature course in 1993 and has been a researcher for the *Australian Dictionary of Biography*.

Rita was born in 1946 in Italy to an Italian family of Austrian descent. Her family migrated to rural Australia in the post-war years. Rita left school at the age of sixteen, worked in factories and restaurants until she met her husband. They have three children and built up a catering business together.

Sage was born in 1944 in Bundaberg, Queensland, to an Anglo-Australian family, one of four children. Her father was a high school principal. Sage completed a degree, became a teacher, married and raised a son and two daughters, **Rosemary** and **Willow**. She divorced her husband, returned to teaching and is now head of a high school English and Performing Arts department. She lives in a lesbian relationship.

Shirley was born in the mid-1940s in Taiwan. She and her husband own separate businesses and have four children.

Shona was born in 1950 in Brisbane to a Celtic-Australian family, one of five children. Her father was a managing director of a medium-sized business. On leaving school she trained as a teacher, working in the profession until she became an academic. She recently completed a Master of Education degree and lives in a lesbian partnership with **Glenda**.

Sue was born in 1946 in Brisbane, the only child in an Anglo-Australian family. Her father was an aircraft engineer, her mother a chief censor during the war, working as a teacher after Sue was born. Sue is married to a teacher and also teaches. She has two sons and has returned to mature-age study to complete a Bachelor of Education degree and enrol in a Master's course in Women's Studies.

Teresa was born in 1949 in Lancashire, England, one of three children. Her father was a factory worker and her mother a spinner. She completed a Bachelor of Arts degree on leaving school in Australia and later enrolled in a Master of Arts course and completed a Graduate Diploma in Counselling. She rose in the education sector to become a school principal and is now a business woman. She has one son.

Therese was born in the late 1940s in Vietnam, her father was a doctor. She gained a degree in politics and economics and worked as a vice-consul. She and her family escaped as refugees after the fall of Saigon. Her husband died shortly after their arrival in Australia, leaving her to raise their three children. Therese has worked in the public service and is active in Vietnamese community organisations.

Valerie was born in 1941 in Mossman, Queensland, to an Anglo-Australian sugar farming family, one of two children. Valerie completed a three-year course in kindergarten training, becoming a kindergarten director before marrying her husband, who is now an Archbishop. She has raised five children as well as working in the church in a voluntary capacity.

The Daughters

Aileen was born in 1956 in Brisbane to an Indigenous Australian family, one of two children. For many years she did not know her father's identity, and her mother worked as a domestic or was unemployed. Aileen was raised by her grandmother, had two children of whom one survives, and is married. She has worked in a number of senior public service positions after completing her Bachelor of Arts degree in Sociology. She is presently an academic and enrolled in a doctoral dissertation.

Berenice was born in 1962 in Newcastle upon Tyne, England, one of six children. Her parents were teachers. On leaving school Berenice returned to England from Australia, completing a Master of Arts (Visual Arts) degree. She worked as a lecturer, artist and community arts development officer before returning to doctoral studies in 1994. She and her heterosexual partner own a small property in a town in rural South Australia.

BIOGRAPHIES

Gladys was born in 1956 in Uruguay, one of three children. Her father was a public servant. In Australia, Gladys has completed TAFE courses, worked as a community worker and ministerial advisor. She is married and has three children.

Indrani was born in the late 1950s in New Delhi, the only child of a communications engineer and amateur actor. She completed a master's degree in India and a doctorate in Australia, working in India before returning to Australia to marry, work as a policy officer and raise her small son.

Jennifer was born in the late 1960s in north Queensland. Her mother is **Helen**. Jennifer completed a Bachelor of Science degree after leaving school, and worked briefly as a laboratory assistant before becoming a police officer. She is married with a baby son.

Kerry was born in 1958 in Brisbane to an Indigenous Australian family, one of eight children. Her mother was a hotel cook. Kerry married and has three children. She worked as a kindergarten assistant, typist, bookkeeper and teacher aide before completing a degree in early childhood education. She is now a senior policy officer and divorced.

Lita was born in 1957 in Lima, one of seven children. Her father was a public servant. Lita completed a degree in social work, and emigrated to Australia where she left her first husband. She has worked as a social worker, remarried in Australia and has no children.

Mayra was born in 1956 in Brisbane to a melded Muslim family, one of ten children. Her father was a refugee from Yugoslavia who worked in factories in Australia. Mayra left school after intermediate, worked in service jobs before marrying and having two daughters. Since leaving her husband she has returned to study, enrolling in a Bachelor of Psychology course.

Melinda was born in 1969 in Ontario to an Anglo-Australian family, one of two children. Her father is an academic and her mother a senior public servant. Melinda completed her High School Certificate and a business course, working as an administrative assistant. She is single.

Nadine was born in 1957, one of three children in a northern New South Wales Anglo-Australian family of tomato farmers. She has completed a Bachelor of Arts degree, a Bachelor of Laws degree and a Diploma of Broadcast Journalism. Nadine is single, has a son, has worked as a sex worker and is now a community lawyer.

Nikita was born in 1957 in Brisbane to a large Indigenous Australian family. Her mother was a service worker. Nikita worked as a secretary before returning to study. She has completed a human services degree, and worked in the clerical, secretarial, welfare, administration and training fields. She is separated and has three children.

Rosemary was born in the late 1960s in Darwin. Her mother is **Sage**. Rosemary worked as a model before returning to university to complete a degree in film studies. She is single.

Willow was born in the late 1960s in Darwin. Her mother is **Sage**. Willow left school in grade 11, completing a secretarial course. She is single and has worked as a waitress, model, labourer and office manager. In 1996 she enrolled in a creative arts/film degree.

Yasmin was born in 1972 in Mount Isa, Queensland. Her father worked in the army and mining industry and her mother is **Audrey**. She worked briefly in an office after leaving school before enrolling in a Bachelor of Psychology course. She is engaged to be married to a Chinese-Australian.

Abbreviations

ABS	Australian Bureau of Statistics
ACTU	Australian Council of Trade Unions
AIS	Australian Institute of Sport
ANESBWA	Association of Non-English Speaking Background Women of Australia
ASEAN	Association of South East Asian Nations
ATSIC	Aboriginal and Torres Strait Islander Commission
CAMP	Campaign Against Moral Persecution
CAPOW!	Coalition of Participating Organisations of Women
CR	consciousness-raising
CWA	Country Women's Association
DEET	Department of Employment, Education and Training
EEO	Equal Employment Opportunities
FNQ	Far North Queensland
IDPOL	identity politics
IUD	intra-uterine device
IVF	in vitro fertilisation
NEAT	National Education and Training
NES	non-English speaking
OPAL	One People of Australia
RSL	Returned Services League
TAFE	Technical and Further Education
TEAS	Tertiary Education Assistance Scheme
UAW	Union of Australian Women
WEL	Women's Electoral Lobby
WICH	Women in Industry, Contraception and Health

Introduction

In 'The Blank Page', Isak Dinesen tells of a Spanish convent where framed wedding night sheets of aristocratic marriages hang on the walls. The blood on the sheets signals the virginal repute of princesses. But there is one sheet which is a blank page:

> It is in front of this piece of pure white linen that the old princesses of Portugal – worldly wise, dutiful, long-suffering queens, wives and mothers – and their noble old playmates, bridesmaids and maids-of-honor have most often stood still.
>
> It is in front of the blank page that old and young nuns, with the Mother Abbess herself, sink into deepest thought. (Dinesen 1957:105)

Sidonie Smith (1993:2–3) suggests that while these sheets are 'signatures of cultural expectations', the stories are not written by the princesses themselves. Rather, women's stories are written from their bodies, 'their bodies have expelled them'. In writing from their bodies, women comply with the cultural expectations of femininity – like being chaste on marriage – and unswervingly follow a biological destiny, to marry and have children. But even in this past time, not all women followed their destinies; one princess is represented by an unmarked sheet. Because her page is blank, the obvious implication is that she has even less to say than those who have followed their expected paths. However, the blankness of her page conjures up questions for all who see it. As I read this story, I wondered what those questions might be. Did this princess, in fact, not marry at all, but became a writer or traveller or Mother Abbess in another convent? If this is indeed her wedding sheet, what does it suggest of her parents and husband that they would permit a blank sheet to hang on the walls of the convent? Did her parents love and nurture a rebellious tomboy and encourage her to read and write? Did her husband acknowledge a woman of difference and encourage her talents?

According to Smith (1993:3), in the blank space 'woman's autobiographical fabrication becomes possible'. However, western women's lives are no longer blank pages on which others may write their stories. In Australia there has been a white feminist movement at least since the last decades of the nineteenth century. Even so, in the 1990s we are still apt to hear some feminist stories more often than others. Our understanding of the women's liberation movement has largely come to us through the women who 'made' it happen. These are women like Anne Summers, who went on from her pathbreaking honours thesis to turn a doctoral thesis into the best-selling book, *Damned Whores and God's Police*. She has worked as a journalist and editor both in Australia and the United States, and was Prime Minister Paul Keating's advisor in the 1993 federal election. Germaine Greer, the errant daughter of Australian feminism, wrote *The Female Eunuch* which became almost synonymous with women's liberation, even as the growing handful of Australian feminists repudiated her and her works. Women's liberation spawned femocracy and academic feminism; its denizens have not been tardy in telling their stories. But what of those women who have not as yet told their tales? This book explores the question: 'What has the women's movement meant to women who were not at its helm?' Despite the growing number of texts on the history of post-war feminism, there is still a blank page in women's experiences on which to write the significant or telling tales of those who experienced but do not claim to have made the women's movement.

Just as the princess whose sheet disrupts cultural expectations provokes our questions about how she made her life different, a key issue for this book is how women made their lives anew. How did they find paths which were other than those they and their parents had anticipated as they grew up? How did they diverge from what their husbands expected of them? How did they live askew from the dominant cultural expectations around them? This book explores the impact on so-called 'ordinary' women's lives of the women's movement, both in terms of the institutional possibilities and the changing perceptions of what it meant to be a woman which were opened up by feminism. These women's lives are influenced by equal employment opportunity in the workplace, gender inclusive curriculum in schools, mature-age entry in universities, supporting parents' pensions so women can choose to leave violent and unsatisfactory marriages, domestic violence protection orders so that such choices do not threaten their lives, cultural contributions like films, magazine articles and women's studies courses which say there are many acceptable ways to be a woman.

Women responded differently to these opportunities and challenges. Those differences were a result of their own generational position, whether grandmother, mother or daughter; their resources and upbringing, which often had much to do with ethnicity and class; the trajectory of their lives, which meant they might live in a capital city or a country town. Ultimately, women also brought their own individual personalities to these possibilities, some of them overcoming enormous structural and situational impediments in the process. Thus, every woman has her unique story to write on the blank page, even as that story is framed by the cultural expectations of her time and the challenges to those expectations from feminism and other social movements. This book tells sixty of those stories, and sometimes only fragments of the stories. But in that telling, it reveals many experiences were shared by more than one woman, that in the 1970s and the 1980s the women's movement and the movement of women intersected in domestic spaces, educational institutions and working environments.

The Study

It is through the tales of ordinary women that a conundrum of feminism can be explored. On the one hand are celebratory claims that women have achieved 'new identities and a new consciousness', that Australia has become a different country – 'tolerant, multicultural, more feminist', that 'feminism is easily the most important thing to have happened in the twentieth century', that the redefinition of gender roles 'has had the most impact on the Australian way of life'.[1] Feminist issues appear so entrenched as to make it on to bestseller book lists (*Generation f* and *DIY Feminism* were ranked in the top ten best sellers in October 1996) and to have found a place in the popular media, even *Who Weekly* which carries stories of celebrities' lives. In an article on 'The 25 most intriguing people of 1995', alongside media, sporting and business personalities, readers were offered Aung San Suu Kyi (Nobel Prize winning democracy campaigner in Burma), politician Carmen Lawrence (described as 'bearing the "additional pressure and honour" of being a role model for women' during the Easton affair) and Helen Garner, author of *The First Stone*, a book to which we will return (*Who Weekly*, 1 January 1996:48–91).

However, this portrait of feminism's success story is questioned in letters to the editor from Marina Bassham and Lauren Ayers in the 9 October 1995 edition of *Who Weekly*. Feminists blame 'men for all the wrongs that happen in life' and don't 'let men and women live their own lives how they want to live them'. However, Lauren Ayers, while 'sick to death of feminists', described herself as 'a firm believer in equality' and choice, claiming a woman should be whatever she 'wants', whether doctor or housewife. These letters capture both the victory and defeat of the women's liberation movement in Australia. While feminism is often linked to the issues over which it has campaigned, like spousal abuse and equal opportunities, feminism is less likely to be applauded for making a positive contribution in raising these issues and changing women's lives. 'Feminist' does not stand for what women accept but what they see as radical. Thus, feminists are not for 'equality' and 'choice', but are 'taking it too far' according to Lauren Ayers. Feminists are man-haters, radicals, lesbians, bra-burners.

> Women whose thought-power, like that of mountain streams, is of little effect alone but which, when run into a general river of purpose, can potentially aid in turning the wheel of time, to grind out a new era. (Louisa Lawson in 1889 in Scutt 1991:xviii)

In talking to the women who participated in this book's project, I discovered a similar ambivalence, at least among those who do not call themselves feminists. Every woman with whom I spoke had something positive to say about the gains of the women's movement, although these were mostly expressed in terms of equal employment and educational opportunities. But a number also thought that feminists are 'taking it too far', for example, in endorsing quotas of women in winnable parliamentary seats or in sexual harassment legislation. In a decade's time these issues may be part of the accepted landscape of equal rights, while other issues will be the mark of the 'radical' feminist. Perhaps, however, in their struggle to 'grind out a new era' feminists meet more resistance for some proposals than others. These issues will be pursued in Part II and the Conclusion, where women's responses to the women's movement are discussed.

Furthermore, while writers like Summers celebrate the gains of the women's movement, others are anxiously pondering a backlash, an idea made popular by Susan Faludi (1991) writing about the situation in the United States. Faludi claims men have beaten back women's gains with increased levels of violence against women, increasingly violent pornography and films, reversals of affirmative action decisions, and repressive and controlling images of women in much of the media. Although Beatrice Faust (1994) disputes evidence of a backlash in Australia, there are signs that women's gains have stalled. While women's educational participation rates now exceed those of men and women's workforce participation rate is approaching that of men, women are far more likely to work part-time and in the lower reaches of the workforce. Women may now earn 83 per cent of men's hourly rates, but their average annual earnings are only 60 per cent of men's (Australian Bureau of

Statistics 1993a:179).[2] It is claimed that women hit a 'glass ceiling' when they reach a certain point in management hierarchies. Women still do more than half the unpaid housework and caring for others.

Women would appear to be exposed to just as much violence as they were thirty years ago, if not more. It has been suggested that the rate of sexual assault in Australia is higher than in any other country except the United States (Evans 1992:198), that in the 1970s Australia had 'the highest incidence of recorded gang rape in the world' (McFerren 1990:193) and the rate of pack rape still remains higher than in Britain or the United States (Looker 1994:217–18). Thus, legal changes in the treatment of sexual harassment, rape, sexual assault and domestic violence have had little impact on the culture of violence in Australian society. Women's liberation has not changed markedly the widespread acceptance that aggression is a component of masculinity; male aggression may even have risen in a backlash against women's increased economic independence.

The return to work in the 1950s and 1960s of married women, prompted by smaller family sizes and an expanding economy, preceded the efflorescence of women's liberation. Kaplan (1996:20) notes that these were disproportionately immigrant, not Australian-born, women. Despite feminism, women continue to be disadvantaged in the workforce. They experience both continuing workplace discrimination and still bear the major burden of caring for dependants, largely children but increasingly aged or invalid relatives.[3] Women's entry into the workforce left them holding the baby as well as a wage packet, the 'double shift' as it was soon termed.

For more than a century Australian governments and unions have disrupted 'free market' decisions to support collective wage bargaining by workers, to ban dangerous goods, to ensure a basic standard of living, to enhance our sense that we belong to a shared national community. Since the 1980s, however, economic rationalism has become entrenched as the dominant government ideology; its full blossoming is promised under the Howard government. To economic rationalists, free markets make the correct decisions about what people and resources are worth, even if these decisions mean the lowest wage paid is below a living wage. Government intervention is seen as inefficient, because governments do not base decisions purely on notions of cost efficiency, but also respond to the needs of people who do not necessarily have money to finance their needs.

In an economic rationalist environment women's capacities to ensure adequate recognition for their labour will be worked out within enterprise bargaining or individual contracts with employers. The relative incomes of weaker and under-represented workers, which includes women, are almost certain to decrease where arbitration and unions do not support the claims of all workers. But women in work are relatively fortunate. Those relying on pensions are likely to be squeezed even further, as economic rationalists call for smaller government and balanced budgets. Women continue to make up the bulk of the poor, particularly as the young and homeless (often forced on to the streets by sexual abuse), and as supporting parents or aged pensioners.

From this it can be see that feminism appears to be something of a curate's egg, successful in parts, or perhaps useful for some women but not others. Indeed, one of the most vitriolic and long-lasting debates within feminist scholarship contests whether feminism has served largely white middle-class women or also responds to the needs of working-class and other marginalised women.[4] This book explores how the women's movement has affected the educational outcomes, occupational success, family experiences and sense of self for women whose stories have been relatively neglected or for whom it has been claimed that feminism has had little value. These are women about whom it is sometimes said that feminism has been marginal or marginalising, women from non-English speaking backgrounds, Indigenous Australian women, women from lower socio-economic backgrounds, and women who do not live in capital cities. The women with whom I spoke are not the 'famous' makers of women's liberation, although a few have been active in the women's movement. Some are feminist fellow-travellers, but most do not call themselves feminist. The focus on women who are not 'notable'[5] distinguishes this project from the plethora of short autobiographies written by women, now amounting to over five hundred stories.[6]

Methodology

While the appendixes contain some statistical data which frame the experiences of the sixty women with whom I spoke, the methodology employed in this book is qualitative rather than quantitative. The raw 'data' are sixty life histories told to me by women living in an arc from Cairns to Adelaide. In asking women to tell their life stories, one is not searching for an 'objective truth' or a mere description of past events. Rather, life histories aim for an understanding of the meaning people ascribe to their lives (Glucksmann 1994:159). In the life histories, women explored how their understandings of the world had changed, while also relating their understandings to wider social relations, to experiences of family, education and work, for example. The method used differs from the life history approach by relating interview material to 'prior analysis of the social structure involved' (Connell 1992:739), and forging a 'link between an individual life and the social and economic structures which shape that life' (Watson 1994:26–7; see also

Shaw 1989:89). This method, described as 'socially theorised life history', identifies a role for social theory in interpreting the interview material. For men who live alternative versions of masculinity, a key aspect of their life path is their engagement with, and response to, the dominant versions of masculinity. For example, gay men experienced an early engagement with heterosexual masculinity but forged their alternative masculinity in the collective practices of a gay community (Connell 1992:747).

However, the theorised life history method poses a hoary dilemma for researchers. If researchers merely relay women's experience there is no room for our input, our training in the constraints imposed by social structures or meanings embedded in cultural texts (Reinharz 1992a:26–31). On the other hand, to assert the superiority of our interpretation comes close to asserting that 'we' have acccess to the objective truth and 'they' – non-academic or non-feminist women – have 'false consciousness'. One answer to this dilemma is to point out that there are many views of the world, and these views quite clearly influence what we choose to research and how we decide to go about it. Thus, I asked women to tell their life histories from a perspective framed by the claims of feminist writers concerning how women's lives had changed since the 1950s.

Furthermore, if we propose to demur from those we interview, perhaps we should offer them our interpretations for their comment (Borland 1991:73; Middleton 1993:71,74; Billson 1991:212). I sent transcripts of our discussion to the women with whom I spoke, asking for corrections and comments. By allowing a space for reflection and editing, this method encouraged frankness at the point of narration. However, on reflection, a number of respondents made themselves appear less racist, less critical or less confused than their transcript might have suggested. While this seems to imply a loss of 'authentic' data, I suspect that if I had not offered the chance to edit transcripts I would not even have glimpsed this personal self who, on reflection, women displaced for a more public self.

Secondly, by sending her extracts from the first draft of the book manuscript, I offered each narrator an opportunity to respond to my (mis)interpretations of her story, how I had used her experiences to buttress my theoretical project. For example, Sullivan (1994:268) had 'not noticed' the theoretical problems in many feminist accounts of prostitution, despite reading them for several years, until 'forced to deal with the angry responses of sex workers'. Through the lens of their anger, Sullivan could see the ways in which feminist theorists 'disparage both sex work and sex workers'. As a result, Sullivan advocated that feminist theorists be both 'respectful of what prostitutes do and yet maintain a focus on gendered structures of power in all work and personal relations'. Interestingly, my respondents maintained a firm sense of their role: to tell their stories and correct any mistakes rather than to offer alternative interpretations. However, this method of response did allow one of the women with whom I spoke, Rita, to finally explain why our discussion had been so unproductive. She had felt 'interrogated' at our first interview, there being 'no connection between you and I'. At Rita's request, I returned eighteen months later to again record her story. During the interviews, and contra some feminist methodology prescriptions, I found that the women with whom I spoke were usually impatient if I offered aspects of my own life story, although I answered any questions they asked. They understood the interview as an 'unnatural conversation' (Lyons-Lee and Collins 1995:7) in which they were given the opportunity to tell their story rather than hear mine (see also Middleton 1993:79).

Reflecting on women's writing in Australia up to the 1980s, Joy Hooton (1990:89) suggests men tend to tell their life histories as a teleological unfolding of events towards one's destiny, as 'a journey to one's current place' (Connell 1992:746), with a focus on individual struggle and achievement rather than structural barriers and frameworks. For women, however, 'it is the process of living that is foregrounded', rather than the achievement or destiny. Many of the women with whom I spoke revealed conflict and uncertainty in their life histories. A number noted paths glimpsed and not followed, either because circumstances (structures) prevented them or because their self-definition as a woman precluded that path. As mothers, they might understand their obligations to do certain things; as women of ideas they might yearn for another life. Once her children were grown, Berenice's mother began to recover herself as an artist. Women could also discern contradictions in their lives, but tolerated these. Rita, while arguing for a form of female power that was loving rather than aggressive, went on to say: 'And, I think, to some extent this is contradicting maybe what I just said, the woman has to have a certain aggression to survive, you know, because the woman's role is very demanding today'.

The stories women told me reveal the effects of the double hermeneutic, that what researchers discover about the world can frame everyday understandings. Such reverberations of feminist ideas in daily speech should give feminists pleasure, while also reducing the problem of imposing the label of false consciousness on those women we 'research'. This is not to suggest that communication problems never occur when speaking with women who are not feminist. I tried to answer honestly all questions put to me, if at times, briefly. Dishonesty is less likely to achieve empathy than a 'respectful distance' (Reinharz 1992:67) which attempts to understand the reasons for disagreement. As an example, when Myra told me about a woman who became a single parent, I asked: 'So you think that, given she didn't find someone to marry, she shouldn't have had a baby?' Myra replied: 'Mmm, I do, especially at that age too . . . But you might not agree with that?' In my response, I noted the problem of the double shift for women, suggesting that this might be an undesirable outcome of feminism. Myra responded: 'Thanks for saying that because that's true. It's good that you can sort of come and say that too'. However, my response to Myra was not the response I would give a feminist colleague. As Myriam Glucksmann (1994:162) suggests, we play roles to secure interviews. But a role is not necessarily a lie – in our daily lives we play a multiplicity of roles, such as commuter, work colleague, lover.

Women encounter prescriptions for ideal behaviour in their family, among their friends, in cultural representations like books and the media, at school and university. Their capacity to choose between future options, for example, various combinations of work and motherhood, will depend on their education, their control over their own bodies, the work sites to which they have access. I asked the women with whom I spoke to talk about their family of origin, their experiences of education (both as girls and later in life), their work experiences and their lives as wives and mothers.[7] Within each of these arenas, I looked for signs of difference or discrimination in their treatment as girls or women. Examples included how housework was allocated in families, parents' career aspirations for daughters and sons, discrimination at work. I asked about their experiences as wives, mothers and lesbians and how these roles intersected or clashed with other roles in their lives, particularly paid work or personal dreams. Where divorce had occurred, I inquired as to the reasons; many women spoke of violence in relationships other than their own, and several in their own. Depending on their suggestions and experiences, we discussed a range of other issues including children's literature, the beauty myth, women and religion, childbirth, issues of contraception and sexual practices.[8] My interpretation of their responses to these issues forms the subject matter of Part I of this book.

In order to discuss the relationship between their own life trajectory and feminism, I asked about the impact of the women's movement on their lives, expanding on this by inquiring how they raised their own sons and daughters (where this was relevant) and the differences they saw between themselves and women of the next generation (this to the 'mothers' and 'grandmothers') or the previous generation (this to the 'daughters'). Some of these women well remembered a moment of engagement with feminism, either of endorsement or rejection, but for others the relationship grew slowly and sometimes painfully. Women's responses to the women's movement form most of the subject matter addressed in Part II.

The Women

Theoretical sampling was used to identify the sixty women with whom I spoke. Rather than select a representative or random sample of Australian women, I focused on the experiences of women who would illuminate my research questions: 'Has the women's movement changed the world as much as feminists like Anne Summers claim?'; 'Has the world been changed equally for all women?' Thus, my attention was on the women who, it is claimed, have been neglected by feminism: women who are not 'white', 'middle-class' and 'cosmopolitan'. A short biography of the sixty women can be found in the List of Women Who Told Their Biographies for the Book at the beginning of this book. Appendix 2 explains how I identified the women.

Secondly, in order to highlight the changes which accompanied or were produced by the women's movement, I sought to speak with women across three generations. The changes associated with the women's liberation movement of the 1960s probably offered the fullest range of opportunities to young women in their late teens to early twenties, women who had not yet made decisions concerning marriage, motherhood and careers. For women over 45 in the 1970s, the women's movement may have been perceived as more of a threat to their achievements than a promise for change. The three cohorts of women whose life chances are compared in this study are the grandmothers (aged 65 to 75 in 1994–5), mothers (roughly baby boomers, aged 45 to 55 in 1994–5) and daughters (roughly 'Generation X-ers', aged 25 to 35 in 1994–5).[9]

Because the women with whom I spoke in no way represent a statistical sample of the several million Australian women with whom I might have talked, I undertook a life chances analysis for women across the three generations (see Appendix 1). The lives of the sixty women who comprise this book are framed by the wider structural changes outlined briefly below, and which is based on data for all Australian women, most particularly a greater role for education as women increasingly expect their lives to combine work and motherhood, the latter more likely to include at least a period of single parenting.

The cohort of the grandmothers were born between 1930 and 1940, generally before the Second World War. Compared with both subsequent cohorts and men in their own cohort, they were much less likely to complete secondary and tertiary education. The gender gap in education has virtually closed by the daughters' generation, only one-third not completing secondary school and 13 per cent completing a tertiary education. A small percentage of grandmothers (approximately 1 per cent) and of mothers (2 per cent) have returned to tertiary study as mature-age students.

However, while the level of education is a reflection of generation, workforce participation is much more a reflection of decade. Grandmothers and mothers had approximately the same labour force participation rates in the mid-1970s, and the mothers have slightly lower rates than their daughters in the mid-1980s. But the projected participation rate for daughters of 85 per cent in the year 2005 is higher than that experienced by the earlier cohorts. Part-time employment was not readily available in the mid-1960s when women's labour force participation rates began to rise (Department of Employment, Education and Training 1991:36). Part-time employment for women has risen fourfold since the mid-1960s (Australian Bureau of Statistics 1993a:123), along with a particularly strong increase in the percentage of married women in the labour force over the last decade.[10] Married women have also entered the workforce as the availability of childcare has improved and real incomes have deteriorated (McDonald 1990:14).

The percentage of women remaining single doubles in each generation, from 5 per cent of the grandmothers, to 11 per cent of the mothers to an estimated 20–25 per cent of the daughters. However, the age at marriage declines over the years, reaching an all-time low in 1971, when 32 per cent of women married in their teens (Office of the Status of Women 1992:10), before rising again.[11] Much of the later and lower rate of marriage for the daughters is due to the development of cohabitation as a normal precedent to marriage (Glezer 1993:17). Across the three generations, the age at first birth has risen and completed family size has fallen. When combined with women's increased longevity, this has meant a lengthening period for women after their last child turns 20 and before they die. This so-called 'empty nest' has spurred women back into education and the workforce.

As is well known, the mother's generation experienced a sharp increase in divorce rates, both prior to and after the introduction of no-fault divorce legislation in 1974. But remarriage rates for women have fallen since 1971. Between 1971 and 1986 the remarriage rates of women aged 25–39 halved from 21 per cent, suggesting increasing disillusionment with marriage. The rate is still falling (McDonald 1990:16; McDonald, personal communication, September 1995). Single-parent households were 9 per cent of households with dependent children in 1974 and 15 per cent in 1990 (Gilding 1994:112). These changes are captured in Tables A1 in Appendix 1 which provides a general context for the life histories on which this book is based. Appendix 1 reveals that the life experiences of the women with whom I spoke do not match those of Australian women as a whole (see Table A1.2). Although reflecting the general trend, the women with whom I spoke tend to be more upwardly mobile than the population as a whole, as can be seen by the improvements in occupational status and educational achievements when compared with each cohort's mother's generation.

Although I spoke with women in each of these three generations, the largest sample of women interviewed was the 'mothers'. This is arguably the generation of women who founded the women's liberation movement, as the regeneration of feminism in the late 1960s is often called.[12] The experiences of the baby boomers[13] are compared with the lives of their mothers and daughters, most of them figurative kin, although five are actual daughters of mothers with whom I spoke.

The Book

> The mayor and the police came to my parents' house and wanted me to come to Toowoomba to go boarding. They saw the potential, but I had so much resentment in me that I wasn't going to do it. Which is a stupid thing when I look back now . . . There was a combination of things. I felt rejected [by the education system] so therefore the resentment came along . . . My mother was very limited too, she couldn't understand the language, she had very little communication with people. The problem was she couldn't cope and the family . . . didn't have that support . . . It's not just one factor, but one factor brought other factors along as well. (Rita speaking of why she did not take up the scholarship she was offered for secondary schooling)

Part I contextualises women's life experiences within the structures which shape those experiences: family expectations, the prescriptions of femininity and its attendant exposure to violence as well as pleasure (chapter 1), education, the extent of which is possibly the greatest discriminator between women's life chances (chapter 2), women's varying work experiences which reveal some of the class divisions between the women with whom I spoke (chapter 3). Chapter 4 explores experiences of childbirth, abortion, marriage and motherhood. In each of these chapters the ways in which educational, work and other opportunities have been broadened as a result of the women's movement is related to the sixty women's life experiences.

Part II explores these women's responses to feminism. Chapter 5 explores how women have discovered or refused feminism through their exposure to the mass media, feminist books, consciousness-raising and women's studies. The relationship between feminism and lesbianism is also addressed, given the widespread popular insistence that feminists are 'hairy-legged lesbians'. Chapter 6 asks whether feminism is solely a white middle-class movement by discussing the reactions of Indigenous Australian women and women from non-English speaking backgrounds. This chapter also explores the impact of feminism in the presumed conservative citadels of church and rural life. Chapter 7 asks whether feminism is a revolution half won by describing how the daughters are carving out their lives. The Conclusion asks questions about the future of feminism through analysis of contentious issues raised by the media during the course of this book's development and discussed by women with whom I spoke.

Several of the chapters conclude with a truncated life history, both to convey some of the rich detail of women's lives and to recombine events which have been dismembered in the book's structure. Women do not experience family and then education and then work; these are interlocking events. As an example, members of a consciousness-raising group reflected that although 'personal power' encouraged better interpersonal relationships, 'financial security' was the most significant change in their lives. This influenced not only their ability to choose partners irrespective of their incomes but also encouraged them to be more assertive in their relations with professionals like doctors and lawyers (Henry and Derlet 1993:150-3). The issues surrounding 'financial security' range across material discussed in chapters 3, 4 and 5.

Structures and Agency: Audrey's Story

In a 1992 focus group survey of the women of 'middle Australia' – those whose personal income was $35 000 or less and whose household income was $60 000 or less – many women saw 'choice' as the key to their daughters' futures. But choice included whether to 'have children or be without children'; it was supported by both 'traditional' and 'non-traditional' educational opportunities; by equal opportunities at work, more women in politics, and changed heterosexual relations. Choice was impeded by violence against women, a consumer-oriented society, the low status of mothering which made paid work almost compulsory and the lack of childcare which meant young women delayed having children for the sake of their careers (Riley-Smith 1992:27, 32, 36–9). In summarising the parameters of women's choice, or lack of it, these women noted the interaction between private desires and public supports for them, and between decisions made by themselves and by others. Similarly, women's biographies reveal how social structures support or impede women's desires, how they open some personal paths but close others. Some of these paths are visible and taken, some are visible and barred. Some once-invisible paths have been made so shiningly clear by feminism's remapping of the known world that a number of women now view past choices and attitudes with amazement.

Thus, the purpose of the theorised life history is to open and explore the space between a conception of individuals as self-determining authors of their lives and an opposite conception of structures as so oppressive they leave no space for personal choice. The former viewpoint, or liberalism, is the more usual rhetoric of everyday life. It offers us the comfort that we have free will, that a woman can be whatever she 'wants', whether doctor or housewife, as Lauren Ayers suggested in her letter to *Who Weekly*. The social sciences emphasise the structures which limit our options, and these 'oppressive', 'patriarchal' structures have certainly been a feature within feminist analysis. Perhaps this is why women who have imbibed the rhetoric of liberalism become so impatient with what they define as feminism. It seems to say that all women are oppressed, that patriarchy is so ubiquitous that there are no alternatives but to be victims of men and oppressed by social structures.

The theorised life history argues, as does Karl Marx, that people make their own history but not under circumstances of their own choosing. More than that, theorised life histories explore the ways in which people carve out their lives or fail to achieve their goals against the backdrop of social structures. These include the opportunities and limitations provided by one's family of birth, one's educational experiences, one's workforce participation, one's falling pregnant or delaying childbirth, as well as the chance encounters with people along the road who open up different paths. Of all the tales told in this book, Audrey's narrative exemplifies the capacity of individual will and self-esteem to defeat the social scientist's predictions. It is told here to demonstrate how the theorised life history method enriches and complicates the social scientific belief that structures are pervasive and difficult to resist.

Audrey's mother was an Indigenous Australian foundling of unknown origin. Her father worked in unskilled jobs when he was not unemployed. His violence gradually crushed Audrey's mother, burdened down by a large family. As a child Audrey was interfered with sexually, probably by a relative although she repressed his face from her conscious memory; a sister was raped at the age of 14. An uncle sexually molested another sister, threatening to throw the whole family out of his house, where they were staying, if she told anyone. Once discovered, Audrey's 'father flogged him within an inch of his life'. But Audrey's father:

> had a terrible problem too because he had a liking for little girls, and all our life he used to be touching us ... He even had a name for it, 'Give me a pow-wow' ... We used to squeal and run away ... We knew from other kids that your parents don't do this ... Mum used to scream at him from the kitchen, 'Leave those girls alone!'

However Audrey has sympathy for her father's dilemma, recounting the story of another sister who fell pregnant and sought refuge with Audrey's father when he was ring-barking trees and 'living in a tent in the middle of the scrub'. One night it became 'too much for him' and he crawled into bed with his daughter, calling her by his wife's name. The next day he sent his daughter away. Audrey suggests: 'It must have been a terrible trauma for him too. He knew he was doing wrong and he knew he shouldn't touch her but he was losing control'.

Needing to contribute to the family's finances, Audrey left school at the age of 12, gradually working her way up from the milk factory, to milk bars and then restaurants. Where more affluent and educated parents prepared their children for the transition to university, in Audrey's family the rite of passage was to work: 'The moment we started work, Mum used to [get] . . . a credit order. One place called the Brisbane Credit Company, £5. We used to get ourselves outfitted for work. A dress or a skirt and top'.

Audrey hid, working night shifts in the milk factory, because she had a 'gummy mouth' (her teeth having fallen out), 'brown straight hair and a runny noise'. After her brother took Audrey to a dentist to be fitted with false teeth, Audrey gained the confidence to leave the factory and work in restaurants. She describes these occupational changes:

> From a very very poor beginning I rose up in the world until I could communicate on a very high level with very rich people, you know, influential people. And I had this good vocabulary and this means of communication, and do you know I was never put down by anybody. No matter how rich they are or how powerful they are, I can speak to them one to one without any feelings of inferiority . . . I've always told the kids this, . . . 'People can only talk down when you go down . . . If they're not treating you right you just walk away'.

Audrey's employment was interrupted when she had a son out of wedlock at the age of 17. When Audrey again became pregnant, rather than face her parents she resorted to an illegal abortion which left her sterile. Miscarrying in the house Audrey was sharing with her parents, she desperately tried to wash the blood down the bathroom plughole, finding the foetus in the process. She could not bear to throw it away: 'perfectly formed, it was a little boy, and I'll never forget that'. When Audrey's mother, who had cared for her son, died in 1953 Audrey felt compelled to marry so she could support her son. Her husband took her to an isolated campsite where 'he punched me, he broke my teeth, he smashed my nose. I've got an eyebrow that won't go straight because it was all split open and no treatment'. With the help of a man camping nearby, Audrey escaped, later meeting and marrying David who worked at Mount Isa Mines. When David died, Audrey had to support her two adopted teenage children and her grandchild.

In Audrey's own teleology of her life, it is her fighting spirit inherited from her mother which enabled her to retain a sense of self in adversity. Audrey says of her mother that even when her father was about to hit her in the face: 'she wouldn't let up . . . she came back at him, same as I do, you know?' In response to her first, violent, husband Audrey 'fought him. I wouldn't be stood on. As much as he punched me, I punched him, until he practically punched me into unconsciousness, and that's the only time I stopped'. One of Audrey's milk bar employers 'liked to feel little girls'. She hit him even though Audrey was so short she had to stand on a crate to see over the counter. The owner retorted, 'Out! Out!', and Audrey replied, 'Not before I get my pay!' Ouraged, he yelled, 'You'll get bloody nothing' as he chased Audrey out with a broom. Audrey notes that such sexual harassment, which will be discussed in chapter 3, is no longer permissible at work. Audrey was misdiagnosed and committed to a mental hospital for a condition which was later corrected with a prescription. She 'was always fully aware of what they were doing to me and that I was being punished with shock treatment'. However, she claims, that she only stopped resisting

> when they sedated me. Otherwise I threw all the bed clothes out the window, I kicked the door, I climbed over the fence, I [chuckles], I just fought all me life, I fought. And that's why I never let anybody get away with anything.

The interactions between home and school in developing and realising women's career's aspirations are pursued in chapters 2 and 3. While many of the women with whom I spoke followed paths predictable by social science, Audrey refused her early lessons. Audrey describes the class and ethnic divisions in her pre-war country classroom:

> Well, what happened was the blacks, the dunces . . . and ethnic people or anybody with a disability were all put in these three front rows . . . The girl with the highest marks . . . well, I say a girl because to my knowledge it was always a girl that was up there, . . . the top left-hand corner, and then they came along the rows . . . As the grades came down, they came down to where we couldn't even be marked, I suppose . . . But then a new hierarchy started there, because I remember, . . . I always tried to keep away from the bottom, bottom of the class, last. And that's where I aspired. I didn't aspire to go up into the back rows, I knew that wouldn't be allowed . . . I actually set out to learn this English, I learned nothing else – oh except the tables . . . That was the best time in my life when the whole class used to sing it, sing the times table. And this was the only time that I was allowed to interact with the class, we were sort of separate . . . And you noticed all the upper grades wore shoes and socks. You came down to those who . . . some wore shoes, some wore sandals, it was sort of a mixture. And down in the front, we were bare-footed

> ... In those days I don't think I even realised [the class implications, but] I was envious of those that had nice clothes, and wore shoes. But we used to have to walk a mile to school, and we had no shoes. And I tell you it was damn hot, this is in Mitchell in Charleville.

Not only was Audrey at the front of the class, but any sense that she might have something to offer was drummed out of her:

> I used to put me hand up sometimes to answer questions in the early part and she used to say, 'Put your hand down Ferris, you wouldn't know anyway, you wouldn't know what time of day it was'.[14] And do you know I was writing poetry and stories at that time and I wanted to show her but I thought she'd make fun of me, so I never told her.

When Audrey hired a tutor for her daughter Yasmin, Audrey thought

> 'I can do this, this tutoring if I only had some qualifications . . . Gee, I can do that, I can do poetry' . . . I thought I could, but when I went to school I realised analysing poetry was an art that had to be learned.

It was this conviction, even if initially misplaced, that encouraged Audrey to complete matriculation English and enrol in university studies. And this was where I met Audrey, in my first-year tutorial. Audrey suggests that she 'got in through the back door', by which she means she was a beneficiary of mature-age entry schemes developed to offer women in her situation a chance which had been denied them as young school leavers. A shift in structures, in the entry requirements for university, opened a window of opportunity. But it was her 'fighting spirit' that allowed Audrey to seize that chance. Despite having no family support and with real disincentives from her own school experiences, Audrey's sense of capacity stayed with her and she completed her degree in 1993. She has tutored Aboriginal children, completed a postgraduate diploma in teaching, is a registered teacher and has enrolled in a master's degree. She is also an elder with the Brisbane Council of Aboriginal Corporation Elders. Thus, although Audrey is 'doing it in slow stages', 'there's just no end to what heights I can reach'.

PART ONE

Women's Lives Through a Feminist Lens

> The invisibility of the historical contribution of women weakens the current status of women by diminishing self esteem and the collective sense that women have 'earned the right' to choose the lifestyle they want.
> (House of Representatives Standing Committee on Legal and Constitutional Affairs 1992:v)

A history of women's liberation written from archives and remembrances is now a flourishing sub-industry in academic feminism (Curthoys 1992; Burgmann 1993; Ryan 1992), including the 'first full-length book in Australia on this topic' (Kaplan 1996:xi). The present text focuses on the impact of women's liberation on so-called ordinary women, but a brief history of Australian feminist activism, achievements and defeats will contextualise the discussion of women's experiences of growing up; of giving meaning to their bodies as sexualised; of education, work, motherhood and marriage.

Nineteenth-Century Feminist Struggles

Had one of the earlier generation of feminists – those who were active in the decades around the turn of the century – looked back over the last forty years from the perspective of about 1920, she too might have written a letter both celebratory and anxious to the next generation. She would have noted that forty years ago women did not have the right to vote or stand for parliament,[1] a right still denied many women in other nations. She might have pointed out that married women did not have the right to own property or sue in court, that women were not admitted to universities (Maroske 1993:20), that most women felt almost compelled to marry because the alternatives were limited to working in domestic service, prostitution, or for the fortunate ones, as a governess. She may have applauded the activism of the 'mothers' of feminism, like Catherine Helen Spence in South Australia, Rose Scott in New South Wales and Bessie Harrison Lee in Victoria, who worked for these changes as well as conducting a more private revolution in changing the definitions of male sexuality to allow for 'voluntary motherhood' in an age where contraception was unsafe and unreliable (Lake 1991:30–1). The average family size in the 1880s was 5.6 children for Queensland's urban-dwelling women and closer to seven in the rural areas (Spearritt 1994:69). By 1911 women had reduced their family size to between three and four children.

This comparison is not written to suggest that there have been only two waves in Australian feminism. Nor is it to suggest that the status of European-background women has ineluctably improved over the centuries of colonisation. Indeed, while Australian women were among the first in the world to win the vote, other countries soon outstripped Australia in the representation of women, which only achieved significant levels from the 1980s (Sawer and Simms 1993:20).[2] It was 1962 before Roma Mitchell became the first woman Queen's Counsel and in 1965 the first woman Supreme Court judge.[3] In 1987 Mary Gaudron became the first, and so far the only, woman judge in the High Court. Only in 1967 in Queensland were women automatically included in jury lists; before that they had to notify the electoral officer in writing if they wished to serve as jurors (Rathus 1993:3).

Australian women have gained a measure of equality in the areas of work and politics – public life one might say – but in the area of bodily autonomy women's struggles have been much more in vain. Just as Sylvia Walby (1990) contrasts public patriarchy with private patriarchy, the 1890s suffrage slogan claimed 'Votes for women, chastity for men'. While women successfully demanded a place in public life, they were much less successful in winning 'chastity for men' or control over their sexuality and its consequences. The power of men as workers and bureaucrats has been regulated more successfully than the power of fathers, husbands and male lovers.

In the face of sexual intercourse made dangerous by venereal disease, and pregnancy made life-threatening by the lack of antibiotics before the 1940s, the Women's Christian Temperance Union, the largest women's political organisation between the 1890s and 1930s, found a ready response in its efforts to encourage sexual self-control on the part of men (Bunkle 1980:62,71; see also Sheridan 1993a:119,120 for Australia). Prior to the discovery of antibiotics five mothers died for every one thousand live births (Spearritt 1994:70). However, from the 1890s the idea that men should control their sexual urges and that respectable women were 'passionless and pure' was gradually displaced by sexological writings which claimed that, to be healthy, both men and women should engage in sex. Popularising and distorting Freud and finding its way into law courts in relation to rape trials, sexology defined women who did not desire sex as frigid and those who desired too much as nymphomaniacs. Women were no longer ravished when raped but viewed as really wanting it to happen.

The mother of nineteenth-century feminism might, like Anne Summers, also have expressed concern that the daughters were not seizing the standard, that they seemed to be relinquishing women's hard-fought claims to political activism and sexual purity to become a 'new woman' (Caine 1992:257).[4] Better educated than her mother and offered a wider choice of occupations, the new woman was defined by sexuality and glamour, pleasure-seeking and romance, although her hard edge was materialistic, a 'gold digger' (Elder 1993:157).

Many of the previous generation of women had been spinsters, but the new woman gave up her childish ways for marriage and motherhood, encouraged to some extent by government payments to mothers. Free clinics for mothers and children, staffed by women, state boarding-out schemes and women's hospitals supported (and regulated) women's mothering roles. Marriage was also redefined as a lifelong companionship based on mutual respect and love, on a sense of equality even if roles were dramatically different (Bland 1987:147). To retain a man's love, women were encouraged to maintain their sexual attractiveness (Lake 1995a:63, 73), placing unreasonable pressures on women, which were the subject of women's liberation actions against beauty pageants in the 1970s. However, this notion of equal worth in the family fuelled ongoing claims for equal pay, renewed regularly from as early as 1913. The first national conference on equal pay was held in 1958 in Sydney, the same year that New South Wales introduced equal pay legislation for teachers (Lake 1992:315; Kaplan 1996:21).

Feminist Activism Since Women's Liberation

> The Women's Electoral Lobby . . . did assess and publicise the candidates' views, and the Labor Party won the election. It was in 1972, the same year I gave birth to my son, David. (Carmen Lawrence 1994:12)

By the 1960s the major women's organisations were the Country Women's Association, religious-affiliated organisations like the Young Women's Christian Association, business and professional women's clubs, the United Association of Women founded in 1929, the National Council of Women, the Australian Federation of Women Voters, the Women's International League for Peace and Freedom, Save Our Sons (which was formed to protest against Australia's involvement in the Vietnam war) and the Union of Australian Women founded in 1950 by Communist Party women. The UAW campaigned for higher child endowment, more kindergartens, government subsidies for childcare centres and against 'blatant sexism' in the media (Burgmann 1993:79). Despite these organisations, Kaplan (1996:6) describes the 1950s as 'constrained and prescriptive years' in which 'young women entered matrimony and then usually suburban boredom'. On to this scene burst an aggressive infant, women's liberation, dismissing their 'mothers' organisations as 'bourgeois and sexless' (Curthoys 1992:429).

Women's liberation in Australia is dated to the summer of 1969–70 when women returning from the United States in 1969 announced the inaugural meeting of the Women's Liberation Group in Sydney. By 1971 there were women's liberation groups in every major town in Australia, clustering in the inner-city suburbs and around the universities (Burgmann 1993:77; Curthoys 1992:430; Kaplan 1996:32). Newsletters and magazines sprang up (Burgmann 1993:91), consciousness-raising groups formed to ponder issues like the myth of the vaginal orgasm (Sawer and Simms 1993:234), demonstrations against beauty pageants were organised (Ryan 1992:58). In 1970 a national conference produced a set of demands which supplemented and expanded the UAW's closer focus on the role of mothers: government-funded childcare, abortion rights, equal job opportunities, equal pay, access to safe contraception, and an end to sexist advertising and images of women in the media (Curthoys 1992:434; Burgmann (1993:82) adds equal opportunity in education).

The Women's Electoral Lobby was established in 1972 as 'the pragmatic wing of Women's Liberation' (Ryan 1990:72), its membership in Melbourne growing from 1000 within a couple of months to 1700 by the end of the year (Ryan 1990:73). Members were mostly in their early thirties, married with children and professional jobs (Burgmann 1993:93). WEL's professional membership produced a formidable publicity machine (Ryan 1990:72) drawing on the skills of media-wise journalists, speech-writing from political scientists, economists who prepared economic analyses, and a survey of candidates' attitudes on women's issues devised by social scientists, including Carmen Lawrence (1994:12). By-lined 'Think WEL before you vote' (Burgmann 1993:93), the survey results received wide media coverage (Curthoys 1992:435), while thousands of people attended public fora in which political hopefuls were asked 'Why should women vote for you?'.[5] First the Australian Labor Party and then the Liberal Party realised that they must woo the 'women's vote' to win office. Childcare became a two-party policy when introduced by the Gorton government in 1970, and by 1990 women's issues were a part of both parties' federal election platforms.

Reflecting their 'utilitarian and egalitarian' principles (Kaplan 1996:61), Australian women added their own variant to feminism, the work of 'femocrats' (Eisenstein 1991:12). The word combines feminist, bureaucrat and aristocrat, denoting the appointment of feminists to senior positions in the public service whose brief is to introduce programs for the benefit of women (Eisenstein 1996:68). According to Kaplan (1996:

194) collaborating in this way with the state was unique to Australia and the Scandinavian countries. Thus, the heady days of the 1970s were replaced by the institutionalised days of the 1980s; protestors became politicians, femocrats, lawyers, journalists, community workers, lobbyists and academics.[6] According to Kaplan (1996:61): 'Per capita, Australia probably had more feminist organisations, collectives, interest groups and social clubs than almost any other nation'. A number of these, like the Leichhardt Women's Health Centre or the first women's refuge (Elsie), were institutionalised by Elizabeth Reid as Women's Advisor to the Prime Minister, giving them legitimacy and government funding.[7]

Femocrats, often in conjunction with politicians, have changed the laws governing marriage, divorce and custody; introduced anti-discrimination and affirmative action legislation; expanded government-funded childcare places; developed changes in the welfare and taxation systems, most notably recognising women's independent right to support as either primary care-givers or worker-citizens. Legislation and services have sought to extend women's control over their bodies, including freedom from domestic violence, sexual harassment, rape and sexual assault, reproductive freedom and better health. State-funded women's information telephone services seek to answer women's queries; task forces in the Office of the Status of Women have inquired into domestic violence, portrayal of women in the media, and non-English speaking background women's issues (Sawer and Groves 1994a:45).

This official story of the women's movement over the last century gives the impression that feminism is the sole cause of improvements in women's lives. But feminism itself responded to structural changes in women's position as well as contributing to further changes. Women entered the workforce in growing numbers prior to women's liberation, fuelling demands for equal pay. The decline in marriage rates has been attributed to a range of factors, only one of them being the impact of feminism.[8] The increased age of marriage and first childbearing has been attributed to changing attitudes to single parenthood, access to more reliable contraception, liberalisation of abortion laws (especially after 1972 when Medicare made abortion much cheaper), and the emergence of cohabitation as a form of trial marriage (Office of the Status of Women 1992:10). While contraception and abortion are clearly women's movement issues, changing sexual values are, at the very least, influenced by other social currents. Thus, increased sexual permissiveness has allowed cohabitation but feminism has also claimed that women do not need to marry and have children to feel 'fulfilled'. However, these values must be supported by structural opportunities. If women cannot choose satisfying and well-paid work instead of marrying and depending on a man, they are more likely to accept motherhood as a life goal. But women's occupational opportunities are a reflection of both changes in economic activity – for example, the expansion of the service sector – as well as changing expectations concerning the kinds of jobs women should be allowed to do. When the women's movement has resonated with structural changes and been supported by other political currents, women have made gains in status; these seem to stall when the claims of the women's movement cannot intersect productively with structural shifts or when confronting hostile ideologies, such as economic rationalism at the present time.

From the foregoing, it is evident that there is a dense interconnection between the impact of feminism and changing structures on the experiences of women in family, education and work. As Carmen Lawrence noted (1994:12), in 1972 she worked for WEL which assisted the Labor Party in winning the election, and she gave birth to her son. While the chapters in this part distinguish women's experiences in these three institutions or social sites, Claudia's story introduces them, revealing as it does the close interweaving of structures, beliefs, opportunities offered by the women's movement and personal happenstance.

Claudia's Story

Most of the grandmothers and mothers imagined a life leading to marriage and the cessation of employment. Yet almost all of them participated in non-household labour after they were married and many returned to further study. Although half the mothers had not completed secondary schooling, many shared the high educational aspirations for their children which fuelled the post-war expansion of classrooms. For such parents there was often a gap between their desires and their knowledge concerning how their children would accomplish a 'good education'. Many did not see that education as leading to independent careers, and neither did their daughters. These issues are exemplified in Claudia's story.

Claudia's father wanted his daughter and son to succeed in their schooling. Claudia's only memory of a hug from her father was when she won a high school bursary. Her parents understood that Claudia, like her brother, should enter Canberra High School; the alternative vocational school signalled a girl was 'on the skids' because 'they were going to work in shops'. As in many other families, parental expectations concerning educational equality ceased at a certain point, often constrained by financial considerations. As parents expected sons to become breadwinners and daughters to become mothers, additional education was the right and need of sons. Many daughters did not question the validity of this belief. When Claudia's father explained to Claudia that he could not send both his children to university, and suggested teachers college for Claudia, she accepted her father's 'universal cosmic plan', even though she did not wish to become a teacher. Some thirty years later, both the world of women and Claudia's world have changed so radically that she adds: 'it was pretty amazing, not just accepting it but actually thinking it was quite the right thing'.

Instead of teachers college, Claudia was accepted for nurse training in Camperdown Children's Hospital. Her aunt, with whom Claudia was staying, noticed an advertisement for a research assistant at Unilever House. Although Claudia 'loved' this job, 'at the end of that year I fell in love . . . and then he got posted to Darwin so I made up my mind that I was going to go to Darwin'. This was the first of two occasions when the future role of 'wife and mother' displaced the role of 'career woman' in Claudia's life. Her move to Darwin did not lead to marriage and Claudia returned to university, taking up her Commonwealth Scholarship. She tried to study medicine, supporting herself by nursing part-time, but it was impossible and she transferred to an arts degree. At the end of her first year at university, Claudia 'got pregnant, got married', returned to Darwin 'and that was that'. 'That was not really that', as Claudia could have chosen a risky abortion instead of marriage and motherhood, a choice explored in chapter 4. Spurred, in part, by female friends and also by the women's liberation movement, Claudia, like Audrey, later seized the opportunity of mature-age university entry. As chapters 2 and 3 show, women often return to their original dreams, by now sometimes carrying a freight of family obligations.

This part, then, explores how the expectations of parents and their daughters concerning the near exclusivity of motherhood in women's lives have been disrupted by events, including women's return to the workforce, increased individual educational aspirations and divorce. While even the grandmothers have been affected by these changes, the disjunction between expectations and reality has been greatest for the mothers, who grew up with their grandmothers' expectations but experienced workforce participation rates more akin to those of their daughters.

CHAPTER 1

Growing Up As Girls

In her essay, 'Throwing like a girl', Iris Young (1990) applies Simone de De Beauvoir's notion that women in patriarchal societies live a contradiction to the ways girls and boys from a very young age use their bodies. De Beauvoir suggests that patriarchal societies define woman as other, as not much more than her body, as 'the object for the gaze and touch of a subject, to be the pliant responder to his commands'. Against this immanence of womanhood, this confining of experience within the body, is transcendence, 'the free subjectivity that defines its own nature and makes projects' (Young 1990:75). Thus, femininity means being something while masculinity means doing things. But given a woman also has a human existence, she too 'is a subjectivity and transcendence' (Young 1990:144). When women use their bodies they express this contradiction between immanence and transcendence. They use only a part of their bodies to accomplish a task, holding back. They react to the approach of a thrown object rather than going forward to meet it. They express a fear of getting hurt. They use up much less space than their bodies are capable of being in. When using their bodies, women are both in them, making them do things, but also standing outside them, seeing them as objects. A woman is 'split. I see myself, and I see myself being seen' (Young 1990:175): 'Feminine bodily existence is an *inhibited intentionality*, which simultaneously reaches toward a projected end with an "I can" and withholds its full bodily commitment to that end in a self-imposed "I cannot"' (Young 1990:148).

As she grows, a girl is given less opportunity and encouragement to deploy the power of her body; she learns feminine bodily comportment, to walk like a girl, to assume herself fragile; she constantly monitors her appearance as an object to be looked at and so judged. She learns to fear invasion of her bodily space, not only in rape but also in the many more frequent touches to which women are exposed in white western society. As Yasmin notes of kick-boxing:

> Women are getting bashed but they won't go and learn any Self-defence ... A lot of girls are so timid ... We would have to help some of the newer belts ... The girls just weren't used to even being touched,[1] that's the word, because the boys had played football and things like that ... You could see why people could have any sort of power over them.

More than just in relation to physical activity, as the young girl acquires a definition of herself as feminine she loses an unalloyed sense of herself as someone who has projects in the world – she moves deeper into the contradiction of doing and being. If she refuses society's definition of what it is to be feminine, she faces ostracism and ridicule. This is because, according to Young (1990:177, 179), the only subject position she can take on is that of a male subject, because in patriarchal society only men are conceived of as subjects, have projects. Thus, women were warned out of education with the claim that they would lose their femininity. When pioneering women in universities proved that they could sustain the rigours of university study without suffering infertility and shrivelled wombs, the final line of defence was that women 'would become unsexed, would lose in womanly grace and charm' (Talbot quoted in Atkinson 1978:100). This threat is still with us, although today it is largely applied to women who choose 'men's' careers (engineering, for example, or physical jobs) or become competitive in sports.

In the generation of the mothers and grandmothers, girls who started life bursting with physical energy and nourishing wide-ranging dreams of future careers often found adolescence to be a time of circumscription to the precepts of femininity. But, as this chapter explores, feminism has expanded the modes of acceptable femininity, so that two of the daughters, Yasmin and Melinda, express their bodily capacities without feeling they are less feminine as a result. More diverse ways of being a girl or a boy allow children to continue to exercise preference for same sex groups, to even continue the category-maintenance work between the sexes,[2] while no longer confining young girls to quite the same narrow roles as their mothers experienced.

Family Influences: Tomboys and Housework

> If it poured with rain the men just sat down and did nothing while the girls are frantically inside helping mother with the afternoon teas, or whatever their highnesses requested. (Margaret)

Both Yasmin and Melinda, who played football with boys until adolescence, noticed the threat they posed to boys' nascent masculinity. Melinda remembers comments like: 'You couldn't kick a football to save yourself', explaining 'the guys didn't like getting tackled by girls, it wasn't tough'. As a young adult learning martial arts, Yasmin encountered a 'patronising' attitude: 'I'll take it easy, you're just a girl'. When both she and her brother were denigrated with taunts from the instructor, such as 'Oh, come on, your sister could beat you', Yasmin 'couldn't do anything about it, it was incredibly frustrating'.

Even so, there are women in all three generations who remember themselves as tomboys. With her sister, Myra 'used to play "Meg and Marge" together and have a stick for a boyfriend, and play pretend houses', but this was part of a bargain in which Myra induced her sister to join Myra and her brother in games down in the gully. Another grandmother, Fiorenza, 'had a train set'. Among the mothers, Deanna and her sisters joined the boys next door to play 'cars under the low-set house in the dirt and made roads and tracks'. The boys came to Deanna's house and played with 'strollers and prams and things like that'. In comparison with the boys, Deanna noticed her fine motor skills when colouring in: 'you never went over the edges like the boys did'. Aileen's childhood was spent 'not being conscious of being female', attributing this to the lack of gender-marked toys (like dolls) in her Indigenous Australian community and the shared obligation of all older children to care for younger children. Indeed, Aileen's training in 'acting like a girl' concerned learning to be a 'woman for the dominant society'. Just as her grandmother transformed herself when she went out, donning matching outfits and accessories, Aileen learned to wear dresses instead of 'big bloomers' and sit with her legs together. Aileen further learned white women's ways by mimicking them, given their refusal to speak to her.

Some grandmothers and mothers asserted their children's equal access to leisure pursuits. Martha's commitment to 'fairness' in her sons' and daughter's treatment was sorely tested when her daughter went camping with her brothers on their surfing weekends. Martha ruefully thought: 'I'll have to be brave about this'. Grace bought both her children fishing rods. Some fathers also encouraged tomboy pursuits in daughters. Claudia's father taught both his children to play cricket. Deanna's father, although the household patriarch, initiated each daughter into fishing by making them a rod when they had purchased the necessary materials. Yvonne's husband, who had no sons, took his daughter 'downstairs and really made a man of her didn't he?', teaching her carpentry and mechanical skills, and going fishing with her.

But time for leisure and for study is constrained by household obligations. The allocation of household tasks to sons and daughters further impacts on career options in the implied messages about a child's future. While Yvonne's sons did the washing up: 'I would tidy their rooms for them . . . Germaine Greer would hate me – I'm a great one for doing the women's job for the men, whether they be children or adults'. In the early 1990s girls spent almost twice as much time on household tasks as boys.[3] As a result, like their mothers who do several things at once (for example, ironing while watching television or visiting a museum to entertain the children), more girls than boys watch television while completing their homework. In contrast, girls in middle-class households more commonly do their homework 'seriously' in their rooms (Gilbert and Taylor 1991:64), pointing to the different expectations concerning university entrance and careers for middle-class girls that have emerged since the 1970s.

Household task allocation often provided an early lesson in equity, or 'fairness' as it was often rendered in the girl's mind. Aquarius knew it was unfair that her mother forced her to do the bulk of household chores, even to cleaning her stepfather's boots. He often helped Aquarius with her chores, saying: 'Don't you tell your mum'. But Aquarius retains a sense of gender role distinction in household chores, criticising an ex-lover's wife because he had 'to iron all his own shirts'. Shona's brothers did the 'dirty jobs', like emptying the rubbish, while Shona and her sister set the table and washed up. Shona and her sister understood the inequity in terms of time rather than gender: 'What does it take to empty the rubbish? Thirty seconds, and it takes half an hour to wash up'. The (unconvincing) parental rhetoric was that all the children were loved equally, receiving the same rewards and punishments, 'except they take a different form'.

Location in the family might temper gender-based unequal treatment, a youngest son or daughter receiving favoured treatment. Yvonne noted that her daughter, born late in life, was not even asked to wash up. However, position in the family might be the explanation offered for different treatment, although gender was the underlying reason. Thus, Jan's brother always received a present from her grandmother on the basis that 'he was the baby'. Contrariwise, Sage's older and only brother was 'the preferred child in the household', but 'because he was the eldest, you just automatically put it down to that, didn't you?'

Pointing perhaps to the impact of feminism, whether or not their own childhood experience was of egalitarian household distribution, most mothers denied that they allocated tasks in their own households on the basis of gender. As Jan said: 'there was no job separate for girls and boys. They were family jobs. Early they learned, they either did that' or Jan would not ferry them to their sporting activities. When she became a supporting parent, Mary and her children 'really did share the household chores so we'd be free to do things together'. Gerda allocates tasks to her thirteen children on a combination of age and roster. Each Saturday they 'all do an extra job for me', including baking the cake for Sunday dinner after church or cleaning the bathroom and toilets, while the 'little ones' 'rake the leaves'. 'It only takes an hour, but it's just something they're contributing to the whole family'.

These images of households with an ordered round of tasks, whether allocated on the basis of gender or age, are generally portraits from middle-class homes. Audrey's family were 'sleeping four to a bed', while 'across the road, you'd hear about half past five, five o'clock, "Come on girls, time for your bath" and there was no such thing in our place'. Audrey's father showed little concern about whether the children washed their hands or faces, although he did insist they washed their feet, to minimise sheet washing which was done in an outdoor copper. Looking back, Audrey notes: 'It was true, we were neglected. We were terribly neglected. And we were dirty, and we did have lice'. One of Audrey's sisters developed a scab on her scalp 'and when the doctor lifted the scab it was teeming with lice underneath, eating her away'. Audrey's father applied home treatments of kerosene, vinegar and Lethane to remove lice and nits, treatments which would 'burn the head off you'.

Similarly, Kerry's extended family did not fit the 'Dick and Dora' model propogated at school. Kerry suggests that school texts denigrated extended Indigenous Australian, Asian, Mediterranean and other families. Lacking material possessions, she remembers 'lots of love'. Where fathers were often absent other male relatives provided care. Kerry remembers three favourite uncles who, as young men in their mid to late teens, 'still cared for us', 'cooked food and made sure you were all right, and if you fell over, they'd give you a cuddle'. In some of her toddler and upper primary years, Kerry's family lived in boarding houses in various inner-city sites. At South Brisbane, the other boarders, as well as the 'parkies' in the park across the road, became part of an extended neighbourhood-cum-family. Sometimes on pay day, the 'parkies' bought the children 'packets of lollies or chips and drinks' and the boarding-house residents regularly cooked 'up a big storm' to share as a communal meal. Kerry notes that her 'Welsh husband couldn't understand what he'd married into eh, trying to keep us as a nuclear family, tell ya'. However, such arrangements had their negative aspects when extended family members reneged on their reciprocal obligations, eating and drinking with Kerry's family but not being around to pay the bills or help with home maintenance. However, Kerry notes that the relationships and emotional support were just as important as these material issues.

Adolescence and Femininity

until you reach puberty, I don't think you take a lot of notice of sex differences. (Sage)

as a kid I thought I was sexless, genderless, and I think I was probably treated that way 'cos my Mum wanted us to do men's things, be professionals. (Nadine)

In a study by Lillian Rubin of almost 1000 people in the United States in the late 1980s, 90 per cent of both men and women spoke of being 'disappointed' with their first genital sexual encounter. Men, however, saw it as an 'achievement' on the path to manhood; women more often felt cheated of 'the romantic fantasy' they had harboured. Phylis embraced femininity when she used her first pay cheque to buy a Berlei padded bra. Later, at an office picnic, a man spiked her lemon squash with gin and on the bus home 'kissed me and he stuck his tongue down my throat . . . it was so embarrassing, it was so rude'. Rather than genital sexual experience, women tended to see their entry into womanhood through menstruation, not as an 'achievement' so much as something often 'frightening, shaming, or at least foreboding'. A study in the 1970s found that girls still reported that periods were 'a secretive affair' and 'a kind of illness' (Segal 1994:229–230). These reports suggest that men transcend boyhood with their sexual encounters but for women the immanence of their bodies propels them fearfully into womanhood.

Studiousness

Many Australian women's autobiographies contrast the autonomy and freedom of childhood with the constraints of gender imposed from around puberty (Hooton 1990:90, 97). In adolescence, many girls leave tomboyhood behind, preferring the differences offered by femininity to the sameness offered by playing and competing with the boys. Martha's daughter, while camping with her brothers as an adolescent and still clear on her role as a person rather than a female, now combines full-time motherhood with community activities. These passages may be played out in Mills and Boon and teenage romances, in which the heroine wins the male away from his obsessive commitment to the public realm to discover his true love for the heroine (Radway 1984:212–18). In one novel in the *Dolly Fiction* series, the heroine throws out her glasses, bleaches her hair and removes her orthodontic band: 'Blind, blonde and dumb, she then conforms more closely to what have seemed to her to be acceptable images of teenage femininity' (Gilbert and Taylor 1991:91). Teen romances, read more avidly by working-class than middle-class girls, favour a domestic future over paid work, and romantic love over academic achievement or independence (Gilbert and Taylor 1991:90).

Some teachers also construct sexuality and studiousness as mutually contradictory, branding girls who flaunt dress codes and sexuality in the classroom as 'promiscuous' and writing them off academically (Gilbert and Taylor 1991:23–4). At Catherine's school, when the more 'mature' girls wore lipstick, the nuns accused them of sexual permissiveness. Catherine also viewed life through this opposition. At her teachers college there were sports-playing girls and boy-playing girls. The boy-playing girls were from middle-class backgrounds and 'looked so smart and mature', but Catherine was really 'smarter than a lot of them'. While Gisela 'eyed' the boys in class, she was shocked at an Estonian friend who talked to the boys playing cricket in the park. Gisela notes the contradiction: her friend was a 'nice' girl and 'very smart'.

Parents also feared the impact of their daughters' sexuality on their academic success. Nadine's mother wanted her daughter to be sexless so she could do 'men's things', Berenice's parents, 'in their attempts to kind of not sexually stereotype us, they actually made us asexual'. Berenice and her siblings disobeyed with 'top secret' romantic liaisons. But other mothers told their daughters to capitalise on their femininity. Sage's mother, for whom Sage's beauty was her passport to marrying 'well', valued Sage for her looks. But Sage could not attract the boys she wanted to, 'And I think behind the face, there was nothing there'. Where Sage's looks undermined her self-esteem, academic achievement replenished it: 'And so I was determined to equal what my brother had got in matric., and I did, I did'.

Sports

There are 1.5 million registered sportswomen compared with 6.5 million registered sportsmen in Australia (House of Representatives Standing Committee on Legal and Constitutional Affairs 1992:110), although the gender discrepancy in terms of informal sport and exercise is not as great. In the past this gender gap has been attributed to the low or trivialised media coverage of sportswomen,[4] and unequal sporting facilities and finances (Mitchell and Dyer 1985:9). In fact, many girls retreat from sport as they enter adolescence, seeing the two as contradictory. Girls' lack of 'movement literacy' (Bennett et al. 1987:369) reduces women's powers to resist rape and domestic battery (MacKinnon 1987:118, 120), discussed in the next section. Because it teaches girls movement literacy and resistance to assault, Yasmin describes martial arts as 'another feminism', even though it is not '*considered* a normal sport' for girls.

Interestingly, as Yasmin points out, as do a number of feminist theorists (for example, Bryson 1987:350; McRobbie 1984; Griffiths 1988b:117–18), ballet and like practices are not seen as physically demanding but an expression of grace. Yasmin was nominated to compete in the Junior World Ice-Skating Championships at the age of 14, although she gave up ice-skating when her father died. By that time, her family had spent about $50 000 on her skating career: 'For a poor family, that's a lot of money'. She turned to kick-boxing, noting that, like ice-skating, it required discipline and balance. Yasmin suffered more injuries from ice-skating, followed a grinding training schedule before and after school, and confronted more bitchiness from the other female ice-skaters.

Melinda was an 'average' person who 'mucked around' with flour fights and so on, in contrast with the squares and the tarts, the latter saying: 'Oh my god, I wouldn't want to get my hair messed up'. When Melinda's grandparents wanted to buy her a dress she responded that 'it wasn't practical to play footie in a dress'. Melinda's movement literacy was underestimated by a patronising physical education teacher when he told the class he was going to teach them how to throw a ball. Melinda said: 'We can already throw a ball'. He asked Melinda to demonstrate, standing 10 metres away. Melinda threw it well over his head: 'And after that he never made the assumption that we couldn't do anything, he always asked'.

A generation earlier, Catherine contrasts femininity with activity. She was 'running around sweating', looking 'like a dag. I was! I still had a pony tail'. In adolescence, participation in sports can also be an excruciating reminder of an emergent unfamiliar female body. Kerry's mother did not have the money to buy her bathers, so 'you're wearing togs that are old baggy-daggy things'. Practising the breast-stroke sitting on the edge of the pool, Kerry realised the action exposed personal parts of her body: 'So I would wear nickers underneath or stay home, ... that was grade six. When you're that age you're really getting self-conscious, that's when your body's changing and you feel like you're living through a magnifying glass'.

Both Rosemary and Willow withdrew from sport during their teenage years, Willow remembering two cases of uncontrolled leakage from her body as instances of shame. Her 'nervousness' brought out 'uncomfortable behaviour', like laughing fits which meant she occasionally wet her pants. She was embarrassed 'having to do gymnastics and do somersaults with pads' when she was having a period. Even getting 'up in a swimsuit in front of half the school' made Willow feel 'beside myself with embarrassment'. Although the shape of her body did not change very much while Willow was in high school, new codes of femininity were being imposed on it. Willow started 'feeling more and more sort of restricted', for example, as girls policed each other in crossing their legs. However, perhaps as an example of de Beauvoir's point that women live a contradiction in their lives, Willow rebelled against the expectation of shaved legs. On one occasion she shaved a spiral up one leg and a chequerboard on the other. In a study of fifty daughters of feminists in the United States, Rose Glickman (1993:91) found that all the daughters discussed unaltered body hair as a testing location of their 'feminism' as opposed to their desire to blend in or feel feminine and beautiful. One, like Willow, suggested: 'I was totally confused. I even considered shaving one leg and not the other' (in Glickman 1993:92). They were also acutely aware that society's message was that if they dressed to 'look good' – in short skirts, painted nails, make-up – they ran the risk of a rape for which they would be blamed or of being 'hassled' (Glickman 1993:94–5).

With the onset of adolescence, sexual reputation might also be at risk. Melinda eschewed attempts to 'have a mystique about you because you're a girl', associating with boys like 'a mate and not necessarily a female'. Commenting on Del's tomboy ways, a neighbour said to Del's mother: 'You were not gifted with a boy child but you have a boy within you'. When a newcomer joined Del's group and mistook Del as an easy girl, Del raised a chair to hit him while her friends leaped to her defence: 'You might do that to other girls but . . . you will be our enemy if you touch her'. The next section explores the construction of femininity and how mothers negotiated their daughters' passage through the menarche, via sex education.

The Seduction of Femininity

In the very infancy of the women's liberation movement, Anne Summers analysed essays about their future written by 126 girls of school-leaving age in metropolitan Adelaide (Summers 1970:73). When these young women mentioned sex, if at all, it was in heavily laden metaphors: one 'experienced the full meaning of love' on her wedding night (Summers 1970:101, 98). In contrast, *Puberty Blues* by Gabrielle Carey and Kathy Lette, published in 1979, is *only* about sex and boyfriends. Walking the tightrope between being a 'slack-arsed moll' or 'a tight-arsed prick-teaser', girls had to carefully time when to 'come across'. Girls who were 'overweight, pimply, a migrant, or just plain ugly' had to choose between the role of prude, which 'was too boring', or moll, in which 'at least people knew who you were' although the moll had to accept 'gang-bangs' (Carey and Lette 1979:74–5). Boys were not categorised by their sexual activity, and 'could screw as many molls as they like during the week' (Carey and Lette 1979:74, 24). Aileen's brief moment as a surfie's girlfriend seems straight out of *Puberty Blues*. The girls 'went and sat on the beach while they went surfing and I just could not believe it'. The other girls in *Puberty Blues* go on from watching boys surf to become unmarried mothers or heroin addicts, but Carey and Lette (1979:118,120) buy a surfboard and take to the waves. Their transcendence costs them their boyfriends, who described them as 'fuckin' bent'.

Puberty Blues categorises 'migrants' as no different from 'ugly' girls in terms of the thing that mattered – attractiveness to boys. Fifteen years later, *Livin' Large* is authored by three young women from non-English speaking backgrounds: Daniella Petrovic, Maria Kokokiris and Monica Kalinowska. Their friendship group generally ignores the 'skips' ('the Aussies') but 'stirs' the 'nips' (Asians) (Petrovic et al. 1994:7, 10). The world has become more complex and dangerous, and provides less hopeful futures. One cannot run away from school at 18 to write a book, the high school certificate being of such importance that 'if you fucked it up, you fucked up your life' (Petrovic et al. 1994:15). Instead of surfing to freedom, the protagonists end up in 'dead-end jobs which are doing nothing for my ego. But I guess these days you have to take what you get' (Petrovic et al. 1994:210). Friends and enemies are given a more complex classification, although the ugly, overweight and gay are still 'outcast' (Williams 1994:14). No wonder one of the girls becomes anorexic (Petrovic et al. 1994:75).

Some things have not changed between *Puberty Blues* and *Livin' Large*: 'Having a boyfriend was more important than anything' (Petrovic et al. 1994:5), girls still carefully calculating the appropriate moment to come across. But now AIDS and contraception inform the girls' bedroom chant: 'Don't be silly, put a condom on his willy' (Petrovic et al. 1994:34). Boys still 'scored' women, but a slut might gain a measure of acceptance: 'Lisa, she did it with all of our guys, and we still gave her respect' (Petrovic et al. 1994:118, 19). In *Puberty Blues*, boys spent time with their girlfriends as a last resort, while the immigrant-descended boys publicly owned their girlfriends with physical contact (Petrovic et al. 1994:11). Girls were still spectators of boys' 'macho' displays; in Sydney's western suburbs these consisted of car races and fights, called 'showtime' (Petrovic et al. 1994:8, 47). Max, both a gay and a skip, was forced into a fight, from which he was hospitalised, dropped out of school, started taking drugs and living with a gay man, finally contracting AIDS. With no bright employment future to lift their morale, 'true love' provides the utopian alternative in *Livin' Large*. While Stassy, the central narrator, drops her boyfriend because of his machismo behaviour (Petrovic et al. 1994:96), Elias, a black Muslim, truly deserves the love of Petra, of Italian background. Petra's father beats and imprisons her, arranging a marriage to an older man (Petrovic et al. 1994:85). With the help of Petra's aunt and a sympathetic teacher, the girls secure Petra's escape into Elias' loving arms.

These texts reflect changing constructions of sexuality since the 1970s, changes attributed by some to a combination of sexual liberation and women's liberation. Thus, Betty Friedan (1965:284) asserted a 'decade-by-decade increase in sexual orgasm' as women won suffrage, careers and education. Women's liberation criticised the hypocritical double standard at the same time as it taught women about their orgasmic capacities. For some in women's liberation groups, learning about masturbation and their bodies 'wasn't trivial . . . I didn't know my own self' (Agnes in Henry and Derlet 1993:54). On the other hand, from the grandmother's generation, Edna Ryan (in Mitchell 1987:76) notes in relation to sex and orgasms: 'Well, quite frankly, I don't let my consciousness get raised on this issue'. The women's liberationists of the 1970s were critical of the sexual revolution as an end in itself (Summers 1994a:253; Densmore 1973:109–10). Even Anne Koedt's (1973:205–6) 'The myth of the vaginal orgasm', which was used by many consciousness-raising groups, argues that men fear the clitoris as a threat to masculinity, largely because it offers the preferable prospect of lesbian sexuality (see also Whiting 1972:192, 195). Such caveats were often drowned out by the attention given to Germaine Greer's libertarian message, Greer (1971:306) saying: 'One wonders just whom Miss Koedt has gone to bed with' as most men are 'aware of the clitoris', 'really frightened of being desired simply as a sexual object' and of 'being expected to have a rigid penis at all times' (see Spongberg 1993 for a discussion).

Sex and Sex Education

The women's movement sought to place in women's minds and hearts contraceptive and gynaecological knowledge which would arm them against unwanted pregnancies and allow them to value their bodies. Peg Hewett (1994:133), born in 1927, considered herself lucky to find out about contraceptive techniques from the Social Hygiene Association, formed in 1916 by Jessie Street for working-class sex education and with the motto 'Knowledge means safety. Give them light' (Finch 1993:142).

In pre-sexual liberation days, women more often remember silence and innuendo shrouding discussions of sex. Margaret's mother 'never told me anything about sex but my grandmother told me everything', including her strategies for contraception given that the church 'never talked about it, not until the thirties'. Myra's mother told her daughters: 'Keep yourself clean and wholesome and when you get married you'll be glad of it', although 'we never knew what she meant really'. When Myra's mother fell pregnant, Myra and her sister thought she was getting fat and so 'missed out on that time of looking forward to a new baby'. During Myra's last pregnancy she experienced a 'beautiful time' when her children joined her in bed and felt the baby. However, Myra is critical that high schools in the 1980s gave children literature on 'condoms and all the rest of it'. One of Teresa's aunts was so horrified by her discoveries on her marriage night that it required three or four months of her husband's abstinence and the priest's counselling before she was able to broach the sex act.

For Helen and Marg in the mothers' generation, the shame and secrecy[5] surrounding their mothers' explanations of menstruation tainted their adult relationships. When Marg had her first period, she was 'incredibly afraid to tell Mum it had finally happened and to ask her what I should do'. Pads were bought from the chemist wrapped in brown paper and then 'kept in Mum's wardrobe . . . it was all very secretive, and you didn't show Dad and you didn't let the boys know'. The only other sex education Marg received was a 'very diagrammatic and highly sterile' film shown by the church on a mothers and daughters night. Marg was not able to share her experiences of childbirth and other gynaecological matters with her mother, the topic being a 'closed' door.

A group of teenage boarders at Mary's girls school, when told by one of their number 'how babies were conceived', would not believe her, describing her as 'filth' and refusing to speak to her for days. Mary's mother did not describe 'what to expect when you got your periods or anything like that'. In contrast, Mary remembers: 'my middle son lost his virginity on the bathroom floor at a party, so I heard about it from the others, it was all joked about and it was all talked about'. Today, as she says, 'my four-and-a-half-year-old grandchildren know where babies come from'. Human relationships education was introduced into schools from the 1980s, and, as Grace notes, parents today have access to 'Family Life Movement' films, and books like Peter Mayle's *Where Did I Come From?*

Indigenous Australian attitudes to sex contrast with the furtiveness and guilt surrounding the sex education many white mothers received. Instead of moral imperatives, Aileen's grandmother suggested that 'it was something that at first could hurt but you could get to . . . love . . . It was a great part of life'. Aileen suggests women on Stradbroke Island look forward to exploring their sexuality as it marks the movement into another stage of the life cycle: 'the unspoken assumption among young women was that you will be sexually active young'. As a mother herself, Aileen talked in similar vein with her own daughter and her boyfriend, explaining that she imagined they would want to have a sexual relationship but that 'at first it may not be successful', saying 'When I tried to lose my virginity I ended up with sticky legs'. When Aileen horrified some (white) guests by recounting this story over dinner, she justified her stance by saying: 'I would rather that my daughter feel that this experience is going to be something that her mother supports, rather than she thinks she's got to hide'. Prior to mixing with white women, Aileen 'thought all women talked about sex', about 'who's rooting who' as well as the pain of their relationships.

Teresa and her friends derided the nuns' message that 'if you touched a boy you had to marry him'. Travelling home on the bus, they 'used to deliberately fall over the boys and grab their hands and say, "Oh, you have to marry us!" The thing was these were the boys from the snobby school up the road'. But Teresa also felt pity for boys who seemed to be akin to animals or werewolves, becoming 'so aroused that at some point they were out of control. And would simply have to keep on going, no matter what, even if you were dead, I suppose. I used to think what a sorry state that was'.

In a study based on discussions with 400 young women in the United States between 1978 and 1986, Sharon Thompson notes that 'sex and love without wedding bells had gained legitimacy in its own right' and that girls could choose their sexual activities because 'it was their life: they had a right; they knew better than anyone else what they needed' (Thompson 1995:23, 172). There were still good girls and bad girls, but there was enormous regional variation in what constituted being bad, for example, oral or anal sex, lesbianism or bisexuality (Thompson 1995:31). There were also class differences, so that some working-class girls staked their virginity not on marriage but on 'true love'. Middle-class girls with further education and careers in view, treated 'intercourse as a kind of growth experience that produces cognitive leaps; romance was window dressing' and love barely mentioned (Thompson 1995:23, 85–6).

In Australia, too, there has been an increasing disarticulation of sex and marriage. In the late 1960s, for Teresa, agreeing to have intercourse with a man was construed as premarital sex. It signalled a 'progression' towards 'a finality which indicated marriage. I don't think I loved the guy at all, and I certainly disliked *intensely* his parents'. Thus, linking sex and love 'didn't really ring true, but there was no other language for what you wanted to do'. The 'sort of "damned whores" stuff' meant 'having sex with someone and not loving him was *extremely* significant'.

For Nadine, born eight years later, the hypocrisy of the 'good girl' message was abundant: 'The problem was the good girl part was so ridiculous, so there was no integrity in the expectations of the good girl bit. It was pure surface, . . . if we as a school appear to be good then we are good, and it just wasn't like that'.

Where Teresa linked sex and marriage – you did not have 'zipless fucks, you had *premarital* sex' – Nadine developed a much more cynical critique of 'good girl' precepts. As she notes: 'Getting pregnant at 16, it's not a matter of opening up the paper and learning about women's issues. I had a real fuck-around getting an abortion at 16 . . . You don't have to have done conducive courses at high school to be aware'. By the late 1980s private school girls also identified this hypocrisy, describing the requirement to 'look expensive, like a piece of material' (Kenway 1990:150–1) and hide (but not refuse) any 'Bogan' or 'tart' behaviour, like smoking or wagging school (Kenway 1990:151). According to Teresa, female high school students in the 1990s still linked sex and love, the only excuse being inebriation: 'Back then when I got married, to have been drunk would have been just as bad, whereas now "I was taken advantage of because I was drunk" sort of thing'. Similarly, in Thompson's (1995:30) study, if girls transgressed their own rules they absolved themselves as drunk or out of control: 'I'm telling you I did it unconsciously because I wouldn't do a thing like that'. In a sense, Teresa suggests that while young girls are no longer held responsible for provoking boys' sexual behaviour, they have ceded their power to control it, negating their agency by becoming inebriated.

Looking Good

> They said, 'Well, we're glad'. And I said, 'Why?' And they said, 'Well a lot of women are older and they wouldn't dream of wearing a swimsuit and also someone who's had a mastectomy, it would show them that they could do it'. And I've got pictures to show it. (Aquarius, speaking of modelling swimwear at the age of 66 for a Tiny Tots Quest fashion parade)

In 1975 Anne Summers (1994a:243–7, 264) identified women's bodies as a colonised 'territory' which is invaded (for example, in rape), from which profits are extracted (for example, in pregnancy and the raising of children forced on women denied sex education and contraception), and which is used to divide women and dominate them culturally (for example, in treating lesbianism as deviant). It is for this reason that early radical feminists launched attacks against beauty contests and advertising which reinforced the notion that 'woman equals body' (Summers 1994a:250). Indeed, the close intersection of looks, sexual orientation and feminism is revealed by the common appellation of feminists as 'lesbian' and 'bra-burning'. They hate men and they hate femininity. The connections between feminism and lesbianism are pursued in chapter 6, while this section explores fashion and femininity.

Women's struggle with fashion is not trivial. If it were, women would not have been so heavily criticised for throwing off their high heels for boiler-suits and unshaved armpits in the 1970s; or for deserting tight corsets for bloomers (long pants worn under a skirt) which gave them freedom to cycle and pursue other physical activity at the turn of the century (Newton 1974:64–5; Oldfield 1992:192). Despite these campaigns, most women have refused feminism's attacks on femininity. One should not merely assert that the majority of women are dupes of a patriarchal culture. Women know the pleasures and rewards which attend emphasised femininity.[6] For example, women, even those who call themselves feminists, have continued to demand cosmetic surgery even when the risks became widely known (Davis 1995:37, 130–1). Some women described cosmetic surgery as the only solution to their problems, even as they knew their problems were 'a symptom of an unjust social order in which women are forced to go to extremes to have an acceptable body' (Davis 1995:57, 162–3).

Looking good is often a job requirement for women, whether explicitly linked with sex, like prostitution and modelling, or not. Naomi Wolf (1990) makes it clear in *The Beauty Myth* that being 'ugly' or 'overweight' can cost women their jobs. When Nadine enrolled in a graduate diploma in broadcast journalism, Pru Goward commented to the women students: 'You need to lose weight', 'Long hair, cut your long hair', and later to the two mature-age women students: 'You're too old for a career in broadcast journalism'. Women were to be flattened into the same acceptable media image. Even to work in private practice rather than a government-funded legal service, Nadine believes she would have to 'change my wardrobe and spend a lot more money on my teeth' and 'probably act like a dutiful daughter'. Her looks limited Audrey's work options to night shifts in a factory. Catherine, for all that she knew she was brighter than the 'smart' girls at teachers college, also felt 'really nervous' about doing class presentations because her looks were devalued. Of modelling, Rosemary 'would say it's my body, my choice. It's not that different from working in a cafe – I mean they hire you, expecting you to look good, and all you do is pump out cappuccinos all day. You just get paid much less'.

We might also ponder dress codes which require women to wear skirts rather than pants. As teachers in the 1970s both Teresa and Shona remember this rule. Teresa wore pants in the winter weather and told the principal: 'if men can wear pants why can't I wear pants? There is no difference, we are teachers'. But she was a woman before she was a teacher. At Shona's teachers college, socialisation 'into good little law-abiding Education Department employees' meant that men wore long trousers and women stockings and skirts when 'practice teaching'; the women 'weren't even allowed to wear slacks for college classes'. In Queensland, following complaints when the Education Department banned both mini-skirts and slacks in primary schools, principals could 'approve' particular outfits. Both men and women are policed by dress codes – indeed men are not allowed to wear skirts in most western workplaces. Pants signify the norm of the worker while dresses signify the abnormality of the woman.

Gerda experienced ambivalence in her training as a model. It gave her self-confidence as a teenager, but she claims that models are 'not treated with dignity'. Additionally, Gerda's boyfriend 'didn't like me up there'. Rosemary hated some aspects of modelling, for example, entering a beauty competition ('I don't want to strut around to see who's the prettiest girl') or being hired as escorts for racing car drivers at a party. Not being a 'body' girl, Rosemary was not required to hang 'all over cars in a swimsuit or something like that'. She was not quite tall enough to be a 'catwalk' girl, and so was promoted as a 'beauty girl', 'a classic kind of look for . . . showing make-up or hair'. Despite the occupation's unappealing aspects, Rosemary 'found that my status kind of rose, once I could say, "Oh, I'm a model"'. Although in retrospect describing this response as 'gross', Rosemary concedes, 'I got a bit hooked on it'. Thus, modelling was a deeply ambiguous experience for Rosemary, 'perceived as glamorous', and indeed occasionally really glamorous, for example, when modelling 'gorgeous clothes' at the Sheraton Mirage in a 'huge ballroom, beautiful long catwalk'. But ultimately, 'it's not *glamorous* because . . . models are just ordinary people', and much of the work is ordinary. Rosemary met women in their forties, formerly successful overseas models, who were now doing shopping centre parades, 'really dependent on that weekly earner'. Rosemary sensed that these 'bright creative women' had lost the opportunity to 'go back to uni'.

Rosemary felt that she was 'intelligent enough to be able to see through it and not get affected by it'. But she did become excessively focused on her looks, and 'never felt good enough'. She got used to 'being treated like a piece of meat', 'going into castings and clients saying, "Can you just lift up your skirt, we want to see how your thighs are?" . . . And it does affect you, even if you know that's what it's about'. Rosemary's access to a feminist rhetoric with which she criticised modelling did not protect her from its effects, although it did help her leave. Referring to Naomi Wolf (1990), Rosemary 'could never justify being part of an industry that perpetuates the "beauty myth" messages to women (and men)' and which coerced models into breast implants. Rosemary knew of ten models who had silicone breast implants. One had to lie in bed for a week recovering, her breasts completely bruised. Rosemary began to hate modelling, and seized the opportunity to return to university before it was too late for her.

Like Kathy Davis' (1995) anguished feminists choosing cosmetic surgery, Sage was ambivalent concerning her own beauty and her daughter's modelling. Remembering the acknowledgement she received for her beauty as a young woman, Sage would tell Rosemary 'Oh darling ... you were wonderful, I was so proud'. But Rosemary overheard Sage speaking to her friends in a feminist voice: 'Oh, Rosemary's modelling, isn't it pathetic?' For Sage the contradiction persists: 'the ageing process is TOUGH!' While some feminists have traded in their boiler-suits for corporate suits, femininity continues to make claims on women. Gerda suggests the dictates of the fashion industry mean that all young girls think about is 'food, fat, food, fat'. Gerda continues: 'We're not meant to be that thin, because they don't even have periods any more' and 'everybody's unique'. But there are limits to acceptable size. While Gerda's daughter fails to value her 'hour-glass figure', she has 'to watch her thighs a bit'.

Growing Up with Sexual Assault and Domestic Violence

According to Joan, social workers were aware of the prevalence of incest in the 1960s, but 'it all seems to have been hush-hush, a conspiracy of silence', figuring in family casework as 'social and economic problems'. At a gathering in the 1980s, of the seven women present two had been abused by their mothers, and four raped by their fathers 'from the tender age of 3 and 4'; only Joan hadn't been abused.[7] Similarly, when rape was considered the woman's fault, even parents might not take action on behalf of their daughters. In Joan's younger days a neighbour was raped but her parents hushed it up, fearing their daughter would be branded a 'scarlet women'. It was not only in Italian communities that these issues remained unspoken, repressed in the interests of *la bella figura*, keeping up face, despite 'kisses going sloppily astray, hugs and cuddles leading to wandering hands, and affectionate squeezes turning into a sexual grope' (Pellizari 1993:133; see also Cavuoto 1993:125).

Women have been emboldened to take action against sexual assault as a result of more widespread acceptance of feminist claims that these events are not the victim-survivor's fault, ideas which have found expression in law; in the provision of hotlines and counselling; in training in social work, nursing, law and other courses (Rehfeldt 1994:170–1); and by women's greater access to an alternative livelihood, either on a supporting parent's pension or in paid work with access to childcare. Even so, a 1993 survey found that 75 per cent of sexual assaults are not reported (Office of the Status of Women 1995a:31), while the attrition rate for sexual asssault charges remains high (Rathus 1993:31) and in 1992 a Supreme Court judge claimed that women should accept 'rougher than usual handling' during intercourse.[8]

Two of Barbara's mother's boyfriends attempted to molest her sexually. On the first occasion, to her credit, Barbara's mother immediately bundled up the children and their possessions and pushed a pram for miles on winding country roads until a passing truck driver gave them a lift back to London. Shona remembers community surveillance making her childhood world safe: 'You really felt as though you were walking in your own kingdom'. Kerry also describes community knowledge and warnings to children as a mechanism for forestalling exposure to dangerous situations: 'when we were told, "Don't go near so-and-so", you knew not to go there'. Rita protected herself from risky situations because she was 'a very sensible mature person, even at a young age'. Working at Lennon's Hotel when the Beatles were performing in Brisbane, Rita was asked to go to their room, but refused: 'Even in those days, like teenagers today, you've got to be at the wrong place at the wrong time, and things do happen'.

Fiorenza now works with older Italians, evaluating their care needs. At times she counsels women who are required to care for fathers who once committed incest and violence against them, frail elderly men who their daughters really despise: 'nobody knew about it, not the Italian community, not the mainstream. Well, there were no services and the migrants were a terribly silent society then'.

Lea describes her father's violence as 'an horrific time', with Anzac Day being one of the 'traumatic' events in the family calendar, when her father returned from drinking with his mates. This would almost always lead to violent arguments and physical confrontations. Thirty-five to forty years later, Lea attended a dawn service as the Member for Elizabeth. When she stepped into the RSL, she experienced a flashback 'that reminded me of the past'. Her father's comrades in arms 'thought very highly of him in the war. He did very well, he became a major very quickly'. But his children did not see this 'good side' because 'happy times were tempered with the uncertainty of when they would revert to the other'. Lea's mother 'had a charade of coping and we just did too', although Lea is convinced that her teachers must have known. 'We were up all night sometimes and it showed . . . our eyes were all puffed up and red . . . but no one ever said anything, no one asked'. Because no one asked, 'it could never be resolved'. In fact, when Lea married and her mother and siblings sought shelter with Lea and her husband 'the cycle was broken'. 'Just imagine if she'd done it twenty years earlier. He got a huge shock and he changed'. In that change a different man emerged and Lea was able to develop a more loving and respectful relationship with him in the years that followed.

But the 'good side' of Lea's experience of violence was that she 'wasn't personally broken by it', standing up to her father and protecting her mother. Unbroken but carrying the experience, Lea became a successful counsellor who recognised children who were as she had been, and understood 'the feelings of helplessness and guilt'. When talking to school children, Lea stressed that it was not their fault, a guilt often taken into adulthood. Thus, Mayra: 'used to feel somehow that I could have done something to prevent it', in fact jumping between her parents and receiving a punch in the face for her intervention. Lea also offered support and advice to children on how to keep themselves safe. She explained that their mothers faced hard options, whether to stay or leave, but that was their mothers' decision to make.

'Looking good' as a description both of emphasised femininity and the encouragement offered to flagging runners, refers to the pleasures and dangers of female sexuality and female bodies, the pleasures of looking good and the dangers of being a woman, whether looking good or not. Yasmin, in contrasting ice-skating and kick-boxing, is well aware that young girls are encouraged out of the skills which will enhance self-protection into equally arduous pursuits which will enhance a sense of femininity. But women like Yasmin seek to transcend their immanence with new definitions of femininity; not ones which mean aping masculinity, and not ones which do not arm them against the dangers in the world.

Conclusion

The 126 school girls who wrote essays on their futures for Anne Summers in 1970 responded to three titles: 'It is [the year] 2036 and you are 70 years old – describe your life' (the private school and Summers' proposed topic), 'Reflections on my life' (high school, topic adapted by teacher), 'My life' (technical school, topic adapted by teacher). The essays covered two major themes: family (marriage, husband, children) and work (training or job/career). Some mentioned 'travel' (Summers 1970:104–5) and half the working-class girls noted accidents and injuries (but only one case of domestic violence) (Summers 1970:106–7, tables following p. 76). Only one-third mentioned no job at all (compared with one-quarter who did not mention children and/or marriage); only 10 per cent mentioned returning to the workforce after marrying, although the majority of them would. Students saw themselves as secretaries, nurses, bank workers, teachers, and occasionally models or air-hostesses. Private school girls sometimes travelled to exotic locales, even if they went in these traditional roles (Summers 1970:78–9, 82). Just over a decade later, in 1982, a survey of female school students found that only 52 per cent desired a career while 81 per cent wanted to have children. However, 54 per cent now thought they would continue to work part-time after having children, although 43 per cent thought it unlikely they would continue their careers. As with Anne Summers' sample, middle-class girls were more likely to envisage a career while working-class girls were more likely to see work as a brief transition to marriage and economic dependence on a husband (Poole and Beswick 1989:16). In the next two chapters we explore the intersections of education and work or career, drawing largely on the experiences of the mothers. Chapter 4 moves on to the issues which were of more significance to Anne Summers' sample: marriage and motherhood.

CHAPTER 2

Training For Life

> That's also my philosophy that we need to work at staying in tune with our Higher Being, be it God or our ancestral spirits or whatever . . . As you are ready so the way is revealed . . . When I finished my studies, I decided – and I'd never considered it before – 'I'd like to teach on the Sunshine Coast and get away from Brisbane for a while'. And when I was ready, I put out my message to God, and the universe reciprocated. I made a phone call, drove up for an interview, and had the teaching job I wanted, all in a week. Here I was, a single parent with three kids living on my own and off we went! No accommodation, knew no one, never been there before. (Kerry)

During the time the marriage bar was in force, young women had to imagine their futures as a choice between becoming a wife and mother or working. These opposing paths are neatly captured in the alternative Phylis was offered by her father. In grade seven, she was taking care of her younger sister and managing the house. He said: 'Okay, you can either go on or you can have this new pair of shoes'. Phylis chose the shoes which were a 'beautiful sort of forest green suede' with high heels, and found a job as a clerk. In contrast, Margaret resisted the media messages and insisted that her daughters 'get the best education you can' rather than impressing people with their looks. Her warning was confirmed when her marriage failed after twenty-five years, demonstrating that 'you never know what the future's going to be for you'. Both these stories suggest, as discussed in the previous chapter, that beauty, femininity and marriage are inconsistent with education and intelligence. Similarly, in the next chapter we will see how femininity undercuts a woman's role as a worker, turning her into a sexualised being in the workplace.

This chapter explores the family and schooling influences which shaped the work and career ambitions of the first two generations of women in the study. While some nurtured the desire to become something, most imagined schooling and occasionally university as a prelude to marriage and motherhood. Mothers, located between grandmothers who were less likely to work and daughters who expected to, entered adulthood with the expectations of their mothers but experienced a working life much more akin to that of their daughters. For this reason (and others), many returned to their childhood dreams as adults, but often along more circuitous paths than they had originally contemplated.

Family Influences

Role Models

People mostly have modest ambitions for themselves and great ambitions for their children. (Kay Setches 1992:73)

In many ways our parents, and I've seen that in other parents, ... their self-esteem comes through the children. Where they missed out on having education ... the children have to achieve these feats, not only for themselves but for their parents as well. (Lea)

In their memoirs and memories, many successful women remember mothers or other female relatives as role models, women who either worked or had an independent outlook.[1] Lisa Quadrio's mother packed crayfish so she could study medicine, rather than do the nursing studies suggested by her teachers. Thus, Lisa Quadrio connects with her mother through 'an academic gown rather than a bridal gown' (in Quadrio and Quadrio 1994:392, 395). Indrani locates her 'staunch feminist' father and 'independent' mother within 'strong women in the myths and folklore' and India's nineteenth-century reform movements which worked to improve the status of women.

A number of women were brought up in 'a company of women' as Noela puts it, sometimes in families where the father had died early (so that Mary's mother, a 'role model', took over her husband's produce and SP bookmaking business), and sometimes in families where men were 'not so striking' (Noela) or were 'gentle' (Pat). Noela's aunt was an off-course bookmaker. Her mother worked with the American Red Cross during the war and later ran the canteen at the local swimming pool. Of Noela's cousins, one joined the army, one was a teacher, and the youngest owned a car and seemed to 'do what she wanted'. Both Noela's grandmother and mother were great readers, a point other women (for example, Claudia) make of parents who have educational ambitions for their children which exceeded their own achievements. Noela comments: 'In her living as a person who continued to educate herself she inspired me'. Noela's grandmother 'had to do dressmaking to keep her family alive'. The eldest in the family, Noela's mother, like Matina, left school in grade six to help support the family, but worked and scrimped for Noela and her brother's additional educational opportunities. While Margaret's mother was 'timid and quiet', her grandmother, who often shared a bedroom with the young Margaret, was a woman of wit and courage. To stop her sea captain husband's wanderings, she threw the 'deep water papers', without which he was confined to Australian waters, on top of the four-poster bed. She invoked abstinence after the doctor warned her that further pregnancies would be life-threatening, and sent deputations of her sons to the ship to extract her husband's wages before he paid them to his mistresses.

Janine Haines (1992b:64, 65) was a teenager before she realised that her parents, who both had careers and shared housework, were behaving in 'quite an odd way for a couple . . . in the 1950s'. Eve Mahlab's father worked at home while her mother enjoyed 'the business', Mahlab attributing this to her own completion of law studies where other Jewish girls dropped out of university to marry (in Mitchell 1984:46–7). However, while Anna's parents gave her and her brother equal educational opportunities, 'traditional roles still prevailed in my household even though both my parents worked in their family business'. So prevalent was the 1950s model of the housewife at home, that Teresa's mother worked but would have called herself a housewife; that women heard on the radio or seen running an office were not necessarily considered 'working' women (Watts 1992:31; Shortlander 1992:31). This points to a need to see the meanings of statistics in daily interpretation. While the percentage of women working had reached the same level by 1948 that it had in the peak year of 1943 (Grimshaw et al. 1994:265), it required a reinterpretation of that fact to plant the seeds of change. Reinterpretation came through changing media coverage and through widening opportunities. Equal pay battles were fought following the post-war reduction in women's wages, but these struggles did not receive press recognition until about the mid-1960s (Johnson 1993:128).

Career Aspirations

> In Taiwan, rich parents would usually give money to their sons and not their daughters. But things are different in Australia. Australians believe that both sons and daughters are equal. (Shirley)

> That's why women have it over men because they go through so many stages. As a mother you do a tuckshop roster, as a wife you 'support' your husband, as a person you adjust! . . . Men just go from there to there and they retire, and it's like dropping off the edge of a cliff for them. (Grace)

Unusual among Australian women, marriage was never in Noela's dreams. Instead, Noela imagined being a jockey and toyed with pharmacy. Ultimately, however, 'I think teaching had always been very attractive to me'. Noela won a physical education scholarship but was appointed to a school in Cairns which did not offer physical education training. Her aunt Mary, 'undaunted, sailed forth to the MP in Cairns' complaining of the injustice perpetrated on young women in the country. Noela's mother was more diffident: 'Oh, I wish Mary would just keep quiet, she's creating all these waves'. Noela and the other physical education students were relocated to Brisbane, a 'powerful example' of someone 'standing up assertively . . . and having something done about it, which was the amazing thing'.

In the generation of the grandmothers, a girl could only be a 'teacher or a clerk'. Girls who 'really had brains' may be encouraged to enter university, but usually 'parents couldn't afford it' (Yvonne). Joan's mother persisted in her desire to become a teacher even though she 'was forbidden the house, and her name was not mentioned for about twenty years'. Little wonder, perhaps, that Joan's mother 'didn't want her daughters to grow up in a country town and be "slushies" in the local hotel'. However, the Depression forced Joan to leave school at the end of intermediate and 'stand in queues waiting for shop jobs . . . seventy, eighty in a queue'. Again her mother intervened, pointing out that the work in a milk bar, which Joan enjoyed, lacked the future promised by a job offer with Australia Catholic Assurance. After nine years, Joan 'married from' this job.

In one of the few stories of direct discrimination, 'there were two slots for girls and twelve for boys' for those who sat the public service entrance examination in 1930. Vera wanted to be a nurse but could not start her training until she was 19 so she worked as a bookkeeper in her father's drapery shop, later realising her nursing ambitions in the Voluntary Aid Detachment during the war.

Glenn's parents and brother worked long hours in the family orchard to pay Glenn's education expenses. Her teachers encouraged her to enter university and train as a doctor, unusual in pre-war days, but Glenn's ambition was to do overseas missionary work as a nurse. Glenn explains this apparent gender role reversal: 'it probably was unusual for me to be educated but my brother was expected to carry on the farm I suppose and I had ambition to travel. We had a more stable lifestyle in those days and perhaps communicated differently'. Faced with her husband's poor health, Glenn upgraded her qualifications and returned to nursing twenty-two years after her initial training.

Among the mothers, Amber had educational ambitions. In rural New South Wales she studied by correspondence 'at night after helping Mum' in her shop-cum-petrol station and cafe, on the understanding Amber would be supported to complete her secondary education. When Amber's mother reneged on this promise, Amber left home and worked in a hospital with a view to sitting the nurses' entrance examination when she was old enough. Although Amber successfully sat the examination, like Claudia, she gave up her career ambitions to marry. 'Of course, at that point I thought, "Yes, this is the love of my life"'. But it was 'probably the biggest mistake that I made', due to the years of incessant hard work and sexual violence Amber suffered before escaping. With a family to support, Amber realised that she would need tertiary qualifications. Thirty years after leaving nursing Amber returned to study, ultimately enrolling in social work, akin to nursing because 'it's close to people who are broken in another way'.

Gisela tried to leave at the end of primary school, sensitive to her mother's struggle to support her, but 'Mother was adamant, and I must admit I thank God that she was', Gisela realising her only option would have been factory work. Ironically, Grace's parents were 'really chuffed' that she attended grammar school, but the school did not offer art classes, which was Grace's ambition. In other homes girls were expected to repress their ambitions for the needs of brothers rather than the wishes of parents. Girls did not always see this decision as unfair. Claudia accepted her father's wisdom, while Margaret realises that her protests would have been heeded: 'But one just didn't, one just followed the path marked out' – as Claudia's story, told briefly in the last chapter, revealed.

However, a handful of women remember, sometimes bitterly, losing educational opportunities because they were expected to leave school and help with the housework (Helen and Matina) or because daughters 'are only going to get married and have a family' (Helen), or because brothers 'might need the higher education' – *might* need the higher education' (Margaret). Like Claudia and the other women who reflect on their acceptance of world views that a feminist lens now questions, Matina wonders whether she could have avoided her destiny:

> the two boys were the most valued, seeing I was just the oldest girl who was dragged out of school to help bring up the other children . . . That's why at 63 I'm now at university . . . I'm really quite angry about it because I really did want to go but I didn't have the, I wasn't strong enough, on my own to fight against my parents on that issue.

Matina married at the age of 22 and has four children. She returned to her ambitions in her early fifties, when the children were old enough and Matina was no longer required to care for her mother-in-law. Valerie, a generation later, successfully 'insisted' that she receive a tertiary education. Although somewhat surprised by her request, Shona's parents readily allowed her to study beyond year ten. Although Shona did not ask, she feels they would have drawn the line at repeating senior, even though two of her brothers did. As Grace notes, parents were the hostages of the times and their own upbringing: 'they just assumed that he would have a "career" in inverted commas whereas mine was a "job"'. Grace told her own children: '"When you go to university" . . . and it wasn't an if'. To flesh out this imagined future, Grace ran her own private holiday program with outings to museums and exhibitions, admitting she probably had more fun than her children did.

Some parents had ambitions for their daughters which, as Lea suggests, would compensate for their own unfulfilled yearnings. Although the first in her family to go to university, Lea's parents 'wanted the best for me, and so they thought university was just the next thing. They never ever said no, never ever'. Lea also remembers a teacher saying: 'She can do anything she chooses'. Nadine's mother, lacking a good education, wanted one for her children: 'so that they would not feel small around people'. Teresa's mother, frustrated that she had to leave school early: 'instilled in us that education was the way to get out of this poverty and this cycle of being part of the lower classes'. Lita's mother married young but constantly said: 'I don't want you to be like me. I've got so many children'. Lita's father was also supportive: 'If anything goes wrong in your marriage I want you to have a career so you can stand on your own feet'. Although Therese's mother had only a primary school education, it was she and not Therese's medical father who insisted her daughters go to university. He would have preferred the daughters to 'stay home, learn cooking, sewing and to be a good wife'. Instead, Therese joined Vietnam's foreign affairs ministry, serving in Hong Kong. Marg's father: 'always said that I wasn't good enough, . . . that I was a failure'. As an adult, Marg 'was *determined*, absolutely doggedly determined they were going to see me in that bloody mortarboard walking up on that stage, shaking hands and getting it'.

To some Indigenous Australian women, ambitions for children made parents appear 'pushy'. Auriel suggests that Aboriginal parents seek to protect their children from the emotional costs of failure. While 'some parents will encourage and nurture and push', Auriel's parents 'encouraged and nurtured without pushing'. In Kerry's family, everyone was praised, either for doing well or 'if we didn't do well we were still praised up for what we already had'. Four siblings and ten of Kerry's cousins have gone on to tertiary study, but as adults. White mothers also try to shield their children from disappointment, as Valerie did when her daughter stood for head girl in a primary school class of largely Torres Strait Islanders. To Valerie's surprise, the class elected her daughter. Mayra became aware that, before she returned to study, she put 'enormous responsibility' on her daughter by 'living my life through her, getting what I didn't get'.

Strong ambitions for their daughters might not compensate for lack of finances or cultural capital to help with homework and educational choices. Pat 'didn't go to university as we couldn't afford it' and Pat felt obligated to help her family financially. Deanna had a vague ambition to become a teacher but sensed her family could not really afford university fees and expected her to 'get on your own feet and you earn your own income'. Deanna also felt: 'You would have been paying for it for the rest of my life, paying back your parents for the notion of what they'd done for you perhaps, you know? That's a dreadful thing to say'. Rita 'always had the thought of going to school, but . . . didn't know how to go and grasp it'. This was compounded by lack of knowledge and support from Rita's mother.

Aileen could not see the point of doing well at school, given that the working future for Indigenous Australian women was as 'domestics. You didn't need to have science and maths to go into that'. Others saw education as the pathway beyond domestic service, although parents' ambitions were often lower than their daughters'. When Mary Ann Bin-Sallik told her mother she did not want to be a domestic worker, her mother replied: 'That's alright, dear. You can be a secretary' (Sykes 1993:25). Instead, she became the first black sister to graduate from Darwin Hospital (in Sykes 1993:26). Just a few years later than Aileen, Nikita 'went through DEET' into 'secretarial school, all Aboriginal girls were put through secretarial school'. Her children, by contrast, are considering the occupations of lawyer, flight attendant and ranger.

Class aspirations also influenced the pursuits thought appropriate and available. Just as Claudia would have been 'on the skids' if she had gone to a vocational school, Alison's parents saw university as the 'only acceptable place' for her after school. However, her father recommended pharmacy rather than the architecture studies which Alison proposed, noting that in the Depression, 'architects were the first to go'. Nadine wanted to be a writer but her mother was intent on Nadine pursuing one of the 'top' professions: law or medicine. Journalism would not satisfy her mother's ambition, being entered by cadetship and not university. Some young women toyed with medicine, but gave it up because mathematics became too hard (Gisela), or because their working-class background meant 'we had no class conception, no business concept of what it was like to be a doctor' (Teresa). Given the long years of study, Lea's father saw medicine as 'a waste' 'because it was going to take six years and I would have children'.

Gisela attributes her limited awareness of career options to her mother's immigrant background and working-class job. Rejecting teaching which 'all the other girls' chose, 'back came dear old libraries'. As a young girl Gisela had discovered libraries, 'there were all these books

... this whole world of just, I suppose, magic'. Not only was librarianship a 'nice profession', but Gisela would be employed and could afford the fees, covering part-time study for professional qualifications and university. The post-war aura of science prompted Lea into science, although 'not really knowing what I'd do at the end'. Teresa won a scholarship to teachers college and one to university. The first person in her family to go to university, Teresa had no 'guidance as to what subjects to choose. So like a typical girl I fell into an arts degree', although she studied mathematics within her arts degree.

Even as a teenager, Glenda noticed the combination of class with gender in defining her options. Grandmothers like Yvonne could only imagine being a 'teacher or a clerk'; a generation later Glenda suggests that a female 'couldn't be anything apart from a nurse, a secretary or a teacher . . . Or you could go into the public service'. Glenda's mother had always thought teaching a 'wonderful' career, because a woman both exercised her talents and had hours appropriate to childcare needs. Glenda won the medal offered for the highest pass in year eight in the region. She suggests that had she been a working-class male instead of a female, 'I think that the Labor Party or the unions would have, as they do, provided scholarships and so on for under-privileged males'. The local newspaper asked her for an interview about her future:

> I had absolutely no idea really about what I wanted to be, but on the way down, I remember riding my bike past the swimming pool and thinking, 'God, I've got to think of something really fast', and I actually thought of law. And I think it was to do with, the interest in just the ceremony of it . . . So I told them I wanted to be a lawyer, which of course I never was for a long period of time.

Schools offered gendered career counselling which rarely extended the commonly known choices. Before the inevitable wedding, Alison toyed with 'doing art, because I could draw and spent a lot of time in the art studio'. Alison mentioned a related possibility of architecture to her headmistress after Alison's final examinations during the few minutes' chat which passed for career advice: 'she made really approving noises. And I thought, she just thinks it would look interesting and different in the old girls' activities list'. Alison did architecture 'because it was the nearest thing to art at the university, and that was the only place to go that I knew of'. Nadine chose law because she was 'good at English':

> the funny thing was I never really equated the legal profession with being a lawyer. I didn't know anybody, I didn't sit around at my parents' dinner parties speaking with barristers and judges. There were no vacation schools or work experience . . . I had never realised it was a desk job.

Career options, then, were circumscribed to appropriately feminine possibilities, if not by parents then often by schools. Moira Rayner (1992:76) was counselled not to study law which was 'unfeminine'. The nuns at Catherine's school were surprised to discover that students like her in the commercial stream could apply for teachers college. In Shona's last weeks at school a visiting guidance officer suggested only the options of nursing, the public service or teaching. The next section explores the more subtle mechanisms by which school experience contributed to the formation of girls' work and career aspirations.

Gendering Education

Barbara notes that 'education would have changed my life completely' and Joy Hooton seems to concur in her comment that in this century and the last 'education plays a large part in female autobiographies'. However, the writers Hooten discusses overwhelmingly complain of 'growing down' in inadequate education, having to leave school for domestic commitments, although a few note their 'lucky privilege' if allowed to enter university (Hooton 1990:224–7). Just as primary education became universal at the turn of the century, secondary education became universal fifty years later. The compulsory school-leaving age was raised to 15 and new comprehensive co-educational area-based schools replaced the old high schools and technical schools. Women now oustrip men in completing secondary schooling and entering university (Marginson 1993:13), provoking claims that schools are becoming feminised and disadvantaging boys. However, there are still more male than female principals, although in 1993 three-quarters of primary school teachers were women as were just over half of secondary school teachers (Office of the Status of Women 1995a:18).

Teachers and Classes

Generally speaking, the women I spoke to do not remember instances of sex discrimination at school, although several commented on the regime of physical punishment. This is quite possibly because, as with household task distribution discussed in the previous chapter, before the late 1960s inequalities were not generally seen through a gendered lens. In contrast, racial and ethnic discrimination is remembered, including teachers who treated migrant children as stupid because of their English language difficulties (Vasta 1992:164–5, 156). Rita was mortified to come to Australia from Italy at the age of 12 and be placed in first grade, where she was jeered by the other children. Her educational experience made her so resentful that she refused a scholarship which would have provided a free secondary education. Gladys was outraged when a teacher tested her son's intelligence without speaking to Gladys first, Gladys indignantly noting: 'wouldn't I have known if I had a retarded child? I mean I'm the mother of the child'. In this environment the children of migrants often tried to fit in, even if it meant battles with their parents (de Lepervanche 1989:50; Loro 1992:16). In the early 1950s in Brisbane, Gisela fought her mother over 'clothing, long socks' and 'plaits'.

Indigenous Australian students experience racism and a learning environment which rubs against the grain of their learning strategies, against spontaneity, against supportive caring rather than judgemental criticism of self and others, against learning through listening and observing rather than talking (Hughes 1987:7–10). This might be compounded by a disrupted home life, for example, Kerry moved schools once or twice a year at certain periods in her school life. As wards of the state, Kerry and her siblings had to 'go with our little slips of paper' for school books and uniforms. When family finances were low they either had to 'book up food' at the shop or 'go over to OPAL[2] to get food, shame, carrying a baker's tray of food and tarts, leftover rolls', a situation Kerry contrasts unfavourably with collecting fruit, food and oysters on her island home. The school loudspeaker summoned Aileen as a 'ward of the state' to collect her textbooks, or to be stripped to her underwear and inspected by male inspectors 'for nits and lice and whether we were clean'.

Kerry's grandparents lived in fear that their grandchildren would be taken from them, and they tried to insulate home from school. 'You were drilled not to talk about home at school' and white school friends were rarely visited. Kerry recalls school was a distrusted foreign world:

> In those days you had those books like, 'Dick, Dora, Fluff and Nip' and Mum and Dad. There was always Mum and Dad and two kids and they lived in this immaculate house and the mother always is cooking lovely meals and biscuits and wearing an apron, and Dad was always working and coming home in his car and mowing the lawns, and everything was so happy.

Indigenous Australians were either absent or represented as such uncivilised ape-like dehumanised people that 'no one would have wanted to be an Aborigine'. Where racism was not blatant, total denial of heritage was common: 'You're too pretty to be an Aborigine'; 'But you're not a real Aborigine' (Kerry).

When Kerry's home life became violent, 'I couldn't be what the teachers wanted me to be because all this stuff was happening at home. I mean a lot of the time we were trying to protect Mum from this fella'. Kerry had 'very positive role models' at primary school and always wanted to be a teacher. Contrariwise, Nikita's senior mistress 'said I'd end up in the gutter' so Nikita proved her wrong and completed junior school. Aileen did very well in primary school but at secondary school, in her 'secondhand clothes', she was ostracised by all but one of the white middle-class students 'who played tennis on the weekend, I didn't know what that was'.

In the post-war period with the extension of secondary education, a number of single sex schools were made co-educational. From the 1980s feminist educators noted that girls often disguised their intellectual capacities in the presence of boys while teachers gave disproportionate attention to the boys in class who, moreover, were often disruptive. Feminist teachers initiated segregated classes, especially in subjects where girls were under-represented or underachieved (Millan 1993: 133). Co-educational schools were 'a rough and tumble place' (Sue), where boys were 'disruptive' (Gisela), or 'just the nastiest, roughest, dirtiest people . . . and cruel, just plain cruel' (Phylis). Catherine and Sue both realised that 'There weren't boys around to put us down and that stuff' (Catherine). Gisela became a good swimmer, which was 'esteem-enhancing', while 'there wasn't the same obsession with boyfriends and being pretty and all those silly sorts of things'. The all-female environment offered 'a kind of breathing space' in which 'there were no barriers, . . . you felt you could succeed' (Gisela).

Margaret's schooling by nuns in an earlier generation developed 'a wonderful sense of self and individuality, which I think my generation was very lucky to have'. Indeed, Margaret remembers an unusual nun who upbraided Margaret's aunt when she complained her daughter had no time to help with the housework: 'But you don't expect a child with Terry's brain to be sweeping and washing up and cleaning, surely?' While the sisters who taught her would not have described themselves as feminists, Noela calls them such in their daily practice of showing women in leadership positions (see also Carmel Niland in Mitchell 1991:11 and Carmen Lawrence 1994:11). Catherine remembers a nun in year eight who taught 'Latin, and French and maths and physics and chemistry', 'domestic arts', 'shorthand, typing, bookkeeping, we all did English'. 'One woman did this!'

However, a number of the women point to contradictions in their convent education. Nuns were 'both confined and free, governed and autonomous, practical and unworldly, gentle and tough, sympathetic and intransigent, female and sexless, they seem to present an alternative way of being even as they suggest its impossibility' (Hooton 1990:232). Teresa battled incessantly at her school for the right to think independently and write critically. At about the age of 13 the students were offered training sessions to become nuns, which Teresa describes as 'the nuns' aerobics'. She quickly withdrew because of a logical flaw in the argument:

> What they were saying was that society needed nurses, teachers, mothers, nuns, doctors, whatever. Mind you, they didn't very often say doctors, it was more mothers and nuns and teachers . . . That bit made sense, our society needed a spread of people . . . But then in the same kind of argument they would put forward this stuff about the best vocation is to be a nun. I remember sitting there saying, 'But it can't be the best vocation, that's a contradiction, the best vocation is surely the one that God has picked for you because that's God's will' . . . But 'Oh, no, no, no, no. The best vocation is to serve God' . . . Mind you, it was no bloody wonder, they were running out of nuns, they wanted a few more.

Similarly, Shona notes 'the nuns always gave us a feeling of freedom and rights and you can basically do whatever you want' although this did not usually include becoming 'doctors or lawyers or Indian chiefs'.

Shona suggests the power of the 'community of women' had geographical limits. They ruled their own territories, but could not enter the altar during the celebration of mass, a space open even to altar boys. They were unable to join the gathering at school concerts and balls, even though they had prepared the students for the occasion. Informal influence occasionally replaced formal power, parishioners colluding with the nuns to ensure that some of the proceeds from the school fete were diverted to keeping the school running rather than going towards the parish priest's coffers which were used to embellish his church.

Through the Half-Open Door of Tertiary Education

While women now make up more than half of Australia's university students, this is not the case in the technical education sector which is rapidly replacing or supplementing apprenticeships as the vehicle for trade and other qualifications.[3] In the 1980s sexual harassment was rife, one woman describing it as a 'sub-rape' atmosphere, with leers, looks, comments, and girlie pin-ups justified as preparation for working life (Pocock 1988:48–9). The National Plan of Action for Women in TAFE, developed in 1991, seeks to improve entry rates, especially in vocational training and to improve the learning and physical environment for women. Recognition of prior learning has also been introduced, both for TAFE entry and to encourage employers to realise the skills which are learned in unpaid labour ('Recognising women's skills', *Women & Work*, Women's Bureau, DEET, 1993, 14(3):11–12).

In the 1980s, to improve the vocational enrolment rates for women, Catherine, as a member of the equal opportunities unit in TAFE, developed a real estate course specifically for women. There was some hostility from the women's studies lecturers at TAFE, themselves struggling for program accreditation. One thought 'that my approach to real estate would detract from the purity of the women's studies program'. In contrast, Catherine believed that economic independence would widen women's opportunities more surely than a raised consciousness. Thus, one woman was studying 'to get some money, and save for a divorce'. In her documentation, Catherine rendered such potentially unpalatable truths as 'a marketable skill, I used to write it all the time . . . The guys would understand that'. Catherine designed an intensive fourteen-week real estate course, 'a fully fledged program, so that they would get their ticket, as they say, and they'd be able to sell property':

> Well did that cause uproar. We were going to flood the market, I mean, this is twenty-one women . . . and how could they possibly do it in such a short period of time . . . Well twenty of those women finished. And I remember the lunch. It was absolutely great. They finished the last exam . . . Everybody is chat-chat-chat, chomp-chomp, and then [one student] said, 'You know what?' And everybody stopped, and she said, 'I've got a brain'. Chomp-chomp-chomp.

From the 1980s TAFE colleges provided senior classes by which women could gain university entrance. In her sixties, Barbara achieved high grades in such a course and although finances prevented her from studying fine arts, Barbara describes 'by-passing junior and getting my senior pass and uni acceptance at 67 years' as her proudest achievement, along with 'raising a good family under trying circumstances'.

While it may still be considered inappropriate for women in Australia to study engineeering (Sydney University's first female engineering student commenced in 1955, according to Alison), this was not the case in either Poland or the Philippines. Agnes enrolled in metallurgical engineering in 1958 when 'a lot of women were doing engineering', although chemical engineering was the preferred option. Agnes wanted to study medicine but her father said the latter was 'such a long course' that he could not 'afford it'. In Poland some engineering faculties had more men than women and some had more women than men: 'You didn't feel like you were a woman in a "man's" job and that you didn't really belong' (Hanna). While Mima Stojanovic also claims there were no gender-typical jobs in post-war Soviet Europe, especially as 'the women were fighting alongside the men', she admits that at the University of Belgrade, where half the geology students were women, 'men didn't like women in the field at first', and she lost her scholarship when she got married in 1951 (in Mitchell 1984:65–7).

Women now constitute about one-third of tertiary educators, although they are less than 7 per cent of professors and associate professors (Office of the Status of Women 1995a:18; *Ita*, August 1992:21). In contrast, during the war women students 'experienced the conviction of being the less listened-to Second Sex' (Moyal 1995:28). By the 1960s, when the privileged or hard-working post-war baby boomers were at university, the climate had changed little. Male and female undergraduates 'derided' (Goldsmith 1994:178) or 'kind of laughed at' (Alison) female academics, Marlene Goldsmith (1994:178) noting both her discomfort and the lack of a gender lens to explore it.

Studying architecture at Sydney University in the late 1950s, the handful of female students in Alison's year felt 'special' because they were unusual, and indeed a higher proportion of them eventually graduated than from among the male first-year students. Similarly, before the 1970s the minority of female students in engineering courses were treated with 'an almost Victorian-era politeness'. Sexual harassment by male staff and students appears to be a response to increasing numbers of female students who are seen to threaten the definition of the discipline as masculine.[4] When Berenice studied Visual Arts at Chelsea School of Art in London in the 1980s, female students were well aware of discrimination, both in class and gender terms. Instead of allocated time with teachers, students had to find favour through what they called the 'star system'. Female students attracted patronage either by adherence to the normative intellectual trends of the art scene or by sugaring their feminism with an erotic coating. Berenice's love of 'good conversation' and intense desire to engage in intellectual discussions unsettled many of her male lecturers. One of them, who sought no further conversations with Berenice, plagiarised her ideas and repeated them to other students as his own. Away from her family and friends, Berenice, 'bereft of a background', 'used to take it personally and feel that I was inadequate in some way'. Although she only attended a few meetings of the School of Arts' women's group, Berenice did not find them very relevant to her own needs, commenting that at one meeting the focus was on sexual harassment.

Nevertheless, Berenice benefited from the appointment of the first woman head of the postgraduate program. She nominated Berenice for the Henry Moore bursary, which provided the financial support without which Berenice could not have accepted Chelsea's offer of a place in the Master of Arts degree course. Berenice and another female student received first-class honours, also unusual in a 'system riddled with sexist attitudes'. Indeed, few of the younger female students whom Berenice had supported congratulated her, while a male student who had received second-class honours confronted the woman who headed the postgraduate program: 'How can you do this to me?' Berenice was 'astonished' that anyone could feel an award was his by right and was willing to voice that conviction.

Although they are gradually changing, universities were experienced by many women as places which only welcomed young heterosexual white middle-class English-speaking background women. Universities are physical and cultural miles distant from Sydney's western suburbs or Queensland's working class towns: 'it was really like being in a different country' (Glenda). Monica Pellizzari (1993:134, 143) was expected to follow the other Italian girls and work in a bank or become a secretary and marry a Northern Italian. Although the nearest university was two hours distant, TEAS (now Austudy) and the abolition of fees under the Whitlam government bridged the miles. She learned to disguise her accent and dress and was no longer branded a 'Westie'. Rhondda Johnson (1994:22) entered university when 'the word feminist had not entered my vocabulary (come to think of it neither had the word vocabulary)'. As Glenda points out, finding oneself as a 'gay woman' or coming from a working-class background would have been 'hard enough'. She had to adjust to both at university.

Universities were also miles distant from Indigenous Australian cultures. In 1988 Aileen had to switch her honours enrolment from anthropology to sociology. The incident which made this necessary is a dense interweaving of sexism and racism, although Aileen premises the story with 'I got out of anthropology because of the sexism'. She came into the departmental tea room one day, her hand in a bandage, to submit an assignment:

> one of the anthropologists said, '[Name] has been sucking your fingers'. And the other guy turned around and said, 'It wouldn't be her fingers he was sucking'. Now these were all male, there was no woman in that room . . . And at that, I turned around, walked into the secretary, gave her my paper and said, 'I will not be back'. Walked out of that department, and pulled out of my honours program . . . I began to realise my role as the exotic . . . I wasn't afraid to engage. I was exciting, an exciting woman, and the fact that I was black and good-looking, to boot, when I look back now, I was their image come true . . . It just blew me away because it was like these are supposed to be people who understand culture, and look at what they are doing to me.

As Aileen notes, she had 'acquired the cultural capital of this institution', working hard and never receiving extensions, but this did not protect her from such experiences, while she still feels 'no matter how well I do, I always have to prove myself'.

Mature-age students, described on one campus as 'the mad housewives' (Haines 1992b:66), were also seen as out of place. Audrey was told during her practical teaching by her supervisor: 'I don't know what the university's thinking of, young people trying to get places in universities'. The convenor in her diploma of teaching program tried to dissuade her with: 'You don't want to go and work out at Longreach or something'. Audrey replied: 'Why not, I was born there'. A dean suggested to Claudia that a woman in her 'position' – supporting children – should not really be considering enrolling in a doctorate. When Nadine returned to classes after the birth of her child, a lecturer said: 'You'll fail, you know', referring to her newly acquired status as 'an unmarried mother'. Added to discrimination against mature-age students, women returning to study often carry an additional cargo of paid work and family obligations, of opposition or incredulity from kith and kin. Often these women struggle with the conflict between the presumed satisfactions of marriage and motherhood and the suspicion that there should be something more. Alternatively, they suddenly find that they must support themselves. The next section explores their experiences.

Training For Life

> It was probably the best thing that's ever happened to me. I often say: 'I started to live when I went to uni. and turned 40, if for no other reason than I stopped playing roles and decided that I'd do something. (Grace)

The ability to enter university as a mature-age student has been profoundly significant for a number of women, particularly those in the mothers' generation.[5] Among the twelve grandmothers with whom I spoke, Joan, Margaret, Barbara, Matina and Fiorenza returned to tertiary study as mature-age students, while Glenn supplemented her nursing qualifications. For Fiorenza it was an escape from a period in which, while she loved her children, she felt 'sort of a useless being' who is 'stupid and empty so you go along with trends'. Fired by Whitlam's 'idea of democracy' at the community level, Fiorenza enrolled in a full-time community welfare course, and then found employment working with the Italian community. Joan was spurred to become a social worker after living on a Northern Territory mission in 1959 and witnessing the appalling treatment of Indigenous Australians. She finished her diploma at the age of 48, returning to the Territory where Don, her husband, worked as carpenter and odd job man and she as social worker. In her final position, at Bermagui, she trained an Indigenous Australian officer to replace her in 1975. Her husband: 'was wonderful ... when I was doing essays, he used to stand at the door and wait until I saw him to talk to him. Imagine. And sometimes he'd say: "Can I talk now?"'. When she and her friends had 'history seminars at home', Don would ring up for the group's take-away orders and bring them home. Joan's husband died while this book was being written, and Joan added to her transcript: 'He was fantastic about it all and often said he was very proud of me! Bless his generous heart'.

Where Margaret's son-in-law and daughter were supportive, some friends were quite hostile:

> I never could believe that making a personal decision like this could engender such strange reactions from people ... 'What on earth do you think you're doing?' 'How ridiculous', and it didn't fill me with confidence, and I needed to be filled with confidence.

When Margaret received her notification of acceptance to tertiary study, she rang her daughter who said: 'Mum, that's great, that's terrific, how do you feel?' Margaret replied: 'I want to throw up, that's how I feel'. After Margaret complained for some time about her anxiety, Margaret's daughter hung up in frustration. Margaret thought: 'Oh God, now nobody's speaking to me'.

Among the thirty-four mothers, sixteen completed tertiary qualifications almost immediately following secondary school, one has completed a TAFE course, six have no tertiary qualifications and seven (Rachel, Alison, Noela, Teresa, Catherine, Shona, Anna) added, or are adding, a masters degree to their tertiary qualifications. Eleven women (Audrey, Martha, Claudia, Phylis, Amber, Deanna, Marg, Grace, Helen, Gisela, Laila, Sue, Auriel) returned to study, in all but one case after having children. However, many young women who went directly to university in the late 1950s or early 1960s went to get a 'MRS', to become Mrs rather than gain a degree: in those days 'you married whoever you wanted to become' (Carmel Niland in Mitchell 1991:12). After gaining a 'MRS' some women went on to a 'PhT', or 'putting hubbie through' (Friedan 1965:14); Teresa supported her husband while he completed his masters degree, and Gisela typed her husband-to-be's honours thesis and corrected 'all his wretched English'.

While women's entry into university in increasing numbers cannot be attributed solely to feminism, women's changing perceptions concerning why they went there owe at least something to the rising debate about women's purpose in life. Thus, Sophia in Henry and Derlet (1993:61), a woman of Italian background, went to university to acquire her 'MRS', but changed her orientations when she saw a poster announcing a women's liberation club. Gisela withdrew from university studies but continued her professional courses to qualify as a librarian, later marrying with 'no more thought at that stage of what was to become of me professionally or even intellectually'. Reflecting on her failure to seize the opportunities for tertiary study when she was young, Gisela invokes a feminist argument, wondering:

> whether that was society, male chauvinism or whatever you like, or whether it was just me and the sort of person I am and the sort of background I had, who knows. I guess a feminist would argue: 'No, it's not you', but some of it must have been, you are influenced by those societal pressures or mores or conventions.

One of the 'conventions' Sage remembers was that with the same results at the end of their first year at university, her boyfriend 'went on to a fellowship and I went to teachers college'. Sage knew it was unfair but thought, 'Oh well', adding 'this was pre-Germaine Greer'. Marriage literally made Sage sick, but 'As a child of the 1950s, I just thought: "Look, you just got married, had kids", you know? I didn't challenge the role I'd been allotted at all'; a point Alison also makes.

Claudia's retrospective surprise that she had once seen the reasonableness of her father's claim that he could not afford to send her to university, Sage's acceptance that one 'just' got married and had children – this puzzlement with which women ponder earlier attitudes indicates how dramatically social expectations about women's education and careers have shifted in a generation. As these women note, feminism has allowed them to see now how they could have made different choices. This suggests that women increasingly brought feminist interpretations to bear on their choices as the 1970s progressed. Thus, Teresa contrasts her experience as an out-of-place working-class girl in the late 1960s with her experience in the mid-1970s: 'There's *The Women's Room*, there's the shift'.[6] In the late 1960s she was 'in trouble in lectures and tutorials for answering back, being cheeky and questioning'. In 1976, returning with a scholarship on full pay to complete a masters degree:

> I went back to university with a bunch of women who are actually the first group of real women who I felt I could relate to . . . We were so strong, we were so strong because we were together. We were so strong because we were financially independent and we were so strong because we didn't have to work. It was just amazing. And we used to go down to the tavern and drink, talk, and talk and talk and talk.

Teresa says: 'I think from that point I was in charge and I have been ever since'. Even 'with a brand new baby', Teresa successfully challenged a decision not to reinstate her in the position as director of a unit, a position she had held for three years.

Grace, Martha and Deanna allude to the empty nest as a reason for returning to study. When Martha's youngest child started school, Martha 'had it in my mind "You've got to get out of this situation"'. Martha went on from a TAFE course to a university degree on the suggestion of a friend, gaining admission on special entry in 1984. When Grace's son married, Grace decided 'it was my turn and I was sure there was more to life at this stage than going off to learn watercolour painting'. Rejecting charity work as absurd when the family was living on the basic wage, Deanna felt that 'part-time study, it just fits into your life' which had become 'not fulfilling enough'.

As well as the 'empty nest' influence, some of these women worried about developing an 'empty brain'. Akin to Fiorenza's experience, Claudia realised that she lacked the concentration to read an entire story in the *Women's Weekly* and thought: 'This is absolutely terrible because my mind is going to fall apart'. Claudia responded to an advertisement in the *Northern Territory News* about external study but the complicated application forms deterred her for another year. Little wonder that she waited apprehensively for her first essay to be returned: 'some distant person that you didn't even know was just sort of assessing this and saying, "Yes, alright you are allowed to be alive"'. Deanna remembers lacking the perseverance to find out about interesting issues, thinking: 'It's okay when you're elderly and you let it go, but here I am only around 40'. Grace enrolled in a senior English course, prompted partly by a feeling that her husband 'had to come down a step in levels of communication' to speak with her. While some of her fellow students had returned to study as part of a career plan, Grace was rewarded because she could 'look at everything differently' and have 'much more interesting discussions'. Like Grace, Claudia says: 'it was something that I was doing just for myself whereas everything else I was doing was about raising children'.

Laila's husband understands that an educated woman is 'an asset for them both and she'll be better for it'; Sage's husband noticed that Sage 'became a reasonable human being to live with'. Joan is unsure whether she would have gone to university without her husband's support. Other women have done without that support. Deanna cannot

> remember a positive response to it. I don't know why I stuck with it; when you think of it, why did I? I'd go off to lessons, as far back as going to the high school to do the senior subjects, I can remember driving to it, in tears from the friction... And he'd come in from work, and the tea would be right, the tea would be there before I went. Not now, I'd say: 'Get your own'.

Deanna realises that her husband was threatened by her studying, while 'It must have been dreadful the clack-clack-clackity-clack-clack' of the typewriter. This problem could have been resolved 'if you'd had the wherewithal to have an enormous home with a wing that could have been devoted to the typewriter' and another to the 'sport and wrestling on TV'. Deanna concludes: 'it's really sad when I think of it, a lot of years'.

Making sure the tea was ready was the first line of defence against potentially recalcitrant and probably insecure husbands. Martha remembers: 'it was quite a shock to my husband for me always going out and saying "Dinner's there"'. Claudia's husband said: 'as long as nothing changes this will be alright'. Claudia 'made sure that apparently nothing changed, outside anyway, but an awful lot was changing inside. And I mean I'm quite sure it's why I ended my marriage'. Study does tend to change mature-age women and husbands who wanted nothing to change were right to be apprehensive. As Grace said:

> put it this way, if my husband came home and suddenly said to me: 'I've decided I want to go out west and raise chickens, become a travelling salesman for Morleys, open a shop selling flowers', you know something totally different, I'd guess I'd be a bit, 'Oh'. And the changes that he'd go through while he was adjusting to that new lifestyle and business would necessitate changes in me.

But he did not afford Grace 'the same courtesy', did not acknowledge the changes occurring in Grace, 'that what was happening to women in general at that time affected me too'. Grace wanted to discuss her new ideas and remembers 'we had an argument once and my husband said: "Oh, this is boring shit, don't talk to me about it"'.

Lacking her husband's support, Claudia found assistance from a friend during a crucial year in her studies, 1974, when she 'had really taken on too much'. Claudia's friend minded Claudia's children and swapped houses with Claudia two or three days a week:

> She had a big polished table which she always put in front of the window for me to work on, and she had this clock that chimed the hour. And I will never forget that sort of sense of just being in a totally quiet house with this clock chiming . . . I will never ever forget that she did it.

Kath Davey (1995:78) was also supported by a network of friends when she left her husband. Another friend encouraged Claudia to enrol in full-time university study supported by Whitlam's NEAT scheme and TEAS funding. In these circumstances, although Claudia's subject choices were constrained to those hours when her children were at school, Claudia 'got amazing results because I worked really hard all day. I didn't waste a second while I was at uni.'

Among the fourteen daughters, a quarter have not completed high school and half completed university studies almost straight after secondary school, while one has recently returned to doctoral studies; two either completed or are completing tertiary studies after a short break from secondary school, and five returned to tertiary studies after a longer break. Three of these are Indigenous Australian women.[7] In her first years at university Audrey 'wouldn't let anybody know I was Aboriginal because they mightn't let me in'. As she says: 'You were a lesser species, a lesser person than others so I hid this'. Later, she realised 'Aboriginals are getting all free tutoring, and Austudy and Abstudy, oh my goodness me, I'm Aboriginal, everybody, I started to be Aboriginal again'. Yvonne has two Indigenous Australian stepdaughters and one white biological daughter, Ceri. She feels that all three daughters were in basically the same family situation, but she and her husband had to struggle on their pension to pay for Ceri's schooling. Furthermore, Ceri, who has completed Aboriginal studies in the health area, is ineligible to apply for ATSIC jobs – this 'is a type of discrimination'. Yvonne says she is not a racist but sees herself as

> indigenous as I have no other country that I call 'home'. I feel that far and away our debt for early treatment of Aboriginals has been paid and now government, with our present multicultural society, should be treating everybody the same whatever their race, creed or colour so long as immigrants have become naturalised and can call themselves Australian.

Aware of society's negative evaluations, Auriel's father refused to apply for Abstudy even though his friend, Captain Reginald Saunders – 'the only Aboriginal you ever learn about at school, who was the first commissioned officer with the army' – tried to convince him otherwise. His apprehension was well-founded. A life member of the Ainslie Football Club, Auriel's father had played, coached and captained there. Despite long years of apparent friendship, when Auriel won a scholarship to study with the Aboriginal Task Force in Adelaide in 1979 several friends asked questions like: 'What are you going there to study with them coons for?' Others no longer spoke to Auriel's father: 'they wouldn't accept him for a man once he had this other label'. Auriel's colleagues muttered volubly 'about getting a tin of boot polish out, and maybe they could get things like this'. Her classmates in the program also suspected that she was really a white woman. Indeed, Auriel had a very hard time because she was fair and was away from home for the first time in her life. Some years later Auriel completed a university degree.

Auriel knows from the statistics and her own experience that she is unusual, the only woman from either side of her family with tertiary qualifications. Contrasting white and Aboriginal families, she understands the path is more difficult without family and friends who have walked that route. But ultimately there is 'something in people's personalities', which combine with opportunities to allow some to succeed. Similarly, Nikita and her female close kin, some of whom have returned to university study, used mechanisms like Abstudy and Aboriginal and Torres Strait Islander support services at university to change their life chances through education. Domestic violence in Kerry's family contributed to her leaving school before the age of 15 and then losing a job as a teacher aide at a school for Murri children. In 1984 when Kerry was working in a voluntary capacity, she was encouraged to apply for a support program to study a degree in early childhood education. She succeeded although she was a single parent caring for a teenage sister and three young children while she studied. To gain more authority among professionally trained team-mates and to understand her work issues more fully, Nikita twice decided to improve her qualifications. However, 'without the support of all my sisters and family, I wouldn't have got through basically'.

Conclusion

When Shona contrasted the influence of private matriarchs in the delimited sphere of convent or home with women's second place in the social or public sphere, she suggested: 'It was almost as though there were two different categories. There was a family category and then there was a social category'. In the home, however, despite the clear sexual division between breadwinner and homemaker: 'there was never ever any indication that women should be second class', 'that they shouldn't have rights' or 'that men could tread over them'. Similarly, Martha suggests of herself and her sisters:

> They have their roles to play but they don't see things from a male–female perspective, but from a person's point of view. And I think that was the way my mother saw it. They seemed to grow up in situations where they had great respect for their partners, it wasn't us against them or anything like that. There seemed to be a better sense of equality in the situations that we grew up in.

However, Martha also says certain 'social attitudes . . . about women' still come through in her household. 'But I just say: "I beg your pardon, just think about what you said"'. Martha's sense of equality was based on a widely accepted understanding of separate spheres in which justice was rarely subjected to a gendered lens. Where men and women were reasonably happy with this situation, a Kantian sense of equal worth could supplement, and to some extent eclipse, the inequalities in economic or political power which marked most women's lives. But such inequalities were often rendered obvious when women sought to change their roles. We have seen the resistance of some husbands to their wives' desire to return to study. On occasions, husbands also objected to their wives returning to the workforce, to which we now turn.

CHAPTER 3

Work

> Because of commitments to family and home, part-time work is usually required which eliminates promotion and many other benefits for women. As many women in my age group are unskilled or have been out of the work place for many years, low paid or menial work has to be accepted. In my case, I am expected to take care of my family, and husband, much of the housework, grandchildren, and, as our parents age, care for them as well. I am also expected to bring in some sort of income. Leisure time does not exist. Even when watering the garden, I am still performing a task. Should I watch TV, I will probably be ironing or sewing as well. (Helen)

In the 1960s about four-fifths of husbands disapproved of their wives working (Gilding 1991:118). By the 1990s the vast majority of husbands and wives approved both of women's labour force participation and equal sharing of housework in such situations (Bittman and Lovejoy 1993:313), while in a 1987 survey 75 per cent strongly supported equal opportunity legislation for women (Sex Discrimination Commissioner 1992:15). These surveys suggest that it is now widely accepted that women should have equal opportunities at work, supported by equal pay initiatives, equal employment opportunity legislation, childcare, education and retraining. However, while men endorse equal sharing of housework, they do not generally practise it. Working women carry the double load of which Helen complains.

The two impediments to women's equal workforce participation which Helen identifies are located outside the workplace. The first is women's obligations to care for others – children, husband and parents as they age – which often limits women to part-time work.[1] The next chapter explores women's experiences of marriage and motherhood. The second impediment is women's lack of qualifications for participation in the workforce, an issue we explored in the previous chapter. This chapter focuses on the formal and informal barriers within workplaces which confine women to the lower echelons and particular occupations.

This so-called sex segregation of the workforce can be seen in tables 3.1 and 3.2. While women now constitute 40 per cent of the Australian workforce, swelled by the return of married women from the 1960s, the Australian workforce has, if anything, become more gender-segregated since the 1960s (for example, see House of Representatives Standing Committee on Legal and Constitutional Affairs 1992:31 on Queensland). Over half the female workforce is in the two pink-collar occupational categories of clerks, sales and personal service workers, two categories in which female representation has increased since 1911. Women are also well represented in some of the professions, particularly nursing and teaching. While the ACTU is committed to 50 per cent women on its executive by the year 1999, only 31 per cent and 25 per cent of available union official positions are held by women in Victoria and South Australia respectively, while for branch secretary the figures are 17 per cent and 6.9 per cent (McCreadie and Nightingale 1994:40).[2]

Table 3.1 Women as percentage of total workforce in different occupational groups, 1911–1992

	1911	1947	1976		1986	1992
Managerial	13	19	15	Managers, administration	23	25
Upper professional	10	9	14	Professionals	39	42
Lower professional	67	60	57	Para-professionals	43	47
Clerical	13	43	62	Clerks	74	78
Shop assistants	23	39	69	Sales, personal service	63	66
Service workers	71	55	62			
Craftpersons	28	8	5	Tradespersons	10	10
Operatives	9	27	27	Plant, machine operators	16	14
Labourers	3	7	10	Labourers, related	33	36
Graziers and farmers	10	10	63	Farm employers[a]	24[b]	65
Rural workers	0	0	30	Self-employed farmers	23[b]	35
				Farm wage, salary earners	19[b]	26
Total women in workforce (%)	20	22	35		39	42

Notes:
a Data is to some extent influenced by changes in taxation laws, although there is now greater recognition of women's contribution to farm work.
b Data is from 1978 figures.
Source: Leonard Broom and F. Lancaster Jones (1976) *Opportunity and Attainment in Australia*, Canberra: ANU Press, p.39; Desley Deacon (1984) 'The employment of women in the Commonwealth Public Service' in Marian Simms (ed.) *Australian Women and the Political System* Melbourne: Longman Cheshire, p.136; Australian Bureau of Statistics 1993a:125; Office of the Status of Women 1995a: Appendix 2.17; Sheridan 1994:20–1.

Table 3.2 Distribution of women across occupational groups, 1994

	1994[a]
Managers, administration	6
Professionals	14
Para-professionals	6
Clerks	30
Sales, personal service workers	25
Tradespersons	3
Plant, machine operators	2
Labourers, related	11
Other	3

Note:
a Expressed as percentage of total women in the workforce.
Source: Australian Bureau of Statistics 1993a:125.

In blue-collar or factory occupations, women are found not in the more skilled and better paid occupations of tradespersons or even machine operators but as unskilled labourers. Reflecting the gender segregation of the workforce, in Yvonne's generation of the grandmothers most young women thought the best they could achieve was to become a nurse, teacher or clerk, none of which at the time involved university training. By the generation of the mothers, the obvious occupational choices had changed little, although now teaching more often meant studying at university, and more young women considered but rejected medicine for one reason or another.

There are two kinds of legislation affecting the status of women. Anti-discrimination legislation protects individual women from acts of discrimination on the basis of their sex, for example, not winning a job because the employer believes the woman will become pregnant and leave. Equal opportunity or affirmative action legislation focuses on improving the position of women in a more collective way, by changing workplace practices so that they are more female-friendly. Examples include providing part-time work with career structures, and providing special job training opportunities for women. Anti-discrimination legislation was introduced first in South Australia in 1975 (most States, the two Territories and the Commonwealth now have legislation) and outlaws discrimination on the basis of characteristics deemed irrelevant for employment, education, or the provision of goods and services. Anti-discrimination legislation includes grounds such as 'sex, marital status, pregnancy, parental status, breastfeeding, age, race, impairment, religion, political belief or activity, trade union activity, lawful sexual activity', or association with a person defined by the above characteristics (s.7, Queensland Anti-Discrimination Act 1991), while in the Anti-Discrimination Act (1977) (NSW) discrimination on the grounds of homosexuality or lesbianism is prohibited. The Affirmative Action (Equal Employment Opportunity) Act (Commonwealth) (1986) covers all workers in organisation of 100 people or more (religious institutions and combat duties in defence forces are exempt). Employers, in consultation with affirmative action staff and unions, are encouraged to devise schemes for the advancement of women in the organisation. The Affirmative Action Agency cannot impose sanctions for non-compliance, but those who refuse to provide annual reports are named in parliament and do not receive government contracts, while successful schemes are widely publicised.

Given over a decade of affirmative action and anti-discrimination legislation, it might seem surprising that Australian working women are neither making it to the top nor out of their traditional occupations. This chapter explores the work cultures which constrain women to stay in their place. We look first at obvious barriers, like the marriage bar and discrimination in selection, and then at aspects of workplace cultures which, at the very least, make women feel uncomfortable and which might be severe enough to impede job performance.

Breaking Down Formal Barriers

The Marriage Bar and Equal Pay

Unequal pay and the marriage bar are now almost universally seen as 'unfair'. However, such notions were less widespread at the turn of the century when Vera's mother was quite possibly part of a deputation which protested, not at unequal pay but the difference between men's and women's wages. The female pupil teachers approached the Premier when he visited Charters Towers in Queensland in 1900, complaining that the discrepancies between male and female teachers' wages had become excessive, especially as the female teachers were required to teach the extra subject of needlework.

Jan was happy to resign from her work when she got married: 'It wasn't a choice and you weren't against it. It was just the way things were going'. Similarly, Shona reflected, although she did not endorse the situation: 'It was taken as a given, this is the Department's way, these are the Department's rules, nothing will ever change it'. When Grace returned to work, 'There were some people' who accused her of 'taking jobs away from a married man'. However, Valerie 'felt very strongly' that marriage did not mean 'you were a no better teacher or less reliable'. In the mid-1960s, in charge of the Darwin preschool, she 'formed a Kindergarten Teachers' Association' and became the first president. It was 'a little challenge to the Welfare Department'. In the same period Gisela moved to Sydney, thus avoiding dead-end temporary jobs in Queensland's council libraries where the marriage bar was still enforced. In the late 1970s Sage was refused a teaching position because she was married to a breadwinner. Generally, however, with teachers in short supply, the marriage bar was evaded by rehiring women in a 'joyful little deal where they made me resign and then I was immediately re-employed but as a temporary teacher' (Sue). Sue actually found this 'the most wonderful thing ever' as she could become a permanent part-time teacher in a high school. However, within a few years the Department abolished permanent part-time positions and it was a decade before Sue's constant complaints to the Education Department secured her a permanent job.

But even when the marriage bar was seen as 'unfair', it was not always viewed through a gendered lens. Shona suggests 'it was the way of the world . . . day follows night, and it was a given' (Shona). Sue notes that, because so many women were teachers: 'you don't ever think it's discrimination against women because they really need women. What you think is, "It's the Education Department", because they're just impossible'.

Women working as temporary teachers received no pay over the holidays. They had no continuity of service which meant no superannuation, no long service leave and no chance to climb the promotion ladder (based largely on seniority). Although not a teacher, Yvonne remembers resigning because she was pregnant with her first child, and 'missed my long service leave by half a year, and there was no pro rata, no nothing'. Thus, the marriage bar meant 'it was almost like you have one life, or another life' (Catherine). Those women who chose the teaching life were unmarried and their 'superannuation just went back into the fund. It was only if you were a male full-time member of the service that your spouse got it' (Shona).[3]

The marriage bar was based on the Arbitration Court's commitment from 1912 to the notion that men as 'breadwinners' were paid a 'family wage' sufficient to support a 'homemaker' and children. Unfortunately, all men, regardless of whether or not they were supporting parents, received the family wage while no supporting mothers did so, many unions colluding in this world view (Grimshaw 1993:101, 102, 107). The Women's Employment Board was formed in 1942 to draft women into essential war work at higher rates of pay. Until the mid-1960s working women's basic wage was a rising proportion of men's (54 per cent before

1950 when it became 75 per cent) (House of Representatives Standing Committee on Legal and Constitutional Affairs 1992:9).

Before and after the Second World War women campaigned for equal pay. The Feminist Club demanded equal pay for women in the armed services and for teachers, taking its lead from the Council of Action for Equal Pay formed in 1937 following a conference called by the Clerks' Union (Booth and Rubenstein 1990:122). From 1950 the Australian Federation of University Women, the Australian Federation of Business and Professional Women's Clubs and a new organisation, the Union of Australian Women formed in 1950 (Grimshaw et al. 1994:276) took up the campaign. In 1967 the ACTU took the test case to the Conciliation and Arbitration Commission which resulted in 'equal pay for equal work' (Booth and Rubenstein 1990:122) in 1969. As this affected only 19 per cent of working women, the decision was extended in 1972 to 'equal pay for work of equal value', which included women working in predominantly female industries, while in 1974 adult females achieved equal minimum wages (Burgmann 1993:99). In 1986 an unsuccessful comparable-worth case was brought before the Industrial Relations Commission by the ACTU to revalue the work of nurses (House of Representatives Standing Committee on Legal and Constitutional Affairs 1992:9–10). The 'minimum rates adjustment process' as part of the Accord (the agreement between the Federal Labor government and the ACTU which operated from the mid-1980s to restrain wage demands in return for reduced taxes and more social welfare payments) allowed comparison of skills deployed in traditionally male and female jobs, while the protection of the Sex Discrimination Act has been extended to cover awards resulting from enterprise bargaining agreements (Agnew et al. 1993:118–19).

Despite all these interventions, in 1991 women earned between 81 per cent and 83 per cent of men per ordinary hour worked. They earn less if overtime is counted, if men's and women's annual incomes are compared (because of women's part-time work), if they are in the lower occupational reaches, and if they are Indigenous Australians.[4] These comparisons indicate the importance of race, class and education in determining income levels.

It was bad enough to be paid less than men, but when women were more qualified or more efficient than their male colleagues the inequity really rankled. Of the 'nice' jobs available to young women completing high school in the 1960s, the most academic were librarian and teacher. On the other hand, as Glenda suggested in the last chapter, clever young men, even those from the working class, aspired to become lawyers, doctors or engineers. The result was that female teachers were being managed by less qualified men, either in terms of their secondary school grades (Glenda), lack of training as teachers (Teresa), inspectorial assessment (Rachel), or by men employed only because they 'had proved themselves during the war' (Shona). Of the male teachers who taught with Catherine: 'not one of them had actually ever passed much at all' at teachers college and 'they weren't good teachers either'. 'I'd never had a bank account – we went down to this bank to open bank accounts and bank these cheques . . . I remember thinking "Gee I've got all this money" and those buggers had more'. Although aware of the injustice, Catherine continues: 'No, we didn't do anything'. On the other hand, Teresa 'was part of the agitation for equal pay for equal work', though she found some of her older female colleagues quibbled about it. Even when Teresa pointed out they could be left as widows with children to support, 'the expectation was still that men will do it', that is, will be there to support their families. Thus, even in the 1960s and 1970s not all working women supported equal pay.

Gaining Great Expectations

> We used to have meetings and put propositions to the poor old principal there. It was a very strong feminist growth. We were passing books around, we were meeting to talk about them, and it was really very stimulating. (Catherine)

While few female teachers before the 1970s 'made it to the dizzy heights of inspector' (Shona), the preponderance of female teachers meant that within the school there was no 'feeling of inferiority' (Rachel of Sydney). 'Very strong female personalities' wielded informal power and knew their rights concerning class sizes and so on (Shona). Shona compared the role of women in the public teaching sector and in the private sector more generally. In the former, women sat on committees and 'were part of the decision-making process'. Visible in an increasingly female-dominated profession and often working below their administrative capacities, female teachers created and grasped the opportunities of affirmative action. Lea recognises she was among the capable women who 'surfed in' on the wave created by the South Australian Equal Opportunity Act in 1987 which abolished seniority. This was supplemented by other 'affirmative action moves within the Education Department to get more women in leadership positions'. In 1988 Lea won a deputy principal's job. This was followed by a principal's job in 1989 and another principal's job in 1993, both in open selection processes based on merit.

Catherine changed from being a compulsive housewife ('I would wash the kitchen [floor] *every* day, . . . I'd vacuum *every* day') to puzzling over people's negative reaction following her return to work when her son was 3 months old ('there I was being a really good teacher, not a bad mum, either, and these people were questioning me'). However, it was not until the late 1970s, as a business senior and through the Business Studies Association (then called the Commercial Studies Association), that Catherine 'started to agitate about how few women were made seniors'. Rather than describing this agitation as 'strongly' feminist, Catherine locates it in terms of the unfairness of women's pay and promotion prospects. But feminist literature and discussions about it with a group of similarly inclined women at Catherine's next school finally gave Catherine the words and terms to connect her disparate experiences of living, teaching and curriculum design. She now saw 'what was going to happen to girls' as related to 'what had happened to me'. She realised that a good secretary looked and behaved nicely, and even more importantly was nice to her boss: 'and it was always a "him". And I remember going through it with the Year 11 kids from the textbooks and we whited out all the "hims", and made them "hers" and the kids got angry' – as do some children exposed to feminist fairy tales. Catherine went on to a career in equal opportunities and management.

Many women in their forties or older remember being questioned about marriage and childcare at job interviews, clearly indicating that the prospective employers had in their minds a woman rather than a worker. Before anti-discrimination legislation women often felt obliged to answer the question, and sometimes did so cheerfully enough. While being offered a job in the early 1960s Alison was told: 'Well, we've got two women working here already . . . We wonder why we would need another one'. As Alison notes: 'A lot of things occurred then like that', but 'you didn't know there was such a thing as discrimination . . . So because this bad thing didn't exist for you, you didn't notice'. From her experience of discrimination, such as being asked in 1979 why such an attractive girl might seek a welfare job in prisons, Giovanna Salomone (1993:59–60) participated in forming a women's group, later working for the appointment of an equal opportunity officer.

Salomone lacked legal redress, but even where such redress exists the female interviewee may be hesitant to exercise it, not wanting to appear troublesome. Teresa was the equal opportunity representative on an interview panel when one of the interviewers asked:

> 'You've just had a brand new baby, what are you going to do if your baby gets the measles?' And I said . . . 'You don't have to answer that question'. And she said: 'I don't mind'. And I said: 'But I do, because if you answer that question then we have to call back every other applicant who we've interviewed and ask them the same question: Do they have children? And I want to know what they're going to do if their kids get the measles'.

Employers hobbled by anti-discrimination legislation sometimes choose to leave jobs unfilled rather than expose themselves to litigation, as happened to Del and Hanna. Hanna had applied for a job for which she had the perfect qualifications, and 'They couldn't say that I wasn't qualified, they couldn't say anything'. But for Hanna, 'being a foreigner, a woman and an engineer on top of it' meant many months of unemployment before she won her present position, in which she had to serve a longer than usual probation period.

Alongside the work of equal opportunity officers, unions gradually took on an agenda which responded to the needs of women in their ranks. Issues like equal employment, maternity leave, flexible working arrangements and retraining (voiced by Zelda D'Aprano's Women's Action Committee formed in the early 1970s; Dixson 1994:237) were incorporated into a Working Women's Charter Campaign in 1977, a moderate version of which was adopted by the ACTU (Booth and Rubenstein 1990:124). Twelve months of unpaid maternity leave were awarded in 1979 (Booth and Rubenstein 1990:126), although many unions still do not provide paid maternity leave for their staff (Shute 1994:175). Despite union responsiveness to working women's issues, women's alienation from unions still appears to be greater than men's – perhaps because much more needs to be done for the specific needs of women workers.[5]

Between Jan's acceptance of the marriage bar ('You became a wife and mother'), Alison's cheery deflection of a sexist question and Teresa's insistence that non-discriminatory interview principles be applied, the world of work was transformed for professional women. In the 1950s and 1960s teaching was a good job to combine with motherhood. By the 1970s and 1980s more women were aware that they were good teachers, often better than their male colleagues who were climbing the promotion ladder, and they began to see the situation in terms of sex discrimination rather than 'the way of the world'. Despite these changes in women's expectations and in dismantling formal barriers to women's participation, women today meet a more insidious challenge. These are the almost invisible barriers of micro-inequities in the workplace, often embedded within organisational cultures which assume and reward one kind of life, the masculine lifestyle. These micro-inequities are aimed at women who are 'out of place', women in non-traditional jobs, women who aspire to climb the promotion ladder, women who are not only women but are marked as ethnically different.

The Invisible Worker Disappears

'The Case of the Invisible Woman Disappears': the idea for 'Invisible' came from a job . . . I had a male manager who couldn't work with women. He dealt with a series of conflicts that arose between us by ignoring me. It made my job impossible to do . . . I overcame the imposition that this situation had made on my life by turning it into fiction . . . I worked on these prints and sculptures for two years. It ceased to be about being shafted in the workplace . . . to become an investigation of how my imagination is an important way of making claims on my identity as a woman. (Berenice)

'G'day love, I'd like to see a lawyer.'
'Please take a seat.'
'So where is he?'
'Who?'
'The lawyer.'
'It's me.'
'But you're a young sheila!'
'My gender does not interfere with my intellectual capacity.'
(Common conversation between older male clients and Helen Durham in Durham 1995:121.)

Sexual harassment and other micro-inequities have been described as 'guerilla action' in the face of anti-discrimination and other legislation, which has won the official 'war against women' (Rowe 1981:155; Walby 1990:52–3; French 1992). Whether men consciously realise this when they harass women or not, so-called 'harmless' jokes, touches and girlie posters serve to retain work areas as exclusively male as one lone woman after another is employed, harassed, and resigns. Thus, sexual harassment is at least as much about preserving job opportunities for men as it is about sex. Micro-inequities make women invisible when their names are omitted from organisation lists, they are not invited to social functions, they are called by diminutives and not included in informal discussions which actually exchange significant information. This 'chill factor' squeezes women out of the organisation's culture (Cockburn 1991:65), while producing both pain and confusion, leading the recipient to wonder whether she has suffered real discrimination or is oversensitive (Rowe 1981:156-63). In such situations women become invisible as workers but all too visible as women, and often as 'different' women, for example, non-English speaking background women.

In her job as an advisor on the arts curriculum Berenice was triply ignored or patronised, young and 'a girlie' because arts was feminine and low on 'the hierarchy of disciplines'. It was, however, her experience as a part-time community arts officer in a small town which prompted 'The Case of the Invisible Woman Disappears'. While she stood in her supervisor's office doorway delivering her reports, he gave 'no sign he was actually hearing me. Except that there'd be some small gesture'. 'It was my first time of ever meeting someone who has immense problems that every time they look at you, they're seeing a woman', and the worker becomes invisible. Farm women tell a common story of being invisible as farmers (for example, see Alston 1995:71), ignored by retailers and tradesmen alike. Women say: 'I'll have half a dozen saddles for the gates' and the retailer responds: 'Does he want galvanised or plain?' and so on through discussions of size and other attributes (Jane Bryant in Rigg and Copeland 1985:162). Lita, experiencing repeated and escalating discrimination, felt too visible as an ethnically marked woman and 'wished I could disappear'. A woman's painful visibility as femininity masks her role as a worker in those jobs (or for those men) which are so intimately associated with masculinity that a woman worker is an impossible monster. Invisible workers are policed through the general workplace culture, refusing to acknowledge women's work and skills, and through sexual harassment.

Workplace Cultures

> When I went there to work, there was a very large contingent of Aboriginal women at senior levels. I was the last one to leave ... There was a particular guy who was a first assistant sec. in charge of Aboriginal programs who just knew how to sweep a broom through, very effectively. We went at transfers, we went at demotions, but we all got out. (Auriel)

> I participated in most of the social gatherings in the office, so they didn't have any excuse to say: 'Oh she doesn't like to participate'. Even things I wouldn't do all the time, like going to the pub, which I think is just a waste of time. But I discovered ... things were being organised in the pub. The credibility of a worker could be destroyed in the pub. (Lita)

Women's invasion of hotel bars is part of official feminism's history. But some workplaces also had their male-only domains. Although teaching was dominated by women, the men's staff room in some schools was a sanctuary forbidden to female teachers. The women's staff room, being larger and the venue for staff meetings, was open to male teachers. Shona and another teacher 'invaded' the men's staff room one lunch time and were policed with outrageous and embarrassing jokes 'to make sure we didn't go back there ... ever again'.

When Alison entered the male space of construction sites, she carried with her the authority of being the architect in charge of the job. She also used a little judicious swearing to put the workers at their ease, reflecting that today a woman's swearing might be construed as an adoption of patriarchal attitudes but then it was seen as a positive act, a way of moving into male language areas. While some architecture offices might be hostile spaces for women, Alison felt the more prestigious offices were not. In the office where she worked in the late 1960s and 1970s 'babies grew up there' because of flexible working hours. Alison shared the professional identity of 'architect' with her colleagues, although she expressed it slightly differently from some. Some male architects saw themselves as 'god architects', 'there for power games' and thinking 'of themselves in a *Fountainhead* way. That book was really popular amongst architects'. In contrast, Alison self-deprecatingly describes the job that gave her 'a reputation' and 'a sense of achievement and recognition' as 'a delightful little Victorian thing, one of the early restorations, "pioneering effort" as a purist said later, meaning it wasn't critically correct, but it was a good effort'. While not a 'god architect', Alison confesses an interest in power: 'you could stop everything dead, you can get walls pulled down. There was a lot involved, and great responsibility'. Alison was disappointed when a female colleague, an interior designer, 'let the side down' by not being professional, failing to attend meetings and depending on her husband's advice.

Lita's story exemplifies how the woman wronged also experiences the pain and confusion of wondering whether she has somehow precipitated the discrimination practised against her. Lita was out of place in the Australian public service on at least two counts. At university she developed a materialist Marxist explanation of poverty, seeing social work as about empowering people to make their own decisions. As she says: 'I cannot keep away from social justice issues. And that's going to make me get into a lot of trouble'. Lita was also constantly reminded that her second language was English, colleagues commenting: 'Who spelled it wrong? It was probably Lita'. In different employment locations Lita was either passed over for promotion because of her 'communication' problems (her lack of facility with English) or because she 'used too much jargon' (her excessive facility with English). On top of this, migrants must 'adapt to a new system that they don't know' and are often denied information which is readily accessible by others (Gladys).

Lita's struggles against discrimination were supported by equal employment opportunity officers and industrial officers. But their involvement also branded Lita as a troublemaker in an environment where her loss of self-esteem made it increasingly difficult for her to judge and claim her rights. At one point Lita organised a NES network and the other two members of the network confirmed Lita's suspicion that her suggestions made in meetings were ignored. Lita was not invited to social gatherings, was exposed to racist jokes from her boss, and yelled at by her boss. When Lita reminded her boss of a grave error of judgement he had made, he shouted: 'I don't remember Lita, and you tend to remember things vividly. I don't know what you're saying. I don't want to speak to you any more. Can you just get out of my office!' His outburst reminded Lita of the abuse she had experienced from her husband. She left his office in tears and decided, on the advice of the union, to place a complaint with the Human Rights Office. As Lita said, her job concerned telling others to assert their rights. Before lodging her complaint

Lita checked it with her husband: 'Do you think it makes sense? I don't want to become too emotional here'. The investigation of her complaint took so long that Lita had a new boss by the time it was completed. Lita's new supervisor was no more supportive, and under the stress of a hostile working environment which meant she had to perform her duties exceptionally well, Lita entered regular counselling. Finally, her doctor would not let her return to work and she took stress leave. As she says: 'days I was in bed and didn't want to do anything, so depressed... So what my clients went through, I think I went through'.

Lita has initiated a number of services for non-English speaking people in Australia, established the Migrant Women Whose Second Language is English network and is a member of both the Association of Non-English Speaking Background Women of Australia (ANESBWA) and the ACT Women's Advisory Board. These have given her strength and since her stress leave she has been able to contribute to their activities 'so people won't have to go through so much of what I've gone through'. Lita feels it will take several generations before the 'very Anglo-Saxon' environment accepts people from other cultures, rather than turning women like her into victims when they do the 'right things to be assertive'.

Lita's experience reveals the limits of the formal arsenal of anti-discrimination legislation, human rights officers and unions in the face of entrenched and sometimes subtle forms of harassment. Legal redress is costly, time-consuming, requires high standards of proof (Thornton 1990:200, 202) and casts the complainant as either a 'victim' who 'needs' support, or a troublemaker. Sometimes women feel they have precipitated the discrimination and are unsure of their rights. However, the very existence of the law and education about it do gradually change working environments, a few well-publicised cases telling not only employees but also employers that practices once deemed perfectly normal and legitimate are now illegal.

Sexual Harassment

> We really didn't know that there was anything wrong in our lives so we didn't object... I've seen some young women get so unnecessarily aggravated about things which they take so bitterly. (Alison describing her working life as an architect in the 1960s and 1970s)

> When I think about it, it sounds like the dark ages and it was only five years ago. (Teresa describing sexual harassment at the school when she became principal)

Where once women might complain of 'indecent assault' in the working environment (Bacchi and Jose 1994:264), Catharine MacKinnon

(1987:70) argues that the legal claim for sexual harassment is the first time that women have defined women's injuries in law. Sexual harassment is now written into Australia's anti-discrimination legislation, and covers any 'unwelcome conduct of a sexual nature' (for example, sending suggestive notes, making lewd comments, touching), whether it is a male or female who is the recipient of the unwelcome conduct. Because men are generally in power over women and male heterosexuality is constructed as active and female heterosexuality as passive, the overwhelming number of cases are laid by women. The Queensland legislation covers harassment in 'the street and anywhere else for that matter', although this is yet to be subject to scrutiny through complaints (Morgan 1995). Sexual harassment renders the worker invisible, constructing in her place the sexually marked woman: 'It was okay to have us all in the boardroom while we were young and attractive, but when we get older we become dragons' (Sally Milner in Ford 1991:88; see also Mendelsohn 1993:145). Margaret describes legal secretaries around 40 years of age as greatly prized as 'workhorses' because they were good, 'but socially you didn't exist'. When selling sweets in factories Yasmin remembers 'you had to be nice, and had to smile' even in the face of wolf whistles and feeling that men were mentally undressing her. Willow was grabbed selling 'raffle tickets in really sleazy pubs wearing lingerie'.

Sexual harassment occurs not only in private corporations, but also in unions (Lewis 1994:109, 108) and voluntary organisations (Pavan 1994:222–3). Sexual harassment complaints form a large and rising part of investigations under the Sex Discrimination Act.[6] Sexual harassment is a more persistent problem for women in the lower reaches of the work hierarchy, suggesting how significant are power relations in explaining its incidence. Some 80 per cent of cases in Victoria involve harassment by a boss or supervisor, prompting Jenny Morgan (1995:101–2) to suggest a common understanding 'that sexual relationships between co-workers are, indeed, more "private"'. Like Audrey (in the Introduction to this book), Helen contrasts a pre-legislative era with the present situation. When patients ran their hands up a nurse's leg or grabbed her private parts, such incidents were 'laughed off or kept to oneself', the nurse being blamed for causing or enjoying the attention. Gladys, aged 18, was sexually harassed in the freezer where she worked. The other women, while 'very supportive', deterred Gladys from laying a complaint. As a legal secretary, Margaret was 'chased round many a desk' and 'you don't know how to handle it, it's terrible'. For Margaret the difficulty occurred not so much at the time of the harassment – one can say: 'Get back there, hands off' – but negotiating the episode the next day, 'because something's broken down, and it's very hard to repair'.

As with rape cases where the issue of consent divides legal and illegal behaviour, judges initially had difficulty understanding why women were not either flattered by these advances or found it easy to refuse them (for example, Einfeld J. in *Hall, Oliver and Reid v. Sheiban* (1988) EOC 92–227 at 77,136). The debate concerning acceptable, or indeed inevitable, sexual relations in workplaces and educational institutions continues with Helen Garner's (1995) best-selling and widely publicised *The First Stone: Some Questions About Sex and Power*.[7] Like Justice Einfeld, Garner consistently fails to recognise the unequal power relations between students in a college and the master who allegedly harassed them, seeing them as powerful wielders of youth and beauty and claiming that eroticism and love are inevitable in workplaces (Garner 1995:163, 59, 148). Thus, Ann Curthoys (1995:210) claims that the debate generated by the book is not a generational debate but a debate between those who have struggled with sexual harassment in a university setting and those who have not, or those who do and do not understand that sexual harassment is a 'management issue', as the young feminist, Virginia Trioli (1996:77) puts it.[8]

But 'struggle' it is, rather than an easy matter. As Rosemary Pringle (1988:89–90, 102) explores in her analysis of secretaries and 'erotic bureaucracies', sexual fantasies and relations are normative rather than unusual in most workplaces. Feminists will probably fail if they attempt to banish erotic relations from workplaces by legislative fiat. As with the definition of rape, the challenge for feminists is to uncover the differences between coercive sex and chosen sex, especially when authority relations conspire with many men's belief that sexual advances are welcome. Thus, according to Pringle, feminists must accept that secretaries derive 'power and pleasure' from their interactions. Margaret noted that some young women in the office responded to the advances of male solicitors, concluding 'I suppose, it's just a case of when the opportunity's there, for both, they used one another'. Both Lita and Halina worked in factories where female workers competed for the attentions of male co-workers.

Auriel's case of sexual and racial harassment started when a member of the service personnel left a note under Auriel's windscreen wiper which said 'Fined – one screw'. The offender boasted of his actions. Auriel

> went to the hardware store and I bought the biggest bolt I could find. And I painted it black, because they knew I was Aboriginal . . . And I went in, and he sat next to a window, and I stood back at the door which was a good 20 feet away from him, and I threw it. He had to catch it or it would go through the window. And we were on the eighth floor of Building A at Russell Hill, and I yelled out in front of everybody: 'That's the only black screw you'll ever get, mate'.

But guerilla action is not always available – or effective. As a probationary police officer, Jennifer worked in a station where the senior officer was wont to make unwelcome comments. He commented on Jennifer's new hairdo with: 'Oh, can I run my tongue through your hair?' Jennifer shrugged it off with: 'Oh, very funny, hah, hah'. He asked: ' "Oh, well can I run it through other places?" I just walked off'. In his probationary report, he accused Jennifer of 'unnecessary smart comments'. In response to Jennifer's complaint, the superintendent of training said: 'Oh, we believe you but we're not going to disbelieve them' which meant Jennifer's training period was extended:

> That's the way it sort of came across to me, because I didn't sleep with the boys, I was to be punished, and that's really how I was treated. And people sort of look at me and they sort of go: 'Well, why did you get extended?' And I said: 'Well, you'd never believe me if I told you'.

While such behaviour has been reduced with the introduction of the 'Anti-Discrimination Act and all that', significantly, it has not reduced at the work-site where Jennifer suffered harassment: 'Unless you're one of the boys, yeah, it's very difficult down there'. While Jennifer suggests there is now an over-zealous prosecution of cases, neither of the examples she cites involved a supervisor and a subordinate, perhaps leaving untouched the work cultures where men in charge are the perpetrators. Jennifer thought it excessive to institute prosecutions when an officer working with his back to Jennifer in the operations room had his shorts undone and shirt hanging out or when an officer greeted another officer, arriving with her boyfriend, along the lines of: 'Oh, you had someone to wake you up today'.

The debate over sexual harassment is informed by comprehension or lack of understanding of systemic power in organisations, a focus on either 'eros' or 'sex' as the motor of heterosexual relations, and the changes women experience in their interactions with men as they age. Many women agree with Garner and Jennifer that sexual harassment legislation has gone too far:

> Doesn't the human factor count any more? All this ridiculous petty complaining does nothing to advance the cause for women. It only increases the agro between men and women and will serve to slow up the process of complete equality. (Barbara citing wolf whistling, calling a woman 'dear' and patting a female on the shoulder)

Similarly, some focus group respondents commented that men 'wonder if they should even say, "you look nice today"' (Riley-Smith 1992:69). If sexual harassment is about work as well as sex, so is prostitution, as will be explored below.

Changing Women's Work Rewards

Because affirmative action focuses on improving women's employment in those areas in which they are a minority, schemes tend to focus on the higher reaches of organisations. Furthermore, it is likely that a greater proportion of educated women have the confidence to use anti-discrimination and affirmative action legislation, contributing to claims that such legislation benefits middle-class career women more than it benefits working-class women (for example, see Burgmann 1993:101).[9] Similarly, maternity leave is more likely to be taken by women in managerial and professional occupations and with higher education and incomes. This is a compound of the greater likelihood that such women will not be casually employed and so are entitled to maternity leave, their greater knowledge of maternity leave provisions and their greater capacity to survive on one income (Glezer 1988:16).

While gazing through the glass ceiling might be painful, such women have more resources and are more richly rewarded for their labour power than women on the factory or restaurant floor. This section briefly compares the experiences of women in factory jobs, pink-collar jobs and lower managerial jobs, and how they attempt to move up the occupational ladder. Some examples of the ways in which women with administrative or managerial authority begin to change the workplace cultures for other women are also offered.

Climbing the Occupational Ladder

> [People are] constantly striving to get more, and acquire more and secure more, and maintain more ... And your life just disappears like that (snaps fingers). (Shona)

> He treated his staff appallingly, he never had any appreciation of what it's like to be an employee ... You control them, you dominate them, you don't give them anything. In particular, you don't do up the staff dining room because they're just the plebs ... If you did it up any better they'd only destroy it anyhow. (Marg, speaking of her father)

Marg's comment is echoed by studies of women working on the concrete floor. Non-English speaking background women are disproportionately represented in factory jobs. The year 1990 was the first year that 'clerks, salespersons and personal service workers' was the major employment category for Non-English speaking background women (at 41.6 per cent), while representation among 'managers and professionals' also increased considerably (Alcorso 1993b:52). Non-English speaking background factory workers suffer appalling conditions. Wages are low, especially for outworkers; the risk of sexual harassment is high; and they are exposed to a higher incidence of occupational accidents and diseases, for example, repetitive strain injury (Collins 1988:173; Probert 1989:120; de Lepervanche 1992:86). In the factories visited by Women in Industry Contraception and Health workers, women could take perhaps two toilet breaks daily, forcing them to wear layers of sanitary napkins, while some toilets did not have sanitary disposal units. Women faced extremes of temperature, or had to eat while working because of targets and dirty or nonexistent canteens (La Marchesina 1994:262–3). Pat and Aquarius, immigrants from England, and Rita, Gladys, Halina and Lita, all from non-English speaking backgrounds, worked in a factory at some stage. Lita's experience in a pasta processing factory was the worst. Lita had

> stomach problems, because you have to eat in a rush. There was a toilet for around fifty women working there, so you have to queue . . . And the toilet was so filthy, full of spiders. There was not enough toilet paper. And then you have to eat, and the dining room was just rough tables and benches . . . All the women feel so abused and mistreated, no one has any respect for anyone. Everyone is just like a machine, and everyone is just looking after themselves, no one cares about anyone else . . . And they treated you like you were a piece of dirt, 'Eey, woman, do that!' They never called you by your names, there was no respect.

Little wonder, then, that a service job was often considered a progression from factory work. Rita noted that working in a restaurant meant higher wages, contact with people – sometimes famous people – while factory work was 'very monotonous'. Martha suggests of her job as hotel receptionist: 'I suppose I was very lucky to get a position like that, because everyone was aware that I was an Aboriginal black girl'. In 1960 Jan, with her high school certificate, 'bypassed the telephone and the tea-making and went straight' into a stenographer's job. However, Jan asserts: 'there was never any looking down to the office girls or staff', while the girls 'didn't want anything different', partly because they were paid above award wages. Jan sought to make her job more rewarding, first by introducing dictaphones which the managers resisted using, and then by becoming skilled on the new accounting machines. She combined this with her role as the manager's private secretary, which included babysitting 'his children when he and his wife went off to functions'. She also did the men's jobs when they were on holidays, describing it as a form of 'enterprise bargaining', given that she received a higher wage and extra bonuses.

However, there were no career paths out of these jobs. Many women married instead, and some, like Rita, pursued the path of upward mobility adopted by many non-English speaking background Australians – into a family 'business of your own'. By 1992 more than one-third of small businesses were owned by women (House of Representatives Standing Committee on Legal and Constitutional Affairs 1992:32), although women's businesses are smaller than men's, concentrated in operations of less than 150 employees (Still 1991:3–5, 60). Non-English speaking background women particularly are employers or self-employed, although in one sample in about 60 per cent of businesses the husband is the dominant partner (compared with 11 per cent where the wife is dominant) (Alcorso 1993a:99, 101, 102). Helen worked sixty hours a week and her husband seventy in their shop, but Helen's work was a 'bit trivialised' in comparison. In that ten-hour difference Helen was expected to 'go home and wash and iron and clean and scrub'. Shirley says of Taiwanese family businesses that the husband is usually the manager and the wife the secretary. Shirley and her husband have separate businesses, Shirley encouraging other Taiwanese women in Australia to do likewise.

Where Gladys and Lita speak from a clear understanding that they were exploited as workers in a capitalist-driven economy, a number of women with whom I spoke deployed the rhetoric of respect rather than of exploitation, although the sense of exploitation lurked behind the analysis. Margaret remembers two law partners arguing over whose work should have priority, when one suddenly stopped and said: 'Well, look, I can't see what the point of all this is, after all we're only fighting over a typist'. Perhaps the Kantian notion of equal worth and Australian egalitarianism fuelled the belief that workers should be equally treated as human, even if they were not equally rewarded. The claims of all workers to respect is behind some of the interventions of women who became administrators or managers and sought to change workplace cultures.

Changing Workplace Cultures

> it's good to have good friends that you can go out and have a laugh with and that, get you to see things in perspective. And it's about learning that it's okay to make mistakes, which is a difficult thing for me sometimes, wanting to be superwoman all the time. (Lea)

Table 3.1 shows that the percentage of women in managerial and administrative positions has increased from less than 20 per cent before 1976 to 23 per cent in 1986 and 25 per cent in 1992, although Leonie Still (1991:1) claims that between 1983 and 1991 there was a drop in the percentage of women in senior and junior management with a small rise in middle management, while the Karpin report in 1995 declared Australia had the lowest percentage of women managers in the industrialised world (Trioli 1996:129). Less than 5 per cent of the Australian Institute of Directors' 9050 members are women. In August 1992 none of the largest 500 companies were headed by a woman (*Ita*, August 1992:21), although since then Janet Holmes à Court has become the owner and managing director of one of Australia's largest companies. Of the directors of companies registered in Australia in 1994 sixteen men earned over $900 000, with Rupert Murdoch topping the list at $5.75 million, while only two women earned above this amount, Janet Holmes à Court ($1 million) and Imelda Roche, owner of Nutrimetics ($900 000) (O'Neill 1995:32).[10] Because of statistics like these, feminist researchers ponder the existence of a 'glass ceiling', an invisible but impenetrable barrier at about middle management level which prevents the graduate from becoming a partner or chief executive officer.

Dressed in a brief authority and willing to use it, women can begin to shift workplace cultures: including all the workers in monthly meetings (Fabian Dattner in Mitchell 1991:65) or working for pro-active measures to encourage women to return to work after maternity leave (Helen Lynch in Ford 1991:51–2). At the age of 21 Auriel became a typist controller, introducing rules for her forty-strong staff to ensure they were treated 'with respect'. She forbade the use of red pen, pencil and scribbling something on a 'scrap of paper' and throwing 'it in to be typed'. Auriel reduced sexual harassment with a roster system, so that officers could not call for particular stenographers, and by insisting the office door remained open. While sexual harassment was limited to unwanted attentions like a hand on a shoulder, as Auriel was well aware the officers were expressing power as much as sex: 'I mean, nothing really bad happened, but we were intimidated in those environments. And they knew it, and they deliberately did it, and we all just hated it'. Armed with the Joint Services Manual – 'the Bible' – which Auriel would freely quote to support her rules, Auriel earned the title of 'dragon lady'.

Hanna suggests that many male engineers 'believe that they know everything about everything', and yet lack management and human relations skills. She used a participatory management style to overcome her subordinates' resistance to a female boss and a foreigner. Hanna promoted a ritual mark of respect for secretaries on International Women's Day and Secretaries' Day:

> I said: 'We have a special day for women where all men have to be friendly and nice for a change'. So we have a special morning tea. They asked if this was only European. I said that it . . . was and is accepted by the entire world . . . They asked when men's day was. I told them that men's day was every other day . . . In Poland it is quite a celebration. We used to get a flower . . . All the women in our section got a little rosette . . . We tried something similar for secretaries' day . . . When we started the secretaries didn't get anything, not even a thankyou. I didn't believe that was right. They deserved some recognition. Without the secretary the manager would not do his job properly.

As an incoming school principal Teresa dealt promptly with widespread sexual harassment in her school. Sexual harassment awareness training was introduced in the school and sexual assault charges were laid in two situations. One of her contributions to improving the gender balance in management was securing a female-only deputy principal's position in her school. Teresa's greatest difficulty was dealing with another female deputy who 'was absolutely and utterly a non-feminist and stabbed me in the back all the time . . . I found that far more difficult to cope with than some of the male games'. With a female principal as role model Teresa developed herself as a '*woman* leader' (italics added), moving away from her 'somewhat masculine' leadership skills to a more participatory style. But, claims Teresa, such management styles suit men as well as women, who are just as unhappy when their skills are wasted, when they are abused rather than encouraged into better performance, when they are not listened to but dictated to. Teresa believes women are more adept at seeing 'both sides of the question' while men often see only their side, assume it is reality and 'then they just barge ahead'. Teresa endorses so-called feminine approaches but she does not endorse a merely 'feel-good' system, believing a good manager will fight with her own supervisors to defend her staff and also make hard decisions about incompetent teachers.

Similarly, Lea says that in politics 'somehow or other there's got to be some sort of accountability for what happens', 'keeping people up to their tasks, getting quality work out of them'. She is critical of the 'incredible ego stuff too, especially with men', the lack of managerial skills and failure to identify the job description of a good politician, which she believes includes 'communication, working with groups, negotiation, . . . flexibility, organisational management'. These skills, which Lea developed as a principal and in her community work, count for little in the party machine where the normal (that is, male) career path into politics is student politics at university, working for a politician or in a union, serving time on committees and other party structures until achieving pre-selection. Women are more likely to enter politics as a second or third career and in their forties, which was considered by many as 'too old'. Lea did what was required: 'I knew if I wanted to get into politics I had to start scoring up the points that they counted, you know, like working within the Party, standing in unwinnable seats, and achieving recognition in their terms'. In April 1994 Lea became the Member for Elizabeth (South Australia), later handling the shadow portfolios of health, family, community services and the ageing. To inform herself about her portfolio Lea built up a large network of stakeholders who shared information with her because she sought to understand the issues and listen to their point of view. Lea was surprised by the comment made by many of these people that she was the first politician they had known who operated in this way. She distinguishes her approach from male fear of self-exposure, which encourages some men to say 'here's the answer, it's decided'.

Unusual women, merely by their presence, offer a riposte to the stereotypes. One engineer asked to come and look at Hanna 'because he had never seen a woman engineer in his life'. Teresa's subordinate 'borrowed a film from the film library which was entitled "So you have a woman as your boss?"', Teresa impressed that he was 'virtually expressing his vulnerability'. When Anna was working as the executive officer of a commission, her superior delighted in correcting meetings of local council managers when they mistook her for his secretary. Even so, given the 'mythology' surrounding women in unusual positions, a woman has to 'work very hard, much harder than a man and do much more to be noticed. Not accepted but *noticed*' (Hanna). For their own part, several of the women with whom I spoke acknowledge excellent mentoring by male supervisors who encouraged them to seek promotions. Anna's boss had better relations with his female subordinates because 'there wasn't that . . . young Turk rivalry'. One of Catherine's superiors taught her 'heaps', particularly how to leave people feeling 'respected, it was sort of like an unconditional regard for people'. Catherine says: 'I suppose if I do anything well, . . . I refuse to let them goad me into anything but respect'.

While some women have been willing to 'work very hard' to be noticed, others have chosen routes which are often less valued and less rewarded than the paths traditionally taken by men. Berenice decided against becoming a studio artist, instead choosing community arts so that she could work 'with people whose art practices were much more integrated with their daily life'. When Berenice resigned from her job and stayed 'at home making art, having exhibitions, and basically organising a market, . . . the gossip [in her former work place] was . . . that I had gone to pieces'. Her former colleagues could not see Berenice's choice as 'another realm of working, a different kind of workplace'. While Alison enjoyed interior design work she chafed at its lower status, so that she 'liked being called an interior architect rather than an interior designer'.

Who, then, is to judge merit when men's and women's sense of merit and what is to be valued are still so radically unaligned? As Lea said of entering politics, it required jumping through hoops designed by men which seemed irrelevant. Ultimately, corporate worlds – and political worlds and blue-collar worlds – will only change when enough women informed by feminist ideas are there to challenge and shift the relationship between consensus and hard bargaining, community work and studio work, child-rearing and corporate raiding.

'Women's Work' Underlined: Prostitution

Rachel: [My daughter] gave me a card for my birthday that said . . . something like: 'Feminism – I myself have never been able to find out precisely what feminism is. I only know that people call me a feminist whenever I express sentiments that differentiate me from a doormat'. I love it.
Chilla: But, do you know what comes after that? 'That differentiate me from a doormat or a prostitute.'
Rachel: I'd agree with the next bit too, now you tell me it. That wouldn't worry me a scrap.

Even a prostitute doesn't like it to be known in public that she is a prostitute. She wants to be treated as a lady. (Lucinda)

As these quotations imply, prostitutes have been aligned both with feminists and against ladies. Indeed, in 1975 Anne Summers categorised 'prostitutes, lesbians and women in prisons and detention homes' as 'damned whores', in contrast with the respectable femininity of 'God's police', particularly married mothers who policed community morals (Summers 1994a:200, 232). Nineteenth-century and post-war feminists challenged this dichotomy, noting that both prostitutes and wives provided sexual services for their keep. Some have argued that all women are degraded and endangered by the institution of prostitution which, like sex right in marriage, accepts that a man has natural and uncontrollable sexual urges and the right to find relief for them (for example, see Hatty 1992:73). This is accepted in the present legislative framework. Prostitution is a 'necessary evil' (men will have their sex) which should, however, be kept off the streets (Frances 1994:38–41), in registered escort agencies in the Northern Territory, brothels registered under town planning legislation in Victoria, and registered brothels in the ACT (Neave 1994:87–9, 85, 90–1). As a 12-year-old, Kerry remembers being labelled as a prostitute when a taxi driver offered her $10. Kerry did not understand the proposal: 'but my instincts told me and I ignored him and turned around and walked away. But that happened, like because you're black, because you're in South Brisbane at that time then you must want to make a bit of cash on the side'. So pervasive is this assumption that an Aboriginal word for woman, 'gin', has been turned into 'whore' in the white man's mouth. Today, the word has been reclaimed by Indigenous Australian women, Kerry noting that she and her friends hail each other with: 'Hey, gin, where are you going?'

In reply to feminists' criticisms, sex workers retort that the explicit contractual nature of their sexual services guarantees them higher payment and greater freedom than most wives receive. By claiming that prostitution is 'women's work underlined', I accept the argument that sex work is work, indeed '*skilled* work' (Sullivan 1994:262). However, this is not to accept fully that sex workers are simply 'workers' who do not feel that 'what they are doing involves both sex and work' (Prestage and Perkins 1994:12–13). One indication of this is that most clients are male and most sex workers are female. Another is the high exposure to abuse that sex workers suffer, including rape, robbery and bashing (Perkins 1994:171). Assaults on street workers include breasts burned with cigarettes or being dragged along the footpath by the nipples (Perkins 1989:346), while a disproportionate amount of abuse is meted out to Thai prostitutes brought to Sydney on contract debts (Brockett and Murray 1994:194, 200, 198).

One woman with whom I spoke, when aged 17 with a baby to support, 'went into a house of prostitution' but was evicted by the police as she was too young: 'I felt dirty, I felt already used'. Nadine also worked in brothels with both an infant and a drug habit to support, taking her university books with her. A small number of workers had to adopt a range of personas, as requested by the client, for example, the French maid or the nanny. Those responsible for protecting the women were 'just a phone call away', in fact, too far to respond to trouble in time. Nadine found that 'once the trouble starts, you've got to stop it yourself, you've got to contain it somehow or else you're fucked (pun intended)'. With experience, Nadine learned to spot at once the clients who would prove difficult, 'the ones that hate themselves for doing it, the ones you can't trust because they don't trust themselves'. Sometimes Nadine could trick a difficult client into leaving; she might say that another client was due to arrive or her moody husband was coming over. When a difficult client was not so easily deterred the situation could become quite dangerous:

> you sense what could happen, so you put up with things that are degrading because you know that will satisfy them and make them feel as though they've got their woman-hating out, and so they got their money's worth without imposing serious physical harm.

But 'for every man that doesn't understand himself, you then have another man who's gracious and loves the company and loves women. So you can't generalise'. Many men 'treat it like business, and for girls it's business, and so that's fine'. In such circumstances Nadine feels her status as a worker is understood: two humans are involved in a transaction and there is 'no pretence as to the transaction'. In other situations, for example, where the transaction was cursory and impersonal or where Christian clients sought to convert her, the sinner, Nadine felt her status as a sex object rather than a contracting worker.

Work like prostitution and modelling (discussed in chapter 1) exposes the sexed nature of almost all women's work: requirements to dress a certain way, have a certain figure, be a certain age, be available either sexually or by offering nurture or a smile, 'forced into servicing, sexualised roles as part of their employment' (Sullivan 1994:257). As with sexual harassment, in these various incidents of workplace culture the female worker may be rendered invisible and her femininity heightened. The struggle of women in the workplace has been to expand the categories of worker which will embrace comfortably women beyond those which are intimately connected with women's presumed roles of servicing, flattering, nurturing, and into those where the pay and promotion prospects are greater, often because of the assumption that this is where the *real* work is done.

Conclusion: Careers, Jobs and a Life

Rachel, reflecting on her own life choices, contrasts the path she could have taken with the one she chose. Her father assumed all his daughters would go to university but Rachel gave almost no thought to what would follow university. While an academic friend of the family steered Rachel into traditional arts subjects, she made an independent decision in second year to study government. Almost as an afterthought, Professor Henry Mayer, having listed the 'gaps' in honours theses on State elections and referenda, said: 'Well, you could do something on women if you like, there hasn't been much done on women'. As a result of working on this 'much more interesting' thesis topic Rachel met Norman MacKenzie,[11] who first 'asked the questions that I simply hadn't thought of':

> He said: 'What are you going to do when you finish?' And I said: 'Oh well, I've applied for scholarships and maybe that will come off'. And he said: 'What if it doesn't?' And I said: 'Oh well, I'll get a job and then I'll go to England'. And he said: 'Yeah, and what then?' And I said: 'Oh well, I'll do a trip and then I'll come back and probably marry'. And he said: 'What then?' And nobody had ever said it... and it was an absolute revelation to me that anyone could keep on asking, 'And what then?' And it did, it totally altered the way I looked at things.

Clearly, 'the wonderful women' at Sydney University's Women's College had not asked these questions. Perhaps, as Ann Moyal (1995:24) suggests, the climate was not 'markedly feminist'. On graduation Rachel became a librarian at the Mitchell Library where she met Jean Arnot, the long-time campaigner for equal pay for women who was passed over for the job of State Librarian in more discriminatory days. Arnot sent Rachel 'off in her stead to the Public Service Association Women's Committee'. Union and political involvement became a central feature of Rachel's life.

Thus, despite 'all those lucky connections' and writing a thesis which 'is still referred to', Rachel was not in the very forefront of the resurgence of post-war academic feminism as she might have been. Instead, she married and between 1961 and 1967 'was with small children, not working. Effectively not reading even'. These were life choices Rachel 'never for an instant . . . regretted'. Again, in the late 1960s Rachel chose not to study for a doctorate as she thought she would either resent her family's demands or not be able to give her total attention to her doctorate. Rachel then 'sort of fell into teaching', another member of the cohort of highly qualified female teachers who would raise the temperature for change in the 1970s and 1980s. Because of Rachel's commitment to her family she 'always felt' she had 'a job, and it was not a career', marking the distinction in terms of where the greater importance lay – inside the house or beyond it. Men, more so than women, are able to combine families with careers, although Rachel's husband, a partner in a legal practice, also had 'more of a job than a career', because 'what was going on here was really the more important thing'. Rachel is not apologetic about the choices she made, but for her it has been one life or another. With different choices she was positioned to make the same impact on the world as the feminist writers who came a few years later, like Anne Summers and Bev Kingston.

Applying this distinction between a 'job' and a 'career' to the lives of the women with whom I spoke, while all of the twelve grandmothers worked after their marriage (two solely in family businesses), only one had a career rather than a job. Joan, who had no children, was a social worker; Matina may consider her late start in ethnic community work as a potential career. Among the thirty-four mothers, three have done unpaid community work and one, Gerda, concentrated on raising a large family. Of the five childless women in this cohort at least four have pursued careers, in the professions of teaching and architecture and in the public service. Additionally, however, six women with children are in the midst of careers, while a further four might be described as in the early stages of a late-starting career. Thus, about half of the mothers have experienced paid employment as having 'jobs', compared with 90 per cent of the grandmothers. A good number of mothers have, or are combining, careers with childbearing. The daughters envisage a life which combines career and motherhood, and many have adopted a 'life plan' to negotiate the potential shoals, as discussed in chapter 7. The next chapter turns to the 'female world of love and ritual' (Smith-Rosenberg 1983), the world of marriage and motherhood, which is not the man's castle it once was.

CHAPTER 4

Marriage and Motherhood

> We were raised with the belief that the answer to all life's problems was the husband, the family, the happy home ... You got a bit older and some bloody bird called Germaine Greer went and 'burned her bra'. And all of a sudden they're saying, 'Yes, the husband, the family, the home, the happy life, you can have that. But you can have a career too' ... I got a bit confused at that stage ... But then I found my prince, my knight, whatever you want to call it, the dickhead that I married. (Jillian, a supporting mother participating in the Jobs Education and Training Scheme, in Arnold 1991:89)

> When their mothers' fulfillment makes girls sure they want to be women, they will not have to 'beat themselves down' to be feminine ... They will not need the regard of boy or man to feel alive. And when women do not need to live through husbands and children, men will not fear the love and strength of women. (Betty Friedan 1965:331 in *The Feminine Mystique*)

Just as Jillian found her prince (who turned out to be a 'dickhead'), in 1971 over three-quarters of surveyed women under 35 years of age felt that a woman's 'most important role in life' was as a mother, whatever her career; the percentage who so opined falling to less than half a decade later (Glezer in McDonald 1990:13). The support for childcare so women could work outside the home and for equal sharing of housework in such situations had risen to around 90 per cent in 1991 (Bittman and Lovejoy 1993:304–5). Such support for 'gender egalitarianism' was greater among younger couples, among middle-class couples, where couples worked longer hours of paid employment and the smaller was the income gap between the man's and the woman's earnings (Baxter and Kane 1995:201, 206, 210). Indeed, the women I spoke with used part-time earnings for their own projects, buying a sewing machine, or in Deanna's and Lita's cases, paying for driving lessons and thus gaining a measure of independence. Myra and Jan remember owning a car as a significant pleasure, Jan still feels 'excited thinking about that first car I drove'.

While all three generations of women have experienced paid work since marriage, the grandmothers and mothers, unlike the daughters, generally expected domestic roles to be their primary life goal. They did not anticipate the high levels of divorce that their generation, and succeeding generations, wooould experience. These patterns are revealed in the tables in Appendix 1. The percentage of women remaining single doubles across each generation, from 5 per cent of the grandmothers to 11 per cent of the mothers, to an estimated 20 per cent of the daughters. Marriage rates are lower where women have more education and higher occupational status, indicating the greater capacity to choose a single life rather than relying on a male breadwinner's income.[1] The percentage who remain childless also doubles between the grandmothers and the mothers, from 11 to 20 per cent. But the divorce rates almost quadruple, from about 10 to almost 40 per cent. In terms of the women with whom I spoke, of the grandmothers, seven were married, four were widowed, one was separated; five had been married more than once. Of the mothers, twenty-one were married or in a heterosexual partnership, six were separated or divorced, one was single, two were widowed, and three were in a lesbian partnership; eleven or one-third of them had been divorced or separated at some time. Of the daughters, five were married, six were single, three were separated or divorced; three had been separated or divorced at some time and one had lived in a cohabitation which had not led to marriage. While the experience of failed marriage did not increase markedly across the generations, it was high in each generation, affecting one-third or more of women. Even so, the majority of women in each generation (except the daughters) were in a heterosexual relationship at the time of our discussions, a number as a result of remarrying.

Given their unhappy experiences, then, 'why do women continue to marry?' as Ailsa Burns puts the conundrum. Despite women's liberationists' condemnation of marriage, women continue to seek fulfilment of their emotional needs in this state, believing their marriage will be different (Burns 1986). As will be seen below, some marriages *are* different and these women's happier experiences are reported briefly here. Some women do beat the structures of an institution which privileges men over women, for example, in terms of allocation of housework and childcare, or because the wife's career goes on hold to raise children or further her partner's career. Furthermore, as Summers found in her survey of high school students' essays, children figured more prominently than husbands, who, in several cases were divorced in exchange for handsome alimony, or died (Summers 1970:102). Thus, women may also marry to have children. Because women, especially as part-time workers, earn less than men, a male income may still be seen as a necessary buttress to the role of mother. This chapter explores choices women made around the 'other life', as Catherine called it, choices concerned with becoming a wife and mother.

The Fruits Are Good

> I had one baby pretty well every two years. There was nothing to stop them; in fact, we didn't seem to worry about it in those days . . . there was no such thing as pills or anything like that . . . You'd ask doctors and they'd just tell you 'no'. (The butcher's daughter, born in 1899, who gave birth to seventeen children, in Carter 1981:55)

> It's a call to holiness being a mother . . . It's the best being a mother and the fruits are good, it's not easy, it's challenging. (Gerda)

One-third of Summers' young essay writers completed their lives with the comment that they got married and had 'x' children (Summers 1970:103). As with these adolescent girls' tales, so too with Mills and Boon stories (and Jane Austen, for that matter): the end is marriage. Feminists have pondered this genre, the difficulty women face in constructing a life beyond marriage that is neither anti-climax, failure, nor a translation of the heroine into a mother who lives through her children. Interestingly, several women with whom I spoke and for whom mothering was a central aspect of their self-definition, made comments which reflect this problem, comments which they subsequently edited out of their transcripts. Her children grown, one woman had said and later deleted: 'Up until then, I never had time for me, because there wasn't time. By the time it was home, husband, kids, family, whatever, there wasn't any time left. So your interests and your things just go'. Another commented on her time before marriage: 'I was determined because I thought: "If I don't do it now, I'll be sorry later". Because [edited out: when you're a mother and wife and all that] it was really a time to be truly myself'. Amber experienced the ambivalence repressed by these women in a recurring dream: 'I would wake up in a cold sweat and I would have forgotten to feed the child I had, and it was the same dream all the time. And I would be doing something really happy. I would be going about my business'. For Amber, the ideology of motherhood weighed heavily on her:

> I always looked after them and bathed them and I fed them myself . . . But I never had the motherly instinct and that was what made me feel so bad . . . But I realise now that there's a lot of women who don't have that . . . And that was a real guilt thing that I've always carried, and I still carry it . . . What you would have liked to have done, is leave the children and go.

Because of the prevailing ideology that motherhood was 'what you did and then you were happy for ever more', Claudia also saw her unhappiness as her own fault: 'maybe I wasn't doing enough'. Thus, Gerda suggests motherhood 'doesn't mean not being yourself, but, once you start thinking, "Me, me, me, me, me", then you start being unhappy'. Let us turn, then, to this experience of motherhood which kindles guilt in the minds of women who do not live it in uncontaminated joy.

Meanings of Mothering

> I didn't consciously say: 'I want to stay home and be a wife and mother' . . . I never had a choice. That was what you did and I felt happy. (Jan)

> I started out not seeing it. I was just blindly going along, and so do so many others. Just blindly go along, and a part of that blindly going along, they don't give themselves education, but they end up also pregnant, and in a financial situation that they're trapped, and they can't seem to make those life choices later on, even when their eyes do open up to it. But some of them never end up at the right place at the right time, to be able to even have their eyes opened to those other life choices. (Auriel)

From the second decade of the twentieth century in Australia mothering, particularly among the working classes, was subjected to increased professional surveillance from the medical profession, para-medical welfare workers and volunteers of the Infant Life Movement (Reiger 1985). Following the Second World War, Bowlby idealised mother love and developed the notion of maternal deprivation. In the hands of his enthusiastic proselytes, maternal deprivation meant that any child not brought up with the constant and unremitting attention of a mother was doomed to juvenile delinquency and psychiatric problems (Riley 1983:89; Gilding 1994:110 for Australia). By the 1970s motherhood had become defined, somewhat paradoxically, as both a more intense emotional experience based on natural relations between mother and child while also being a chosen experience (due to the wide availability of contraception) which took up fewer years of the average woman's life (due to smaller family size) (Crouch and Manderson 1993:63, 140–1). As an example of the greater demands made on motherhood, the regime of feeding, waking and bathing by the clock in the 1940s and 1950s gave way, by the mid-1970s, to a mother learning 'to interpret her baby's needs' and thus offer the security which will lead to regular feeding times (Knapman 1993:116–17).

Myra's birth was recorded in her father's diary in 1928 as 'got ring on 'phone from Blackwood Hospital, a little girl . . . Finished shutters, doing skirting boards, kitchen rail boards, canopy etcetera, went to hospital'. By the 1970s pre-natal programs were held at night so fathers could participate, although apparently in 1984 only a few white middle-class fathers availed themselves of this experience (Knapman 1993: 118–19). By the 1990s, according to Michael Gilding (1994:117), fathers' attendance at childbirth had become 'overwhelmingly the norm'.

While fathers are now expected to be more involved in this intense emotional experience, the fact that it is also chosen is indicated by an *Age* poll in 1981 which found that over three-quarters of those polled felt it was reasonable for couples not to have children.[2] The average and ideal family size (Evans 1992:25) is now two children, although only about a quarter of women will actually have two children.[3] Given the two-child norm, Claudia often feels criticised for producing seven children, while Gerda, perhaps defensively, told me that it was not irresponsible to have a large family in Australia (as opposed to 'the Third World situation'); none of her family are on the dole, three are 'full-time taxpayers', and her 'calling' as a mother is an 'inspiration' to others. Claudia feels feminists who do not have children are more prone to see her choice as incompatible with feminism. Gerda also senses criticism from the women's movement, that 'if you're a housewife, you're suppressed'. Gerda believes that women are now 'starting to realise, wow, wish I could stay home'. Gerda, via the adage 'the hand that rocks the cradle does rule the world', claims she is 'doing something really fantastic for the future of Australia through my children and through who I am and by my example'.

On the other hand, having no children can evoke criticism or pity. Gerda suggested that 'to become a career woman is great but it's not better than being a mother, it's just different'. However, having established that I was childless, Gerda said 'I feel sorry for you, I can't help it'. Joan, who 'never regretted' not having children, was 'furious' when a doctor once asked what the 'investigation' had revealed as the cause of her childlessness. Joan angrily replied that she had initiated no investigation. Alison remembers a friend talking about her children and then saying: 'Oh but you don't know anything about that'. The implication is 'you haven't passed the full woman exams'. These examples offer support for Robyn Rowland's (1992:276–7) contention that IVF and surrogacy programs express a social expectation that all women should have children.

Only three of the 126 essays Summers (1970:92–4) analysed referred to reproductive choices, including one girl who had test-tube babies, avoiding the necessity to marry. In the 1960s two-thirds of Australian women in their reproductive years used the pill, the highest proportion in the world (Gilding 1991:113). This proportion fell to a quarter in 1989–90, 15 per cent for women from non-English speaking backgrounds (Office of the Status of Women 1995a:Appendix 2.13). A number of women with whom I spoke divided their contraceptive experiences into pre-pill and post-pill days. Pre-pill, in the 1950s at Women's College, the requirement to obtain passes to stay out late was an excuse offered to males, an alternative form of contraception

(Alison). In the early 1960s the risk of pregnancy out of wedlock fortified Gisela's refusal of men's advances. Pre-pill, Pat relied on abstinence or the far less reliable Dutch cap. Mary's three children in three years were all conceived 'on different contraceptive things', but she had no more children 'after the pill in 1961'. However, there have been ongoing doubts raised as to the long-term effects of the pill (Gisela's husband convincing her they should use condoms after she had been three or four years on the contraceptive pill), as well as the IUD (Teresa attributing her miscarriages to it). Reflecting these and other issues, during the 1980s the number of registered abortions rose, female sterilisations halved, male sterilisations rose by about one-sixth and IUD insertions fell by two-thirds (Australian Bureau of Statistics 1993a:71–2).

Claudia 'sort of threw' herself into mothering, spending 'the whole sixties having babies', and seeing no choice in the matter. For many years Amber was stunned by the idea that there might be a decision, a way of controlling the outcome of intercourse. Catholic women with whom I spoke limited their family size because of their health or their desires for children's educational experiences (Margaret) or because birth control was 'my only resistance to religion' (Martha). Teresa decided that contraception was everyone's responsibility and began to take the contraceptive pill. As she could not live with the 'cognitive dissonance' she left the Catholic church at the age of 18.

However, for Gerda and Claudia taking 'responsibility' for contraception meant natural family planning. Worried that she was sterile, Gerda prayed for children when visiting Lourdes and 'drank so much water that my stomach just sloshed all the way back to the bus, I made a real pig of myself'. Because of her 'false ovulation symptoms', natural childbirth planning was unreliable, and 'really worried my husband for a while, but because we're Christians, the Lord just said, "Look, I will provide", and He has, so much, unbelievable'. Gerda remains a staunch advocate of methods like the saliva test and the Billings method. Unlike contraception, natural family planning is a 'good discipline', which makes intercourse 'more special'. One's husband expresses that he 'loves you enough to do that'. Similarly, Noela suggests that in her Catholic girls school 'we do sort of hold the line that, *ideally* natural family planning, ideally is the way that many people would choose to go if they could. Because of the lack of side-effects etc.'

Claudia had not associated her Catholicism with failure to use contraception 'until a Catholic priest said to me after I'd had the fifth child, had I read anything about contraception'. After an unhelpful response from her doctor Claudia turned to library books and, with a friend, established a branch of the Childbirth Education Association. Natural family planning offered self-empowerment in that 'women taught themselves and could teach other women'. They gain knowledge about 'how their bodies are working and how they can actually read the signs, then they can make up their mind what sort of form of contraception they are going to use'. As another form of discipline and bodily self-knowledge, Claudia learned the Lemaise method, a breathing technique which counters the physiological effects of anxiety, increasing a sense of being in 'control' during childbirth. Again her doctor, this time a woman, was unhelpful, saying: ' "Oh, it's early days yet", patting me on the hand'. The Association drew in 'these really good women', two trained nurses and a physiotherapist, who became interested as a result of their own pregnancies.

Anna, like Claudia, refers to women's self-empowerment through knowledge about childbirth and nursing. She is one of the new breed of career women who postpone childbearing until their thirties, daunted by the experiences of women around them trying to manage high-powered careers and a young family. Anna gave up her public service career to join her husband in a family business, and 'What does one have in a family business but a family?' Her sister-in-law recommended the Childbirth and Parenting Association, which Anna and her husband attended. The childbirth educator was 'very much into empowering the woman' to not be 'threatened' by the hospital, 'where most of us would choose to have our children'. Their childbirth educator recommended finding a GP who would not 'intervene unnecessarily', 'walking around during labour and doing whatever felt best – hot showers, baths, back massages, squatting etc.' For her deliveries Anna chose 'kneeling as if praying to Allah'. The childbirth educator highlighted the 'stupidity' of the 'traditional' position, flat on one's back, drawing an analogy with defecating; Anna noted this position had been introduced by one of the French Louis kings who wanted a good view of his wife giving birth.

Anna's childbirth educator tried to focus her class beyond 'THE BIRTH' to 'what you're lumbered with for the rest of your life', but with little success, given their anxiety. Anna describes driving home from the hospital:

> that time in hospital, you're really cocooned away from the wider world. You don't go out much at all, and you're there just focusing on your new baby and your husband and friends come in and all that sort of thing. And then suddenly you're in the wider world again . . . I remember, that really strange feeling of this little precious bundle coming back.

The Nursing Mothers Association provided Anna with breastfeeding advice, a mail order service for baby-friendly products and 'was a very worthwhile mechanism of getting to know other young mums in the area'. This helped her to avoid loneliness and provided 'reassurance' and 'practical feedback' on the variations among children from 'somebody else who will empathise and not judge necessarily'. In contrast, Laila found the focus on 'your child' and your 'housework' somewhat limiting, but notes that she was up to twenty years older than the other mothers in her group, and 'maybe because they were put in a bit of a box, . . . young mothers'.

Anna describes the Nursing Mothers as a 'feminist organisation if you like, in the bottom line' because it offered women's empowerment through knowledge. Anna approached her work as a trained breastfeeding counsellor in the same way Claudia approached natural family planning, pro-breastfeeding but with the primary aim of providing information so that women can 'make the choice that's appropriate in their situation'. Because breastfeeding is a learned skill rather than one that comes automatically, it can be difficult to acquire:

> and the counsellors have probably the best practical information they'll get from anybody, unfortunately, because a lot of GPs are horrendously ignorant . . . The amount of information that they get in their medical training can be ranging from zero to a reasonable amount.

For Anna breastfeeding was a defence against the family histories of eczema, asthma and hay-fever. It also cemented the bonding process: 'a quiet time where you can relate positively with your baby', while night feeding releases hormones which relax both mother and child. Kerry refers to the strong bonding and the 'indulging' of Aboriginal children through breastfeeding. Kerry continued intermittently to breastfeed one of her daughters until she was about 3 years old. The drawback of breastfeeding, as Anna notes, is the lack of the father's involvement, a problem not really resolved until the birth of her second child. She resented that her husband was 'reporting in for duty [but] he was equally responsible', while also realising that her routines and his unsureness excluded him from more involvement.

Anna, with her characteristic fervour for each of her life stages, threw herself into parenting. 'You want to be good, whatever that is', sifting through childhood experiences and 'fitting within the constraints you have in your own life'. Even so, Anna experienced 'a postnatal depression' stage, 'a real black hole', which she probably saw also as a failure to realise the ideal of motherhood. Eventually the infant welfare nurse 'gave me permission to sort of see a psychologist or get some help'.

Three women described the searing loss of an infant, either through a miscarriage or shortly after birth. After her miscarriage Yvonne could not handle the presence of her 3-year-old step-granddaughter in the house, 'there and alive and I'd lost my baby that I'd wanted so badly'. The doctor would not allow Vera to touch or bring home her spina bifida baby, saying she would neglect her husband and her other children. Indeed, for the three weeks of the child's life, 'I used to rush up to the Cairns Base Hospital every day as soon as I'd done my housework. It was like a magnet'. When Pat lost a baby at the age of 2 months, 'I just woke up in the morning and he was dead ... To me, it was my fault ... It seems I had a breakdown, I don't remember'.

Amber's experience of pregnancy and childbirth was ensnared in a life of psychological and sexual torture. Her husband allowed none of the rituals of buying clothes and preparing a room for the baby. The 'work was so never-ending, I mean I would be out roping a cow down or feeding pigs or whatever it was ... knowing full well I was going to have to go and have the baby that night'. Meanwhile, 'he would still be pushing me for the sexual side'. While such experiences would hardly make childbirth appear attractive, Amber also feels she doesn't 'really like children'. Amber constantly compared this lack of special (excessive?) affection mothers are meant to feel towards their own children with her own responses.

Other mothering, as African Americans call it (James 1992:47), can be a rewarding substitute for biological mothering. Other mothering ranges from adoption to step-mothering to versions of aunting. Yasmin was Audrey's first adopted child, offered by a friend who said: 'The reason I'm giving it to you is because I can't give it a decent life'. The two went to Charleville for the birth where her friend registered under Audrey's name. She asked that her 'sister', Audrey, be present for the birth and be the first to hold Yasmin:

> She wanted me to feel that I was the mother, so, I couldn't have been any closer ... So I stood there and watched Yasmin being born. It was a beautiful experience ... She just slipped quietly into the world, a little thing all covered in butter, not a sign of blood.

Two years later, Audrey's second adopted child was offered to her by a girl who could not 'bring meself to walk away from the hospital without it' and who had been told how much Audrey loved her 'own little girl'. Auriel describes herself as a stepmother, 'eccentric aunt and great-aunt'. For some women motherhood is 'a driving force', but for Auriel 'the driving force' is the Indigenous Australian agenda. Lita was always aware that she 'didn't want to have children', although her second husband regrets this as 'all of his friends have got children'. Instead, Lita shares in the care of her niece, and, knowing what it means to raise a child, feels she 'got the best of the two worlds'. While Alison says not having a child 'doesn't worry me' as there are 'too many other interesting things to do', she remembers a child adopted by friends: 'I really loved her, I hated to see her go home [to her parents], I got a bit funny about that actually'.

In imagining and describing their work with the Childbirth Education Association, the Childbirth and Parenting Association and the Nursing Mothers Association as feminist-inclined, Claudia and Anna have applied the messages of autonomy, choice and information developed in the women's health movement (Broom 1991: 13, 41) to the role of mothering. Such work goes some way towards repackaging feminism which has, at times, expressed ambivalence about mothering, although, as Rich (1977) makes clear, it is generally the institution of motherhood in a patriarchal society rather than women's experiences and roles as mothers which feminists attack. The women's movement's commitment to reproductive autonomy, and especially women's acccess to abortion rights, might also contribute to the widespread perception that feminism and motherhood don't mix. Thus, in 1903 a Birth Rate Commissioner in New South Wales bewailed the women's rights movement as a 'formidable adversary to fecundity' (de Lepervanche 1989:43).

Abortion

Throughout history women have chosen to limit the number of children they rear. In Australia between the 1880s and 1910 reproductive strategies included abortifacients, infanticide and baby farming, after which abortion, although illegal, became more popular (Allen 1982). In 1933 the first birth control clinic was opened in Sydney, which became the Family Planning Association in 1960 (Weeks 1994:16–17). One of the largest campaigns of the contemporary feminist movement was to return control of abortion decisions to women, who had exercised it before the late nineteenth-century campaign by the medical profession to prevent women's long-held practice of aborting a foetus before the 'quickening' (at about 3 months). Indeed, it is still the case that no woman has a complete right to choose, but must, at the very least, consult a doctor. The Australian rate is slightly lower than termination of one in four pregnancies, 'affecting at least a third of all Australian women and the majority of families' (Expert Panel of the National Health and Medical Research Council 1995:62, 42, 46,). Even so, resistance to abortion continues.[4]

Gerda describes non-natural contraception as an 'abuse' of the body's 'perfect machine', and abortion as taking life. Even in a case of rape, it is not the fault of the 'little child . . . and it is a child, I don't care what you say'. Both Noela and Claudia oppose abortion on demand, Noela describing it as 'the one area of feminism' she finds 'difficult', Claudia asserting that feminists do not call for abortion 'on demand' but rather that abortion not be a criminal activity. While Noela finds 'the church's stance ... very acceptable', she points to the continuum 'from a frightened 14-year-old girl to a woman who will choose an abortion because she knows she's going to have a daughter and not a son'.

Although evidence is scanty and unreliable, there is some suggestion that it is not the rate of termination but the dangers and costs of the procedures that change when abortion is made legal (Expert Panel of the National Health and Medical Research Council 1995:62). The women with whom I spoke revealed fear of death from abortions that went wrong and fear of arrest and conviction from being discovered. Helen recalls hospitals in the early 1960s where 'women who had miscarriages were often accused of promoting an abortion' by both male and female staff. Alternatively, doctors refused to perform curettes following a woman's report of a miscarriage for the same reasons. For one of the women with whom I spoke, here called Jane, this resulted in the 'most incredible bleeding, I mean the whole placenta and everything like that came away, all over the carpet'. In 1961 when she became pregnant, student friends offered to raise the money for an abortion for Claudia but she was 'really scared' 'and didn't want to do that'.

Jane also reports a friend's experience of nearly dying from an illegal abortion. For three days before her friend finally agreed to attend the hospital, Jane was 'carting up these blood-stained sheets and trying to wash them out in the bath, it was just horrendous'. When, a year later, Jane was able to share this experience with another person, she 'just went into convulsions, sort of shaky things', which she experienced when she spoke about the event for many years. The 'shakes' were due both to her own recent miscarriage and the 'the secrecy and fear of prosecution, which were far stronger than the loss of an unplanned child'. She remembers: 'When I took her to hospital, we planned in the taxi what I would say. We really thought I would be arrested as an accomplice'. Jane fell pregnant again while on the pill, newly introduced and unreliable. In a more accepting climate, she went to 'a nice abortion clinic in Double Bay' and confided her experience to friends afterwards. They told long-past stories: 'none of us talked, none of us knew, because we ... couldn't tell anybody, that was the worst part of it, we couldn't tell anybody'.

Audrey preserved the foetus from her illegal abortion because she could not bear to throw it away. Perhaps because abortion is still tainted with illegality and secrecy, Australian women have not developed rituals which acknowledge the loss of an alternative choice, however convinced they might be they have made the right choice. Jane says she never felt she had 'destroyed a child' nor has she regretted her decision. However, visiting Japan many years later she wondered about her response to the shrines for aborted foetuses:

> The mizugo are the little statues that you find, often at shrines to jizo. They're small Bodhisattvas, like little children, with little red hats on them and little shawls, and people bring offerings. At that first place we saw them in Tokyo, they all had little windmills. Rows of them, these little yellow and pink windmills going round and round and round, funny and pathetic and tragic too, but cheerful as well. I thought about it a lot then, wondering whether I did really feel bad about my own happenings. And I think it's really more that there was a home there for them, a home for each of them. It was sort of a bit sentimental in a way, but, I guess perhaps to deny it would be unnecessarily tough. Beyond that, when I thought about it a bit more, I thought: 'Oh well, perhaps there was a feeling there that I didn't even know was there'. (Jane)

The Stolen Children

> But everywhere we went, people were crying ... overjoyed. They were crying because this girl had come home to her country, to her people, and to her Mother. It was the deepest thing. (Marjorie Baldwin-Jones in Sykes 1993:44)

Judith Allen (1989:235) argues that women's central battle qua women has been for reproductive freedom, the freedom to limit their fertility. But as women of colour point out, this is a white women's battle. Over the years, white feminists' demands were for abortion rights, while Indigenous Australian women were fighting against enforced sterilisation and abortion by the state and the medical profession (although the Women's Abortion Action Coalition included no forced sterilisation in its list of demands). In a survey of thirty-three Koori women in Victoria, only four were in favour of abortion, fifteen were in favour of it only in special circumstances and fourteen were strongly opposed to it (Nathan 1980:61). Kerry suggests that the spiritual connections of the child meant there was 'some reason behind' the child's conception. Because the child has a kin identity through its mother, the shame of illegitimacy is a white shame and a white label, reflecting a patriarchal society in which patrilineage is more important than matrilineage. White children still commonly take the father's name and all children are described as illegitimate unless the parents are married.

Lisa Bellear (1992:57, 59), the first Koori to be elected to local government in Victoria in 1988, opens her biography: 'Since the invasion, one in six Aboriginal children has been removed from their natural family. I was one of those victims'. Others argue that there are no 'Aboriginal families untouched by that system' (Goodall 1990:8).[5] Indigenous Australian children may also be welcomed in the face of the generations of stolen children, removed to missions, the girls taught a limited vocabulary and sent out to service in white homes (Fesl 1989:31). As Joan describes the scheme: 'cheap servants in Adelaide to these good Catholic families that wanted to be kind to these poor, *coloured* children. I tell you'. Roberta Sykes described the tally of deaths of teenage girls in a Protection Board list made in 1938 as 'perhaps the earliest list of black deaths in custody', one in twelve dying between 1916 and 1928, most often of tuberculosis, linked with poor living conditions and social upheavel (Walden 1995:14).

From the 1970s the practice was increasingly condemned by independent Aboriginal childcare agencies, organisations established to reunite families, and findings of the Royal Commission on Human Relationships in 1975 and the Royal Commission into Aboriginal Deaths in Custody, reporting in 1991. Legislative reforms from the 1980s increasingly focused on providing indigenous childcare for Indigenous Australian children (Sweeney 1995:4; Lyons 1984:148–9; Chisholm 1985:8). Given the trauma reported by white mothers who relinquish children for adoption, the pain of Indigenous Australian mothers must be incomprehensible to those who have not experienced this loss. Some of this pain was revealed in 1995 and 1996 to a national inquiry on the subject.[6]

Women as Carers

My mother can sort of feel brave enough that she, she's in her late fifties, to say: 'I don't want to be a mother any more'. But you have to wait that long. (Berenice)

My daughter said: 'Mum, you're more than a mother, you're my best friend', and I thought: 'Oh wow, that's great'. (Gerda)

Not only does household income often plummet when women have children, but expenses rise.[7] Parents of a first child up to the age of 13 spend between $186 and $220 a week in support (in 1994 prices) (Jean 1994:16). When a mother withdraws from paid work the timetable of her spouse's working life often becomes the rationale for the family's waking, eating, sleeping, leisure and geographical location. Thus, Catherine and her children 'follow[ed] our "keeper"', as the family moved from location to location with her husband's promotions. Without kin support to help with childcare, Darwin was a 'wonderful man's world' but 'when you've got a baby on your hip, you can't quite do the same things' (Valerie). Valerie established a baby-sitting group to provide 'an extended part of the family' and which 'made a little bit of money for the church'. Sage recalls that nuclear families participated in leisure activities as a whole, mothers minding each other's children.

Before the 1980s government payments to mothers were small and they were seen as a gift, like the £1 'baby bonus' introduced shortly after Federation which was paid to white women for each baby. The Maternity Allowance Act 1912 gave £5 for the birth of every child to mothers of European background. The Child Endowment Act of 1941 paid allowances (of two shillings a week per child) directly to the mother (House of Representatives Standing Committee on Legal and Constitutional Affairs 1992:9), while a widow's child allowance was introduced in 1956. In the early 1970s these benefits were extended to all single mothers as the supporting mother's allowance, and extended to supporting fathers in the 1980s (Neave 1992:800). A pioneering study by Meredith Edwards in 1981 demonstrated that money paid to the husband, for example, as a taxation rebate, was not necessarily given to the wife to spend on the family. In the mid-1980s Professor Bettina Cass (1986), as head of the Social Security Review, further analysed intra-family inequity, recommending payment of family support pensions to the primary caregiver, usually the mother.

It is no longer a 'slur' on a man to have a wife in paid employment; rather the wife who stays at home might be seen as a 'bludger'. Deanna goes on to suggest that if she had stayed in the workforce she could have stuck 'up for my rights', for example, over sharing housework. The Australian welfare system presently reflects this somewhat schizophrenic approach, that women both deserve support as caregivers but are better off in the paid workforce. Women receive 95 per cent of sole parents' pensions, about a quarter of unemployment allowances and almost a third of sickness benefits (Neave 1992:800). During the 1980s government schemes sought to remove women from the category of 'supporting parent' and place them in the category of 'paid worker', by providing retraining schemes for supporting parents or rehabilitation schemes for those on sickness benefits. In the 1990s social security payments became gender neutral at the formal level so that men and women can receive payments as either carers (including carers of the elderly or disabled), or unemployed workers, or a combination of both (Bryson 1994a:298). Spouses of unemployed workers or low income-earners (below $231 a week) are eligible for social security allowances (Office of the Status of Women 1995a:10), including a parenting allowance to care for children under the age of 16 (Bryson 1994a:305).

Not until the 1890s in South Australia was a woman who left her husband after persistent mistreatment legally entitled to maintenance (Castles and Harris 1987:190). However, maintenance orders were always difficult to enforce. Since 1988 the Child Support Scheme has garnisheed supporting parents' wages at source.[8] It is men, more so than women, who bear 'the deadly combination of childcare, marriage and serial polygamy practised by persons of modest means' (O'Donovan 1985:153). Thus, some feminists have argued that responsibility for raising the next generation belongs to the community as a whole (the state should pay for it) and that poor fathers, particularly, should not be penalised for starting an extra family (Yeatman 1990:92–4, 96–7). According to this argument, femocrats who supported the Child Support Scheme allowed themselves to be incorporated by the state as 'God's police', enforcing obligations on errant fathers to 'protect' women.

When Laila first arrived in Brisbane less than a decade ago, Australia struck her as more 'like a housewife society' than Scandinavia where nobody considers staying at home and further education is an unquestioned expectation for women. Laila suggests that, more recently, attitudes have changed. The rising demand for childcare places indicates the spreading expectations or need of women to work. Childcare has become a pressing issue, ranked alongside violence and breast ancer in one national consultation process with women.[9] The first allocation of childcare support wrong-footed feminist activists, because it was paid largely to pre-schools which did not offer full-time childcare and so were unsuitable for many women in paid work. Today, indicating changes in expectations, childcare provision is linked almost entirely to the needs of mothers in paid work, extending to long-term day care, vacation care and out-of-school care. The growth in childcare places has been phenomenal, even if most of them have been in the cheaper day care option.[10] Gisela, a supporting mother, remembers that when her son was due to go to school 'there was no such thing as after-school care', noting 'It's within living memory for me and it's almost like another century'.

Despite the widespread use of childcare, in 1989 not very many more than half the respondents in a national sample agreed that a working mother can establish just as warm and secure a relationship with her children as one who doesn't work (Evans 1992:45). Similarly, a number of women in my study suggested that childcare is 'sterile' and gives a message of rejection (Valerie), that work-stressed parents cannot give their children enough attention (Myra, Valerie) which may lead to undisciplined children bought off with presents (Lucinda) or 'cranky' children who are rejected by day care and passed on to 'poor grandparents' (Barbara). Jan's children 'appreciated that mother was there', Jan suggesting that the first ten minutes when children come home are the revealing ones, and children are not interested in sharing their day after that.

While Deanna believes that children benefit from interactions outside the home in a childcare situation, she advocates part-time work, a strategy adopted by many working mothers. Grace echoes Glenda's mother's credo that teaching is the perfect occupation to combine with raising a child. Working at her children's school offered Grace all the advantages of workplace childcare: 'if they fell over or did anything wrong, I was there, on the spot'. A generation earlier, Sue light-heartedly notes she was 'a latch-key kid', but she only ever sat on the front steps like a 'little waif' if she forgot her key and only for the few minutes until her mother returned from her teaching job. 'But the women in the street . . . were horrid, really, really nasty to her . . . She was taking a job from somebody else.' Some of the mothers who took occasional part-time work felt 'incredible' guilt or 'worry'. Deanna made it up to the children by 'buying them toys and spend[ing] all the money you earned'. Margaret was always worried, especially if she had to leave one of her children at home.

In and Out of (Heterosexual) Love

Dymphna Cusack told us once that, as a small girl, she had stood under a peppercorn tree at a big family Christmas dinner watching her aunts slave over steaming fowls and puddings, while the men drank beer. Finally, an uncle asked her: 'And what are you going to be when you grow up, little girl?'. 'Not married', snapped Dymphna. (Rigg and Copeland 1985:185)

It was the old story, you know, I used to rubbish it all the time with my poor old mum, I gave her heaps. She used to say: 'He's a good man'. It always used to make me laugh. 'He's a good man, he doesn't beat us, and he doesn't drink.' He was sort of defined by what he never did. But, you know, in reality, for the times he was actually a good father, and a good husband. (Teresa)

Given the *Age* poll discussed earlier which found that over three out of four Australians felt it was reasonable for couples not to have children (in 1981, West 1987:41), what then was the point of marriage? Surveys in the 1980s suggested companionship was the most popular answer, followed by sexual relations, with factors like housework or bread-winning skills of less significance (Gilding 1994:117; Evans 1992:12, 13). But to feminists, the companionship of marriage masked slavery, economic and emotional, where women had only 'petty retaliation(s)' like nagging and refusal of intercourse (Summers 1994a:194–5). Indeed, in a 1989 survey only 47 per cent held that married people were happier than unmarried (Evans 1992:12, 13). As Deanna says of the 1960s: 'that was the idea of when you married, you were under the control of the husband'. The constructions of a patriarchal society which placed men and men's projects above women and their 'immanence' was amplified, given that the majority of men marry down in status, education, age and occupation (Bernard 1972:31–4). Thus, Gisela married a man a good ten years older than her, who at the time seemed 'just so much more sophisticated and I suppose well read and charming', while now she sees 'just an ordinary guy', who in fact 'was very unsatisfactory' in some ways.

Auriel's decision to marry was worked out in the context of being both an Indigenous Australian and a woman, as well as the daughter of her parents. The marriage celebrant, Juni Morosi, advised Auriel that she could keep her name, although Auriel, 30 years old, knew this. She notes: 'it's a symbol of the whole patriarchal white society that you change your name'. If Auriel is introduced to white people as her husband's wife, this elicits the response of 'just as his wife, instead of this other person, who has a brain'. 'They don't hear the name, they hear "the wife", and they forget to hear that I'm also Aboriginal', which means merely that Auriel is 'married to a black fella'. Auriel notes that her Aboriginal identity is signalled by her surname 'Bloomfield', a well-known Aboriginal family, so that:

> even though I'm fair, people will listen to my voice. They hear that I'm black. They can't see it, but other Aboriginal people can hear it . . . So, it was partly my passport, without a sign on my chest, it's a sign that I am Aboriginal.

Auriel was also 'proud' to keep the name her father gave her, adding 'after all, we're only swapping whitefellas' names', even if they have 'become black names in their own right'. Auriel's husband was not perturbed, white marriage ceremonies not being 'high on the black agenda'.

Why then did Auriel marry? In short, it was important to her parents, born 'in 1918, 1922 as my parents were', they had 'a certain set of expectations'. Auriel and her husband chose to marry in April, as her parents had. Auriel 'wore mum's wedding dress, that she'd had the train and sleeves cut off' and Patrick wore a pin-striped suit as Auriel's father had. 'Dad gave Mum a string of pearls as a wedding present, Patrick gave me a string of pearls for a wedding present. But they got married in a church. We drew the line at that.' Auriel and Patrick 'had fun doing it', a gift both to their parents and a ceremony to 'suit ourselves as well'. Thus, Auriel's definition as wife is a purely familial one: 'Half the world doesn't know that Patrick and I are married, because we don't wear conventional wedding rings, and we don't use each other's names. And, I mean, it's not their business'. Auriel and Patrick translated a white ceremony into something meaningful for them but which also allowed Auriel to maintain her public persona as an independent Aboriginal woman.

Falling in Love

When you are young, your demand is for a man who is tall and dark. He has to be handsome. He has to have wealth untold. He has to idolise and worship

> you. This is the Mills and Boon image. Yet these are not the reasons for a real relationship. (Joyce Clague who interprets her MBE as More Black than Ever – Clague 1993:162, 156)

> I had four men who wanted to marry me during that first couple of years of being separated ... I used to say to people, 'It's interesting, isn't it? There's this mythology around that women are the ones who want to get married'. (Teresa)

In Margaret's generation 'a lot' 'didn't marry', instead pursuing 'wonderful careers ... all over the world'. Margaret went to Papua New Guinea where the single men would 'get as drunk as could be before they'd approach a girl'. This meant it was more fun to 'go to bed and read a book'. The safety of courting environments was often linked to the banning of alcohol. In pre-war Cairns there were 'unwritten laws that you didn't go off in pairs' while 'Not having the drink, I think, was the big thing' (Vera). In post-war Sydney Mary attended dances where alcohol was banned and after the movies the streets could be safely walked at night. In the mid-1960s Deanna met her husband at a 'sound lounge', 'a safe respectable place – "no fights" and no grog (although the men carried flasks and slipped alcohol into the drinks)'. One could dance 'extra close and things like that' to the recorded music, but women could also 'set the limits'.

Following an engagement in her youth which was called off, Alison continued to look for a relationship. When she met her present partner at the age of 48, Alison 'was really sick of being on my own, I was still yearning for that companionship with someone, and suddenly it became possible'. Sage was 'extremely lonely' during her first year of teaching when she 'could not find a man I really was attracted to at all'. In this frame of mind Sage's father was successful in convincing Sage to renew her relationship with an unsuitable suitor. Sage was:

> on anti-depressants before I got married. There was every sign I shouldn't do it. But I was unable to live my own life ... So off I went to Darwin with my husband ... And had children ... I thought: 'This is the next thing you do'. And I mean, I don't regret that part of my life at all.

Teresa escaped her marriage before she had children. After her divorce Teresa 'fell in love many times, I fell in sex many more. I think the word for it would be promiscuous but I didn't think it at the time'. Kerry's marriage was a more pressing economic necessity. Her mother died at the age of 46 leaving Kerry with the responsibility of her young son and two young sisters as well as her own second pregnancy. 'There wasn't the support services ... that they've got today', and Kerry married the man she had been dating since she was 14 years old. He was a good provider and a good father but they were ill-suited. When Kerry felt ready, she left him.

Marg's parents sent her to a private school so she would 'marry that middle-class professional boy from the nice family across the tracks'. Instead, she married 'the boy who lives three streets away', his mother an alcoholic and his father a house painter. Marg's close relationship with her husband has not prevented, has perhaps enhanced, role-experimentation, including partner swapping and extra-marital relations. 'We talked it through and we both accepted that that was something we were quite comfortable about.' On social occasions Marg felt that she was 'perceived ... as Frank's wife', 'so why bother to go and talk to Marg ... she's not in the market, as you might say'. Marg put her wedding ring in the bank vault, at first feeling 'disgustingly naked without it on'. But, akin to Auriel's comment, 'it made a difference', people approaching Marg quite differently. When Marg's decision was raised at a family dinner, her father accused Marg of being 'disrespectful' and 'insulting' to Frank, her own mother and 'the institution of marriage'. Matina also felt she was treated as 'justa wife': 'When you don't work you are just your husband's partner, you don't have any real respect in your own right'.

Following a violent marriage, in 1970 Yvonne married her childhood sweetheart. When I spoke with Yvonne it had not been long since her husband died. He had spent some of his last months at home and, as his condition deteriorated, Yvonne and Merv developed a ritual: 'I'd say to him, "Ready" and he'd sort of brace himself and I'd slide him back up the bed.' On his last day of life:

> I went over, and he put his arms up around me and ... he said: 'Ready' and I said: 'Yes' and I sort of pretended to pull him up the bed ... That was the last word he said to anybody ... And then he hung on to me, wouldn't let go, and about half an hour later they extricated me.

Housework

> I hate housework ... People who go round and wash the floors every day and dust the furniture every day make me feel guilty, but drive me crazy too because I'm not that way inclined at all. (Yvonne)

When Naomi Wolf was in Brisbane promoting her book *The Beauty Myth*, someone asked her how she could both endorse women's pleasure in looking good and attack the demands western culture made on women in terms of youth and beauty. She answered with the analogy of housework, drawn very possibly from Betty Friedan's (1965:297) claim that housework is 'not a career, but something that must be done as quickly and efficiently as possible'. Before women's liberation women did housework not for pleasure or even out of necessity, but because they were centrally judged as a wife and mother on the state of their houses. For some women, as Aileen points out for her grandmother, that judgement by the white authorities meant an Indigenous Australian woman might see her children taken away.

Even so, and even in the 1950s, housewife was a poor second to mother in terms of central role definitions. Houseproud women make Yvonne 'feel guilty', echoing Amber's comment that her lack of mothering love made her feel guilty. But whereas Yvonne can be driven 'crazy' by houseproud women, one cannot claim that dedicated mothers drive one crazy. Gisela describes herself in the early 1970s as among '*just* the dreaded housewives, ... I mean I was really nothing', but women do not describe themselves as 'justa mother'. Kerry describes herself as a 'good' mother without being a 'good' housekeeper. Indeed, the children of her Welsh in-laws enjoyed escaping from their 'houseproud' mothers' homes and cooking 'up cakes and biscuits together, ... playing games building around the furniture, getting into dirt and water'. Helen 'stood up to' her mother-in-law's complaints about her housekeeping skills, saying: 'No, I'm sorry, I'm not inviting you to eat off my floor. I'm inviting you to eat off my table, which is clean'. After a five-year freeze in relations Helen's mother-in-law said: 'Yes Helen, you're quite right'.

In the 1930s Myra's mother washed all day on Mondays, using a copper. On Tuesdays she ironed all day, using an iron heated on the stove. 'Mum seldom went to town, and Dad often bought her clothes', asking a shop assistant who was his wife's size to test their fit. Surveys in the 1940s and 1950s revealed that parents shared some tasks, like setting the table, buying groceries, childcare and control, social activities. But such activities were 'mandatory' for women, while other possibly shared activities like income-earning were mandatory for men (Gilding 1994:107; Summers 1970:73). Couples who tried to frame their marriages in more equal terms often ended in chronic disagreement (Gilding 1994:111). As in 1965 so in the mid-1980s and in 1993: women who worked spent considerably less time on housework (Summers 1970:86; table 4.1 below; Baxter forthcoming).[11] Women performed 65 per cent of the total of unpaid work in 1994, valued at $139.4 billion (Townsend 1995:2), so that the demand for recognition of this labour in the national accounts and for accreditation of associated skills has spread beyond the women's movement to the wider community.[12] On the other hand, the data for 1994 in table 4.1 reveals that men whose wives work full-time spend only six hours less per week on the combination of paid and unpaid work than do full-time employed women in the same situation (64.2 hours for the husbands and 70 hours for the wives).

Table 4.1 Mean hours per week spent on childcare, housework, paid work

	Child-care	1980s House-work	Paid Work	Total	1994 Total
Full-time working husbands with wives in paid employment	7.6	15.2	41.6	64.4	64.2
Full-time working husbands with wives not in paid employment	8.5	12.5	41.6	62.6	n.a.
Full-time working wives	14.7	28.3	37.0	80.0	70.0
Part-time working wives	18.2	38.2	16	72.4	59.5[a]
Women with no paid employment	24.1	41.1	0	65.2	56.0[a]

a Possibly skewed because these are the wives only of men in the same employment situation.
Source: Adapted from Baxter and Gibson 1990:19, 22, 24; Lewis 1989:20, 104; Bryson 1996:214.

While feminists often focus on the symbolic significance of inside and outside work, men's and women's household chores might more appropriately be divided into work which takes hours (for example, feeding children, cleaning the house) and work which takes minutes (for example, changing nappies, taking out the garbage, grocery shopping), women doing much more of the former and men more likely to share or dominate the latter (figures from Lupton et al. 1992:113 citing Janeen Baxter's doctoral dissertation). Interestingly, housework surveys show that men make more housework than they do. Single mothers spend less time on housework than partnered mothers, even with the same amount of paid work (Burns 1994:274).

As table 4.1 reveals, only full-time home carers have a 'working week' similar to men's. The table also reveals why women favour part-time paid employment over full-time employment. This is how Margaret describes combining even part-time paid work with housework:

> I was out the door ready to go to work at 8.30 of a morning and I was home with the children on the train by 3 in the afternoon, or 3.30 I think we got home. Then I'd start with the homework, helping them with their assignments and what have you, doing the washing with one hand. Standing, have one of them stand outside with a torch sometimes at 10 o'clock at night so I could hang out the washing in the dark ... And my mother used to say to me when she came to visit: 'You know Margaret, you're overdoing it, you're working too hard'.

Margaret knew this but had set herself the goal of seeing 'all the children through high school, and further if they were so inclined'. Her health finally 'cracked under the strain', Margaret's doctor telling her she had to resign from work. When combined with childcare, housework and paid work made a full day: 'It was just a constant thing, I mean you were feeding one and then next thing you were pregnant again' (Amber); 'you couldn't do anything, wherever you went you took the pack with you' (Deanna); 'I find that sometimes, there's four people talking to me at the same time' (Gerda).

In the 1990s, as in the 1950s, families in which both partners share in childcare are unstable, only 37 per cent still practising this arrangement two years after the initial survey (Gilding 1994:115 describing Russell's findings). Men know what they ought to say about shared housework – it too taps a fundamental sense of the 'fair go' when women work (Gilding 1994:117; Bittman and Lovejoy 1993:313). Women increasingly know that they want this equal sharing and that they are not getting it, men often conflating 'helping' with responsibility or 'equal participation' (Bittman and Lovejoy 1993:313).[13] Some studies suggest the gap between men's and women's housework and childcare contributions has changed little, although one study suggests a radical reduction in the hours full-time employed wives devote to the 'double shift, thus narrowing the gap.[14] In rural Australia, although in the second half of the 1980s young husbands claimed to share in childcare, data indicate few differences from their fathers' generation (Dempsey 1992:102), so that rural women define leisure in terms of farmwork, voluntary community work and children's activities (Alston 1995:107).

Anna has an extremely supportive husband and they both have relatively flexible hours working in the family business. Even so: 'the bottom line is it's the mother who is ultimately responsible for the kids, no matter who the father is or how good he is'. As an example, Anna's husband suggested he would like to go out with Anna more often as a couple. Anna pointed out that it was 'a good idea' but, as she would have to earn the baby-sitting credits required, she would 'have to pay for it in the end'. Her husband accepted the force of her argument. Although they are both teachers earning the same amount, 'it really gets to' Sue's husband when he is doing the housework and she is reading a book, because it might be university study related but it might not. One wonders how often it annoys Sue when she is doing the housework and her husband is relaxing.

Divorce and Property Settlement

It's the basis of life, to feel safe. (Woman in the 1992 focus group survey of the women of 'middle Australia' in Riley-Smith 1992:53)

As the Industrial Revolution gained pace the rationale of romantic attraction increasingly replaced uniting family properties as the reason for marriage. The expectations of marriage were raised, while the economic consequences were diminished. If love died or was not forthcoming, all the more reason to search somewhere else for it. About fifty years ago legal separation or divorce gradually became more accessible, although still hampered by the costly and guilt-provoking adversarial divorce system in which one party had to prove the fault of the other party through adultery, cruelty, desertion and so on. In the mid-1960s about 10 per cent of marriages ended in divorce. In 1974 the Whitlam Labor government replaced this system with no-fault divorce, based on 'irretrievable breakdown' or living separately for twelve months. Divorce rates rose dramatically before stabilising, so that today about 30 per cent of marriages end in separation within thirty years of marriage (McDonald 1995:52–5). Previously 'Only *Englesi* (Anglo-Australians) divorced, Greek people never did' (Quadrio and Quadrio 1994:388), there are now more separations and divorces among migrants in the 30 to 50 years age bracket (Rossi 1990:139).

As children became an economic burden, especially while young, custody rights gradually shifted to women. From the 1970s women who returned to the workforce faced the loss of custody, although today this is unlikely. In the the majority of divorces women have primary custody rights, but studies reveal that where fathers contest custody they have a good chance of winning.[15]

The phrase was coined in the United States that 'a woman is only a husband away from poverty'. A survey in 1987 established that men on average were $60 a week better off after separation but women were $78 worse off (Edgar 1989:8). Given the poverty into which many divorced women are plunged, Deanna seriously considered her financial situation before separating from a husband who 'basically' had not mistreated her:

> If there is a pay packet coming in regularly that's a very very comfortable situation . . . Before we had our split, I sort of weighed it up. I could get an income with Austudy which would take me through – I mean a very small income – which would tide me over until I got this piece of paper which hopefully would get me a job in some area in teaching . . . A lot of women, you hear of them taking off with nothing. I was never brave enough to think of that.

Aquarius and Barbara received nothing like a half share of the homes they had helped buy. A generation later Teresa was insistent that she took equity in the house as her part of the divorce settlement even though it meant she 'was absolutely flat broke'. The operation of the Family Law Act has required courts to take into account non-financial contributions to the marriage when making property settlement, even in terms of women receiving a portion of their husband's superannuation entitlements on divorce. This has not included a woman's sacrifice of career or future income earning capacity, while equity as equality was much more likely to be enforced where there was very little property and not a significant family business (Charlesworth and Ingleby 1988:34).[16] One daughter, at least, endorses the notion that women's unpaid work is of less value than paid work. Melinda is 'annoyed' when women who stay home with the children demand half the house on separation unless that was explicitly agreed between the couple.

While women's economic situation may be worse as a result of divorce, most report growing emotional self-worth and independence, even if some women, like Lucinda, are critical of women who divorce for such reasons. Lucinda says of a sister-in-law who left her husband because 'she has "grown apart", what kind of a thing is that?' When Margaret bought her own house, it was 'the first time I'd ever lived alone in my entire life, and I was absolutely terrified of it. Now I love it'. Nikita, growing up with no sense of 'control over my life', has gone 'from strength to strength'. Kerry has 'gone on to being more of myself', whereas she 'found in a relationship that it's a bit threatening to your partner that you'd want to be off doing a book project and not drop everything to watch a movie or spend time with them'.

Such growth in self-esteem was no doubt greater for women who had suffered violent marriages, even if retrieval of self might be longer coming. At university in Lima, Lita was an assertive student participating in 'rallies and demonstrations to support the workers'. She was drawn to her ex-husband's 'progressive' understanding of social issues in developing countries, and only later discovered 'he hadn't come to his understanding about women's rights'. Lita found her ex-husband changed with marriage, but in Australia she lost self-esteem through unsuccessful job applications. It was not until 1988 when her sister joined her, and with support from the Migrant Women's Lobby Group in Adelaide, that Lita found the confidence to leave her first husband. She tried three times to 'be fair' and 'give him the opportunity to change', but finally went to the police and left him when 'he threatened to kill us'. Similarly, Aquarius' husband changed after marriage – 'then I was just the mother of the kids, you know how it is' – in escalating violence and rape which included frequent threats that he would kill her. The price Aquarius paid to escape was leaving her children behind, knowing he would care for them.

Once married, Cliff turned his violence on Amber who lived through a nightmare of extreme isolation, endless hard work, continual childbearing and sexual, physical and psychological experiences so 'horrific' that Amber spared me most of them. Amber became 'a prisoner', Cliff taking her child endowment, collecting the mail, and later, when Amber learned to drive, monitoring her petrol consumption. 'If anyone came to the house he would abuse them, and abuse all the friends of the children.' Amber had 'child after child' because 'He just saw that as a way of keeping me in check ... It's hard to explain, but I just didn't know what I could do about it, to stop it'. The sexual violence was something totally beyond Amber's experience, 'really frightening, when you're young. It's hard to comprehend and you don't want to tell anyone about it. You just try to keep it to yourself and hope that as they get older they'll tire of all these actions'. Finally, when she realised the marriage would not work, Amber withdrew emotionally and mentally:

> Because we're talking here, the numbers of times as well as the type of sex ... And if it wasn't going on, he was talking about it ... I just no longer was his wife, so to speak. And I think at that same time, I was no longer anyone's mother either, it was just me, one of me.

Not only was Amber ashamed of the sexual violence, but she doubted she would be believed had she told anyone about it. As Amber says: 'you do think about going', but she 'wasn't strong enough in' herself to believe she could leave, especially as 'your self-esteem must take a battering'. She feared that the children might be taken from her on the grounds she could not provide 'a proper home' for them. Cliff had also threatened to kill Amber if she left. Meanwhile she had learned coping mechanisms to limit Cliff's violence, 'and you always go back to what you feel safest with'. Amber notes that 'I could have killed him and done less time than I did' but she was 'not a violent person'. She resisted suicide because of the 'foolish' thought that came into her mind. Her grandmother 'always used to say: "If you commit suicide you never enter the kingdom of heaven" ... and I thought: "Don't think I'm going through all this for nothing"'.

Ultimately, Amber's eldest son started to repeat the cycle of violence, and the boarding school education Cliff had promised the children was refused: 'I had no option but to leave'. The children successfully begged Amber to return but she left again, working in a shop and cleaning at night, while the property settlement went through court. When Cliff died of cancer, ownership of the farm was contested and most of its value was paid in lawyer's fees, Amber receiving almost nothing after years of hard labour building up farm after farm.

Betty Friedan's ([1963] 1965) classic text, *The Feminine Mystique*, is written to post-war mothers: 'healthy, beautiful, educated, concerned only about her husband, her children, her home', 'respected as a full and equal partner to man' but who felt empty, incomplete, desperate, non-existent (Friedan 1965:16, 18–19). For Friedan (1965:17, 24, 29), the 'problem with no name' resulted from combining women's higher education with horizons limited to housework and husband-care.[17] This chapter has told stories of women who were not rendered desperate and empty through their dedication to motherhood, although far more of the women with whom I spoke have combined motherhood with further education or work or both, despite the increased time committed to the 'double shift'. Mayra's story marks a transition to Part II which deals with women's discovery (or rejection) of feminism. For Mayra, the path from marriage and housework to freedom lay through feminism.

Conclusion: Mayra's Story

Mayra's mother, widowed and pregnant with her fourth child, entered a marriage encouraged by her brother-in-law, the Imam of the mosque. Mayra's father, a prisoner of war, carried with him from Yugoslavia the brutalities and insecurities of his past to encounter a 'terrible time' of racism and factory work in Australia. As Mayra's mother said: 'They worked your father so hard, they broke his back'. He took his frustrations out on his family:

> They do that, they come home and kick the dog and scream at the wife and tell the kids to shut up. And that's pretty well what he did, he just dumped all his bad feelings on his family. He was very cruel and very violent. And he was aimless, he died very young too.

Defining herself as an Australian rather than a Muslim, Mayra resented that she could not attend dances, expose her arms, and do 'a lot of things that girls my age took for granted'. When she was aged 5 Mayra's father punched her in the face for 'flirting' with a boy. She and a school mate were sitting on a swing after school. Mayra's father was later than usual leaving the pub, so she was pleased finally to see him:

> I ran over to him: 'Daddy! Daddy!' And as soon as I got near to him, I saw that – I'll never forget it – I saw the anger on his face and couldn't understand what I'd done wrong. And as soon as I got close to him, he just swiped me and knocked me to the ground. And gave me a big lecture about flirting with boys. And I didn't even understand what it was all about at the time. So that's the sort of strictness I was brought up with.

Furthermore, 'we weren't treated the way we should be treated when we reached the mosque'. Mayra and her sisters disclaimed Islam.

Mayra's mother brought her up on: 'When you grow up, you'll meet a nice man and he'll look after you . . . And he won't be a mean, cruel awful person like your father'. In Mayra's rejection of dependent wifehood, her story marks a transition from the fruits of marriage to the more dangerous and mysterious fruits of feminism. This is not to suggest that these paths are incompatible, although there are reasons in our society why they are in tension. As Mayra notes:

> No one showed me that I could be an individual myself and that I could depend on myself to look after myself and I had this conditioning that I was supposed to have a man to look after me . . . that was very much the trend in the fifties . . . And I think now: 'God, I can look after myself better than most men'.

When motherhood is combined with wifehood, personal interests and intellectual stimulation are often crowded out as Jan, Mary and Deanna note. Pat recalls attending her first WEL meeting in 1972 which gave her a glimpse into another world. She had 'never had this opportunity to be involved with women before. All I seemed to do was work and keep the family going'.

Mayra's husband had his own brand of cruelty, constant criticism which provoked Mayra into increased attempts to meet his expectations. Ultimately she realised 'that he needed me to be somebody and I was never going to be that somebody, no matter what I did. And that didn't make me wrong'. Mayra lost a great deal of self-esteem in the relationship, but comments: 'I guess to start the relationship in the first place I obviously didn't have as much self-esteem as I should have had'. While grappling with a man who refused the protection and identity Mayra's mother had promised her, Mayra also grappled with another contradictory message from the 1950s: 'We need someone to look after us but all we do is go and look after everybody else'. Satisfaction was meant to come through looking after a husband and children:

> I tried and worked very hard at those sorts of things, and it didn't give me any satisfaction. It only made me feel worse. And, the more I lived with my husband, the more I realised I was living his life, not mine. And one day in my early thirties, I went: 'Is this what life is?' . . . I started seriously thinking about what I wanted to do with my life. And, as soon as I started feeling that way, I sunk into depression. I was severely depressed, I was crying all the time.

Mayra visited 'an old lady doctor', asking whether 'she could recommend some counselling so I could start to figure out who I was'. The doctor replied: 'I think the best way that you can learn to understand yourself is to get a point of view from a woman', recommending Marilyn French. Reading French brought self-understanding to Mayra but not peace:

> The more I started to understand where I was coming from, the more trapped I felt, and the more I knew I had to get out... But... there was a tug of war with what I was taught, that, you know, I had these two children, who were precious to me, who adored their dad, and I was going to ruin this family... But then, I think, what over-rode it for me was, I realised I was important too... I actually materialised those words for myself... I wasn't put on this earth to make all these other people happy. I was put on this earth to live my life... and reach my own potential... I'll never forget the day I drove out of the driveway with the two girls in my car, and just packed up to the top, and the girls were crying, and I was crying. And I watched my husband run out of the house with tears streaming down his face... And I remember the words I said to myself as I was driving out, ... 'I'm never going to put myself in this position again'.

From laughing with her husband at the images of bra-burning feminists portrayed on television, Mayra now believes that 'the feminist movement' helped her come 'out of my underprivileged background'. Mayra contacted the women's health centre, saying: 'I really want to do something with my life' and 'Can you give me some direction?' Through working there as a volunteer Mayra gained the self-esteem to believe that she could enrol in a university, although she had left home and school at 15 to escape her father. Even her father might have played his part in this. He used to bounce Mayra on his knee saying: 'I was his little girl who was going to university', a 'horribly mixed message' when combined with the Muslim message of 'grow up to do what your husband tells you to do'.

While Mayra's story should warm the cockles of any feminist's heart, she draws a distinction between the 'woman doctor... in her seventies', a 'tender loving woman' and mother and an implied 'raving feminist or butch person'. Mayra says of feminists like the doctor: 'You start to realise that those women were always there'. Indeed. Images of bra-burning radicals brandishing *The Female Eunuch* have hidden from view 'those women who were always there', turning the majority of women away from feminism, the word, even as they endorse feminism, the practice.

PART TWO

Present and Future Feminisms

Although change can travel at the speed of thought, it certainly depends on who's doing the thinking.
(Carmelle Pavan 1994:221)

Defining a Women's Movement

In 1994 International Women's Day was celebrated in twenty-three cities and towns in Queensland, and the annual 'Reclaim the Night' march in October is held in capital cities and provincial centres. By the mid-1990s traditional feminist organisations like the Women's Electoral Lobby had been joined by groups as diverse as networks of businesswomen in the ASEAN trade bloc, eco-feminists, 'feminists in cyberspace', and women joggers 'running the country' (Sawer and Groves 1994a:87-8). But do all these organisations belong to the women's movement?[1]

Judith Grant (1993:4) suggests that the core concepts of feminism in its various manifestations – 'woman', 'experience', 'personal politics' – have each posed dilemmas. That to define 'woman' would be a problem might seem strange, given that in most societies most of the time social members are only too aware of who are the women and who are the men, performing much boundary work to keep these distinctions clear. Postmodernists question the notion of 'woman' to disrupt these taken-for-granted distinctions, a reason for their interest in border-crossing sexual identities such as hermaphroditism, transsexualism, non-heterosexual identities and practices. More central, however, is the question of who feminists mean when they use the category 'women', given that women's experiences of oppression differ so widely across time and space. Moreover, some women benefit from the exploitation of other women, for example, managers of their secretaries, rich wives of their hired domestic labour, immigrant Australians of the dispossession of Indigenous Australian women (and men) of their land. Thus, working-class women and women of colour have challenged white middle-class women's definitions of a 'common oppression' and common vision of feminism's goals.

Gisela Kaplan (1996:202, 201) suggests that 'success for some Anglo-Celtic, Australian-born and largely middle-class women has indeed been impressive'. For most of the rest any gains, for example, in terms of better health or better education, have been shared by men in their socio-economic categories. Thus, for almost all Australian women feminism has produced a 'meagre harvest'. Previous chapters have revealed that women who are not Anglo-Celtic and middle-class share some experiences and gains with privileged women, but these are often inflected differently. Examples include Kerry's family's exclusion from the 'Dick and Dora' nuclear family model in school books; the experiences of recently migrated women in factories; the triple discrimination Lita encountered as a non-English speaking background woman with a radical social agenda. This part explores the effects of these experiences on responses to the women's movement from those who are not Anglophone, middle-class, heterosexual women living in urban centres.

The liberationist slogan 'the personal is political' sought to disrupt the notion that politics only concerned public issues, like elections and economics. It argued instead that power battles between men and women and patriarchal structures can also be found in the bed and in the kitchen (Jaggar 1994a:475). But such a sweeping definition of politics has been criticised as implying that every time a woman acts she is 'acting up', so that the women's movement becomes 'what women do' (Nancy Cott in Sharon Sievers 1992:320). This can be seen in Naomi Wolf's (1993:59) definition: 'Feminism should mean, on an overarching level, nothing more complicated than women's willingness to act politically to get what they determine that they need'. This definition would encompass an association of female corporate directors establishing a mentorship program to enhance their promotion, women for ordination in the church, Right to Life anti-abortion activists, and Women Who Want to be Women. The first group Kaplan (1996:38) dismisses as 'career feminism', whereas for her, as for the early women's liberationists (Summers [1975] 1994a:72, 73), feminism challenges dominant female roles; striving for 'the formation of new and different gender relations that lack the ingredient of domination on the basis of essentialist assumptions of difference', and which may entail 'a transformation of society as a whole'.

Thus, it is not so much a matter of roles or issues that distinguishes the feminist and the non-feminist. Indeed, maternal feminists, together with women like Claudia and Anna, have worked to value and reward women's mothering and nurturing roles and to empower women in these roles. Rather, one should ask: does this woman or group seek to empower women with more choices in their lives, to decrease the resource inequality between men and women, to expose and change the economic and cultural structures which systematically disadvantage women or other groups? Or does it seek to confine women to roles in ways which have traditionally disadvantaged women (for example, statuses in which women receive less financial resources or where women are defined legally and socially as under the protection of men)? Does it focus wholly on individual agency and lack an analysis of the social and cultural structures which constrain women's actions? Thus, a conservative response to violence might seek law and order protection but only for properly behaved women (who do not dress provocatively or who are good homemakers), while a feminist response might encourage women to act on their own behalf in self-defence, rape crisis lines and women's shelters, while also guaranteeing women a living wage with which to make real choices (see Campbell 1987:148–9).

However, by this distinction, when the Women Who Want to be Women asked that housework should be included in the Gross National Product figures they made a claim later echoed by feminists. Yet, their first act was opposition to the National Council of Women as undemocratic, unrepresentative and discriminatory, because men did not have a special council 'interfering' with elected MPs (in Rowland 1984:132, 135). Furthermore, while businesswomen's groups may be self-serving, women's presence in greater numbers can change organisational cultures. Because of their own needs and experiences, businesswomen may force workplaces to grapple with women's obligations as housewives and carers; they may find expectations for woman-centred responses are placed on them by female clients and the women's movement; they bring at least some remnants of the experiences of growing up female into organisations which are premised on growing up male (Pringle 1996 in relation to female doctors).

I suspect every feminist has a different answer to what makes the women's movement, one reason why I have deferred discussing the issue until this point. However, it is interesting that there is an often-unexamined assumption that feminism is somehow more radical than the women's movement. The distinction I would make is that the women's movement encompasses women acting to improve the status of women (however, wherever). Feminists' commitment to improving the status of women is contextualised within an understanding of the structural impediments faced by women and how these impediments vary between women depending on class, ethnicity and so on. The limits of the acceptability of feminism in the popular imagination – somewhere before systematic structural disadvantage is understood – will be explored in the Conclusion to this book.

There Has Always Been a Women's Movement

Irene Greenwood (1992:113) says of the 1970s 'famous' feminists Germaine Greer, Betty Friedan and Anne Summers, that they were not a 'new phenomenon. I had read the books of my mother's generation'. What was new was their 'higher education, knowledge of the realities of economics and politics, experience in student militancy, and financial independence'. Eve Higson said to Margaret Reynolds (1993:122): 'The trouble with you young women is you think you invented feminism'. Indeed, in its early years the story of women's liberation was the story of Athena sprung fully-formed, although clearly not from her father's brow. Women's liberationists wrote histories in which their activism was wrought from their own experiences, as though the post-war generation were 'the first to know' (Rachel). Rachel, born on the eve of the Second World War, gets 'very irritated by the assumption that there is this huge gap between the 1890s or the winning of suffrage and Anne Summers et al. because, I know that there were the Jean Arnots and the Muriel Heagneys and it never stopped'. Suggesting: 'It's all very well to give Edna Ryan a doctorate when she's 80', Rachel points to women in the 1930s who fought for equal pay, for married women to retain their jobs, earned their own living, or, like Edna Ryan, won local government office. 'And then further back, you know, the Jessie Streets, imagine the social pressure on Jessie Street. What might she have done nowadays?' Many post-war feminists know of the United Nations Decade of Women meetings, far fewer know that Jessie Street was a moving force in the foundation of the League of Nations and had attended post-war reconstruction meetings as Prime Minister John Curtin's delegate (Greenwood 1992:116). For her part, Irene Greenwood (1992:118, 116) attended meetings of the International Status of Women Commission and the International Labour Organisation in 1965. Greenwood's activism spans the pre- and post-war feminist generations (Baldock 1993:2–3), and she acknowledges the benefits she derived from an earlier generation of feminists, noting there were kindergartens for her children to attend as well as some information on birth control (Greenwood 1992:110).

Dale Spender (1982:4–5) claims each generation is forced to invent feminism anew because men have repressed women's ideas from textbooks, libraries and common knowledge. Perhaps rejection of the mothers by their daughters is another factor, despite the reminders from Greenwood, Rachel and others.[2] In the 1920s and 1930s the glamorous sexualised 'new women' rebelled against their 'mothers', the nineteenth-century 'old school of fighting feminists who wore flat heels and had very little feminine charm' (Ware 1993:126). A little more than a generation later, in the early 1970s, women's liberationists pejoratively applied the term 'feminist' to earlier 'bourgeois' activists wedded to a 'despised reformist tradition' (Caine 1995:9). However, as the women's liberationists mellowed they applauded their foremothers, like Edna Ryan (in Mitchell 1987:75, 76) and Dame Roma Mitchell (in Mitchell 1987:43), but only to be spurned in their turn. Now the mothers are ageing radicals pitied by a new generation of women as 'a bunch of sad and lonely people who lived only for their jobs and their politics' (Summers 1993:194). Rightly or wrongly – more the latter, I suspect – generational differences have become the tag for current controversies concerning victim feminism versus power feminism, and prudish Victorian feminism versus libertarian feminism, which will be discussed in the Conclusion to this book.

In these next three chapters we consider the impact of the post-war women's movement, not so much on women's lives but on their hearts and minds. How did 'ordinary' women find out about feminism? How did they respond? Why do so many women seem to endorse feminist goals and yet far fewer women are willing to call themselves feminist (chapter 5)? Secondly, we explore the responses to feminism from women beyond the Anglo middle-class confines of capital cities. Is this a movement also for them, or is feminism a small movement for an elite few (chapter 6)? Thirdly, we ask about feminism in the daughters, both in terms of different experiences of education and work, and different expectations concerning marriage, motherhood and careers (chapter 7).

CHAPTER 5

Finding Feminism

Passages To and From Women's Liberation

brought up to please, we are without a sense of ourselves. (Deborah McCullough in 1975 in Chesterman 1993:185)

It took a while for women in general to take the opportunities the feminist movement offered up for them. Look at me, tentative about going on to uni. study, didn't learn to drive until I was in my thirties, never went to the movies by myself till I was married for about ten years. It's scary to step out and say, 'Yes, I'll have some of that freedom', it required a decision – how much freedom? Where does it stop? It required accepting responsibility for your own actions, decisions and life I guess. (Grace)

Feminism was suggested to women by incidents as major as the shame of rape or an unwanted pregnancy, as pressing as equal wages, or as apparently superficial as unequal access to leisure facilities. As people act they change, if but slowly, the structures in which we are embedded. We create and recreate our own identities, as working-class women, as Greek–Australian women, as urban Indigenous Australian women. But in the process and by our own practices, we add to society's repertoire of ways of 'doing' those identities. From their encounters with feminism, the 'mothers' in my sample went on to divorces, secondary study, asking husbands to share housework more equally, demanding better conditions at work, or going to the movies alone.

The options which Grace explored in her imagination ran ahead of the changes in her practices because 'not enough was known about what happened *after* you made your choices – especially radical ones'. Or as one member of a former Melbourne consciousness-raising group notes, attitudes are the 'big gap' between legislation and its implementation (Helen in Henry and Derlet 1993:182). Women have come to their awareness of feminism in diverse ways. Where most non-feminists have relied on the media, newspapers and television, feminists have more often come via consciousness-raising, feminist books and, from the mid-1980s, women's studies (Rowland 1984:228), although paths to feminism are more often private than public. This section is about consciousnesses raised, both in and out of the consciousness-raising groups which were so popular in the 1970s.

Consciousness-Raising

> I remember my husband having his birthday, and I went to a meeting ... during that period nothing could have kept me away. I lived for it. (Helen in Henry and Derlet 1993:55)

A newsletter in 1973 listed thirty-four consciousness-raising groups in Melbourne, one in Geelong and two in the western suburbs (Henry and Derlet 1993:64). In a survey of women in the United States involved in consciousness-raising groups, everyone agreed that her life had been made 'richer for its expanded possibilities', a number saying that CR saved their lives (Shreve 1989:74, 75, 221). Reconvened members of a Melbourne group ruminated over personal growth, class analysis of society, violence against women, protesting on the trams over equal pay, and a sit-in at the office of the Minister for Housing over Housing Commission flats (Henry and Derlet 1993:74–5). However, Bernadette (in Henry and Derlet 1993:58) was both excited by her personal development and disappointed at the lack of larger political actions:

> Getting to know each other with no men present ... that was the big thing. We could just be women, no matter who our husbands thought we were ... Although I do remember at the time being disappointed that it wasn't more political. Because I thought we were going to change the world.

Dawn Rowan (1992:141) was taken to her first Women's Liberation meeting in 1970, and sat up in bed reading '"Why I want a wife", "Christian oppression in the family", "The myth of the vaginal orgasm" and "The politics of housework". I needed no more convincing'. In the Adelaide Women's Liberation Centre Rowan and others established the first crisis counselling service for women in 1970.

Generally speaking, however, women did not go almost straight from reading about the myth of vaginal orgasm to establishing a crisis counselling service. As Grace suggests, the women's movement is 'so opposite to what you are taught to believe' that 'most people would test the water a little bit'. The possibility that there was another ocean in the world was often presaged by what Anita Shreve (1989:54–5) calls the 'click' of recognition, possibly only a 'split second of recognition', but one which opened the door on to large 'life-shattering, life-enhancing matters'. The click might be a sudden realisation that their husbands did not listen to them, that their older brothers had been taken more seriously than they were when growing up, that men expected and accepted women's housework without saying 'thank you'. Grace remembers this last example of the click experience in an article tucked away in a women's magazine among pieces on ' "How to please your man" and "How to make a perfect apple pie" '.

Helen's 'click' also occurred over domestic labour. On a busy evening she was preparing her children to attend a school concert when her husband came home:

> It was very hot, it was in North Queensland, and he sat down with the bottle of beer. And he said: 'Gee I'm tired, I really don't feel like going to this concert tonight'. And I said: 'Oh, you have to go, it's for your son', and he's saying: 'Yes, yes'. And in the meantime I had cooked tea, I bundled the kids into the bath, I had fed them . . . I dried them and dressed them . . . Then I got my husband's tea and gave it to him, and still, and in the meantime, I'm trying to eat my meal and clean up. So he got dressed then, and I'm standing at the sink washing up and I hadn't even got changed . . . And he came into the kitchen, and he said: 'Oh dear, I'll help you with the dishes'. And I said: 'Oh, thank you, thank you' . . . I suddenly thought: 'Really, I shouldn't be that thankful, I should expect it'.

Helen then refused to clean the garage, saying to her husband: 'It's your toys, you put them away'. Following a pitched battle, she also trained her children to do a share of the nurturing and housework. Helen's last two pregnancies were difficult because of toxaemia. One morning she refused to get up until she was brought a cup of tea, staying in bed with a 'good book' until the early afternoon: 'I didn't make them breakfast and I didn't make them any lunch, and they needed this and they needed that. And I said: "Oh, well, when I have my cup of tea, I'll be quite willing to do this for you" '.

For Deanna the 'click' came with Helen Reddy's mid-1970s song, 'I am woman, I am strong':

> 'I am woman, hear me roar'. I can remember standing in my kitchen doorway, and I mean, just where the proverbial door mat would be [both laugh] . . . I don't know how I could have been feeling at the time, for that to have made an impression on me . . . I know I've changed, I mean even in the last twelve months, I've sort of changed my ideas of what you should do. Really, the sky's the limit. If I could change the past, just what would I have done? . . . The 'I am woman' thing, that was probably the little [makes sound like 'ch-ch-ch'] that started things off and made you aware, and so you kept your mind open to different things. And that which fitted into your situation,

you . . . let it have an influence on your life. And that which you felt, okay, may have been acceptable to you but wasn't acceptable to your situation, you sort of set aside and gradually you stood up for yourself more as a woman.

Helen Reddy's song 'opened her [Deanna's] mind' to 'different things'. From then on, Deanna kept a look-out, as it were, for alternative ways of thinking and living, storing those ideas which appealed but which were not yet 'acceptable' in her situation. Gradually she changed her situation as she stood up for herself 'more as a woman'.

Many women who were sympathetic to feminism described their responses in a similar way, as a shuttling backwards and forwards between changes in their desires and changes in their material situation. In the first forty years of her life Grace accepted 'what was handed out to me' while 'always knowing inside that there's got to be something better than what you were doing'. Women's liberation offered Grace a choice she did not previously have: to be as 'liberated as I choose to be for the moment'. Teresa changed 'one cell at a time'. When she was told that 'girls are not good at maths', Teresa replied: 'But I've got a degree in pure mathematics'. 'And the exact response was "But you're different, you think like a man."' Teresa's actions concerning equal pay and dress codes, other issues which did not 'sit right' with her, were discussed in chapter 3. But each cell has to be replaced, has to be undone as well as remade, working over the 'indoctrination' with new ideas, so that some 'cells . . . are still not feminist cells'. Like Deanna, Teresa links desire with structural possibilities, 'knowing what you want' with the ability to get it. Gisela, too, notes the relationship between interior changes and external exigencies.

Half a decade before the official dawn of women's liberation in Australia, in 1965 Merle Thornton and Rosalie Bognor chained themselves to the public bar at the Regatta Hotel in Brisbane after they were refused a drink. This is treated as a founding moment in Australian feminism by Ann Curthoys (1992:430), Verity Burgmann (1993:77) and Gisela Kaplan (1996:32). The link was also made by Aquarius and Margaret. Margaret remembers in the 1950s in Melbourne that women ordered their lunch in the bar 'and then we'd take our lunch and walk outside to the garden where we were allowed to sit and eat'. In 1957 when Margaret went to work in Papua New Guinea, she noticed both that women's opinions on topics were 'listened to' and 'it was the first time I was able to walk into a hotel and order a drink from the bar without everybody stopping dead'. Aquarius contrasts the Australian situation with the English pub where 'you play darts with the men and nobody takes any notice, because they got educated', while judging by the reaction from the hotel patrons in Australia 'you'd have thought we'd walked in there stark naked'. In her own protest action Aquarius and some friends broached the 'holy of holies', the bar at the RSL club:

> I'll never forget that day . . . We said: 'Well, what are we going to do?' I said: 'I'm going to have a beer at the bar'. I said: 'It's been proclaimed. It's been announced'. I said: 'If we don't, they're going to say, "Aahh, they don't need it" and we won't be allowed it'.

Aquarius' group went to the bar where the 'lovely' barman inquired: 'Yes, ladies, what can I get you?' They sat there for two hours, joined by other women who came in.

Other women in my study suggest that feminism was always there, even if not by that name. Glenda's mother explained that 'publicly the father was supposed to be the head of the family, but really Mum was the head of the family in our house'. With messages like this Glenda developed a long-term 'gut feeling or perception that women were unequally placed' and did not deserve to be. In Alison's working life as an architect, feminism has 'been a constant mainstay and support'. Sue notes that as 'a happy watcher of the ABC and I watch SBS . . . it's all, it's *there*'.

Berenice explicitly contrasts an organic way of reflecting on one's life among friends with 'organised discussions about things' which she finds 'really quite bizarre', as do most of her friends. 'Organically grown' feminism is often fed by feminist literature, to which we now turn.

Feminist Books

> Feminist publications also end up in libraries – where they are tenderly received by feminist librarians. (Dann 1985:127)

> She stood alone then and she always has . . . But she wasn't condemned for that by her teachers or her fellow students, she was just different, and they recognised it. (Margaret, discussing her cousin's memory of Germaine Greer at her convent school)

Judging from women's reminiscences, books have pride of place in the process of reconceptualising the world (Lynne Spender 1992:49–50; Kay Setches 1992:72, Gisela, Nadine, Phylis and Kerry). Gisela's walk to school took her past a building with a library in it, 'and one day I plucked up the courage to peep in the door and there were all these books . . . And I just discovered this whole world of just, I suppose, magic'. Fortunately her mother could afford the 'piddling sum' required to join. Kerry explored her local area, swimming, visiting relatives, libraries and the museum. Phylis remembers the 'very first book I read', 'picking out the words, "Uncle Tom's Cabin"'. Phylis still has 'a fascination with knowing things', which helped her overcome her fears and return to university as a mature-age student. In contrast, Mayra did not discover reading as a child and reflects 'My life would be very different now, I can't get through enough books'.

From the mid-1970s feminists were appointed to Writers Week committees; publishing houses made space for more women's writing after Literature Board grants were offered by the Whitlam government (Westwood in Watson 1990:225–6,228); women's presses, often short-lived, focused specifically on feminist writing. Since the mid-1980s Anglo-Australian women's writing has been joined by the biographies of Indigenous Australian women, while second-generation immigrant Australians reflect on the difficulties of experiencing racism and disadvantage in an alien culture or the pleasures of a 'double vision' drawn from both cultures.[1]

Feminist children's books influence a younger generation of girls. When Sage read a story to her pre-school daughter about a female protagonist who led the other characters on a bear hunt, 'within ten minutes Willow's downstairs saying: "Come on, we're going on a" – she didn't say bear hunt, it was a buffalo hunt'. Grace, a school library-aide, refers to a spin-off from feminism in the range of issues addressed in children's books: 'My daddy is a nurse', 'My mother drives a truck' . . . 'Meet my stepmother' and 'We're getting a divorce'. She concludes that if children 'grow up with any bias at all, it's in their own mind and of their own choosing'. Grace notes, however, that there are still books written specifically for the teenage girls' market, like the Babysitter Club series, while there are still books to which boys more readily respond, information books on cars and boats or joke books. Similarly, Bronwyn Davies (1988:64–7) found that the children in her study were disconcerted by stories without a 'proper ending' and which challenged 'traditional' models of masculinity and femininity, for example, boys who wish to do ballet, girls who rout dragons but in the process become dirty and unkempt and are rejected by their princes, princesses who refuse to marry. Even so, young writers have learned to play with the genres of children's stories.[2]

Verity Burgmann (1993:80) in her overview of the development of post-war feminism cites three key texts: *The Feminine Mystique* (1963) by Betty Friedan, *The Female Eunuch* (first published 1970) by Germaine Greer and *Damned Whores and God's Police* (1975) by Anne Summers. This list does not include Simone de Beauvoir and her book *The Second Sex*, which 'literally changed thousands of women's lives' (Moi 1994:3). De Beauvoir was among the first generation of European women educated on a par with men, women like Hannah Arendt, Alva Myrdal, Margaret Mead (Moi 1994:1). Even though in 1949 'women's issues were not central to the political agenda of any major party or faction', 'the very moment she realized she was an intellectual *woman*, she started to write *The Second Sex*' (Moi 1994:189, 2). In proposing that woman is the 'other' to man's essential and transcendent self (see chapter 1), de Beauvoir 'poses a radically new theory of sexual difference' (Moi 1994:155) while also advocating access to contraception, readily available childcare as well as changes in the social images of femininity (Moi 1994:174–5, 191).

Fiorenza, who grew up in Milan, describes Simone de Beauvoir as 'my sort of mentor'. Later, at university when she was introduced to Greer and other writers, Fiorenza could compare the position of continental European and English-language women and feminisms, reflecting that in Australia and New Zealand women voted fifty years before Italian women first voted, in 'the referendum in 1945'. However, Kaplan (1996: 10–11) notes there were more women in Italian parliament just after the war than there are women in Australian parliament today. Marlene Goldsmith (1994:178) also read de Beauvoir, and Ann Moyal (1995:26) remembers that in 1943 Virginia Woolf's *A Room of One's Own* 'spoke to me directly'. Although 'One had no real inkling of feminism', Moyal 'stood eager on the brink'. Years later in 1984, Beth Yahp came to Sydney and 'discovered Virginia Woolf and feminism', slowly unlearning a fear of speaking instilled through her Malaysian education (Spender 1990:463). For Fiorenza and Yahp, unlike Moyal and Goldsmith, feminism came in several languages. Rather than being limited to the 'backward' stereotypes in which they have so often been located, they knew two cultures and blended these in ways appropriate to their own lives.

Burgmann's list also excludes Dymphna Cusack's *Come in Spinner*, based in part on Cusack's experiences at the children's court where she worked, and dealing with illegal, dangerous and expensive abortions, doctors often gouging the system. The book 'shocked the world' (Cusack in Rigg and Copeland 1985:61, 60), including Margaret's mother who forbade her daughter to read it. Margaret immediately took the book out of the library again, realising that it was 'the implied sex' that had horrified her mother, Margaret remembering that 'some soldier raped a girl or something'.

Feminist books resonated with and amplified women's half-formed articulations of their experiences. They made women aware that they were 'not alone', as Marlene Goldsmith (1994:178) reports of de Beauvoir and Friedan. Friedan (1963:33) claimed that sharing 'the problem with no name' meant women knew they were not 'completely alone'. This point was also made in relation to Marilyn French, particularly with *The Women's Room*: it was 'like reading my own life history' (Chris Momot 1994:240); 'personal meaning lay in each page' (Giovanna Salomone 1993:63); 'the experience was totally related to my experience. And I can remember so much falling into place' (Teresa speaking of *The Women's Room*).

Sage remembers 'crying' when she read *The Female Eunuch*. Greer 'said what I felt, expressed what I didn't understand was wrong, that I couldn't have articulated'. Then Sage knew 'why we read. We read so that we know what we really feel'. Not surprisingly many women, like Sage, after encountering feminist literature become avid readers: 'I just couldn't stop reading'. Greer's book had 'an enormous impact', articulating for the successful entrepreneur, Mariana Hardwick, what she had instinctively thought about her 'typical patriarchal European family' (Ford 1991:128). Irina Dunn, of Russian and Irish-Chinese heritage and entering the Senate in 1988, describes an influence so 'profound' that she became a 'committed feminist' (*Broadside*, newsletter of the National Foundation for Australian Women, 16 (May) 1994:5). Barbara Lewis (1994:107) recalls 'a powerful book' and comedian Rachel Berger an 'extraordinary' one (*Courier-Mail*, 4 October 1993:16–17). Phylis 'thought that she was just wonderful', while Shona suggests she saw issues differently after reading Greer: 'And suddenly I started to think about it then, "This isn't right, this isn't fair. Why should this be this way?"'.

In Papua New Guinea Gisela became a member of a reading group instigated by female academics. Possibly because of the group's informality, Gisela 'felt the equal of anybody there', experiencing an audacity to speak that she doubts she would now have in academic company. 'Everybody just came out with their opinion, and this wonderful discussion would ensue.' The group read *The Feminine Mystique* and *The Female Eunuch*, Gisela saying of the latter that she 'can't remember much about the book, except that it opened my eyes'. Akin to Shona's response, Gisela asked: 'Oh, why didn't I think of that? Why didn't I realise that? ... Well, yeah, okay I can do that'. Gisela links reading *The Female Eunuch* to leaving her husband. The marriage had become increasingly unsatisfactory as his involvement with another woman often left her 'transportless looking after a child'. Formerly supportive of Gisela's talents, he was less enamoured of the feminist ideas she brought home from the reading group. Gisela realised she had to leave to regain control of the situation:

> I don't know how much ... feminism had liberated me, I don't like to use that word. But it certainly had made me think and obviously made me realise that I couldn't hang round waiting for somebody else to do something about my life.

In 1979 Germaine Greer asserted: 'women really aren't liberated', even those who say 'Your book changed my life' because they are still 'half-tanked, with their nails bitten down to the elbows'. While Greer was accused by some feminists of being too libertarian, she was also too radical for many women, either at that time or for all their times. Margaret Whitlam (in Mitchell 1987:25) describes Greer's 'wonderful' and 'disastrous' pronouncements, linking Greer to 'aggressive feminism'. Dale and Lynne Spender's mother found the book 'awful' until she talked the issues through with her daughters and 'got herself a life' (*Courier-Mail* 6 October 1993:8). Although Teresa tasted her menstrual blood after reading Greer,[3] she comments: 'I don't think I really engaged completely with the arguments. I don't think I was old enough, I don't think I'd lived enough'. Similarly, when she first read *The Female Eunuch*, Claudia thought: 'that's absolutely terrible, it can't possibly be right'. Within a year Claudia re-read Greer and was able to drop some of the preconceptions and faith 'in all the things you should be doing as a woman, all the things I had been taught to do as a little girl as well as being a Catholic'. Thus, it is not 'the best book in the world', 'but it is a very challenging book', a challenge Claudia was only ready to meet on her second reading.

Re-reading *The Female Eunuch* while writing this book, I can see why Greer is described as libertarian and 'was a libbie a man could like' (American feminist, Claudia Dreifus, in Spongberg 1993:409). Indeed, the very term 'female eunuch' refers to women's conditioning to deny the quest for self-knowledge through her sexuality (Greer 1971:68). Greer claimed that men are no more the enemy to women than soldiers in different uniforms are the enemy to each other; it's largely a matter of getting 'the uniforms off' (Greer 1971:297). One can see why her book was experienced as 'awful', when Greer (1971:75, 294) used terms like 'female faggot' or derided overweight women. But it was also 'brave': 'To be free to start out, and to find companions for the journey is as far as we need to see from where we stand' (Greer 1971:20). While Greer addresses issues still with feminism, like the myth of love which impedes girls choosing independent careers, or the misery, resentment and poverty many housewives experience, the 330 pages which cover these and other issues are free-wheeling rather than rigorous, and packed with the prejudices of the time, including racism and a comment that lesbianism arises from the woman's 'inability to play the accepted role in society' (Greer 1971:37, 50, 294).

For Berenice the signal significance of feminist texts is in the way they build bridges of communication between women: 'I think for women to read is almost like an act of feminism, and for women to read and to discuss with other women about reading is a feminist act'. Books are 'a territory for our ideas'; exchanging them with other women expands our territory of understanding in both the appropriation of the ideas and the discussions with friends. Writers speak to readers across enormous cultural and geographical distances. Berenice marvelled that Simone de Beauvoir wrote something in a French library 'years ago' which Berenice devoured in the Australian desert after a counsellor told Berenice to read her way out of a personal crisis (akin to Mayra's story in chapter 4). Almost in reverse geographical contrast, Catherine read Doris Lessing until 2 or 3 in the morning in a campervan travelling through Europe with her family: 'I remember days and days thinking about these books, and I really hadn't read anything in any shape or form which made me think that the life experiences of other women might reflect any of my own'.

Musing on the uses of the Internet,[4] Berenice notes that books are relatively cheap, readily transportable, promise completion within their pages and advertise themselves as a commodity on their covers. An example is the impact of *For Better, For Worse And For Lunch* (Hindhaugh 1992) on rural women, discussed in the next chapter. As Berenice notes, and is exploring in more detail in her doctoral dissertation at the Australian National University, the book is also an object, more than 'just the words within, and it has many values'. Books become icons, filled with meanings produced beyond their pages. To have read a certain book and liked it proclaims both your cultural capital and ideological position. *The Female Eunuch* has entered college curricula and been used by young students for high school essays (Fiona Giles in Scutt 1985a:166). Opinions of Greer and her book circulate among far more women than have actually read *The Female Eunuch*, some women reporting their encounter with feminism in terms of *not* reading Greer (Glenda, Deanna) or of learning about Greer's book through newspaper articles (Grace). The *Courier-Mail* (1 October 1993:16) asked: 'How was the sexual revolution for you?' and reported responses to *The Female Eunuch*, with its classic cover. The cover signifies the book's widely-shared meaning in Joanne Travaglia and Elizabeth Weiss's (1992:126–9) lampooning of the traditional Italian gifts of 'bomboniere'. At baptism, instead of pure and frilly sugar-coated almonds (the traditional sweet), the baby girl receives a copy of Greer's book. As a result, when she reaches her majority she celebrates with a university degree rather than a wedding.

Women's Studies

> Women's College . . . was extremely proud of its role in women's education and its traditions and getting so many women out into the community. So that was there, almost like a women's movement before us, before we even knew there was a women's movement . . . I felt as if I was a person at last, I really did. (Alison, speaking of her experience at Women's College, Sydney University in the 1950s)

I've only experienced the feminist movement in a gentle sort of way in my own life. In fact, the first lecture I attended was one you gave here, and I went to collect my car at a friend's place ... She's in her seventies, and she said: 'Well, what did you learn on your first day?' And I said: 'I learned all about penis envy', and she said: 'Oh, my God'. [Both laugh, Chilla somewhat guiltily] (Margaret)

The most famous text of Australian feminism, *The Female Eunuch*, was not written by a feminist academic (although Greer was previously and briefly a tutor at Sydney University), and nor are many popular texts with which women explore women's issues. However, women's studies has combined the female presence in academia (through institutions like Women's College at Sydney University) with the outpouring of ideas on women's liberation to define an academically accepted institutionalisation of feminist knowledge. Women's studies is now established as an academic interdiscipline which researches, records and teaches feminist knowledge. From the perspective of the activists, women's studies 'sold out' its radical constituency as early as 1976, becoming the preserve of a privileged elite isolated from practice who concentrate on abstract research which will advance them up the academic hierarchy (Yeatman 1990:68; Sheridan 1993b:42). From their perspective, women's studies academics, like femocrats, claim their survival is premised on an adaptation to the organisation's goals and structures, reframing claims in terms of the institutional culture in ways which still meet the needs of their female clientele.

Whatever the success or sell-out of women's studies, 'woman' is still not commonly equated with 'intellectual',[5] even though three-quarters of higher education institutions now offer women's studies topics. The first course to be named as a women's studies course was offered in 1973, and the first program established in 1975.[6] None of the senior feminist academics came from non-Anglo backgrounds, while very few women's studies academics come from non-English speaking backgrounds. This is reflected in a predominantly white British, United States and Australian feminist curriculum, not always relevant to 'other' women (Huggins 1994:78). External studies, now in the Open Learning system and requiring the payment of up-front fees, and outreach programs offer courses to women who might be reluctant or unable to broach campus life. Sue Schmolke (1992:137), appointed in the 1980s as convenor of the Northern Territory's Women's Advisory Council, felt that reading the prescribed external studies text, *Damned Whores and God's Police*, 'in the 1970s in Tennant Creek was like an illicit act'. Melba Marginson (1992:120–1), after attending the Deakin Women's Studies Summer School in 1990, formed the Collective of Filipinas for Empowerment and Development.

Women's studies courses often challenged marriages (Kath Balfour 1993:106) as moments when contradictions fell out of place and explanations for women's lives emerged (Crosby 1993:183). Berenice notes that contact with women's studies continues to be an 'earth-shattering' experience for some women. Women's studies courses, like feminist books, 'speak to' women (Nadine), 'profoundly' influencing Berenice's 'understanding of my own identity'. Nadine suggests that apart from the love of and from people within the women's movement, 'probably the most significant thing which has become part of me as I go along is the theory'. Theory gives women the words and ideas with which to counter the barbs of males (Cathy Henry in Scutt 1985a:68). When her husband says 'extremely disparaging things, *extremely*' about women's studies Sue notes complacently: 'I don't take any notice of those'.

During her early married life, with four young children Fiorenza 'had left Simone de Beauvoir a bit behind'. She returned to university and 'caught up with the real political side of feminism'. When Claudia studied the first women's studies subject at the University of Queensland, she encountered the treasure of 'a proper reading list'. As an academic Claudia braids feminist theory with politics, astonished by resistance in her first appointment to studying John Stuart Mill instead of Machiavelli as 'the major political figure' in the first year course: 'It seemed to be such a modest request about Mill that if I was going to argue about it, I might want to argue for someone else who was a bit more difficult for them to swallow'. Though Claudia went on to become a feminist academic and Fiorenza a feminist activist, for Martha there was really nothing new at university 'from a woman's perspective', she having previously read things about Aboriginal women like *We Are Bosses Ourselves* (Gale 1983): 'I didn't see that as any revelation because that was the way I had seen women generally, black or white'.

Some women have found the radicalism of women's studies out of kilter with their own personal circumstances. Marg felt overpowered by the 'big', 'extreme', and, 'for want of a better word, butch feminists'. She felt their demands for 'militant' political protests were inappropriate for someone like her, in a 'fairly senior position in my chosen career'. Almost a decade later, Phylis was surprised at the lack of 'solidarity among the women'. Some women's studies courses provided a retort for mature-age students who described themselves as 'justas' – justa housewife, justa secretary (Margaret Henry 1993:79) – but Phylis did not think she was 'justa housewife', and especially not 'justa mother'. This seemed to be the message from her women's studies subjects. As women's studies have become more institutionalised within the curriculum, it is likely more women have chosen the course for reasons other than a burning desire to change the world. Sue enrolled largely by 'default', her first preference not on offer that year. While Sue has 'learned lots', she doubts that 'it has made me a rabid feminist. I don't think I'm a very rabid person'.

In chapter 2 the importance of mature-age university entry and the abolition of fees under the Whitlam government in providing a path to university was noted by a number of women. By contrast, in 1987 up-front fees were introduced, although payment could be delayed until one's income reached a certain threshold, and school leavers were given preferential treatment. According to Gisela Kaplan (1996:155) this signalled a retreat from access and equality of opportunity in education, further sealed by the Howard government's first budget in 1996, which reduced university funding, increased both fees and their rate of repayment and introduced fee-paying places for Australian students. The role of women's studies in opening the options for other than middle-class Anglo-background Australian women is likely to diminish in the face of these changes.

Women's Organisations

> Good heavens, women! All women! (Pat recalling her first encounter with WEL in 1972)

Claudia distinguishes women's liberation from philanthropy in that the former was self-help and taking 'responsibility' for issues which were both your own issues and those of other women. Sage's first feminist actions were 'a couple of protests' in the early 1960s at teachers college, as a result of which Sage believes she was failed in one of her subjects, given that she passed the supplementary examination by submitting exactly the same piece of work. In the 1970s in Darwin, Sage became part of the local women's liberation movement. She co-edited the papers from a conference at which Sara Dowse, the first appointed femocrat, spoke. Women from across the spectrum attended the conference, 'even the CWA'. While this meant 'dreadful debates on abortion . . . it was really good that women of such diversity could come together, and even bothered to'. The local women's liberation movement also offered an adult education course on Germaine Greer, established a refuge and after-school care. Claudia, who was a member of this group, suggests that self-help is both vital and effective in small communities without facilities. Because of links with the local powerbrokers, who were sometimes the husbands, 'you could do something about' almost everything. But it was also the case that 'you had to do something . . . otherwise nothing was going to happen'.

WEL provided a 'synthesis' for women's diverse activities, allowing women to retain their own positions and interests even as interaction with other women shaped 'how you were in the world' (Claudia). Pat says that a 1975 meeting organised to celebrate the United Nations Decade of Women 'changed my life'. Following a speech by Senator Margaret Reynolds, the women who responded to a call to establish a Cairns branch of WEL overflowed the house at which they met. Pat, who has been awarded accolades such as International Woman of the Year for the district in 1995, describes the issues they tackled as including 'DDT in breast milk, flammable nightwear for children and elderly people (labelling of same), tubal ligation and the law, women in government', and lobbying candidates for local elections. They also improved the appalling conditions for women prisoners in the watch-house after WEL members supported 'a young Aboriginal women who was in the watch-house charged with murder of her violent partner'.

For several years Pat and her friends opened their homes to women escaping domestic violence, some 'referred' by a local doctor. For Cairns to have a shelter attitudes had to be changed, both those of other women in WEL and the wider community. Between 1976 and 1978 Pat's sub-committee campaigned for federal funds and publicised the issue, Pat remembering that in Innisfail 'these men all sat round and they said: "What about a men's shelter?"'. Pat's major ongoing contribution to the shelter was to establish a second-hand bookshop which guaranteed a secure funding base. A local businessman provided shop space in the centre of Cairns. In 1980, because the shelter workers were spending so much time on the telephone with crisis and other counselling, WEL opened the Women's Information Referral Centre which later spawned a rape crisis centre.

For Sage the establishment of a local chapter of WEL, prompted by a friend bringing news from Canberra: 'was a turning point, and that's where I decided I could do anything . . . We felt enormously powerful, you know. We'd get quite heady at times thinking what we could do'. Pat shared a similar belief in the near-invincibility of women:

> We were discovering each other, we were discovering the pleasures of being with other women . . . We thought that we would come to the fore, . . . feminists would improve the situation through new laws and new ways. And women would be strong, and men would have to toe the line. I mean, I don't know what we were thinking of.

Those heady days are gone now, displaced to a large extent by evidence of the enduring nature of patriarchal structures, or more negatively 'dead years, dead intellectually, dead in public debate' (Kaplan

1996:154). Furthermore, not all experiences in women's organisations have been positive.

Bega's women movement was split into acrimonious camps over philosophical differences which found expression in debates over the use of the premises and the funding of the refuge. Nadine was a founding member of the Southern Women's Group which had a financial membership of eighty women in the mid-1980s. Nadine remembers the women as vibrant and interested in making things happen. 'We didn't need "help"; we wanted things.' Out of their own possessions and contacts, the group established a resource centre, a refuge, a library and a newsletter:

> Most of us called ourselves feminists but we all meant something different ... Actually we weren't keen on calling ourselves this or that, we didn't have to. We just concentrated on what we wanted, and what we thought we lacked in the area as women.

Government funding meant that women were no longer doing things for themselves but were providing 'services' for which they were accountable to femocrats.

For her part, Joan (like Pat) believed the Bega refuge would not survive without a secure funding base, particularly after only being saved from closure in 1988 by anonymous donations. She felt there was a contradiction between the refuge's need for security and safety and the open door policy of the Resource/Information Centre on the same premises. Furthermore, the Bega Women's Group were 'a lot of middle-class twits', talking 'about poetry' and 'What are we going to do for the Bicentenary'. Joan felt that the needs of 'abused kids, and abused women' were far more important. Just as Pat's business experience helped her secure a funding base for the Cairns refuge, so Joan's experience of bureaucracies stood her in good stead when dealing with local councils. A member of a delegation to a councillor in Moruya, Joan said:

> 'Look, Mr Johnson, there's six women here' ... there were teachers, health workers, health nurses, graduates in health education, myself, we all had something. And I said: 'Do you think women of our status are going to turn around and behave like idiots?' So 'Oh, no, no'.

When the Resource/Information Centre was evicted, Joan was astonished by the 'savagery' and 'backstabbing' in relation to 'women's work'. She felt: 'I don't ever intend getting involved in this type of exercise ever again'.

One of the strengths of feminism has been the truth of the slogan 'the personal is political'. Women can make some changes in their own lives without joining an organised movement, even if those changes quickly meet barriers when there is no collective political action to remould structures. Thus, Helen suggests:

> I really don't think of myself as a feminist but I think deep down I really am. When I say I don't think of myself as a feminist, I can't really see myself burning my bra, I can't see myself marching, but I can see myself taking a stand for myself and taking a stand for my fellow women. And if I can see something that isn't quite right, now I would speak up whereas years ago, when I was first married I would go with the flow. (Helen)

Similarly, Halina felt she 'wasn't altogether in the feminist circle' and 'didn't go on marches, that's not my type of thing'. But just as Helen will now take a stand for her 'fellow women', Halina 'made an awful lot of noise'. Because of her 'noise', Halina was awarded the Order of Australia Medal for her community service work.

The women discussed above would call themselves either feminist or pro-feminist, at least in some respects. But many of the women with whom I spoke have never read a feminist book or entered a women's studies classroom or attended a WEL meeting. These women have come to their understanding of feminism through its representation in the popular media.

Popular Feminism Versus Bra-burning Man-hating Lesbians

> Popular feminism, . . . the errant daughter of capital F Feminism, is all around us . . . We hear it on the radio, read it in the newspapers, and watch it on TV. (Andrea Stuart 1990:30)

> I had some exchanges with chauvinists on my programs and I tell you, I am as proud as anything, because I could have really squashed them to smithereens. I said to myself: 'I'm not going to give you bastard the pleasure, because then you would go "ho, ho, this feminist"'. So I . . . said everything that I wanted to say in a very quiet nice voice and they couldn't find anything against me. (Halina)

Surveys indicate that while three-quarters of women and two-thirds of men read, almost every Australian watches television every week and about three-quarters listen to the radio (Australian Bureau of Statistics 1993:253, 258). Clearly feminist books reach far fewer people than Channel Nine's nightly news. The mass media is an outer trench of contest, even if some of its ammunition comes from feminist texts and femocrat citadels. But as the letters to the editor of *Who* magazine mentioned at the beginning of this book indicate, this 'popular feminism' might be doing a disservice to feminism rather than spreading the word beyond those who read *The Female Eunuch*, attend consciousness-raising groups, enrol in women's studies or join women's organisations.

In 1971 *Refractory Girl*'s readers, presumably among the most radical women in Australia, were equally divided in their response to women's liberation: 42 per cent totally approving and 42 per cent totally disapproving (see Refractory Girl, 1993:17). In 1980 a hundred women in Adelaide were asked: 'Do you believe it is necessary for women to strive for changes to their position in society?' While 69 per cent said 'yes', they often made qualifying remarks such as: 'as long as they are not militant', 'but they shouldn't be rabid or feminist and hate men', 'I'm not a women's libber though' (Snowden 1981:52). Only 19 per cent wanted to become involved in an organisation with the aim of changing the position of women (Snowden 1981:55). In 1994 surveys and polls found that 96 per cent of young women expected equal pay, 95 per cent that all housework should be shared, 70 per cent believed their lives were more satisfying than their mothers', 89 per cent would be happy to financially support their partner, but only 33 per cent felt comfortable calling themselves feminist.[7] While many secretaries in Rosemary Pringle's (1988:250–1) study 'felt strongly about equal pay', they distanced themselves from feminists 'who have BO and hairy armpits'. Focus groups with 224 women from 'middle Australia' in 1992 found that 'only a handful of women' were comfortable with the term 'feminist', which was associated with a bygone era (the 1960s or 1970s), unattractive women ('butch', 'dykes' with 'hairy armpits' and 'really short hair') who were anti-men and overly militant. On the other hand, only a minority of older women thought women had gone too far, while most thought 'it can only get better' (Riley-Smith 1992:40, 41).

Similarly, the women with whom I spoke approved at least some of feminism's victories, even though many rejected feminism, which was associated with bra-burning, radical lesbians and Germaine Greer. For many, feminism was almost synonomous with Greer: 'Germaine Greer, burn your bra and all that' (Gerda); 'all the burning bra bit' and Germaine Greer (Aquarius); 'I remember Germaine Greer, and burning bras and whatnot and coming from a very starchy family thought, "That's not for me"' (Helen). For others bra-burning was the key concept, sometimes linked with lesbianism: 'You ran the risk of being labelled "bra-burning female"' (Grace); 'bra-burners and lesbians' (Nikita); 'I wasn't going to get up and be a bra-burning feminist, I mean to use all those stereotypes' (Gisela); 'When they burned their bras. That's the only thing that came into my consciousness. I couldn't see the point of it' (Jan). This section explores the repulsion of these terms for so many women, and why Greer, lesbianism and bra-burning have come to signal an undesirably radical movement.

Greer Meets the Press and the Women's Movement Loses?

Not pursuing a traditional academic career, Greer raised the ire of most feminists, 'conspicuous by her absence from' the feminist magazines *Mejane*, *Hecate* and *Refractory Girl* (Spongberg 1993:414–15). Unlike some American feminists who deliberately avoided the press (Spongberg 1993:408; Heilbrun 1995:168), Greer's free-wheeling publicity-seeking found a ready response for her more acceptable message of sexual permissiveness, Greer even being awarded 'Playboy Journalist of the Year' in the United States in 1972 (Spongberg 1993:407–8). Beatrice Faust described Greer's media victory as 'pyrrhic' (Spongberg 1993: 416), in that her message was twisted to bra-burning and a 'sexual challenge rather than a political threat' (Spongberg 1993:412, 413).[8]

Greer (1971:308–9) notes that the press lapped up women's liberation movement stories for their 'atmosphere of perversion, female depravity, sensation and solemn absurdity', creating 'a suspicious and uncooperative attitude' in response. Thus, women's memories of feminism in the media and of their own scoffing responses to them, include women burning their bras (Jackson 1994:71); 'the butch type of woman and the extreme version of feminism' (Mayra); 'Germaine Greer . . . crying her ability to say the "F" word' (Lucinda); Greer as a 'really tough-looking woman' (Catherine, who now, however, sees Greer as 'such a brave person').

While the press sensationalised and trivialised feminist issues, either deliberately or through ignorance, an increased percentage of articles have canvassed women's issues since the 1950s;[9] there has been a movement of feminist voices out of the letters to the editor columns and into the main body of articles as expert spokespersons;[10] articles on the negative consequences of masculinity, like aggression and bullying, are appearing in mainstream newspapers.[11] However, a newspaper survey in 1993 revealed that women were represented in only 24 per cent of all news references, where they were most often the victims of crime.[12] The fervour with which women's groups have taken on the role of media watchdogs, writing to the Australian Broadcasting Tribunal with cases of sexual or racial harassment or discrimination (Schultz 1993:173), indicates the pervasive influence of the media and women's willingness to engage critically with its messages. Teresa directed the production of school curriculum materials in South Australia to develop greater sophistication in media consumers:

> We actually did whole segments of programs that were concerned with the images of women, images of race, and basically images of class . . . In fact, those media documents . . . were the most successful publication that our

Education Department had ever done, in terms of sales. Very practical, very hands-on, but also it made a lot of sense to people and it helped people work through the issues themselves. Teachers and kids.

Greater press coverage of feminist issues or general news items from a more gender inclusive perspective can be attributed, at least in part, to the greater number of women in the media industry, even if they are still disproportionately in the lower ranks.[13] Irene Greenwood (1992:109, 111) was an isolated woman's voice on radio in the late 1920s and again between 1935 and 1973 discussing 'women in the international news' and feminist writing. The 'Coming-Out Show', now 'Women Out Loud', was launched by the Australian Women's Broadcasting Co-operative on International Women's Day in 1975 (Westwood in Watson 1990:225), going to air on Saturday afternoons so men could 'eavesdrop' (men apparently make up half the audience) (Rigg and Copeland 1985:5). In the summer of 1994-5 'Life Matters' ran a series on men and masculinity, dealing with issues which have arisen via feminism's agenda, and to which Glenda refers (see chapter 7). The subject was returned to periodically throughout 1995. In 1981 Halina began her radio broadcasting career as panel operator, producer and interviewer for a women's program of weekly interviews with 'women from the point of view of women'.

The bra-burning feminist was an image created by the press. At the 1968 Miss America pageant feminists threw make-up, girdles and bras into a 'freedom trash can'. In an analogy with draft card burning, a reporter wrote that women burned their bras, although 'no feminists are recorded as having actually burned their bras and relatively few even threw them away' (Jaggar 1994b:148). If bras were not burned the pervasiveness of this pejorative label might seem surprising. It is not only about the cost of bras and the consequent stupidity of burning them, although Peg Hewett (1994:133) and Aileen both make this point: 'I couldn't even afford bras. And I thought "What are these people doing burning their bras, like, they're so expensive?"' (Aileen). It is not just a challenge to standards of white femininity, which was the meaning of bras to Aileen – a part of her armour when entering the white public world – and to Kerry: 'there was nothing such as burning the bra, I mean our people walked around with their susus bare anyway, proud to exhibit their source of nourishment to the young'.

Iris Young (1990:189-91) suggests that breasts are the signal of a woman's sexuality, but they do not belong only to men. When a woman derives erotic pleasure from breastfeeding she is gaining a pleasure independently of men. When women refused to encase their breasts in bras (which made all breasts the same) and instead released their variability and fluidity, they presented breasts as their own rather than objects for the pleasure of men. Thus, 'bra-burning' was a rejection of constricting fashion and a rejection of looking good for men, and even, therefore, potentially a rejection of men. But many heterosexual women like men, and like them a lot, though they may wish they were better behaved. Bra-burning thus becomes connected with lesbianism and being anti-male. As Fiorenza notes: 'while I certainly was very much about feminism I wasn't anti-male'. Marg suggests: 'I still like the feminine aspects and I don't find myself identifying or feeling comfortable around the butch sort of females'.[14] Frustrated perhaps by feminism's failure to change men, the label of lesbian is tagged to feminists who seem insufficiently interested in making men better behaved.

Are Feminists Man-hating Lesbians?

It's natural, whether you're lesbian or whether you're gay or whether you're heterosexual, you've got to engage in some sort of sexual act as part of your being, unless you're crazy, or unless you're going to be a monk ... So to hide it or to deny it is to treat it as though it isn't a part of your life. (Aileen)

I think that's something that has to happen. It's happening now isn't it? Recognition from the Governor-General, no less, of gay marriages[15] ... Because there are other issues of greater importance to the greater majority of the population, I think these are sensed to be minor issues. (Glenda)

Reminiscing about the Women in Labour conference in 1984, Halina contrasts the lesbians 'thundering' in the formal presentations with 'treating themselves so lovingly' at the dance. In this section this apparent contradiction between public and private presentation by lesbians is explored, and why it is that lesbians' presumed man-hating rather than their concern for women receives so much popular attention.

In the quotations above, Aileen, an Indigenous Australian heterosexual woman, rather than Glenda, an Anglo-Australian lesbian, points to the centrality of homo/heterosexual identity in contemporary western society. We do not divide the world of sexual activity into rapists and non-rapists, or celibates and the sexually active, but rather into the gay and the straight (see Sedgwick 1990:8, 25). This is strange, given that it is presumably just as important for a woman to know whether a man prefers forced or consensual sex, as it is to know whether someone might be attracted to oneself.

The appellation 'lesbian' is used to police the boundaries of acceptable femininity, as can be seen by the associations it conjures up: nice moderate women/feminists versus radical mannish lesbians/feminists, God's police versus damned whores. The protagonists in *Livin' Large* used this distinction (see chapter 1); Bronwyn Davies' (1993:130, 135) pre-adolescent girls used it; at Melinda's high school 'the guys' used to call Melinda and her girlfriend lesbians, even though the 'guys all hang out in groups'. Shona's male colleagues dismiss her questions, apparently concluding: 'Well, what would you expect of this hairy-legged lesbian?' In contrast, the heterosexual women are 'sort of bona fide' (Glenda) or 'a real woman' (Shona). Lesbians' views are discounted because they are assumed to be man-haters and biased.

Today feminine dress provides no absolute deflection of the label 'lesbian'. At a seminar I gave to North Queensland's Peninsula Branch of the Association of Women Educators (27 July 1995), one teacher, Karen, with a shock of curly light hair and bright red lipstick, pointed out that she was called a 'lipstick lesbian' when men discovered she played sports or asserted her own opinions. Gayness has been extracted from beauty and applied to women with attitude, however they look. As Aquarius suggests, 'independent' women, women with 'a bit of intelligence', are accused of being butch, 'a smart-arse' or 'out of their tree'. When refuges were first established their proponents were called 'sluts or lesbians or both', wanting heterosexual sex either too much or too little (Rhondda Johnson 1994:25).[16] In Cairns in the 1980s Pat and other women who were working to establish a refuge were reputed to be 'radical feminists', 'lesbians and hippy type women'.[17] Lita suggests that some refuge workers are radical lesbians who 'don't believe anybody else who could have ideas about being in the middle. Some men are horrible but some men could be alright' (Lita).

However, the women's movement and lesbians in it have made of acceptable femininity a moving edge, ever outward, one hopes. Today the border traverses 'non-traditional' occupations where once every woman who remained unmarried in order to maintain a career was seen as a 'sour spinster'. At a north-west mining site, a woman who became active in affirmative action was redefined as a man and a 'dyke' (Eveline 1995:99). Lucinda is surprised when attractive women take jobs digging the road when they could be 'dressed decently' as receptionists or park rangers.

Why should women worry if we are called lesbians? Eve Sedgwick (1990:36–8, 84–9) argues that we hold two contradictory views of sexual orientation at once. We believe both that there is a distinct population of persons who are 'really gay' and that we all have aspects of same-sex orientation in our sexual personae. The repression and projection of this latter produces attacks on the 'really gay' or the periodic attempts by straight women to purge the women's movement of lesbians. The Hobart Women's Action Group at the Women's Liberation Conference in 1973 claimed that lesbians should not have to 'wait' until after the revolution for their liberation (Burgmann 1993:172). Despite recommendations made by the 1974 WEL conference to end discrimination against lesbians (Kaplan 1996:99), there has been misunderstanding between heterosexual and lesbian women on occasions ever since, Kaplan (1996:91–121) in her chapter on this relationship pointing to the forbearance of lesbians in the women's movement. Straight feminists complain that they are accused of 'servicing men' (Peg Hewett 1994: 135) or 'colluding with the enemy' (Paula Gallagher in Williams 1995:26).[18]

While the heterosexual women with whom I spoke often claimed that lesbian sexuality does not worry them, they also use the tropes of 'butch lesbian' to define and deplore particular kinds of behaviour. Both of Barbara's daughters prefer male to female bosses because the latter are 'inclined to be bitchy and over-bearing'. Melinda contrasts her 'butch, very stern, very serious' boss with the subsequent male boss who was 'such a nice guy to work for'. Unlike gay men who do not want to 'show those women' – 'I don't think that even crosses their mind' – lesbians are 'not going to put up with any shit from men'. Such a comparison reflects a gender inversion model of homosexuality, the mannish lesbian, the effeminate gay man. Deanna describes a childhood gay male friend as 'gentle', but Amber describes 'effeminate' men as androgynous, claiming they have 'more manliness in their little finger than the Australian men who tend to be violent'. In contrast, for Melinda, lesbians are both 'forthright about their opinions' and their sexuality, sizing up Melinda's mother when she walked into a gay bar. Melinda wonders whether 'they've just had bad experiences with men'. Phylis, despite her ambivalence towards men as sexual objects, remembers a 'not very good' childhood experience when she was left with 'a very butch lesbian'. When Phylis read about a homosexual relationship she 'was physically sick'. But she also remembers 'nice' lesbianism, 'a couple of old little ladies' in a nursing home.

Gayness was and is something foreign to many straight women, not helped by events like the Gay Mardi Gras according to Glenda, who retorts that what 'straight people do in the suburbs . . . is quite lewd'. Teresa says of a school friend: 'we knew she was gay because of the way she related'. She also suggests: 'I would never have been able to sort of articulate what she might do when – I had no idea'. When Helen announced she was 'going nursing' her grandmother warned Helen's mother that she would 'lose her innocence', apparently a dark reference to learning about 'homosexuals'. Helen had not even heard the word before, it being some further time before she 'heard about lesbians'. Helen feels 'it's a lot healthier' now that 'it's very much out in the open', although she suggests it will never be 'fully' understood.

Clearly there has been and continues to be discrimination against lesbians: pejorative understandings of homosexuality, denial of the same rights as heterosexual couples to superannuation, inheritance or job relocation, questioning in courts about their ability to be proper parents, denial of jobs if they 'come out'.[19] Compared to heterosexual couples, it takes much longer for homosexual relationships to be accepted by friends and family. As Glenda said: 'God spare us, yes, twice as long'. Given these costs, as well as the ability to disguise one's lesbian orientation, Eve Sedgwick (1990:34, 68–73) claims that living in or out of the closet is 'the fundamental feature of social life' for gay people. Coming out almost always alters relationships and produces either a threat of rejection or a threat of sex. Joan's gay friends 'all love' her because she doesn't 'think "Oh God, she's going to rape me", as one friend put it'. Halina asked someone whether she was gay, thinking she would inform the woman of a conference as it might interest her. To Halina the question meant no more than 'Is it raining?'. But for Halina's interlocutor the question was much more heavily freighted. As Glenda notes: 'I think you become very paranoid because you expect to be discriminated against as a gay person'.

Glenda's *bildungsroman* of coming to knowledge of her lesbian sexual identity involved experimentation with men between the ages of 13 and 24, 'the number of encounters decreasing with age', and the last being 'very unsatisfactory really'. Glenda became aware that she was different in puberty:

> Maybe my strong feminist perception at a young age is also associated with my interest in women as sexual objects at a very young age which was probably when I was 12 . . . I was aware of really liking women and being interested in women and preferring them as company. At the same time, clearly, there is an impetus from your peers and from your family in relation to establishing relationships with men, with boys. And of course, because I grew up in a country town which was very very conservative, . . . I spent a number of years trying to get on with boys in a sexual way, and really failing to do so . . . It wasn't probably until, I suppose, about 16 that I was convinced that I certainly wasn't heterosexual. Whether or not I was convinced at that stage this was a long-term circumstance, I'm not sure. Because it was really viewed as a disease and an illness, whether of the mind or the body they couldn't determine.

Glenda suspects that at this time she too saw homosexuality as a disease; in the 1950s and 1960s the 'cure' included electric shocks, emetic agents which produced vomiting and frontal lobotomies (Kaplan 1996:96). Disease or not, homosexuality was clearly 'problematic' and 'you weren't getting any approval for it'. In response to the disease model, Glenda visited a psychiatrist when she was 18 and had moved to Brisbane. He suggested she could 'pass' by marrying a homosexual man.

Glenda rejected this possibility and moved on to a political trope of self-definition at the time when the Campaign Against Moral Persecution was formed: 'it was the beginnings of the gay movement in Brisbane ... I think it's just really enjoyable to have been part of that embryonic movement'. CAMP, formed in 1971, was 'possibly Australia's first gay and lesbian public group' (Kaplan 1996:93). It provided a vehicle by which Glenda could redefine herself from being ill into a person who deserved human rights and acceptance of her sexuality.

Shona's progress into a lesbian relationship was more a happenstance. In her teens and twenties she did not 'think I'd even heard the word' but feels that had she been aware of the activity it would be 'like another game of cards'. Shona enjoyed the company of girls and women at school more so than boys, who were categorised as being about sex and romance: 'a vast field of exploration and adventure, but it wasn't necessarily something that I ever felt was quite right'. Shona did not 'fall in love' and was surprised when two successive male companions proposed marriage. But Shona was also not 'looking out for the right woman, or any woman'. In fact, Shona suggests that had she met these men later she 'may have been married'. Instead, she worked in a remote school, removed from her friends and normal networks, and 'thought there was a possibility that I might be interested in homosexual activity. I didn't really know if I wanted to label myself homosexual'. Shona came close to a homosexual encounter with a friend on several occasions, and had a brief affair with a woman thinking, 'Well, I've done that', and 'Yes, but'. Glenda, with whom Shona is now partnered, was first seen as one in a group of new and interesting female work colleagues.

Sage grew into her lesbian identity after marriage and motherhood. Sage's 'first sort of sexual experience at school' involved 'lots of kissing' with a girl, which she says 'wasn't really sexual but it certainly wasn't platonic either'. Sage's mother 'stopped that' which Sage 'just accepted'. Sage is not aware whether her mother was conscious of prohibiting same-sex activities, although 'she picked up something'. As an adolescent Sage became 'caught up in that male world', although she thinks she may be bisexual, still finding some men attractive but being 'so much more comfortable with women'.

The two major sites of becoming uncloseted are at work and with one's family. Glenda says of the Education Department: 'it was something you had to hide all the time, ... something that I think one has to hide even now'. In the professions, however, gay members are accepted, 'particularly if they are valued members', but only as long as they stay closeted. While work relationships are made complicated and dangerous by a closeted gayness, relations with family carry the heavier threat of pain and rejection, Glenda asserting: 'If your mum and dad think it's alright then I think you can do whatever you like'. Thus, Glenda believes that only when families are won over will the culture against gayness change, and only by 'support groups for mums and dads' winning over other parents of gay children. Women from non-dominant ethnic backgrounds can also experience considerable anguish over the thought of being rejected by their communities if they come out, and often resent the Anglo-lesbian community for not understanding this potential loss (Pallotta-Chiarolli 1992:147, 150, 142-3; Kuh 1995:106, 108; Awekotuku 1991:28, 32-3).

Sage's mother is 'appalled by me, absolutely appalled, because of my relationship with Stephanie . . . because you see, she feels it's a waste. Isn't that terrible?' Shona was warned of the possible price of coming out to her parents when, over dinner, her father described a friend – 'poor bloody Harry' – who had just discovered his daughter was gay. Glenda did not discuss her sexuality with her parents but believes they 'suspected' or 'probably knew'. Glenda's father 'used to say, "This girl is not like any other girl that I know"', which was probably right'. However, it did not stop him grabbing Glenda's girlfriends' breasts. Shona's parents clearly know and accept the relationship:

> It is taken, I live with Glenda. Glenda and I go away on holidays together. Glenda and I invest in things together . . . It's not as though Dad goes: 'And this is Glenda. She's in a relationship with my daughter and they live in a house together' or anything like that. But he trips over himself to introduce Glenda to his friends . . . They'll come over here and Mum will say: 'Is it in your bedroom?' and that sort of thing. That's all natural, but in terms of actually stating the obvious that's never happened and I don't think it ever would.

However, with her brothers' children Shona suggests: 'It's much more a normal sort of a process for them'. 'They just acknowledge that Glenda and I are in a relationship even if they don't spell it out, and come around and say, "Gidday lesbians!" or whatever'.

Glenda's relationship with Shona, now of twelve years' standing and without any 'wanton or criminal or deleterious' aspects to it, constitutes a nice 'ordinary suburban life, where we've just got on with our jobs and our careers' (Glenda). For Glenda, in their demonstration effects, it is this 'very unremarkable kind of relationship which has the strongest force' in the long term.

Given the widespread construction of feminist women as lesbian, and the policing of lesbians as criminal or deviant, it is perhaps little wonder that closeted lesbians may be diffident about expressing their feminism:

> I must say, now I'm gay I find it really hard . . . At first I was frightened of exposure, you know. Before I knew I was gay, I used to quite happily say:

'There's nothing wrong with being a gay, what's wrong with you kid?' I can still say it, and I'm getting better. (Sage, commenting on her role as a teacher)

On the other hand, lesbians have a strength in their feminism which is perhaps harder for heterosexual women to achieve, Glenda suggesting that women who are interested in men are possibly more 'prepared to make certain compromises or negotiate power' than are women who do not 'rely on men for sexual gratification or sexual status' (Glenda). Lesbian women and lesbian lives have allowed heterosexual women to see that there is life beyond a man and marriage – if this is their fate or choice, and that this choice can still involve love and intimacy. Aquarius stated: 'There used to be a choice, didn't there, either get married or on the shelf, and as long as you were married to something that had a pair of trousers, you were alright . . . and they hang on to them like grim death'.

Women-Identified Women

I suppose I'm a separatist really. And I would like that to be the way I live. I love women, I just think they are just beautiful . . . I love their generosity just so much. They are also very beautiful to look at, their forms and their colours. (Phylis)

In an attempt to dissolve some of the antagonism between 'gay' and 'straight' feminists, in 1980 Adrienne Rich (1983:257) suggested a lesbian continuum to denote 'women-identified experience'. This ranged across lesbian love, 'the bonding against male tyranny, the giving and receiving of practical and political support', marriage resistance and female friendship. As Shona says: 'I don't really think that there should be such a huge gulf', that is, between lesbians and heterosexuals. But many heterosexual women writing in the 1970s longed to join the men's domains and not the women's, to be where they saw power, status, interesting conversations and romantic appeal. Thus, sex segregation at parties was the sign of Australian women's 'doormat' status (Dixson [1976] 1994:11; see also Greer 1971:285). Women who have recently arrived in Australia have similar reactions. Hanna and Laila both noted gender segregation and men's disparagement of women's intelligence in their social encounters.[20] Contrariwise, in some situations women are prohibited from being together. At an RSL Club dance women unaccompanied by men 'were told to sit on a table and stay there . . . like people in a market'. When no men asked them to dance Aquarius and a friend danced together during a rock'n'roll number. They were soon policed out of this activity with an official's comment that 'Two women can't dance together'. However, Aquarius concludes: 'Now you see fellas dancing together' as well as women.

But women have seen the value of the lesbian continuum. Claudia attributes her growing self-confidence and community activism since 1962 not to reading Germaine Greer, but to her female friends. They gave her confidence 'about being able to change things' and created a world in which she felt more like herself. Paradoxically, however, her friends helped her 'block' out the 'terrible' aspects of her marriage and 'stoically' persevere with it. Berenice notes that female friendships provide an 'immense kind of connection and support'. Sage's 'wonderful' friendship with Claudia is 'pure' and 'strong'.

Having changed the emphasis from white colonisation's emasculation of Indigenous Australian men to a retrieval of Indigenous Australian women's traditional power,[21] Indigenous Australian women now say 'the Anglo-Australian feminist movement' wants 'what we had, and which their society destroyed for us' (Miller 1993:67; see also Wirrpanda 1987:75; Huggins 1994:74; Eve Fesl in Rowland 1984:110–11): 'When you see a lot of feminists together and they think they're making a statement, they're actually not, for us Murri women have been doing that for thousands of years... Aboriginal women were the original feminists anyway' (Kerry).

Thus, women's business is accepted as an autonomous sphere, by adults and young men alike (Lilla Watson, 1994; Aileen). Women's and men's business is linked to 'showing respect for the opposite sex' through avoiding certain kinds of sexual subjects, sexual jokes and body contact. This does not obviate 'physical contact', like hugging and dancing and fathers unselfconsciously extending physical affection to their sons at public meetings (Kerry). Women's matriarchal power (Nikita) and assertiveness in the family domain extends into public venues, for example, contributing women's knowledge about paternity to men's more formulaic statements, resolving disputes in public and participating in native title claims (Aileen). Martha remembers 'one woman in particular would be always propounding the Bible about justice, to her employers, her unfortunate employers'.

According to Lilla Watson (1994) white women's business was a private domain enclosed by the public (and more important) domain of men's business. The women's movement has expanded women's business to abut the circle of public business, but only by accepting co-option into 'equality' and 'individual rights and freedoms'. Instead, white men must also learn to redefine men's business, to adapt it to the women's agenda. Interestingly, despite their understanding of Indigenous Australian women's autonomy, some Aboriginal women do not align this with white feminists' demands for separatism, which they see as anti-male rather than pro-autonomy (Oodgeroo Noonuccal as Kath Walker in Mitchell 1987:198; Eve Fesl in Rowland 1984:109 criticising the expulsion of a young man from a women's meeting).

Indigenous Australian women are increasingly vocal concerning misogyny in their communities, whether it is an extension of ancient inequalities or a product of white patriarchal colonisation. Pat O'Shane (in Mitchell 1984:156) suggests that: 'Australian men – black and white – are basically misogynists. They just cannot relate to me as an intelligent, articulate, human being'. Aboriginal men in the black political movement set women against each other by demanding sexual favours in return for membership of their 'little power clique' (O'Shane in Mitchell 1984:155). Other articulate Indigenous Australian women have been called 'Black power bitch'; 'treated like a smart-assed girl from art school'; been ganged up against.[22] Thus, while Indigenous Australian women's business may be respected in many situations, Indigenous Australian women who mean business are not always treated any better by black colleagues than are assertive white women. The next chapter explores the responses to feminism from women who live beyond the Anglo middle classes in capital cities.

CHAPTER 6

Is Feminism a White Middle-Class Movement?

> When we used to have the media, and the government which didn't want to know anything about migrants, things were much more difficult. It was as if migrants are there but they don't really exist, like the Aborigines, I mean they are *there* but we try not to *think* that they are there. (Gladys)

When Muslim women in purdah came to the women's movement to request support so that they could meet for their traditional prayer sessions, or non-English speaking background women wanted their children taught their cultural traditions in their mother tongue within the state school system, they received little understanding from Anglo feminism (Kalantzis 1990:40). As Jeannie Martin (1991:126) notes, Anglo feminism often constructed the 'other' as victims of greater oppression, offering to 'help' them but only if they threw off their patriarchal traditions (Vasta 1991:163). In 1973 Anne Summers suggested that rural women were 'puzzled by the anti-organization, anti-leadership slogans being parried at them' from the Women's Electoral Conference in Canberra (Rowbotham 1992:265). Of the nine women firefighters in Carol Finlay's (1994:3,8) study, two 'discussed the achievements of Germaine Greer' while the others 'knew little to nothing about her', suggesting that their 'Amazonian concept of femininity' and their awareness of gender discrimination had come from other sources.

This chapter explores the claim that the women's movement has not only been a mainly urban Anglo middle-class phenomenon – which is probably largely true – but that this is the only constituency which has responded to feminism. In fact, while the exchanges between women in different cultural locations are often troubled, they are also potentially productive.

Fashions of Feminism

Like many Anglo women, there are non-Anglo women who see feminism as rejecting men. While not all non-English background migrants are family-oriented (Vallesi 1993:77), migrants to Australia may suffer the keening loss of an extended family far away as well as prizing the remnants of the family close at hand which offers a retreat from the racism and difference of Anglo society (Vasta et al. 1992:216). It was 'la famiglia', 'It was "them" and "us" – "them" being that cold, cool Anglo-Saxon world out there' (Giuffré 1992:93). Fiorenza suggests that most women, 'especially migrant women', put their families first and themselves last: 'So they don't have a lot of spare time really to dedicate to their own thinking, or becoming active in society or anything like that. Sometimes, of course, their own community won't allow that, especially their own husbands and family'.

Where Anglo feminism often reduces women's liberation to personal fulfilment and individual demands, Latin-American norms recommend a community response, reintegrating the woman into the community and her family (Aldunte and Revelo 1987:2). Similarly, Auriel as a senior Indigenous Australian bureaucrat feels that instead of women-oriented programs, a community focus is required. She understands 'there are certainly Indigenous women's needs that are specific to Indigenous women' but is not 'into feminism', because 'I'm not prepared to put women's roles separate to men's'. Indigenous Australian women think 'of the whole community framework' (Auriel), 'of the collective' (Kerry). 'That's where we are different from feminists, ...we always include the males – fathers, grandfathers, brothers' (Nikita). This is reflected in their responses, both to the Anglo-feminist women's movement and to its projects for dealing with issues like male violence.

The Significance of Ethnic Communities

> We, the Vietnamese women with our traditional values and the influence of Taoism and Confucianism within us, always strive to be a good wife and mother with the best interests of the family at heart... We feel it is our duty to contribute as much as possible to the development of a country which has kindly opened its doors to refugees... at least half of this contribution can be attributed to Vietnamese women. (Anh Thu Thi Tran, Acting President Vietnamese Women's Association in 1995, Vietnamese Women's Association in NSW Inc, Annual Report 1994–95,1995:7–8)

In the 1970s Gladys escaped a politically disturbed country to be confronted with the barbed wire fence and huge lights of Wacol, a reception hostel for immigrants in Brisbane: 'so much like a concentration camp' that Gladys 'burst into tears'. Therese and her husband were diplomats until the fall of Saigon. Their house was confiscated; after three attempts they escaped to Malaysia where they were at the mercy of the immigration officials, unable to discern or question the reasons for acceptance or rejection. Halina's property-owning family was declared 'enemies of the people' in Soviet Poland: 'all that was familiar, whether it was people or things or environment, was left behind never to be seen again'. As Cora Gatbonton (speaking at the 'Herstory' Workshop organised by the Ethnic Communities' Council Women's Issues Committee, Brisbane, 27 October 1994) says, immigrant women 'come by any means', including means unacceptable to the Australian immigration authorities.

Halina points out that assimilationist policies often encouraged chauvinist responses among migrants 'with very little education' who wanted to fill the 'vacuum' of dislocation:

> All the little Poles together, all the little Germans together ... And the government, ... they said 'Now you are Australians, forget about what has been'. That was another mistake because the moment they said it, ... all our energies went into fighting it. And you see, it shouldn't be a fighting situation, there should be ... a smoothing situation, but it wasn't.

While Halina and her husband developed links in both the Australian-born and overseas-born communities in Brisbane, for many the choice seemed stark: assimilate or be inferior. Italian and Greek children were called 'Ities' or 'wogs' and even Teresa's Lancashire accent branded her an outsider. Sometimes parents were physically assaulted if their children spoke their parents' language, as Matina remembers. Little wonder then:

> when you grow up not belonging, you try as hard as you can to look like everyone else and be like everyone else ... We actively chose our Australian group and friends, and the golf club ... But we were ashamed, ... I was ashamed until I was about 30, of being Greek. There was all this pressure of not being quite good enough ... Now I'm really proud of my Greekness. (Matina)

Gerda also suggests she 'always felt a *little* bit inferior' as a migrant, a feeling in tension with her belief that 'we're all equal'. Inferiority could persist, the foreign name outlasting the foreign accent. Matina's son was not allowed to try out for the school cricket team because his name was Mottee. Matina 'was furious, and he knew I'd be furious, that's why he didn't tell me' until years later. It may be this sense of inferiority as much as a real rejection of their ethnic background that encourages second-generation migrants to tell Melinda they are uninterested in learning their mother-tongue: 'What's the point? ... I've got no intentions of going back there'. For Melinda this is a good sign, multiculturalism meaning a diversity of looks but not of languages: 'their kids will ... blend in a lot more here'.

The importance of community, as well as different theoretical approaches, is indicated by the tactical responses to domestic violence among Filipina, Italian, Vietnamese and South American community workers. Domestic violence occurs throughout Australian society and male violence is a preoccupation for women,[1] with increasing condemnation indicated in surveys.[2] The response of the women's movement has been to establish refuges and, later, supported accommodation assistance,[3] to campaign for the introduction of protective court orders against violent husbands,[4] to argue that a background of violence constitutes self-defence when women turn on their batterers and kill them (McGregor and Hopkins 1991:xix, 22; Rathus 1993:87; Office of the Status of Women 1992:59).

The women who find it most difficult to leave domestic violence situations have no independent incomes, no friends or family close by, and are often isolated either in rural areas or because they do not speak English. Both Indigenous Australian women (19 per cent) and immigrant women (41 per cent of Sydney refuge users) are over-represented in women's refuges (Office of the Status of Women 1995a:31; Vasta 1993:11). Despite the greater client need among these groups, the services devised by Anglo feminism have been less suitable to their particular needs. Shelters are often experienced as alien, in terms of food, group living, the language of communication (McFerren 1993: 157), the anti-male culture. As Lita suggests, some refuge staff 'were just anti-male, just to the extreme', saying things like 'No, you don't need to see that bastard'. Unfortunately, racism among workers and residents in women's refuges continues (Vasta 1993:11). Women who go to the police for a protection order may be rejected by their community, and survivors do not want to lose that 'cultural bonding' (Lita). One Vietnamese woman, described as 'brave enough to break through the cultural barriers and obtain an order', was killed by her husband who was outraged at the 'loss-of-face' of the intervention order (Durham 1995:118–19).

Melba Marginson (1992:116, 122) links the high levels of violence perpetrated against Filipinas with media images of the 'manipulative mail-order bride, docile domestic helper or a wandering prostitute'. Filipinas in Australia have higher education levels than Australian-born women, but however they met their husbands, they are often stereotyped as 'mail-order brides' – as Del found. Various reasons are offered for the higher incidence of violence among these marriages, besides the racism and sexism of Australian-born husbands. For example, separation is considered more of a failure in Filipino than Anglo-Australian culture (Del, a welfare volunteer with Filipinas suffering domestic violence), Filipinas feel disempowered in Australia where they do not control household finances, lack extended family support and may not know their rights (Agnes). Agnes further notes that, due to the poverty in the Philippines, many women 'will do anything to get out', including being less than honest with their Australian husbands concerning their family circumstances or that their husbands are expected to remit money to their family in the Philippines. For Agnes, the solution is to improve the economic prospects of Filipinas in their homeland.

The Vietnamese Women's Association in New South Wales, founded in 1984 by women like Therese, works to help 'the whole community, but especially the women'. Domestic violence was identified as a major problem in 1990 and the association lobbied successfully for funding to build Mimosa House, an Indo-Chinese women's refuge in the western suburbs which has six bilingual staff who speak Vietnamese, Cantonese, Mandarin, Lao, Thai and Khmer. Therese notes:

> Women, victims of domestic violence, are often advised by workers of the mainstream refuges to take legal action against their husbands. But in our policy we avoid that. Because sometimes it is not only the husband's fault, sometimes it is the woman's fault as well. We try to let them interact, to bring them to counselling, and to console them and to reconcile . . . We would only advise them to go to take legal action if we have no other alternative.

This policy of unity, or reunity, is based on the interpretation of Confucianism in Vietnamese immigrant communities as a set of reciprocal duties and obligations (in which white feminists might claim some duties are more equal than others). The husband as the 'leader' must provide financial support, 'protect' his wife and children, and help his wife 'in every way possible' with her household tasks which are her primary duty. Parents and children also have reciprocal obligations of support and respect (Cung 1995:48).

While her co-worker supported the wife, Fiorenza devoted her energies to the perpetrator. Her message was: 'I am against your violence but I care about you as a person', using a model inspired by Gandhi's *satyagraha*, or principle of non-violent resistance, which has elements of compulsion and coercion (Jones and Diack 1987:3). Fiorenza sought to remove the perpetrator from the house rather than the survivor. A woman who enters a refuge is really 'running away' and cast in the mould of 'victim'. If a woman can stand her ground just a little longer, 'with the right help, you don't have to move'. While removing the woman might be the easiest immediate solution, many women return and, Fiorenza says:

> they haven't really learned very much at all, in spite of all the support and the information they were given, because nothing has really changed inside

them. But even if they don't want to go back again, for some of the women it is almost impossible to survive and function in mainstream society.

Fiorenza also used the community network to 'shame' perpetrators, visiting them at work sites and talking to the man 'before his friends . . . You break the silence straight away'. Gladys said of Fiorenza: 'she's magnificent'. Fiorenza was awarded an Order of Australia Medal for her services to the Italian community.

Raquel Aldunte and Gladys Revelo (1987:2) approach domestic violence from a Marxist and feminist perspective, seeing women's status reduced both by colonialism and machismo. Machismo might be further heightened by insecurity in a new country, the man desperately trying at least to master 'his' woman. Gladys worked with the Migrant Women's Emergency Support Services as one of the bilingual workers. They placed migrant women in mainstream refuges after providing training for the refuge workers. At the same time, ethnic communities were educated to see that 'men didn't have the right to do that'. Gladys received many threatening calls from men, claiming that 'we were destroying families'. Her husband's encouragement was 'the only support that I had doing the job'. Gladys paused and said: 'You don't realise how stressful it is until you are out of it all'.

Links with the (Anglo) Women's Movement

Mary Kalantzis (1990:39) suggests that the 'practical struggles of immigrant women' are more personally demanding than those for 'leaders of the EEO industry or the feminist film-makers on their government grants'. Certainly, the agenda for non-English speaking background women in Australia is often larger than the Anglo feminist agenda, including the need for English language classes, culturally appropriate and multilingual welfare services like refuges and aged care homes, concern about class inequalities and appalling working conditions, and different orientations to a family and culture besieged in foreign soil.

As Indrani says of multiculturalism in organisations: 'you're expected to know everything from A to Z about over a 100 nationalities, and it is assumed that you don't understand what Anglo feminists are on about'. Labels like 'migrant women' or 'ethnic women' lump a diverse range of women together and place them after Anglo women: 'as an addendum in the back pages of every book, or every directory' or solely as a 'welfare thing' (Matina). Some of this has changed with the development of multicultural women's organisations and the representation of non-English speaking background women together with Anglo women on more committees.[5] While Matina's 'formal relationship with the women's movement has been spasmodic', she saw her role on the National Women's Consultative Council as that of a 'sensitisor', 'because I believe that they influenced me but I believe that I influenced them'.

Fiorenza also describes a two-way exchange in the Women's Electoral Lobby and the trade union movement:

> I was not as knowledgeable as they were of the Australian situation. And then when I went to the migrant women, Italian, and others, then of course, I found that most of them were even less knowledgeable than I was; it was all very new to them . . . You couldn't discuss things the same as you would in the mainstream, because they already had all this history behind them, sixty years or so, whereas the migrant women were coming new into it. Apart from someone like Raquel or Gladys, the others had no experience of feminism whatsoever. And it was very frightening to some of them (for example, Muslim women).

Hanna drew some support from the Business and Professional Women's Association, so that through 'being together with working women' she learned about local mores.

Both Matina and Fiorenza derive strength and information from working at the 'grass roots'. Fiorenza's grass roots' support is a counterweight when the organisational leadership thinks to contain Fiorenza's activities. Working in grass-root positions brings Matina 'back to the reality of what is happening with the women' because 'the easiest thing is to speak for women without really hearing what they want to say'.

Many in the Anglo community perceive that women from other backgrounds are shackled by the traditions of arranged marriages, polygamy, Catholicism or Islam, and by the economic and intellectual poverty of their peasant backgrounds. Indrani has been accused by feminists as well as other Australians of being 'too traditional' and 'not traditional enough'. She was too traditional – 'too feminine' – when she wore a sari to feminist conferences. She was not traditional enough when she replied in the negative to a co-worker in a feminist organisation who asked, not about feminism in India, but 'if I practised meditation and chanting and believed in wearing charms'. In Brisbane, although not Canberra, people were surprised Indrani had a university degree, no doubt because of 'media images of poor Third World women who are starving and oppressed and illiterate'. When CAPOW! was organising a working bee to clean the office Lita was asked how many non-English speaking background women could come and help. She said: 'I'll ask them but they have to clean their homes as well and may not be keen'. The reply was: 'Of course, we know, NES men are so chauvinist'. As Lita notes, if she and her colleagues complain: 'They will just think we are being emotional NES women'.

Indeed, many non-English speaking background women come from countries with a feminist tradition at least as long as white Australia's, and encountered feminism and its debate with Marxist-inspired male students at university (Indrani in New Delhi and Lita in Lima). South American feminists grapple with the same dilemmas of working for women-specific issues like abortion, sexual discrimination and rape, and calling themselves 'feministas' only to be accused of 'burning bras, smoking like a chimney in the street, drinking hard spirits or refusing to have children'; 'being lesbians, anticlerical' (Margarita Muñoz of Panama and Marie Frantz of Haiti (where many women are very devout), in Küppers ed. 1994:11, 36).

While Anglo-Australian women are ready to condemn dowry deaths, female foeticide and genital mutilation, they rarely link these practices to their own dilemmas over cosmetic surgery or 'how far very intelligent and otherwise quite independent women would starve themselves, to conform to pretty unrealistic expectations'. As Indrani goes on to note: these are all issues 'about the control of women's bodies by a patriarchal system'. Such ethnocentrism raises 'the hackles' of women from non-Anglo cultures 'who might initially have been willing to discuss it'. They are hesitant to launch straight 'into these public forums' and tell Anglo-Australians 'what they feel is wrong about their own culture' because they wonder whether it will be used 'to reinforce stereotypes'. 'There's also a time and a place for raising sensitive issues'(Indrani). Straight off the aeroplane from wartorn Eritrea, Somalia and the Sudan is not the time and place to discuss genital surgery, when to these women 'sheer survival', 'combating loneliness and isolation and learning about the system' are more pressing issues. However, while women from non-English speaking backgrounds are critical of Anglo ethnocentrism, they also criticise patriarchal practices in their own cultures, often advocating a judicious mixture of their cultures of origin and their culture of adoption. Therese notes discrimination against women in Vietnam; Agnes that her father was a womaniser, acceptable in Filipino society with its double standard and where men are very 'chauvinistic'; Shirley, that Taiwanese 'women should not be too dependent on their husbands' and women can and should learn to be 'strong'.

Women migrating to Australia have noted the appalling ignorance of Australians, ignorance of the diversity and specificity of the cultures from which these women came. Fiorenza was born in Milan, a modern, European, industrial city with women doctors and primary school principals. Rita moved from an Italian city where she was attending opera and ballet to a country location where the only cultural activities were barn dances. This seemed a 'low sort of culture' in contrast. For such migrants it was Australian culture rather than their mother culture which was archaic or, as Fiorenza said, lacking in 'complexity', despite the 'openness' and 'generosity' of people:

> Australia gives you a sense of freedom and equality, but . . . when you start looking deeply, what you take for freedom sometimes is lack of concern about things . . . Australians are not terribly politically minded the same as in Europe. The fact that you always had just two major parties, one can't tell the differences between the two, perhaps you can, but it is difficult to pick the differences.

Similarly, Indrani suggests that Anglo-Australians' approach to other cultures is often a kind of lazy liberalism. It 'acknowledges the right to be different but doesn't try to achieve a deeper understanding of the bases of these differences'. When combined with anti-intellectualism – which Indrani contrasts with a deep respect for learning in many Asian cultures – Indrani finds herself 'repeating the same basic stuff' at forums. On the other hand, at least 'Australia's come to a point where it's beginning to accept, at least at a certain level, different voices'.

If Australians do not accuse the migrant 'other' of being bound in tradition, they seem to invest them with all the culture they feel Anglo-Australia lacked. Beatrice Faust (in Mitchell 1984:11) remembers 'the great thing' was the 'cosmopolitanism' and 'reality' brought by the migrants. Halina suggests that, as a result, many migrants not only came with a vacuum but they came into a vacuum: 'we find an empty place here that cannot fill our vacuum'. Halina claims that the government should have promoted Australian culture which might have made it more visible, seemingly less bland, less like white bread and cheese slices. In fact, Anglo-Australian culture often feels like the expression of power and not difference, particularly if one is an Indigenous Australian.

Indigenous Australian Women Reflect on White Feminism

> There was great interest in trying to involve Aboriginal women and we learned some very sound lessons out of that that I have never forgotten . . . We would organise things in a way that Aboriginal women would be able to come. But as if there was no question that this was a good thing to do and they would nicely agree to come, . . . but they never had any intention of doing it because it didn't have any value to them. And it just takes a little while to work out that that's what is happening and it isn't that they have no sense of time or they're really disorganised or they have no sense of responsibility, just that they don't see the point. They thought we were nice when we organised to go mud-crabbing with them, . . . but they didn't see much point in being involved in this organisation. (Claudia)

> Other women don't really know what the issues are. Like for black women most of the time it's just a case of survival and surviving, with racism and everything else that goes on. (Nikita)

It was 1983 before the first and only government-funded national consultation with Aboriginal women was carried out (Daylight and Johnstone 1986), and 1989 before any response to this report was launched. In 1984 the Department of Aboriginal Affairs formed an Aboriginal women's unit, upgraded to an office in 1986 (Sawer 1990: 133–5). In its 1991–2 budget of $158 million the Aboriginal and Torres Strait Islander Commission allocated only $1.3 million to the 'indigenous women's initiatives' program (Moreton-Robinson 1992:8; see also Eve Fesl in Mitchell 1991:196). Even so, most Indigenous Australian women find the idea that they might work with white women for common goals inconceivable. While Indigenous Australian women share some of the concerns produced by white feminism, these are often overshadowed by events which touch far fewer white women. Institutionalised race relations have caused dispossession of land, kin and culture. Families have been disrupted when children were taken from their parents, when Indigenous Australian children were defined as wards of the state, requiring the Protector's permission to marry, move or leave a mission (to attend funerals, for example). This continued until the 1980s for many Aboriginal people in Queensland (Jackie Huggins in Huggins and Huggins 1994:25). The early deaths of parents and siblings is captured by Aileen's comment that she had been dealing with death since she was about 2: 'Death was just such a part of the Aboriginal community, because there was always someone dying, it's a sad fact'. Thus, in contrast with the growing preoccupation with ageing in the white women's movement, Auriel notes that juvenile issues are far more important for Indigenous Australian women.

Marcia Langton (in Sykes 1993:163) remembers 'Severe brutality, such as horse-whipping Aboriginal people, was normal, even when I was a child'. Pat O'Shane, the first Aboriginal female teacher in Queensland, the first Aboriginal lawyer in New South Wales, magistrate and head of the New South Wales Department of Aboriginal Affairs, felt her education was constantly at risk because of Queensland legislation. Until 1972 she could be removed to a reserve by any person in authority who deemed it necessary (Mitchell in O'Shane 1984:148). As Martha recalls:

> Anyone who caused trouble was sent off . . . When I was a child, in the 1930s, we were aware of people being sent off. So that pressure was there. I mean I never ever felt threatened or anything, or insecure, but that probably had to do with the fact that I was there with Mum and Dad and uncles and aunts all around us. (Martha)

Martha knew that her family had the right to vote, whereas some cousins 'who married people from Cherbourg or Barambah had to go to the Director and get a permit to marry'. Similarly, in some places:

'Aboriginal people had to sit on one side of the picture theatre . . . They weren't allowed to go into hotels'.

In a situation where 'assimilation' was closer to genocide through stealing children or removing people from their land to reserves, the struggle to keep indigenous culture alive was less than totally successful. Martha's grandparents and great grandparents 'adapted to the situation, . . . for the sake of staying in their own country', so their descendants 'know who we are, know who our relatives are'. To stay this way, Martha's mother 'always made sure that we conformed in every way to what was expected of us, from the white population'. The fear of being sent away also meant that family members policed each other not to speak their outlawed language. Contemporary language retrieval faces twin hurdles of forgetting and past conditioning. One of Kerry's uncles speaks his language quite well but 'you can see by the body language' his reluctance. Some of the young children in Kerry's family and extended family now proudly bear Indigenous Australian names. Martha, like Aileen, remembers the surreptitious expression of customs and language at women's social gatherings, where the women smoked clay pipes, imbibed 'a couple of drinks of rum and they'd start talking', passing on songs and legends to the children.

Claims like 'they have no sense of time' are among the 'pathetic excuses' given by white feminists when Aboriginal women do not come to their conferences. Like Claudia, Jackie Huggins (1992:130) suggests that 'perhaps they're [Aboriginal women] just too smart to enter into yet another alien discourse designed by and for whites without any consultation with Black people in the first place'. Valerie says: 'They'll say what they think you want to hear, until they really know you. So do Torres Strait Islanders'. But should a white woman then respond with what Indigenous Australians wish to hear, or her own truth? Speak in the idiom of the other, or retain the idiom of self but learn the meaning of the other's idiom? Valerie has learned to accommodate to advertised feasts on Thursday Island that don't start on time, walking into a room and finding she is the speaker on an issue, being asked in the afternoon if she can host the Mother's Union meeting that night. As she says in the face of such requests: 'What would I have gained by saying "No"?' Thus, she has learned from interactions with Indigenous Australians to 'ride with the occasion'. For Vera, on the other hand, the 'conditions reported in the south' about Indigenous Australian issues are out of line with 'our experiences in the North [where] many of us had been employers'.

Valerie, who has completed a rape counselling course, was tested in her cross-cultural understanding when a young Indigenous Australian man, whose family was known to Valerie and whom Valerie had encouraged to broaden his horizons, raped a white nurse 'in almost every way imaginable' as she was returning from an aerobics class. Later the nurse returned to the community where the rape occurred, and 'it was very very difficult because they all said: "You deserved it, your white men have been doing this to us for centuries"'.[6] Just as Audrey could feel some sympathy for her father's temptations (see the Introduction to this book), so too can Valerie see that imprisoning the 'promising' Indigenous Australian man does not settle the accounts or contribute to improving Indigenous Australian communities. In some ways, his punishment precipitated outrage against the nurse, even if it was based on white men's unpunished sexual exploitation of Indigenous Australian women. Valerie seems to feel that if she could pierce the mystery of his behaviour, find the explanation, she would be closer to opposing or accepting his punishment of imprisonment.

As a result of their position, it is argued, white women perforce participated and continue to participate in racist domination of Aboriginal women and men: 'Many Aboriginal children have suffered brutally at the hands of white women who have always known what "is best" for these children', as welfare workers, institution staff, school teachers, adoptive and foster mothers (Huggins 1994:73); 'The major obstacle to totally effective Black feminism is white racism in the feminist movement' (Lucashenko 1994:23). As late as 1980 some white women refused black women admission to a refuge in Alice Springs (Burgmann 1993:120). Roberta Sykes also reports 'the most virulent and racist comments that I had heard publicly for some time' came from white feminists when she opposed relaxed abortion legislation (in Rowland 1984:65). Pat O'Shane ([1976] 1993:73) recalls that members of WEL resisted a resolution of congratulations on her admission to the bar because 'she is not really an Aboriginal'.

Auriel has been a member of Indigenous Australian women's groups (for example, the Australian Capital Territory representative on the Aboriginal Women's Advisory Council) and mainstream women's groups (for example, the Aboriginal representative on the establishment committee for the Australian Capital Territory Domestic Violence Service). Auriel commends Ann Wentworth, who invited Auriel's participation, for her responsiveness to 'the diversity of the needs of women in the community' which 'makes it so much easier to get in there'. Kerry notes that Indigenous Australian women will 'reap the benefits in a way of the feminist movement', but women's movement issues pale in comparison with 'everything else'.[7] Just as women from non-English speaking backgrounds have additional burdens to those shouldered by most Anglo-Australians, so do Indigenous Australian women:

> Aboriginal women have had to fight not only racism but the sexism. A lot of them are living beings because of an act of rape on their mothers, grandmothers and great grandmothers, and they had to put up with rape themselves and then they had no legal recourse available, and then their children were legally stolen and were responsibilities of the state, and then they couldn't educate themselves any higher than domestic and ancillary staff, and they were not even classed as Australian citizens until the 1967 referendum. And you want to go to an Aboriginal woman and say: 'Come and join our feminist group' . . . Until our culture is accommodated or accepted a bit more, there's always going to be barriers. And attitudes haven't changed really a lot and it's still going to be a long time before attitudes change. So Aboriginal women have still got to have a lot of other issues, than just feminism. (Kerry)

A fall-out of colonisation has been the perpetuation of the violence by which whites subjugated Indigenous Australians in indigenous communities:[8]

> People were belted up, people were flogged, things were manipulated. If a local white fellow wanted a certain woman and she was married sometimes it was arranged that the husband got sent out of town for a while . . . So there's lots of bitterness, fear, or there's lots of hate, there's lots of anger or frustration. But at the same time I'm not excusing violence in any way because we women have had to survive, Aboriginal women have had to do or die, and a lot have died. A lot have done, through all the adversities, and there's a lot who have gone to alcohol or other addictive behaviours. (Kerry; see also Matchett 1988:258–9; Langton et al. 1991:481; Atkinson 1990:7)

It has been said that the idiom for women bashing is 'blackfella loving', jealousy indicating love (Lucashenko and Best 1995:21). Aileen reflects: 'because violence was a part of the culture I didn't see that as being abnormal'. Aileen's first husband, a white man, told Aileen she deserved his violence because she was black. 'Right deep down I never bought his bullshit', but Aileen's 'awakening' came when she visited a white woman whose husband slapped her. She immediately packed her bags, gathered up the baby and left. Aileen said: ' "Are you really going?" And she said: "Yes, no man will ever hit me" . . . it was a real dawning, I didn't have to put up with that, I could leave, this wasn't normal from white men'.

Nikita notes Judy Atkinson's findings: 'There's actually more deaths on Aboriginal communities of Aboriginal women than the whole of the black deaths in custody and it's still continuing'. Indigenous Australian women are more likely than white women to resist violence both with public shaming strategies and with a retort of violence.[9] In such circumstances, one might say that there are 'batterers' but there are no 'battered women, they have not learned helplessness' (Burbank

1994:176). However, partly because of their greater proclivity for offence and self-defence, Aboriginal women suffer disproportionately in the white judicial system.[10]

Some Indigenous Australian women stay in violent relationships because they do not want to also raise children in families where fathers are largely absent. Kerry, witnessing her mother's experiences, 'would never put up with a man who was violent', but says of other women who do: 'We didn't judge them and we tried to support them . . . we could see the whole picture – the powerlessness, oppression, being made scapegoats for out of control lives'. Nikita suggests that it is largely in her generation that women have found the strength to overcome the victim mentality. In combating violence Indigenous Australian women focus on 'walking with the men' (Baldini 1995:129), for example, banning alcohol from their communities or setting up alternatives to separatist white-run refuges (Goodall and Huggins 1992:417; Timaepatua 1992:32).

It is not only Anglo-Australians who are racist, although they have the power to perpetuate their racism in discriminatory institutions. As Aileen says: 'Within all communities, there are racists'. Thus, there have been debates between Torres Strait Islanders and Aborigines – the Torres Strait Islanders 'do not like being lumped with the Aboriginals' (Valerie). There has been antagonism between Chinese-Australian women and Indigenous Australian women, for example, Shirley Smith's denial of Irene Moss's claim that Australia is 'an Asian nation with a European heritage' (in Curthoys 1993:19). Recent migrants to Australia can be as racist as the Anglo-Australian stock, one saying: 'three paces behind a man and all this rubbish, that's crazy. Like some countries, they're still very much second-class citizens . . . I think Arabian countries are still very much like that, and in China you know'. Kerry remembers that chants of 'Blackie this', 'Blackie that' came more often from recent migrants to Australia, who to Kerry did not 'even come from here'. Kerry notes that she now works in cross-cultural training where Indigenous Australian and migrant women share experiences and stories to build cultural understandings. In Shirley's Multicultural Women's Group 'we encourage members to learn more about each other's and their different cultures. It is hard'.

Martha advocates reconciliation with white society, partly because 'there's no such thing as vacant land in south-east Queensland'. Aileen suggests:

> What I'm constantly trying to do with my mob is to sort of try to get them to see that being racist in return is not the answer. And it's more about trying to get them to understand where they're coming from.

However, reconciliation will require a remembering of the past, replacing ignorance with honest appraisal (Lucashenko 1994:21). The remembered past must be reinterpreted so that white women (and Indigenous Australian women) find a mutual respect, a sense that learning and assistance can flow in both directions, even if not necessarily always of the same kind. However, there have been instances of mutual support. Two instances in Oodgeroo Noonuccal's life capture the different relations between white women and indigenous women. The second most published Australian poet (after C. J. Dennis), Oodgeroo Noonuccal (as Kath Walker in Mitchell 1987:202, 195, 201) once worked for Lady Cilento as a domestic cleaner; she was also assisted by Mary Gilmore in becoming a published poet. Louise Liddy-Corpus (1992:28) remembers that Margaret Reynolds (senator for Queensland) 'was the first Australian politician to fly an Aboriginal flag in a formal ceremony'; Margaret Reynolds (1993:121), in her turn, was influenced by Bobbi Sykes to make her first political speech. Faith Bandler (1992:170, 171, 173) helped form the Aboriginal Australian Fellowship, with Jessie Street at the helm, which campaigned for a decade to change the Constitution. Later, Bandler joined WEL to help agitate for abortion law repeal. Pamela Ditton's (1992:25, 26, 27–8) introduction to feminists in Alice Springs in 1977 was facilitated by Pat O'Shane; in 1983 Ditton and her feminist colleagues mediated between the interstate peace activists and local Aboriginal women who also vehemently opposed Pine Gap. (See also Terry Stewart, a youth worker at Wakefield Street Aboriginal Community Centre (in Hanlon and Stewart 1992:13–14) and Eisenstein 1996:123–5.)

Donna Awatere Huata (1993:127) says of cross-cultural learning in Aotearoa: 'We always knew instinctively that Pakeha women would support the Maori struggle'. In anti-racism courses, when a Waitangi Tribunal report is read 'the women will often stand there with tears running down their faces' (Huata 1993:127). Similarly, Pat recalls a meeting:

> I knew very little about Aboriginal people and when Rose Collis spoke about her people and conditions for them, including the removal by force of the part-Aboriginal children – and she was one of these – I was stunned. All around me were women weeping, as I was.

As Aileen says, cross-cultural conversations are only possible because of our likeness, our shared experiences and mutual understandings: 'You understand that there are differences but what you're trying to do is search for likeness'. This does not eliminate the risk of speaking across cultures. Even identifying what are the likenesses and what are the

FEMINISM: A WHITE MIDDLE-CLASS MOVEMENT?

differences is no mean feat, let alone building coalitions and shared understandings upon them. The next section explores feminism's tentative entry into the worlds of rural and religious women.

Frontiers of Feminism

Feminists have expanded women's imaginable possbilities, even if many women shelter behind the lines before moving forward into the new territory. As Mayra says: 'I love the way Marilyn French describes it, "We needed those women to bring the middle forward"'. Or the 'top rated feminists [who] did nothing for me at first', they opened doors 'by risking ridicule because of the fierceness of their beliefs' (Grace). When Fiorenza says: 'Strong feminist views were not always acceptable to migrant women', it should be remembered that they were not always acceptable to many woman. Valerie links the women's movement to the women's ordination movement, saying both are 'expressing a lot that those who aren't involved are also feeling, and I think it's been great'. In this section we explore the moving frontier of feminism in the countryside and the church community.

Outback and Outspoken[11]

> The president welcomes everybody, and we'll say our Motto and our Creed, have a minute's silence for those bereaved and then we go into minutes and correspondence and general business, which can be anything about how many cows did you sell last week to how to put a collar on a dress to . . . what do you think of the politicians. (Jan describing the teleconference meeting of the Cairns Aerial Outpost branch of the Queensland CWA)

> The women's movement didn't really touch those people that lived out in rural communities. (Jan)

Besides fear of their partners and economic insecurity, in country New South Wales women facing violence often have no means of escape, no place to go, little or no assistance from police (who are often 'mates' of their husbands or even known to be violent), face family and community pressure to stay as well as 'a prevailing attitude that "you made your bed, you lie in it"' (Healthsharing Women 1994:97–8; Shannon 1994:200). Mary felt that her mother would respond to her situation with this adage, incorrectly as it turned out. Aileen's kin knew of her situation, but Aileen felt shame because 'I also knew that I'd made my bed . . . and it was therefore my responsibility to get out of it'.

Audrey, Amber and Mary all experienced violence in isolation, although in Mary's case it was verbal violence. Mary was fortunate in that her mother-in-law gave her all the money she had in the house which, with Mary's endowment cheque, enabled her to buy train tickets to Sydney. The children were 'like ponies that had been locked up in a stable that were let go in the paddock. They just blossomed and they galloped around'. Despite their gambolling, the children 'wanted to stop in the country'. Mary tried again to make the marriage work, feeling guilty for a long time because she could not: 'and I saw lots of women with alcoholic husbands. At that time to me it seemed that they could make it work'. Because it never occurred to her to 'take' money from the government, Mary found what work she could: 'the most terrible job . . . sorting the mail at *Reader's Digest*'. It was only when she enrolled in a TAFE welfare course that Amber realised that other farm husbands, like her own, controlled their wives' movements by monitoring petrol consumption or letting down tyres, that the local policemen and ministers of religion were also sometimes wife-bashers. In her own isolation she knew about feminism because 'it was obviously mentioned on the ABC and things like that', but Amber 'always thought, to get help I'll have to get away from here and go to a town'.

Rural women, as the media reiterates, are facing a 'crisis' and shouldering much of its costs. Service delivery in rural communities has always faced the difficulties of distance and lack of anonymity (so, for example, young women cannot avail themselves of the local doctor's services when seeking contraceptive advice – Wilkinson 1995:60). The rural crisis takes its social toll in marriage breakdown, stress due to financial straits, suicides of children at home without jobs or money. Although there is a greater demand for services, economically rationalist governments and private companies have responded to population decline by closing post offices, schools, government office branches, court houses, hospitals and banks, forcing community groups to fill the gaps with additional voluntary labour (Teather and Franklin 1994:6–7) and mothers to help with distance education at home.

Since 1953 the number of farms has almost halved while the contribution of primary production to exports has fallen from around 90 per cent to about one-third (Alston 1994:27). Many rural women have always been farmers rather than farm wives, now reflected in statistics (influenced also by legal moves to spread the taxation burden).[12] Women's unpaid contribution to the rural economy is some $6 billion each year (Alston 1994:27). Even so, only 14 per cent of women in Alston's study felt they had an equal say in farm production decisions (Alston 1995:66, 127), while women rarely have equal financial equity in farms on divorce.[13] Although by the early 1970s one-third of agricultural students were women (compared with none in 1965) (Kaplan 1996:179), women have little visibility in the professional sector which services agriculture (Teather and Franklin 1994:6).[14]

FEMINISM: A WHITE MIDDLE-CLASS MOVEMENT?

Women's participation in the economic and physical burdens of farming is not matched by men sharing the domestic labour (Alston 1994:29). Mary reports the minor intransigences by which women can allocate at least some domestic tasks to their husbands. She never learned to milk a cow and was 'the greatest ham-fisted cutter of wood' if anyone was around. The woman next door put her message in the raw steak she served her husband. When he said, 'What's that for?' she replied, 'Well, I asked you to leave wood for the stove before you left and you didn't'. The advent of electricity eliminated wood-chopping, clothes boiling, lamp filling and lighting. Remembering the endless nappies in her young motherhood, Mary's mother insisted Mary have a washing machine so that Mary did not have to boil nappies in the copper. However, because of the lack of electricity, Mary still had to kick-start the washing machine's motor. After the birth of Mary's first child her mother bought her a slow combustion stove so that Mary rose for the night feeding into a warm room. The nearest doctor, chemist and nurse were '40 miles away on a dirt road of corrugated sand'. Once Mary became bogged three times when seven months pregnant and had to walk 3 miles carrying an 11-month-old child to the closest telephone.

On the other hand, as Jan points out, a farm mother can control her children's activities because they rely on their parents for transport. Jan 'kept them occupied, you kept yourself exhausted and they didn't get into trouble'. At the local primary school all the other children shared a farming life, but in Cairns Jan's children encountered kids who had jelly-beans and potato chips for breakfast, who used 'bad language', were more 'street-wise' from spending time outside the home without parental supervision. In two-income households they had 'the latest watches and T-shirts and gym boots', perhaps as a compensation for their parents' absence. Suddenly Jan's children discovered that not 'everybody ate and lived like us'. Jan's message was 'Nobody was right, nobody was wrong', although subtly suggesting some preferred alternatives. For instance, she explained the use of bad language as: 'wasn't it a shame the children didn't know the right words to use . . . You had to really work at it'.

Jan remembers small-town life as 'Everybody was the same, and no woman was any more important than another woman'. This ideal of harmonious rural communities is questioned at both the privileged and under-privileged ends of the spectrum. As the daughter of the town's general practitioner, Rachel remembers his importance elevated her own existence in various ways, including her ability as a small child to 'charge' icecreams at the cafe. The daughter of a labouring man, Glenda suggests: 'if you were the daughter of a doctor or chemist, you were just like royalty. This must be a pretty familiar story'. Aquarius asserts that the story persists into the present: 'on the pension, you're below the poverty line', while those at the other end of the income scale have never experienced 'what it's like to wonder if they're going to get the next meal', although she asserts 'it's part of what makes you more independent'.

In the common imagination – perhaps more so in the feminist imagination – rural communities are often seen as patriarchal, places where 'men run everything' and look 'after their mates' (Roberts 1995:69) and women's group organisers can be branded as 'witches' by the local press (Davey 1995:81). However, such impressions are, no doubt, 'a gross generalisation' (Finlayson 1995:208). Thus, Berenice at first saw Pekina in South Australia as an apparently 'traditional conservative society where women and men had their own spheres', a 'self-maintaining' closed community which Berenice feared would dismiss her as an artist and an outsider. Through the 'formal' meeting points of pub and shops, Berenice was gradually accepted, eventually organising a dance at the hall which she and her partner had restored.

The supposed conservatism of country women is often associated with the assumed conservatism of the Country Women's Association, established in 1922 in New South Wales. The motto, creed and grace of the CWA (supplied by Jan for the Queensland CWA) might reinforce this supposition. All dwell on service and sharing, and within a context of crown, country and Christianity, as the motto clearly articulates:

> Honour to God,
> Loyalty to the throne,
> Service to the country,
> Through Country Women,
> For Country Women,
> By Country Women.

Strength of silent suffering seems to be recommended in one line of the creed, followed immediately by courage to move forward:

> I would be strong, for there is much to suffer;
> I would be brave, for there is much to dare.

Women of the CWA have been called 'strong, powerful matriarchs' (Carmel Niland in Mitchell 1991:20) epitomising 'both the competency and conservatism of farm women' (Teather 1994:135). Women explain their involvement in the CWA and other voluntary organisations in terms of being 'community minded', wanting to serve the community (Yvonne – regional president; Jan – President of the Far North Division and awarded the Premier's Award for community service in 1995). In return, the CWA is 'like a family' (Yvonne). In Mareeba, 'the Country Women's Association adopted me. And the women there were wonderful' (Halina). Signalling the significance of voluntary associations in women's identity, when Vera married she wore a gold Girl Guide badge on her wedding dress. When Jan first joined the Queensland CWA in 1968 the monthly meetings offered an opportunity 'to get away from those home household obligations' and 'talk about something different'. That 'something different' encompasses the study of a different country each year, and arts and crafts activities like dressmaking, floral arts, drama and public speaking. But, as Jan says, the ethos of the CWA means 'you can do anything you want to do'. As women's interests have changed so have Queensland CWA activities. Recently Jan's group 'learnt self-defence, would you believe . . . because some of the younger mums said they wanted to learn', the classes ranging from 'the little girls up to the grannies'. The Queensland CWA provided classes on nutrition, menu planning and food budgeting when some supporting parents said they had not learned this while growing up.

The 'competency' of rural women is displayed in the skills acquired by executive members of the CWA, including public speaking, meeting procedures, budgeting: 'If you didn't think you were worth anything before, you do afterwards' (Jan; see also Tom 1993:27). The CWA owns and manages significant property, mainly rest rooms and halls (Teather 1994:138), while the Far North Division of the Queensland CWA owns holiday, convalescent and respite units. In New South Wales, according to Teather (1994:138), the CWA perhaps shies away from other needed services like women's health centres, rape counselling and refuges, because it fears alienating the male support it has always attracted to its projects. Jan contests this explanation, claiming the government offers such services and voluntary associations fill gaps in service provision; and that the clientele of women's refuges require specially trained counsellors, given their experiences and in some cases the use of language that is 'very offensive to some women'.

Since the start of the rural crisis, the Queensland CWA has become involved in providing an Emergency Housekeeper Scheme, and supplying a Rural Crisis Fund which pays for expenses like vehicle registration, telephone rates, school fees and household necessities. Communication is a key issue, the open 'galah' sessions on the radio now superseded by the less community-oriented telephone, while some women have neither a telephone nor a satellite dish to receive television. Jan has spoken with women who have no sheets for their beds, but cheerfully added: 'But it's in a nice hot area. We don't really need anything'. After meeting basic needs, the Queensland CWA offers something to meet women's emotional or intellectual needs, a book, curtains or cassette tape.

For Jan the CWA is 'political' but not 'party political'. Women are 'in there now', members of local councils, school committees and government corporations because they want to contribute to decisions affecting their lives and their families. However, they can be outspoken because they are members of a voluntary organisation and do not fear losing their jobs. Women are 'in there now' both because the present situation requires their participation and because 'women want more now than their grandmothers and great-grandmothers did'. Under the leadership of a woman like Jan, the Queensland CWA has expanded its horizons beyond the often assumed constituency of 'old grey-haired ladies' (Yvonne), and offers women avenues into greater self-esteem, more skills and political participation. More generally, however, membership is declining and ageing.[15]

Berenice argues that younger women are drawn to new organisations like Women in Agriculture (Alston 1995:129, 136). Berenice explained how this division is represented in a book which has achieved iconic status among farm women in south-eastern Australia: Christina Hindhaugh's *For Better, For Worse And For Lunch* (1992, reprinted in 1993 and 1994). Jessie, the protagonist, is an English literature graduate, who, like many farm wives, comes as alien blood into the family, place and culture of her husband. Within a year she has become a farmer's wife – taking on the house and garden as her own, and a farmer – taking over the bookwork, protecting the wheat crop from birds. At first Jessie longs for her female friends and the city, describing the farm as 'Hard Labour! I might just as well be in prison. Am I, in fact, in a prison?' (Hindhaugh 1992:52). The reader knows she is transformed when she refuses Edward's offer of a weekend in the city, claiming she is too busy with meetings and her garden planting program (Hindhaugh 1992:183). At a microwave cooking demonstration Jessie offers a throwaway comment to the other wives. They say they left their husbands a casserole or quiche for lunch. Jessie says: 'Oh, I left Edward a note!', which brands her 'as a real women's libber' (Hindhaugh 1992:73).

The events which cross Jessie's path resonate with feminist-oriented discussions of farming women's experiences. A representative from one of the chemical companies asks Jessie if the 'boss' is in. Jessie ponders that media images show country women always in the kitchen and never working outdoors (Hindhaugh 1992:87; for example, *The Land*, a newspaper published by the United Farmers and Graziers Association of New South Wales, portrays 'macho men and domesticated women' – Teather 1994:135). Ruminating on Edward's Moreton Crop Discussion Group, Jessie 'wish[es] I had a group too. A people group. To discuss the human issues of farming' (Hindhaugh 1992:139). Jessie finds her 'people' group in Women in Agriculture: 'We organise seminars and discussion days on such subjects as strategies for decision-making, coping with change, women's health, time management, stress control, how to handle isolation – and many other areas of personal development as well' (Hindhaugh 1992:152).

Gently feminist, and determinedly heterosexual in that Edward's rod finally delivers the pregnancy Jessie at first resists, the book reverberates with many country women's experiences: their forgone education (the book is studded with poetry quotations), their introduction into an alien life, their sharp criticism of patriarchal assumptions without becoming self-named feminists. Jessie's odyssey is to join Edward rather than oppose him, the latter often rejected by farm women as feminism's goal. Because the farm is an economic unit rural women pay a high price of dislocation if they refuse a 'family consciousness' (Alston 1994:26), of working 'shoulder to shoulder with their husband fighting drought, flood pestilence and the economy' (Richards 1995:152). Similarly, Valerie describes the purpose of Cape Women Meet as to offer 'some feminine confidence' in the lives of women who bear the costs of family life and death while contributing their rural labour. Even most members of Women in Agriculture remain leery of feminism, as they define it (Hogan 1994:37), even if 'intrigued by what it means' (Mitchell 1994:143).[16]

Before her talk with me, Jan saw the CWA and the women's movement as 'totally opposite in what they did'. But Jan had repeatedly described the CWA as 'women supporting women', 'there's a place there for every woman'. When Jan mentioned the self-defence classes, I thought how women's liberationists had organised self-defence classes to empower women against rape. When I said that the CWA sounded very much like some aspects of the women's movement, she replied: 'Yes, it is, but . . . they've already been doing that all their lives and they'll go on doing it in a quiet practical way, not out in the public as a radical type of thing'. Jan associated the women's movement with long-gone 'public' protests and 'radical media hype': 'the women's movement to me is way back in the sixties with Germaine Greer. I switched her off thirty years ago'. While the CWA responds to women's needs, it is not a feminist organisation, as Hindhaugh's distancing it from Women in Agriculture attests.[17] The CWA is committed not only to women but also to family, crown and country. Yvonne, in accordance with the results of popular analysis in the United States (see Stacey 1990:12–3), 'blames' the women's movement for family fragmentation in which divorce has produced street kids and irresponsible parents. Furthermore, behind the wishes of members, which may change with the times, is the 'secure' structure of the CWA and its 'discipline' (Jan). In another relatively new territory for feminism, the church, women have also struggled with its discipline.

Feminism in the Church

If everybody lived the ten commandments, we'd be the richest country in the whole world, wouldn't we? There'd be no stealing, there'd be less gaols . . . But we're sinners, we fail a thousand times. (Gerda)

Sometimes seen as backwaters from the feminist mainstream, both country women and church women have offered feminism some of its most moving battles and demanding issues over the last decade. This should not surprise those with an eye to history. Last century feminist sympathisers were nurtured in the dissident religions like Unitarianism and the Quakers (Levine 1990:38; Rendall 1987:10). Judith Stacey (1990:57–8, 117–21, 139, 140–5) explores an 'evangelical feminism' in the United States, advocating equal pay, equal rights, equal marriages (including greater support for male participation in childcare), welcoming single people into their communities, discussing self-defence against rape, criticising social pressures on women to be slim. Only more conservative views on abortion and homosexuality distinguish the communities Stacey discusses from widely understood feminist positions.

In 1968 the inter-church group, Christian Women Concerned, was formed, addressing women's role in church and society as well as poverty, peace and racism. In 1973 the Australian Council of Churches (New South Wales) set up a Commission on the Status of Women under the presidency of Marie Tulip (Dixson 1994:241). This provoked Jean Skuse (1995:166) and her colleagues to prepare a proposal that one-third of lay people appointed to all commissions and committees by the then forming Uniting Church should be women. Partly because of the exemption of religion (along with the military and voluntary organisations) from the Sex Discrimination Act in 1984, no bishops are women, although women can serve as ministers of the Uniting Church, where they comprise fifty-five of 383 ordained ministers. The Quakers (Religious Society of Friends) have always had equality between women and men in ministering. After a long battle which drew in many supporters and antagonists, on 7 March 1992 in a moving service, ten women were ordained as Anglican priests in Perth; the Melbourne and Tasmanian synods since voting to allow ordination of women (Office of the Status of Women 1992:89–90).

The impact of these ordained women is revealed in some of the stories I was told. Mary, an elder and parish chairperson, has a 'lovely woman minister' in her Uniting Church, who has made the congregation multicultural as well as supporting the church's 'work within the community'. However, well before the ordination of women, in Normanton in outback Queensland, Valerie and the parishioners 'took the service' when Valerie's husband, Tony, was absent. He left them 'something interesting to read' in lieu of delivering a sermon. The gathering seemed to enjoy a more lively atmosphere than my memories of church, discussing 'whether we agreed with it, or what did that mean'.

Although it is a generalisation, Noela feels that ordination in the Anglican church has been won at the price of conformity with male clericalism, which 'the Catholic movement towards ordination for women . . . have never wanted'. In their battles with the Catholic church some feminists choose to leave and some to stay, those staying claiming: 'it's my church, and I'm going to stay and I'm going to change it' (Noela). Agnes notes that women, as pastoral associates, members of parish councils and so on, can 'do a lot of things in the parish except say Mass'. Others who stay design their own liturgies. Margaret remembers the homily delivered by a young parishioner on Mother's Day who claimed that the 'sisterhood' of female relations is 'the best thing God ever made'. She warned that the male hierarchy, claiming to be Christian, must recognise 'the role women have to play and will play in the future', as she did not know 'whether I can carry on with this'. Inside or outside the church, women are united in a 'great friendship' and 'common vision' (Noela). Thus, Lilla Watson (1994) is only partially correct when she expresses surprise that western women would ask men's permission to be ordained, while Indigenous Australian women would establish their own churches.

Agnes Whiten walked down the aisle 'side by side' with the archbishop at the Mass which commissioned her as Women's Advisor to the Catholic Archbishop of Brisbane. Members of the congregation noted that 'you never see' a priest walking alongside an archbishop, much less a woman. While some criticised the post as tokenism, referring to Agnes' lack of theological qualifications, Agnes saw herself as a 'conduit' for women's views, pointing to her ability to assert her own views gained as a consultant for mining companies and membership of the University of Queensland Senate and the National Women's Consultative Council. While 'the ordination of women comes up every now and then', the issues which preoccupy 'the broader spectrum of women in the archdiocese' are violence in the family and the media, transmission of faith, sexual abuse of children, unemployment and 'morality of society as a whole'. Agnes notes she occupied the first position of its kind in Australia, possibly unique in the world, although no one has been appointed to replace her since her term finished.

A religious vocation has long been an alternative to marriage for women, not only in the west but also in Asia. Noela never imagined a married future, although it was some years before she imagined a future as a nun. Noela admired the 'dedicated life' of the Sisters of Mercy who taught her, joining them after travelling and teaching in England. Viewed as a radical order in many quarters, the 'Mercies' have been nicknamed the 'seminar sisters' because of their thirst for knowledge. The Mercy Order responded promptly to Pope John XXIII's encyclical which recognised the women's movement as a 'sign of the times', as the 'movement of the Holy Spirit', and to Vatican Council II which allowed nuns to stop wearing habits and 'mix with the world' (Agnes).

Before she went to Fordham University in New York, Noela was aware that women 'who seemed to have equal abilities and competencies and intelligence just didn't get there' which was 'very strange'. But studying for her Masters in Religious Studies was 'probably the most stimulating wonderful time of my life', in which 'the largest part of it was the women's movement and the whole sense of meeting these incredibly dynamic sisters'. Their turmoil had started in 1968; nuns had stopped wearing religious habit, were leaving schools, entering social work, withdrawing their labour when injustices were not redressed.

Having realised she was a teacher before she was a nun, Noela decided to leave the Order. She found it difficult to break away from a life of 'fourteen happy years' and 'people I really loved' and introduced a practice she had learned in the United States, regularly returning to visit. Noela now teaches in a Catholic girls school, balancing her Catholicism and her feminism in what she calls 'a Christian feminist approach':

> Because we are employed by the church in a sense, there's a loyalty due to the institution of the church. But we try to help the students think through things and we raise very strongly questions of the justice or injustice to women within the institution in the way this operates, particularly in years eleven and twelve.

On abortion and contraception, Noela points out that these are issues of 'personal conscience', one of the church's 'strongest teachings, but it's not always one of its best publicised teachings'. Indeed *Veritatis Splendor* (The Splendour of Truth), the papal encyclical of 1993 which took an emphatic stand against contraception, has received far more publicity than the issue of a Catholic woman's conscience and how she trains and accesses it.

Besides 'personal relationships', the important thing in Noela's life has been

> knowing the extent to which I've really influenced so many young women ... you just don't realise what the ripples in the pond do until you meet

somebody many years later and they say: 'The fact that you were the only one that encouraged me and helped me believe I could, meant that I did'.

The next chapter addresses the impact of both the mothers and feminism on the daughters, who represent feminism's future, as well as aspects of its present.

CHAPTER 7

Beating The Backlash

> I was of an era of women who were perhaps dominated by males, or had a pretty raw deal in life. And these days there is so much that women can do, I find it difficult to understand why women allow themselves to get into situations where they are dominated. (Martha)

In the early 1980s Robyn Rowland (1984:18-19, 132–8) identified a backlash by conservative women against Australian feminism, women who opposed abortion legislation or protested at the devaluation of the homemaker role by feminism. Today, the term 'backlash' is more popularly understood as a backlash by men (Faludi 1991), although Beatrice Faust's (1994:48) short polemic *Backlash? Balderdash!* contests the claim that Australian feminism is suffering a backlash, largely because of the country's institutionalised welfare system and compulsory voting. The women of 'middle Australia' noted the existence of a welfare state which encompasses alternatives to violent marriages in income support schemes and work opportunities for women, and of a public discourse which asserts women's educational and occupational choices. They commended greater economic choices (as managers, police-women and in the defence forces, for example) and equal pay, a welfare system allowing a woman to raise a child apart from the father (Riley-Smith 1992:16–24). While these women did not believe women were equal, they were 'more equal than we were'. They referred to their mothers (both 'mothers' and 'grandmothers' according to my nomenclature) as 'doormats', 'slaves' and 'subservient', women who 'had to sit back and listen', 'stayed home and raised the kids', and 'did everything for my father' (Riley-Smith 1992:16–20).

The backlash has occurred at a more personal level, particularly greater male violence, a result of men's insecurity in the face of women's gains. 'They don't know what to do with equality and feminism' (woman aged between 25 and 32 years in Riley-Smith 1992:42–4); 'a lot of men can't talk, so they attack (woman aged between 40 and 55 years in Riley-Smith 1992:51); 'men today probably feel more vulnerable now . . . due to the increasing demonstration of women's strength' (Nikki McCarthy

1993:16, an Indigenous Australian artist); 'feminism scares the shit out of men' (Grace); men are 'frightened, scared that women, women frankly have got to come up [that is, improve their status]' (Aquarius). As one woman said: 'You may have been safer and more secure, but back then you were NOTHING' (in Riley-Smith 1992:54, 41). Men, even if not violent, still look down on women 'on a personal and social level' and treat them 'as appendages' (Riley-Smith 1992:34, 35).

These ruminations on the backlash suggest that feminism may be a revolution 'half won', or perhaps only a quarter won. Young women assume formal equality in their access to education, to work, to politics, but they also understand that substantive equality in these areas has not been achieved. Moreover, they are disappointed that men have not changed, are still violent, are still unloving, are still reluctant to do housework, are still afraid of women.

New Issues in a New Century

I do think feminism has changed all generations of women, from my mother down to my daughter and of course me in the middle. However, it's been a more gradual process in the older generations like my mother's. (Grace)

I don't know that things have changed all that much ... Really, in a lot of ways, if you look at teenage girls ... it just seems to me that there's the ball rolling, but they're not grabbing any bits of it, but maybe it takes a lot longer. (Gisela)

Women express nostalgia for the certainties of the past, when femininity accorded women the right to protection – to 'lie down on the floor and have somebody take care of me' (in Shreve 1989:76) – and respect, expressed in the chivalry of opened car doors and proffered bus seats. Thus, of women's traditional roles Deanna says: the 'mother was more, revered – you don't want to be revered – but the mother was more of an icon in the household' (see also Slattery 1993:152). Feminism's victories have produced 'a deep-seated ontological fear that ... [we] are dealing with nothing less than a profound change in what it means to be a woman' (Summers 1994a:28). Young women today wonder 'just who they are' (Liz Dangar in Ford 1991:20), while older women 'don't know what it means to be a woman any more' (in Shreve 1989:72). The opportunity to 'practically be doing what she liked' 'can be intimidating' 'because you're taken from this lovely little path that you had' (Grace).

But freedom, even at this price, can still be sweet: 'I come and go as I please and can make my own decisions' (in Riley-Smith 1992:18). Mothers often refer to expanded social and geographical horizons in their daughters. Helen 'got what [her family] thought would benefit them'; 'It was unthinkable that I would leave home and live on my own as my daughter did . . . I would be considered a loose woman', especially to become a policewoman as her daughter Jennifer did – 'unheard of in those days'. Valerie's parents were 'horrified' that she wanted to leave home to pursue her education, her own daughters 'go off on overseas trips and play hockey away from home, and do all the rest of it'. Marg is similarly proud that her daughter is 'confident' 'that what you want to achieve is possible no matter what'.

On the other hand, a career is now almost an obligation or a necessity, both economically and to avoid being 'justa' housewife, but it remains difficult to balance career with motherhood, a desire many women still harbour. Armed with better education and higher career aspirations, the daughters are imagining the kinds of domestic environments that will support their double dreams, issues their mothers rarely considered when they were young.

Education

> My grandparents didn't get the chance to go to school, my parents certainly didn't get the chance to go to high school, and yet within that one generation or so I've had the chance to . . . go through to university (Sandra Eades in Coolwell 1993:37).

As early as the mid-1970s recommendations were made to overcome the gendered educational choices by which girls studied languages, arts and literature and boys studied mathematics and science (with the exception of biology) and later, computing. Two decades later girls are encouraged with transition training schemes, awareness campaigns, girls-only classes and better access to equipment.[1] Women in non-traditional occupations also speak to students as role models (Millan 1993:134), Hanna, as a female engineer, stressing that 'everyone has an equal choice to study whatever they'd like to'.

Feminists also attempt to change the curricula and teaching methods in 'non-traditional' subjects to make them more attractive to girls (see Lewis 1993:275 for science teaching in Victoria). As deputy principal, Teresa created and taught single-sex classes in mathematics:

> Some of the men still didn't know how to teach girls maths and that was a problem. They still used the same old techniques; all they thought was that they had a more compliant group of clients. They didn't consider what girls' learning styles might be like anyway. I think, to a degree, girls and women do differ. We like to talk about things, we like to explore. We don't see things in such black and white.

In Teresa's classes, mathematics learning was via 'group work' and 'fun', 'kids helping other kids. I mean you get two girls who are sitting and talking about maths and a lot of male teachers will tell them off'. However, such learning styles are probably preferred by most students, male and female, especially as 'there are no right answers any more'. Rather, society now needs people who can 'explore problems'.

Feminist educators have expanded the formal curriculum, the text and images in school books, to represent women in a greater variety of roles. Feminist educators have challenged the hidden curriculum of subtextual cues, like time and space allocated to boys and girls in classrooms and school grounds, teaching methods and teachers' assessment of boys' and girls' capacities.[2] In primary school, Rosemary 'always felt, sort of smaller than the boys in a way . . . subconsciously', but could not remember thinking: 'Am I being treated fairly or equally?' Willow and Rosemary suggest that most teachers allowed the boys to dominate, Willow contrasting her timidity with the boys' greater confidence. Both also remember teachers who made an effort to encourage the less confident students, Willow describing one such teacher as 'a bit of feminist' who 'was really supportive of the girls'.

Yasmin also had a 'feminist' teacher who 'used to give the boys hell. Like the girls could do anything, right, and the boys weren't allowed to'. The teacher upbraided the boys if they referred to 'check-out chicks', made the boys sit at the front and would not let them 'dominate all the time'. Yasmin hastily points out that the female students were not favoured with 'higher marks or anything like that, I think she expected equal from all of us'. However, posters around the room proclaiming 'AMP Insurance for women', 'Women can pot black' and 'Women can drive cranes', left 'no doubt on what she was trying to say to us', that girls could 'do whatever they wanted'. This contrasts with the memories of mothers which do not even encompass gender bias in their schooling, although it is hard to believe it did not exist, given the discoveries of feminist educators when they set out to quantify classroom interactions and the contents of textbooks.

When she became a school principal Teresa discovered decades of investment and $200 000 in annual salaries spent on technical studies teachers for thirty-two boys and 'not one girl', while the school had no humanities program. The standard reply was: 'Girls are perfectly entitled to enrol in technical studies'. Teresa understood the need to create an environment which would be conducive to girls studying 'non-traditional' subjects like technical studies and expand the curriculum to include computing and Asian languages. Both Yasmin and Melinda were aware of the significance, in terms of feminist struggles, of subject choice at school, Yasmin remembering that in grade eight she had no choice but to do home economics. Melinda chose as her electives 'home economics and woodwork, so it was kind of like doing the mother bit and the father bit'. Indeed, boys on the whole chose the 'father bit' and girls 'the mother bit'.

At the school where Teresa became principal, sexism and violence, both physically and in the language used, 'was rife'. It was directed at both students and other teachers, so the female staff 'hated going into the staff room ... If women got pregnant, they left the school immediately'. Besides biases in the hidden and formal curriculum, girls are policed by sexual harassment. Harassment of girls in schools includes 'dakking' (pulling down their pants), teasing girls about their breasts and periods and calling them 'slut or dog'. Jennifer, who describes herself as 'a big-busted person', remembers a male student who filmed Jennifer's class presentation and focused the camera on her breasts. The class laughed during the video screening and Jennifer was 'dying of embarrassment', but rejected the options of 'abusing' the teachers and telling her mother. Jennifer felt that the teachers should have stopped such behaviour by which boys treated girls as 'just objects'. Elsewhere girls reveal little faith that official procedures will change harassing behaviour in the long term (Cameron 1995:10). At the school where Bronwyn Davies (1993:35–7) conducted research, girls avoided institutional channels, instead mounting their own guerilla actions.[3]

Teresa stresses that in her role as female principal she effected changes in the entire school: changed curriculum and teaching methodologies; retrained teachers for different classroom dynamics; enforced equal opportunity legislation; improved the aesthetics of the school. In Teresa's school the football oval and basketball courts were dominated by boys and there were no communal places for sitting and talking. Teresa completely refurbished the school, much of which was 'disgusting, dirty and dark'. Her school suffered no graffiti or vandalism (with its associated costs) after the redecoration. To a large extent, these changes must be introduced concurrently. It requires staff with different skills and attitudes to implement new curricula and abide by anti-sexual harassment programs; it requires different environments and expanded resources to encourage girls to feel they have a rightful place in a school; it requires a different approach from management, not just the principal, to implement changes, and continue to do so after the feminist principal has moved on. Indeed, women educators have been so successful that girls now complete secondary studies and enter tertiary institutions at a greater rate than boys, provoking a backlash by men (and some women) educators. Visiting schools in the early 1990s Susan Cameron (1995:10) 'always had the opportunity to write ... down' 'It's gone too far now and boys are actually the ones who are educationally disadvantaged'. The issue has concerned feminist educators and appeared in the press.[4]

Given the rapid rise in female participation rates in both secondary and tertiary education, perhaps it is not surprising that access to education was often suggested by the 'mothers' as the major difference between their own prospects and those of their daughters. Education is no longer 'a choice': 'They expect to have an education, and a good one' (Valerie). Willow and Rosemary grew up in a home where they were unquestioningly expected to 'go to university'. Consciously or unconsciously, some mothers focused unequal emphasis on their daughters' education, so that a number note their daughters have educational achievements well in excess of their sons' attainments. Deanna told her daughters: 'As long as you're doing your homework, I don't expect you to help in the kitchen'. This also reinforced for the girls that their studies were important. Matina notes: 'I feel guilty now that I didn't expend the same energy on the boys, not because I didn't want to, but there were four of them, you know, how thinly can you drag yourself, and I had three children under 2'. Girls who grow up 'angry' at their own oppression, as Matina describes her responses to discrimination, may become mothers who compensate for a patriarchal world by nurturing their daughters. Matina remembers one of her sons saying: 'You're only punishing us because we're boys'. Matina reflects: 'That really pulled me up, and I probably was'.

In contrast, in Jennifer's home, from her father 'it was always: "Jennifer go put the tea on, Jennifer go do this, Jennifer do that, Matt's got to study"'. While Jennifer's father initially disclaimed preferential treatment towards his son, Jennifer's mother, Helen, confirmed Jennifer's perceptions. Nevertheless, Jennifer and her brother were equally encouraged to attend university where Jennifer studied science: 'not I suppose traditionally a girl's subject, is it?' Berenice and her siblings were 'brought up to go to university' (which was 'an imposition of another sort' had they wanted to become plumbers). But again, while both sons and daughters were told that 'everybody works, for their own development and to keep themselves', Berenice's desire to become an artist was unquestioned. In contrast Berenice's mother was concerned when Berenice's brother said he wanted to become a photographer because such a career would not support 'yourself and a family'.

Kerry always felt that the path to Indigenous Australian emancipation was through education. In her first post as a qualified teacher Kerry challenged the racism of her white colleagues, some of whom were using outdated texts with images like 'a little Aborigine in a laplap, standing on one leg with the other leg bent with foot on knee, holding a spear'. Working with a friend who co-ordinated a cultural centre, Kerry planned the first cultural day in her school. The Indigenous Australian tutors and performers covered oral history, dance, the performing arts and the visual arts:

> When the bus and the cars pulled up with all my friends, there were a few teachers in the staffroom and one in particular who made comments about

> ... 'And here comes the boongs to teach us a thing or two. The boongs are taking over' ... And one old uncle, proud to share his culture, got up ... dressed up in his laplap and painted up and singing and doing corroboree and boomerangs. And then he said: 'Right, I'll do my specialty' and then he played 'It's a Long Way to Tipperary' on the gum leaf. And the kids couldn't get over it, they just totally loved the whole day, although the old uncle was definitely the favourite.

Following this experience Kerry taught at an Independent Murri school which she 'totally loved'. Many students had 'closed' attitudes towards white people, learned through their own and their parents' experiences of discrimination. A demographic study of West End businesses in Brisbane both enlightened the school pupils as to their community's ethnic diversity and broke down some of the prejudices of shopowners against Murris.

Daughters do not always follow the paths towards university which their mothers chart for them. As a supporting parent now completing a doctorate, Phylis 'worked bloody hard' to keep her girls in a private Catholic school ... but they're not academic'. Melinda's parents and sister are university educated, but Melinda chose to 'branch out and do something for myself'. Daughters sometimes take up their parents' aspirations later in life, Barbara noting the greater range of educational pathways today: 'you don't even have to go to university to get some advancement these days' (Barbara).

Young Women's Work: Traditional and Non-traditional

> Really, just look at Mum. When she was a nurse you got married, you had to quit then and there. I mean, heavens to betsy, can you imagine? (Jennifer)

During the legal struggle in which Ansett's first female commercial pilot, Deborah Lawrie (also known as Wardley), successfully used Victoria's recently passed Equal Opportunity Act (McKenna and Lawrie 1992:46) to gain employment, Ansett justified its refusal to employ her because pregnancy may make a woman unfit to fly and she would waste her expensive training by taking time off for childbearing (McKenna and Lawrie 1992:100, 94). Today such defences are totally laughable to most women, who contemplate a range of employment opportunities. Just as Sandra Eades, quoted above in the section on Education, charts the enormous generational changes in educational opportunities for Indigenous Australian women, Nikita notes the changes in work prospects. Her mother's generation could be 'domestics or cooks or cleaners' or 'a station-hand working on stations'. After leaving school, Nikita could aspire to office work; later, her generation was able to enter university as mature-age students. Her daughter, still a child, toys with the idea of becoming a lawyer or a doctor, and is the first member of the family to have access to such a 'luxury' as playing music, the 'things we may have wished to do but couldn't do because it wasn't the norm and we didn't have the money to do it'.

In 1992 the ratio of women to men in the workforce was approximately three-quarters (.75:1). Some occupations are 'feminised', in that the female-male ratio is well above .75, for example, cleaners (1.9:1), school teachers (2.2:1), stenographers and typists (86.7:1). In male-dominated occupations the ratio is well below .75, as low as one to three women in a hundred among the building trades and professions (like architecture), construction and mining labourers. While not as low, women are still disproportionately under-represented among natural scientists (.35:1), police (.12:1), amenity horticultural tradespersons (.12:1), investment, insurance and real estate salespersons (.3:1) (Australian Bureau of Statistics 1993a:158–9). These latter occupations, described as 'non-traditional' for women, have attracted efforts to increase female representation, for example, the TAFE real estate course Catherine developed (see chapter 2).

Young women draw a distinction between their more or less equal opportunities to enter gender-neutral work environments, and their struggle should they decide to be pioneers in 'non-traditional' work areas. Three fitout and finish female apprentices (interviewed 8 August 1994), training for the building trades, asserted that women must have a strong commitment to overcome the minor but pervasive barriers of harassment and sexist criticism, disapproval of family members, and the loss of stereotypical indicia of female beauty, like a soft skin. All three were pleasantly surprised at 'how easy it was to get in', which they attributed to affirmative action policies.[5]

Yasmin suggests a slight discrimination against the male students in her psychology course, given psychology's image is as 'a helping, caring, nurturing profession'. Lecturers imply that 'women are more caring or more self-aware'. In this environment, Yasmin had believed that discrimination against women was a thing of the past until she took a holiday job at Dreamworld. When the male supervisor resigned the most experienced and knowledgeable worker was his subordinate, a female. Yet everyone 'sort of knew' that the supervisor's job would go to a male worker, 'basically because he was a male'. It was not only the blatant discrimination which angered the female worker but the fact that she would be required to give her new supervisor advice and carry out many of his designated tasks. Yasmin now knows there are career paths, like health and safety inspection, which she would only consider if she were really committed, because 'no one would take me seriously, being young for one, and being a girl'. Thus, like the female fitout and finish apprentices, Yasmin is aware that male-dominated areas, like engineering or driving a crane, require high motivation 'because I know it's a fight... I have to really, really, really, really want to do it'.

Young women who 'really, really' want something are extending the frontiers of women's work. Gerda's daughter is a jeweller, Willow had a labouring job and Jennifer is a police officer. The jeweller's products may be beautiful but the work is 'dirty' and requires strong arms. When Gerda's daughter approached jewellers to become an apprentice: 'They would just blatantly say, "Sorry, we don't have girl apprentices"', perhaps adding, 'All the girls we've had dropped out after two years'. Such explicit sexism amazed Gerda in 'this day and age'. Finally Karen was made an offer and determined to complete her apprenticeship for 'the ones behind me':

> And now she's reaping the benefits, she's there in the middle of Brisbane, everyone can see her work ... But it was four years, it was hard. I said: 'Look what were the alternatives? Check-out chick at Coles', I mean nothing wrong with check-out chick but you wouldn't have felt like you developed your talents the same way.

Willow was the only woman on the site when she joined a team responsible for landscaping a golf course. The first (twelve-hour) day was 'unbelievable hell', Willow's limbs 'shaking from fatigue on the way home'. As she grew stronger, she started to enjoy the rapid changes in her body, just as the fitout and finish apprentices referred to their muscles and sun tan as a fair exchange for soft skin. Although 'wearing really frumpy clothes' Willow was either wolf-whistled or treated with exaggerated courtesy: 'don't swear around her or anything'. Like Alison a generation before her, Willow told 'a few really rude jokes' which 'really warmed them up'. At first Willow accepted her lower pay because she wanted the experience and felt she would not be able to work as hard as the men. In fact, she worked as hard or harder, on one occasion digging more holes than her team mate. Because of her achievements Willow 'could have stayed on, so there is a place for women in those jobs too', although 'it was really physically hard for me and ... I was tired'.

Jennifer's career as a police officer was suggested by her mother, Helen. The doctor marked Jennifer 'temporarily unfit. If you can lose 10 kilos, you're in'. The next step was an interview before 'the panel' which included a psychologist and an inspector. The 'big' question was: '"Can you shoot someone?" And I had to be honest, ... "Well, I've never done it." I said, "If you had to, I'm sure you can, it's as simple as that".

You can't say, "Yes, I will", "No, I won't"'. Jennifer found the physical training so difficult that 'there were times at the Academy when I could have quit'. 'Never an athletic person', Jennifer was placed in the 'remedial PE class', 'appropriately nicknamed "fat boys"'. She initially failed her final physical education test. Along with four men, she repeated it successfully with the support of several female cadets in her squad. The test included a 2.4 kilometre run within a certain time; the 'dummy drag' – dragging four dummies weighing about 50 kilograms across a line in three minutes; the push-pull – pushing and pulling a trolley containing three times the cadet's body weight around a course marked out by four cones. Jennifer and the other five women in her squad of thirty graduated. One of the women was a 'rejoiner', a woman returning to the police force after having children. After Jennifer's time as a cadet she avers 'they started bringing squads that were half and half' (that is, half men and half women, though this has not been confirmed). Though the gender balance is poor, since 1981 the percentage of policewomen in Australia has doubled from 6 to 13 per cent (Office of the Status of Women 1995a:31).

When Rosemary returned to university, she chose film studies as 'the best choice out of the bad lot'. Within weeks she was 'really excited': 'I just love the ultimate challenge of it', the combination of the visual, working with people, and even the 'technical stuff', with which Rosemary is the least comfortable. In fact, women in the industry avoid non-traditional areas like 'camera operators and DOPs' (Director of Photography) for creative roles like director, producer or writer, or assistant roles. Rosemary is 'always frightened when I first go into a new editing suite and see buttons everywhere . . . But I actually really feel empowered by sitting down and forcing myself to learn that stuff'. Such empowerment emerges against the sexist grain in teaching environments where male students get more time with the equipment, their comments are treated as more valid, and one lecturer has asserted: 'Girls aren't good camera operators'. Boys are more cavalier with unfamiliar equipment, trusting themselves to pick it up, while Rosemary needs 'three days to research the camera and make sure because I don't want to stuff it up'. This is not only a sex-differentiated way of gaining confidence, as Rosemary notes. If she 'stuffs up'

> we've got another woman stuffing up camera, you know. But if the boys stuff it up, they say: "Well I was never taught the camera". It makes me angry . . . But basically it doesn't sort of outweigh the positives of being there.

Akin to Alison's image of the 'god architects' who thought 'of themselves in a *Fountainhead* way' (see chapter 3), Rosemary's male student colleagues have 'amazing' egos, and construct 'enigmas' or 'entities', for example, as a 'fabulous director of photography'. In contrast, the female students 'are more committed to the product', and go about doing the actual work in a 'more collaborative' fashion.

When girls choose to enter the building or mining industries, the engineering professions or the police force, they are told to ask themselves questions about their femininity, a modern-day variant of the shrivelled wombs used to threaten women entering universities a century ago. Hanna suggests girls drop out of engineering courses because most men 'believe engineering is a male profession and that it is not normal for a woman to be an engineer'. Consequently girls in engineering cannot find boyfriends. In a study of working-class girls in the mid-1980s parents policed girls away from career choices like mechanic or plumber as 'no job' and one which would impede their daughters' marriage prospects (Wyn 1990:122). Many young women wish to combine a career with motherhood through dint of delayed childbirth, part-time work and a helpful father. They may feel more able to control the former two contingencies, but the last continues to elude many women.

Relationships

> I see daughters of women in their forties, they're all just typical teenage *girls*. I know that sounds awful but just all make-up and boyfriends and – I guess that's . . . adolescence. (Gisela)

Sage remembers inviting Quentin Bryce, a high-profile femocrat, to talk to one of her classes, a 'wonderful dialogue' going sour when Quentin Bryce responded to a 'little naive one' who asked, 'Why couldn't the women play golf on Saturdays, Mrs Bryce?':

> she sort of stopped and there was this very very uncomfortable silence while she debated with herself, I could tell . . . And then she looked at them and she said: 'Well, do you think Australian men like women very much?' The girls couldn't handle that. I saw that they were learning so much and responding so well to her, but at that suggestion she became this radical feminist. It's such a shame, but see that is just too threatening, isn't it?

As Anita Shreve (1989:77) suggests, young women still expect their 'prince' or the 'right man', only now he will 'share the chores and the breadwinning'. But young women are also more cynical about finding their prince. Grace's daughter asks only for a 'reasonably intelligent, heterosexual' man, 'not suffering from traumatic withdrawal symptoms from somebody else . . . that I can have a normal relationship with', who will treat Grace's daughter 'first as an intelligent person, then as a woman'. Even with this minimal blueprint she has 'despaired' of finding anybody at the moment, although not 'madly wanting' to marry and raise babies. Fiorenza says her daughter has 'decided she has not met the right guy and so she's not married, and probably might never be'. Kerry has said to her daughters: 'I wonder if youse will ever get married because unless you find the fella who's going to do everything you want, you won't marry him'. Several years ago Willow withdrew from relationships, focusing on her own personal development: 'I'm not going to have a relationship until I feel like a contented, happy person'; 'So I might have to wait until I'm 30'. When I spoke with her Rosemary was also taking 'a break from it' while she worked through her attraction to men who are almost 'bastard'.

As young girls, Yasmin and her friends told each other: 'Aren't we lucky we don't have to get married straight after school?' Of two friends who plan to marry, 'the general consensus is "Why? You don't need to" and "We'll be going to the divorce soon"'. Yasmin contrasts her present supportive boyfriend with a previous controlling boyfriend:

> I was going to the adult education and I started going out with this guy, Shane. He would just like sulk, literally sulk, every time I said: 'I've got to go back and study'. He didn't mind me doing it, but if it meant not spending as much time with him . . . It didn't last long.

Given rising divorce rates, the daughters may have to negotiate relationships which carry 'extra baggage' of 'an ex-wife or kids'. Melinda went into such a relationship with equity in her own home. Thus, unlike her mother who has never had a bank account in her own name, Melinda kept her income and property separate. She was unwilling to consider altering this arrangement without 'an airtight agreement' acknowledging her greater equity in the house. Melinda was also cautious about motherhood in such circumstances: 'I need to know that I'm not going to have kids and he's going to disappear off to shift work and be left to do it myself, and for the kids to grow up with him as a stranger to them'. Melinda was also hesitant about 'relying on his salary'. As well as a prince who shares the housework, some young women still imagine a man who will be the sole breadwinner, at least for a short time. The next section explores how feminism has changed the daughters more so than the sons.

Changing Their Inheritance

Now my daughter's generation is more discerning because they have the power that knowledge gives – the knowledge that their mothers didn't grow hairy chests, take up men's mannerisms, ruin the country's economy and create a generation of gay men because they initiated the feminist movement. (Grace)

Despite Grace's claim of feminism's 'demonstration effect', that it has not 'manned' women, unmanned men and ruined the economy, most feminists are disappointed by their daughters' attitudes to feminism. This is often expressed in the trope of a generational rebellion. In the United States commentators suggest that mother-bashing occurred in fiction, films and universities in the 1950s and 1960s; possibly a reflection of the propaganda which sought to return women to the home where they were dangerously balanced between virtuous self-sacrifice and devouring possessiveness. Contrariwise, the generational rebellion by young women in the late 1970s and 1980s might be from daughters who felt neglected by mothers who reshuffled family commitments and responsibilities to attend to a new feminist agenda.[6] Judith Stacey (1990:214, 264, 219, 222) notes daughters distancing themselves from the 'excesses' of their mothers' earlier feminist views, although all the daughters had incorporated some feminist principles into their work and family strategies, even if often unaware that these were feminist-inspired. Rene Denfeld (1995:247) experiences 'condescension' and a 'patronizing tone' 'when feminists bother to address young women's alienation from the movement'.

In contrast, women autobiographers in Australia (Hooton 1990:99; Rayner 1992:75) and New Zealand (Middleton 1993:86) seem more responsive to the significance of the mother/daughter bond and the unfulfilled talents and ambitions of mothers. The mothers and daughters in my study also tell stories of companionship, advice and mutual encouragement. When Helen 'takes a stand', Jennifer says, 'Whoa Mum, way to go!', recognising that 'by me taking a stand it's made her stand easier'. Jennifer and her brothers 'come back' and talk things over with Helen, Helen carefully offering 'options' rather than 'judging them'. Yvonne adopts a similar approach with her daughter, commenting that she has never believed in generation gaps. Melinda, citing a loving intimacy with her mother, suggests that the 'real change' was between her grandmother's and her mother's generation. While Melinda does not always follow parental advice, she takes it seriously, saying: 'I see them as my friends rather than necessarily as parents'. Fiorenza and her daughter share a political activism which has not touched the men in the family. They took to the streets in the Bjelke-Petersen years, and Fiorenza relates with pride that her daughter flew the Aboriginal flag over the rural school where she is principal: 'and in Charleville it was pretty heroic to do that I suppose'.

Compared with herself, Rachel's daughters were 'even as young women, much more independent of thought'. Kerry reports approvingly that her daughters are 'strong and outspoken' and also 'respectful to other people', 'generous' and 'truthful to themselves most of the time'. Mayra remembers that her mother always called her 'stubborn' and 'pig-headed', a trait she suspects carried her out of poverty. While Mayra's daughters share this personality trait, they also have a greater freedom of expression: 'I wouldn't have dared speak my mind like they do when I was their age'. Mayra's daughters tell her, indeed everyone: 'what's on their mind, and what they think very quickly'. Valerie was brought up to accept that adults are older and wiser so when Valerie's daughter 'talked back' to a visiting church dignitary, Valerie felt 'as small as could be'. But then Valerie thought: 'Why should he have challenged her in her own home?' As a daughter, Berenice remembers 'this unwritten assumption in my growing up, that you could think, and you could write, . . . and you could always talk'. This assumption caused 'trouble' for Berenice at art school because the wider world did not always like a woman who 'could talk'.

Feminism in the Daughters

> They want all the advantages we've won for them over the years, but at the same time, they want to be nice and accceptable. It's terribly disappointing. (Leonie Still in Williams 1995:22, 19 of the younger generation of women)

The mothers who created women's liberation have noted the 'chasm' (Summers 1993:196) or 'generational rebellion' (Grimshaw et al. 1994: 301) between themselves and the grandmothers as they rejected 'old-fashioned ideas like women's rights' (Summers 1993:196) for the more radical claims of women's liberation. Somewhat forgetful of this rejection of their predecessors, the mothers, in their turn, now complain of rejection by their daughters. The daughters are ungrateful and ignorant of the gains that have been made on their behalf, which could become losses if young women do not 'reach out for the torch' (Summers 1993:197). Like Leonie Still, Dame Beryl Beaurepaire (in Mitchell 1987:96) suggests the younger generation are 'so complacent' in 'good jobs with a lot of money and that seems to be all they care about'.

As Anne Summers (1993:192–4; Summers 1994a:28) and Robyn Rowland (1984:228) suggest, older feminists are 'pitied' by younger feminists as lonely and unfashionable. Like many women of any generation, younger women are unwilling to give up men or femininity. Many young Australian women agree with the populist young United States writers, Rene Denfield and Naomi Wolf, that one can be sexy *and* a feminist.[7] To some older women such 'popular feminism' is the product of magazines which reduce feminism to 'the entitlement rhetoric of consumerism', 'looking good, having lots of hetero-sex, and being entitled to education and work' (Skeggs 1995:477, 478).[8] Popular magazines in Britain aimed at young women 'carefully don't use the label of feminism' while covering feminist issues, and adopt a 'pragmatic' 'streetwise' language which makes these young women 'much tougher and more together than my generation were at the same age' (Winship 1985:44). The feminist publication, *Spare Rib*, by contrast, seems to disempower women by reducing masculinity 'to its lowest and worst common denominator – domination over women' (Winship 1985:43).[9] Naomi Wolf (1993:319) dwells on finding and expressing one's 'inner bad girl', who 'is entitled to have her ego, her power, and her way' (every mother's nightmare, one would imagine).

As Gloria Steinem (1983:212) points out, young women have the highest exchange-value in western culture (which values female youth and beauty), they have not yet experienced that marriage is often an unequal partnership, and that equality of opportunity does not exist in the paid workforce. This may be why Steinem says that nobody under 25 'could reasonably call themselves a feminist', a comment which provokes further ire from young women (Jenny Brown in West 1987:70), including the claim that older feminists have resented the upcoming generation rather than acting as mentors for them (Trioli,1996:54). But the gains of feminism are the very reason a young woman need not 'be self-consciously or stridently feminist because her feminism was *integrated* into her self-image' (Stuart 1990:32); feminism is an ethos 'so accepted by a younger generation of Australian women that they don't even bother to explain it' (Trioli,1996:9). While Yasmin and her friends joked about feminists: 'in principle, we still used to think that girls should be able to do anything'. Only as she grew older did Yasmin begin to realise 'there were certain things girls weren't allowed to do, certain careers'.

But some young women do define themselves as feminist, as Scutt's collection (1985a) and more recently Trioli (1996) and Bail (ed.) (1996) explore, although they may distinguish their feminist issues and strategies from those of the older generation. Yasmin associated feminism with 'bra-burning', flower-power, anti-nuclear demonstrations and rallies 'back in the sixties'. For her and her friends the big issue was the environment (see also Nicholson 1993:17 and Hutchinson 1993:10 who adds anti-racism). But younger women's issues are not so different from the older generation's, if inflected by new concerns and their stage of the life cycle. They include the painful consequences of femininity (the 'beauty myth', eating disorders), violence against women (both date rape and in the media), access to safe sex and abortion, equal pay and quality education (Trioli 1996; Bail (ed.) 1996; Nicholson 1993:18; Hutchinson 1993:10; Australian Council for Women 1995:81–2).

Anna Donald (in Scutt 1985a:23) learned the term 'sexist' from her father but not the meaning, and saw her mother writing pamphlets for the Anti-Discrimination Board, the Women's Coordinating Unit and the Women's Advisory Council. As a small child, Willow was taken to women's meetings with her mother and can still remember the charged atmosphere. In their different ways both Willow and Rosemary rebelled, at least for a time. As Rosemary ironically remarks: 'The feminist message came through strongly, but it wasn't necessarily about liberation, you know, and doing what you wanted to do. It was about doing what she wanted us to do'. Berenice, who remembers 'feminist' being in 'our family vocabulary' when she was a teenager, also notes its application was sometimes 'contradictory or a bit ad hoc'. As an example, Berenice's sister was characterised as a tomboy and Berenice as an artistic 'girly-girl'. 'So the tomboy gets the boxed set of Simone de Beauvoir's *The Second Sex, Memoirs of a Dutiful Daughter*... I got... the art appreciation book, the history of fashion books'. In Sage's family an early battle was over clothing. The daughters wanted 'sexy or tough clothes' that would allow them to fit in at school, while Sage asserted that they did not have to conform to 'the image that everyone else says you have to be'. On the whole, however, Rosemary repeated her mother's 'feminist messages' 'in essays and conversation until I was about 18 or 19. Then I started rethinking it for myself'. As a fashion model, Rosemary challenged her mother's feminism:

> Can you imagine how that went down with me? I used to say all the time: 'I hope you won't do anything that will compromise you', but she was doing it all day every day, wasn't she?... she was pushing into a territory that she knew was forbidden by me... But you have to do that to throw your mother away, to get her out of your life a bit, don't you? (Sage)

Similarly, Willow also decided 'to do something that's not accepted by the feminists in order to know, in order to expand myself, and know the experience'.

According to Sage, Rosemary's commitment to feminism increased dramatically when she experienced the institutionalised sexism in her film studies degree:

> Rosemary might deny the fact that she was hostile to feminism, but she was, she was. 'Oh Mum, you exaggerate blah, blah, blah'. And I thought, 'Wait and see dear', but you can't, until they're ready they don't see it. And when Rosemary actually said today that the political struggle isn't over, I thought, 'Wow, it's the first time I've ever heard you acknowledge that it's important to

fight it at that level' and not just at the personal level. And it's only because, yeah, she's now into an area where she can see the political struggle is still not over.

Rosemary, who 'definitely' calls herself a feminist, agrees that she has 'felt like more of a feminist since going to university, because I've actually had more direct experience of sexism at university' and this sexism threatens 'something I really want here'. Rosemary has made two films, one of which won a national award. The first one involved 'mostly young women actually, who were really into their cars' and who told 'stories of getting ripped off by mechanics' and discovering the satisfaction of becoming 'independent as far as their car goes'. Rosemary describes the film as 'lighthearted feminist', 'not hard-hitting', because she wanted men also to relate to the issues, which they have. Of the second film, a dramatic comedy based on chaos theory, Rosemary is a bit 'ashamed' that the film has four male characters and two females, although she notes: 'the women are both incredibly strong characters and the men are a bit stupid'.

Willow is ambivalent about the gains of feminism, applauding women's greater independence and choices, but thinking 'we have (in some ways) pushed ourselves too far and, in trying to be equal and have some power, become more like what we dislike in men (materialistic, self-centred, self-serving, egotistical)'. Willow advocates a more androgynous solution to women's and men's dilemmas, one in which men can choose to stay at home with children and women to pursue careers, if that is what they desire. She maintains the need to focus on male-female differences in terms of 'political' issues like rape, but which should be combined with a humanism in which men and women learn to identify and follow their overlapping 'natures', being assertive or placid as their selves require and not their genders.

Melinda, like Willow, also suggests that there may be some basic bodily differences which thwart women's claims for equality, instancing physically demanding jobs and studies which suggest that women adapt one side of their brain and men the other. However, Melinda then steps back from this line of reasoning:

> well obviously guys have the potential to be stronger than a woman, not that it doesn't mean a woman couldn't do it. But likewise, you know, men, if it comes down to even things like housework, sometimes they don't even think about it, like it doesn't even enter their minds.

Phylis believes that each generation has to learn feminism's lessons 'over and over'. She wanted her three daughters to be independent and avoid 'that romantic sickness thing'. But each married, the eldest now concerned that she 'can't leave my husband because I want the children to be happy'. Like Sage, Phylis sees: 'there's nothing that I can do. I have to stand by and watch her go through that until she learns'. The second daughter, focused on her beauty, has married an older richer man who has boosted her confidence and 'can give her all the things that she needs'. But Phylis hopes 'he drops dead before the bad parts come'. The third daughter is 'a really conservative young girl, and she's never going to be a feminist', instead putting life into conventional boxes. Deanna also notes some young women are still 'in the dark ages'. Gisela suggests of young women she knows, both in their thirties and as teenagers, that they seem little affected by feminism, choosing stay-at-home lives or being 'just typical teenage *girls*, all make-up and boyfriends'. She comments that perhaps a revolution like feminism 'takes a lot longer'. And perhaps it takes a change in men.

Mothering Sons: Men and the Backlash

> It's funny, there's a bit of a double standard, and I try and watch myself here because I'm very likely to say: 'Oh, they're just all bastards' and stuff like that. Whereas if a man said, 'All women are bitches', you know, it's like so unacceptable and awful. And men are, kind of, being laughed at a lot and I think that increases their defensiveness and inability to come out and express themselves. (Rosemary)

Joan 'had lovely brothers, and my father was a wonderful role model'. Phylis has 'a son and I love him dearly'. Barbara experienced violence in two of her marriages, so when I asked her how her life might have been different, she replied: 'Marriage to a different type of man, a nice home and children', going on to itemise the support her daughters would receive if they confronted domestic violence. Even so, Barbara claims: 'Very often these days men are suffering for what women do'. Barbara cites what she considers to be a vindictive protection order taken out against her son by his wife, when Barbara's son had done most of the childcare and housework, and provided his wife with economic support after he left. He was advised not to oppose the protection order because generally magistrates grant an order.

As these comments reveal, women interact with men as brothers, fathers, sons, friends and work colleagues, even if they choose not to have men as lovers. Thus, it is not only heterosexual women looking for their 'prince' who rebel against what they perceive as 'man-hating' feminism. It is also women who love their sons, have affection for their brothers and fathers, wish their male colleagues would make life easier; women who seek from feminism the other half of the revolution, a revolution in masculinity. But, just as women relate to brothers and sons, so do men relate to women as mothers, sisters, daughters. Given this, besides the many structural changes that feminists and their fellow travellers have instituted, women can also work at a more familial level for the other half of the revolution. As Sage notes, a mother's battle is also with a masculinity produced at least partially 'out there', beyond her love. She can only change her son within these constraints:

> He's been sent to me, I'm sure of it, because he's been such a challenge. And I love him so desperately. And I see his pain, and I'm constantly surprised . . . I really do understand male feelings but at the same time, having suffered from them, I can't tolerate them either, in the sense of wanting to be with a man like that.

Anna's sons have also been sent to try her. When her youngest says, 'Girls can't do that', Anna 'can only assume [such comments] come from his observations'. Anna responds: 'Well, I do those sorts of things' and tries to put it in the context of the home situation. Anna is convinced 'that there really is something that drives babies who are boys' to be different, more noisy and active, for example, which is why boys and girls naturally form same-sex play groups. As a means of redressing this:

> up until about two years ago, I've always insisted that there be at least two or three girls added to his [elder son's] list of who he wanted at his party. In the end I decided there was no point in that, the girls felt threatened almost by being invited to a party with these gung-ho boys and his interests are so clear-cut in those sorts of areas. I mean not many girls are into collecting basketball cards or power rangers or that sort of stuff.

Instead Anna has focused on encouraging her elder son's 'softer lines, he really likes drawing and things like that'.

Furthermore, if the object-relations theorists are correct, the very structure of producing masculinity in our society requires the son to separate from his mother (see, for example, Chodorow 1978; Benjamin 1990).[10] Because parenting is done largely by women, boys and girls have quite different responses to it. Girls grow up experiencing themselves as more in relation to/with others than do boys, and perpetuate the boundary diffusion of the mother-infant relationship in adult life. However, because his mother is a woman, the son can and must separate from her in ways that daughters find much harder. Boys develop a more distinct sense of self and more rigid ego boundaries, expressing their masculinity through a denial of connection and femininity. The mother participates in this process, identifying more strongly with her daughter as an extension of herself, while encouraging her son to become autonomous and separate.

Men grow out of a world where women are all-powerful into a world where men are supposed to be all-powerful. But while patriarchal culture tells men that women are weak, they remember women/mothers as powerful and dangerous. When men express contempt for women they may be disguising both their fear and repressed love. Heterosexual girls experience another kind of contradiction when they grow into a world dominated by the opposite sex. Women also collude in the rejection of mothers; they too have felt helpless before maternal power. Girls long for the power of the father to 'beat back' the pervasive presence of the mother (Benjamin 1990:94). In adulthood, through romantic attachments to men and through maternity, women seek connection with this patriarchal power. But their collusion in paternal power is much more ambivalent than men's, for that collusion is also a rejection of themselves.

Object-relations theory tends to blame the mother as 'bad', the person who 'rejected' her children, even if this might be seen as 'necessary' for the child's development. In response, feminist object-relations theorists argue that parenting can be arranged differently – and indeed, should be. Fathers should bond physically with their daughters and sons, offer the excitement of the outside world to their daughters as well as their sons; mothers should offer role models of separation and agency in the world (Benjamin 1990:112; see also Dinnerstein 1977).

Object-relations theory appears to be borne out in Babette Smith's (1995) exploration of two generations of Australian mothers and their sons, sons raised in the 1950s and sons raised in the 1980s and 1990s. The older generation of sons remember no love and describe cool relationships, have little respect for their mothers who are interested only in trivia (even where mothers had interesting and responsible jobs) and spent time with them as a duty. While their sisters felt their brothers received special treatment, these sons took it as 'the natural order of things' (Smith 1995:34). The younger generation of mothers explore the agony of separation. Once sons go to school if they openly display affection for their mothers or are even seen in their company in public, they are denigrated as 'mummy's boys'. Mothers react to their sons' withdrawal by becoming tentative, losing self-esteem and handing over the initiative for affection to their sons (who as adults often resent the loss of physical contact) (Smith 1995:138–43). Others succumb to their sons' 'delightful but dominant force' in which flirtation and affirmation of their femininity might be a reward.

Mothers seem to be more emotionally 'unsparing' with their daughters, making them responsible for their actions, while not confronting sons with their weaknesses, their fragile masculinity, their financial problems.[11] However, the emotional distance between mothers and sons seems to have narrowed for some in the younger generation. Where the older men said they 'knew' their mothers well because they were 'predictable', some of the younger men 'knew' their mothers as 'kindred spirits' (Smith 1995:107–8). In the earlier generation even a working woman was treated as 'justa' mother. In the later generation, after a period of tension when a young boy is exploring his manhood, sons may be able to return to mothers with something akin to the intimacy that daughters more often report.

As a child, Del was not above hitting a boy who cheated her in a game. However, Del has tried to instil pacificism in her son. Although a friend advised that 'the Australian way' is to fight back, measure for measure, she told her son to turn his back on verbal taunts like 'chocolate' and 'ching chong' or to reply with witticisms. When children asked, 'You want to fight?', Del's son sensibly replied: 'What for? You do not know me, I do not know you. I haven't done anything against you. Why would I fight you?' Del reinforced her message by saying, 'Remember your father was respected for that attitude', admitting that her own childhood as a tomboy denies using herself as a role model. Del had to face the pain of separation when her son asked her to stop calling him 'bunso', which means the 'youngest son'. His reason was that Del was 'babying' him. Del now calls all her grandchildren 'bunso' 'because that is like a call of love'.

Mothers like Del confront not only the dynamic of mother and son but also the tension between their own culture and the Australian culture. Del links a lesser respect for adults in Australia to children's unwillingness to heed their mothers' advice. She notes that children-in-law address mothers-in-law by their first names, indeed, even 3-year-olds address adults thus. Shirley tells her sons: 'If you want to marry, please marry a Taiwanese girl'. Her second son has promised not to marry an Australian woman, cheekily asking: 'But may I have an Australian girlfriend though?' Therese has greater difficulty with her son than her daughters, attributing his disobedience to his centrality in the household.

Eva Cox (in Williams 1995:22) says: 'We want to change the world, not get the men to do half the bloody housework', but many women would settle for half the housework as a good start. Few would agree with Barbara's estimation that 'Most women are happy to continue with their careers, not expecting their partners to change overnight', but are willing to gradually 'break husbands' into new jobs like washing and 'cooking simple meals'. Mothers in this study report an obligation to bring up their sons with a better attitude. Margaret feels her sons were 'very glad later on' because she taught them to 'love being in the kitchen'. Their wives have said to Margaret: ' "Thank God, you've done this". And I think it gives them more of an interest together'. Hanna encourages her children 'to do all different tasks and not separate the tasks into "women's and men's"'. She tells her son: 'We all have to eat so we should all know how to prepare a meal'. Grace's son will 'bring the washing in, go home and cook the dinner, his wife will go out on the town with the girls, it doesn't worry him'. Jan has noted that 'quite often the man is the homemaker and the woman's out there earning a living and they're sharing'. Jan says that homemaking men have turned to the CWA to learn domestic skills like cake-baking, 'making chutneys, jams, growing vegetables', exhibiting their new-found talents in agricultural shows.

Lea, Barbara and Catherine describe sons similarly competent on the domestic front, almost a parody of daughters being raised in the 1950s. Adept in housekeeping skills, they shy away from their parents' stressful lives which combine careers and child-rearing, and seem unwilling to exchange their freedom for marriage and parenting. Barbara's son offered to prepare the evening meals when Barbara took up lawn bowls (which however 'came to an abrupt end' when he got his first car) but 'lacked ambition' to seek 'advancement'. One of Catherine's sons has developed quite a patter on his exploitation in the domestic sphere:

> 'When I started school', he said, 'I had to make my own sandwiches' – which is true. He said: 'Now, I was a little kid and it's not surprising, because you're making sandwiches like this [mimes hands above head trying to butter bread on a bench top], you miss a lot'. And then he'll say: 'Oh incidentally, see these burns on my hand, they're from ironing my shirts'.

The fact that Catherine's son tells this story against himself reveals that he is not diminished by it. Indeed, her sons were quite scornful of friends who revealed abysmal domestic skills on camping trips. But, suggests Catherine: 'I'm sure there are other times when they wish somebody would do it for them. I mean, it's quite nice to have people running around after you'. She would not claim that they have no 'resentment at all'.

Catherine's sons also police male acquaintances who make sexist comments. Catherine was told about one evening when her son and his friends were at a pizza bar. A new member of the group made a sexist comment and was told: 'That's not a very good thing to say about a woman'. This was reinforced by another: 'Nup, you shouldn't have said that', and another 'You're lucky my mother isn't here'. The friends then discovered that their mothers were all successful career women, concluding 'No wonder we've got a lot in common'. In contrast with an older generation of sons who hardly knew what their mothers did even if they worked, Catherine notes that her son's friends talk to her about marathon running or 'ask me how my work is going', their questions revealing 'These kids know a lot more about me than I know about them'.

Because she and her husband haven't 'pushed our sons like our parents pushed us', Lea's sons don't have 'the drive that I've got'. Catherine suggests that she and her husband might be a negative role model: 'I often wonder whether we've done them a disservice, because we both work pretty hard at what we do, and I think our kids actually don't want to work that hard, in fact they say that sometimes'. Catherine's sons have not had 'strong relationships with any women at all', being 'really into independence'. Catherine is concerned that they may never take on the 'traditional' responsibilities of fathering, a 'tradition' she has not rejected. Similarly, Judith Stacey (1990:217) notes of a postfeminist son: 'If Frank cannot imagine dominating a wife, it is also difficult for him to imagine having one at all'.[12]

While the social commentator, Hugh Mackay, notes the impact of feminism on the Australian way of life, he describes it as 'the redefinition of gender roles which has taken place in the minds of roughly half the population – the female half' (in Sawer and Groves 1994a:83). Rosemary and Willow believe that men are both worse and better than they were in their mother's day. They are worse where they have felt threatened by feminism and are 'clinging to what they have left' like male-dominated occupations (Rosemary). They are made better if they 'have gone with the change and accepted it more' (Willow). But those who have gone with the change are exposed to 'gender vertigo' (Connell 1990:470–1), alienated from familiar ways of being male but receiving little guidance in an unknown territory. A new array of more complicated expectations has probably made men more confused than 'back then' (Rosemary). Grace suggests that feminism should mean 'freedom for *both* sexes', although it will require men to 'step into uncharted waters, possibly with ("horrors") a female captain'. In this vein, Glenda sees the backlash as a necessary path to more open dialogue between men and women. As in any dispute, if one party will not communicate, resolution is impossible:

> men have never expressed their viewpoint . . . They've never ever been open to women, they might have been open to their mates. And if they want to be open to me and tell me all these things, which they're doing increasingly on radio, I'm quite happy to accept that. As long as they don't want to go on with all this idiotic nonsense about claiming power to which they don't have any merit . . . I think in fifty years time they'll look back and say: 'Holy shit, how did we exist in this vacuum of communication?' (Glenda)

Interestingly, Bob Connell (1995:140–1, 236–7) suggests that men cannot create new masculinities in sex solidarity because masculinity is based on dominance. This is why feminists are rightly suspicious of men's groups, which tend to either reproduce or merely reform patriarchal practices. Rather, men need to embed their anti-sexist strategies in wider political actions which affirm and unite them, for example, as trainee nurses, in the environment movement, in labour politics.

Conclusion: The Life Plan

> Heather at 26, she's just doing so well . . . I know ultimately she wants to get married. And Judith is funny, she said: 'Oh yeah, about 26, I'll have a baby when I'm 26'. And, of course, she's 24 now and she says: '26 is too close, I think I'll delay it a bit longer'. There's just too many things. (Deanna)

Jan feels like a 'mugwump bird, you're sitting on the fence with your mug over one side and your wump over the other'. She straddles the traditional values of her grandmother's generation and the need to adapt to the little known environment her children will face: 'They have different stresses at school and the workplace is totally different'. Jan's daughter, presently focused on her career, sees marriage if it 'comes along' as only on 'an equal basis' with her career. Margaret, a grandmother, 'sort of floated along through life' until she determined to do further study. But her daughters have 'got the confidence to go and get what they want'. Instead of feeling threatened their male partners 'see the importance of it'. At college Kerry 'was proud of these young people who were coming up, and especially some of the young black women who were so much surer of themselves'. Where Rita had no defined sense of a working future, Rita's older daughter and her boyfriend each completed an arts and a law degree. Now married and almost 30, she is pregnant: 'She's going to work until about six months prior to the baby being born. But she is going to stay home twelve months with the baby, and then he's going to stay home twelve months'. The couple ensured such shared parenting through taking flexible jobs and buying 'a very modest house which is almost paid off'.

Jan is glad not to be 'in a high-pressured job, trying to be a wife and mother, trying to raise a family, trying to be everything'. Similarly, Rachel describes her eldest daughter with 'a partner, three children, a mortgage, an unfinished PhD and a full-time job, and I don't really think it can be done'. Given these difficulties, young women's first manoeuvre is often to delay childbirth while they establish their careers, although 'that has other unlooked-for consequences, I think' (Rachel). Barbara suggests the unlooked-for consequences include medical problems associated with giving birth, 'little children' who try the patience of parents who have spent many years in the workforce, and grandparents who are 'gone' when children reach their teens. Young women are more likely to return to work when their children are quite young. While Melinda disapproves of women who 'shove' a child into childcare six weeks after giving birth, she plans only something like a year's break from work, after which 'kids are better off being out, socialising with other kids the same age'.

Strategically, many young women develop a life plan which charts a balance between the demands and desires in their lives. Kerry suggests: 'we didn't know how to plan for anything eh?' Murri people of her generation tended to live for today, especially in response to a paternalistic white system which 'planned' everything for Indigenous Australians. At college, Kerry learned about formal 'goals and aims'. As Rachel says: 'my daughters, they're much more conscious of their life plan ... They are much more able to look at it and say to themselves, "Is this the sort of life I want?" I don't ever remember doing that'.

The life plan may be the mark of independent self-assured young women taking charge of their futures. Or it might be the sign of a central dilemma for women who want both careers and motherhood. Thus, a mid-1980s study of working-class girls, 80 per cent from homes where English was not spoken, found these young women were not attracted to university study and 'put a high priority on establishing a relationship with a male'. But they were not 'romantic', instead describing 'marriage, and particularly child-rearing, as an important feature of their future life' (Wyn 1990:121, 123). And not one which should be allocated to grandparents while the couple worked and travelled for twelve hours each day: 'It's no good for the child and it's no good for the mother as well' (in Wyn 1990:123). Similarly, Aboriginal girls 'have few expectations and illusions about happiness as future wives and mothers. But what else is there?' (Dudgeon et al. 1990:87). Thompson found class differences in the romantic scripts of the 400 girls in the United States with whom she spoke. For working-class girls pregnancy meant passage to their futures, 'something important to do'; for middle-class girls it stood between them and their 'obligation to fulfill their own potential'. Romance was envisaged as a leisure-time pursuit; they never imagined going professional in romance and love as working-class girls did (Thompson 1995:119, 106, 23, 85–6).

For young women at university, the life plan still promises a solution. Yasmin says: 'I love psychology, it's always what I wanted to do'. Yasmin's 'personal plan will be to finish uni, travel, I really want to travel, and then build up a career'. Although she is dating someone who owns a house and will marry him when she finishes her honours year, Yasmin wants 'to be able to support myself'. This is her goal: 'no matter who I get married to, no matter what, even if I have children'. In contrast to Yasmin's prospects, Audrey interjected: 'See, I saw my mother, unable to leave home, brutally bashed, day in, day out, by a drunken over-sexual male . . . she had ten children and she couldn't walk away'.

Life plans require a judicious choice of career. Thus, one of Gerda's daughters works in a bank because 'they're very open to women promotions' and part-time work when she gets married. Jennifer, who now has a baby boy, notes that while the police force does not offer paid maternity leave, they reduced her shift work during her pregnancy. Of a mooted creche, Jennifer appended: 'I'll believe it when I see it'. Her immediate plan is to use her paid and unpaid leave before returning part-time, an option only recently introduced but 'which is like a heaven sent'. In contrast, Jennifer notes her mother's lack of choice, forced to resign on marriage. Psychology offers Yasmin a way of blending her goals:

> I think I've always had in the back of my mind that it is a job that I can gel with having children because if I have my own practice, I could again leave for a little while or do part-time and still have children . . . Because I don't think, personally I don't think I would have children until I'm ready to give them the time that I need to.

Rosemary's life plan is not dissimilar to Yasmin's:

> I feel I want to start having successes in the world . . . I don't mean money or anything like that, but feeling like I've developed skills and a talent and a career, I want all of that, and travel . . . I want to have achieved a lot on my own before I sort of decide to commit to a relationship, I think. Especially to children, because . . . I can imagine once you have children then you really have to put yourself second, I think. And I want to do that for my kids if I have them, so I can't see it for another ten years, really.

Both Yasmin and Rosemary imagine negotiating career and motherhood without sacrificing the former to the latter. However, as Aquarius suggests, today 'a woman can choose whether she wants to have a family or not'. This is the choice Berenice has made, claiming: 'To take any creative pursuit seriously you have to get the time to be on your own to do it'. Of her mother, Berenice writes:

> Once, to describe the imbalance between her personal life and her marriage and family life, she drew a picture in the air. She swung her arms around to make a big boulder and called it her marriage and then she poked her hands into its imaginary crevices and said that the rest, herself and her art, happens in these spaces, growing like mushrooms. For her the art of living has been to work out the contingencies that are possible.

Berenice 'did what she wanted to', while her mother 'has done what she could'. Berenice could leave England for Australia, leave a secure job to pursue her creative work, reckon with no other person's financial needs. But the boulder compressing Berenice's mother was more than the role of motherhood; it was also the invisibility of a woman artist's role. Berenice's mother lived in a time when the woman artist was often seen only as 'self-indulgent or as [having] a hobby'. Berenice can more readily define herself as a professional artist, buttressed by opportunities and avenues that did not exist in her mother's day, such as funding for women's art and different ways of exhibiting and sharing work.[13] More than this, Berenice suggests that today there is greater capacity to innovate the roles like 'mother', 'professional woman', 'artist', which formerly were more fixed. 'I think that that's quite extraordinary, that jump between one generation and the next.'

Yasmin's and Rosemary's lives have traversed new tough and beautiful versions of femininity in modelling, ice-skating and kick-boxing. They have not refused the pleasures of their bodies, as some feminists of an older generation seemed to recommend, but nor have they neglected their minds, seeing these as a much more likely basis for a secure future. They grew up believing that women could do whatever they wanted, and found out that this was not the case. In their struggles against sexism, they have naturally to hand strategies of resistance found in popular feminism and forged in activist feminism. As an example, a lecturer's 'feedback' on Rosemary's work as a director was: 'You're too emotionally unstable to be a director'. Rosemary's immediate response was: 'Please, can we talk about the product I have here'.

Many of the daughters believe they can combine motherhood and a career, and they want both. They are 'traditional' in this respect, as Catherine defines it. And they know the weakest link in their chain of dreams is other mothers' sons:

> I don't like the thought of having children on my own. I'd like a supportive man there too, who I know that I'm going to be with for the rest of my life. And I feel like that's a long way off, me being ready for that kind of relationship and, yeah, finding that person. (Rosemary)
>
> And hopefully the father will have a lot of role in it as well. Hopefully, but I don't know. I know, I think it's changing, I think a lot more men want to as well, to a degree. (Yasmin)

However, if their 'princes' fail to materialise these women will survive much more successfully than their mothers did. Their mothers were raised to complete themselves in marriage, hardly imagining a career, returning to university later in life if at all. This is why the other half of the revolution is so necessary. Men, less needed, must learn to be desired:

> There's all these men at the moment who are sort of leading men's revolutions, and some of them are really gross I think. They're quite angry at what feminism has done, but instead they should be looking to it as a way of liberating them. (Rosemary)

Of course, many mothers said much the same thing to their own husbands, and some of them had their liberation and some of them had a divorce. This would seem to support Phylis's claim that feminism's lessons have to be learned 'over and over' in each generation. The Conclusion to this book evaluates both the immediate past and prospective future of feminism, reviewing the structural changes which have widened women's prospects and the contemporary debates concerning whether feminism has already 'gone too far'.

Conclusion: Feminist Futures?

> If generally the term 'postfeminism' implies that gender equality has been achieved, or was a misguided aim in the first place, . . . it can be used positively to denote a more sophisticated and multifaceted women's movement, or more negatively, to describe a recent tendency in the media to put 'liberated' women firmly in their place. (Lyn Thomas 1995:4–5)

> I'll be a post-feminist in post-patriarchy. (T-shirt message quoted in Trioli 1996:164)

In the quotation above, Lyn Thomas suggests four meanings for postfeminism, the first a true postfeminism beyond the structural inequalities which divide men and women; the second an antifeminism in which feminism's project was never necessary; the third a more complicated understanding of sexual difference contrasted with the simplicities of a universal oppression of women; and the fourth, the backlash against feminism, articulated by Susan Faludi (1991). From the stories and statistics in this book it should be apparent that gender equality has not been achieved at home, at school or at work. Even in the educational sector where such an achievement may be most plausibly argued, women are still under-represented in those disciplines which will lead to higher paying careers. While many young professional women in the workforce today may only substantially confront the challenges of their gender when they decide to have children, women in so-called non-traditional areas – which cover a range of skilled and unskilled pursuits – experience harassment and discrimination.

This book has been a deliberate testament to the claim that gender equality was not 'a misguided aim in the first place'. It has traversed the relationship between changing structural opportunities and women's changed perceptions of themselves and their choices. Structural changes have occurred aside from the feminist movement in some ways, but have also been interwoven with legal and policy changes which enhance women's capacity to seize structural opportunities. The impact of feminist educators in producing the greater success rates of young women at school and university cannot be measured, but is surely significant. Another example is women returning to work in growing numbers before the declaration of Australian women's liberation. But before and since 1969 women have campaigned for equal pay and the removal of the marriage bar. Anti-discrimination and equal opportunity legislation, maternity leave (though generally unpaid) and permanent part-time work have enhanced the working prospects of many women, and not only an elite minority as Kaplan (1996:202) claims – although these may have harvested the greatest benefits. But some women who have benefited from new attitudes to women in the workforce, women like Teresa or Hanna, have made changes in workplace cultures, reformulating management styles and protecting their staff from sexual harassment.

Less difficult to measure, but also articulated by the experiences of the women with whom I spoke, has been the change in attitudes, self-definitions and expectations for women. Indeed, for Kaplan (1996:205) this is perhaps the major exception to the 'meagre harvest'. The previous 'absence' of women from 'public policy and consciousness' and the 'cultural infrastructure' is not only reversed but would now be 'unthinkable'. Feminists campaigned to change attitudes, to expand the acceptable boundaries of femininity to include lesbian and single life choices, to change the acceptable boundaries of masculinity to preclude sexual violence and aggression. The stories of how women responded to the women's movement, told in chapter 5, reveal many women shuttled backwards and forwards between an external world of expanding opportunities, new threatening messages about the 'liberated' women and their internal familiar self-definitions and lifestyles. In changing their lives these women gradually changed and realigned both their practices and their self-definitions. Minor revolts concerning housework reverberated in changed self-conceptions; apparently innocuous decisions to return to study led to divorce and a new career; belief in their daughters' equal right to an education produced self-assured young women who devise life plans. In some of its manifestations at least, feminism has increased the choices for a majority of women – if not equally – for example, in relation to state support for women who leave violent husbands, or the opportunity to improve qualifications and occupational rewards. As suggested by the experiences told in chapter 3 on work and chapter 6 on the responses of women from non-Anglo backgrounds, the women's movement has not undone the inequalities based on class and ethnicity, although it has smoothed some of them.

In relation to the last two definitions of postfeminism offered by Lyn Thomas – a more complicated understanding of sexual difference and the backlash against feminism – one might ponder whether some of the contemporary popular debates are a positive indication of the complexity of feminist thought or an expression of a backlash. When women say: 'I'm not a feminist, but . . .', are they rejecting something which they see as unsophisticated and unidimensional (for example, 'man-hating') or are they rejecting something which is still seen as too radical, but which feminists hope will one day be just as widely endorsed as equal employment opportunity and shared parenting? This question is explored in relation to two issues which emerged while I was writing this book – quotas for women as candidates in winnable parliamentary seats and sexual harassment. The first points us to an individualist versus a collectivist orientation to women's rights; the second explores the way a focus on sexuality issues has been rendered as 'victim' feminism.

Entitlement Feminism and Social Justice

> I'm a girl, so I'm a feminist. As a woman on her own, whether you call yourself a feminist or not is immaterial. As a single parent and then in a profession where you've got an inappropriate background so you're professionally alone, the fact that you keep going in that profession means feminism has to be part of you. (Nadine)

Anne Summers (1994b) inveighs against qualifiers like 'I'm the sort of feminist that wears lipstick and likes men' or 'wants to have children', because feminism 'always was about women having the right to do whatever you want'. Adjectival feminists call themselves feminists, but with a caveat that distinguishes them from more 'radical' feminists. Thus, Mayra says:

> I know I'm feminist right through to the core – but sometimes you find yourself clarifying what type of feminist you are. I really believe women have a right to be who they are, to be individual people. They're not some appendage to a man. That's where I am with feminism.

Agnes defines herself as a 'hands-on feminist', a woman engineer who went into underground mines in the 1960s but has only recently started reading feminist books. For Agnes, feminism means 'if I have the ability to do it then I am allowed to do it . . . regardless of my gender'. Fiorenza, Halina and Aileen describe their feminism in almost identical terms. Halina, 'always a feminist', claims 'whatever I wanted to do I was going to be allowed to do'. Fiorenza has always been 'a natural feminist', 'insofar as I have always felt that what I wanted to do, as long as I was capable, I would, regardless of whether or not it was seen as relevant or not to women'. Aileen initially felt feminism merely reinforced 'what I believed about myself anyway and the way I'd been raised, that I could do anything that I wanted to'.

At first glance it would appear that these women are referring to what Beverley Skeggs (1995:477) calls entitlement feminism, 'individual entitlement' to 'decent work' and education, which she contrasts with a commitment to collective entitlements. Indeed, Gisela Kaplan (1996: 154) seems to suggest this is the major difference between the women's movement in its radical phase which peaked in the mid-1970s and the 'dead years' of the 1980s. Kathy Bail (1996:3–4, 16) rejects 'institutionalised feminism' for 'DIY feminism' in which feminists are identified through their passions like music and publishing fanzines (magazines produced in small numbers with home-based desk-top publication and distributed by their authors) 'before their gender' and in which 'individual practice' and 'personal challenges' are much more important than 'group identification'. Thus, Trioli (1996:64) suggests that 'young women are being encouraged to go it alone – and without ideology'. Sociological discourses explain disadvantage in terms of structural inequalities and were well represented in many public policy formulations up until the 1970s when they were radically sharpened by New Left explanations of the persistent class inequalities inevitably produced by capitalism. By the 1990s economic rationalism became the dominant discourse in public policy, asserting a user-pays principle for all commodities, including water, food and shelter. Claims that inequalities are based on inherited differences in intelligence are re-emerging to justify growing discrepancies in income and increasing poverty (Kaplan 1996:159, 160, 204).

Feminisms are influenced by the societies which host them. The politics of change must find a successful purchase through the values already endorsed in society, even if those values are renegotiated by feminist intervention. Thus, it is not surprising that the most enduring brand of feminism in the Anglophone west has been liberal feminism, even if qualified in countries like Britain and Australia by some purchase gained through social democratic referents. Individualism imagines a society of more or less equal opportunity, a conception of the world which denies deep-seated divisions between groups of people. According to Kaplan (1996:13), Australia's belief in egalitarianism may undermine rather than support collectivist or class-based understandings of inequality. It operates as a 'culture of concealment', disguising class and power inequalities from those who do not experience them.

Some of the women with whom I spoke, even as they articulated the right to equal opportunity in their own lives, also noted that Australian women seemed to have no conception of class and 'were really shattered by anybody who wanted to talk about stuff like that, thought you were a communist!' (Fiorenza); 'in a society like this you cannot make radical changes because people ... are programmed not to move the status quo' (Gladys); 'the word [Marxist] didn't exist in their vocabulary' (Lita); 'there is also a lack of awareness or a reluctance to acknowledge what the international market economy does to the position of women from Third World countries' (Indrani). Anne Summers reports that some migrant women saw her strategies as 'Anglo-elitist shit' (in Eisenstein 1996:119). Women activists from a South American background view Australian women's organisations as politically backward and suffocated by the presence of male government ministers invited to address meetings (Kalantzis 1990:40–1). When Lita, as the ANESBWA representative on CAPOW!, tried to raise issues about the inclusion of disadvantaged people and the unemployed, the 'self-interested middle-class' members resisted her suggestions. Australian-born women from working-class backgrounds also criticise the middle-class orientation of many feminists (Walker 1991:106; Joy Baluch in Mitchell 1984:103). Nadine suggests that 'it's been so easy for them [some feminists] to take on a feminist stand', in comparison with her issues as 'a girl who doesn't have good teeth or the right accent'.

Mainstream feminism is accused of being individualist, lacking an understanding of the class inequalities which divide women. From within this individualist orientation, some women define feminism as personally irrelevant because they were already strong, already had the opportunity to do whatever they wanted. Such women deem feminism as a 'misguided aim in the first place', as unnecessary, in terms of the typology with which we started this chapter (Thomas 1995:4–5). Dame Mary Durack (in Mitchell 1987:190) 'never agitated for women's rights. I've always taken it for granted I've got them'. Nikita describes herself as 'not a feminist but a strong woman within my own family and within myself', who has not been 'personally' affected by the women's movement. Similarly, Jan did not need the women's movement because she was already 'liberated', 'treated equally' and 'could do what I wanted to do'. Jan adds that the women's movement has given other women choices, changed expectations, put women on an 'equal par' in the community. Jan's distinction between her own needs and those of other women might explain the tension in her remarks. She says: 'I feel now that we're accepted as equal to men', but immediately qualifies it with 'But I've never felt inferior to men anyway'. She notes that older women agree with her that the women's movement has not 'made any difference whatsoever', but also comments that women can now drink in bars, and 'in rural areas the hotel is the meeting place'.

Like Jan, Joan and Margaret also initially encountered feminism as something other women needed. Margaret suggests that *The Female Eunuch* made her aware of 'the brutal lives other women led and that something was actually being done about it', but it seemed to have little relevance to Margaret's life as a married mother. But this changed when Margaret 'came back to being a single woman again'. Margaret gave as an example the condescension she experienced when buying a car, before she returned with her daughter who knew all the technical jargon. Joan took little notice of the women's movement at first, thinking 'What the hell are they on about?' In the mid- to late 1970s, she told another woman: '"I think I've always been liberated". But as she knew my life story a bit, you see, she said, "No, Joan, privileged is the word". And that helped me, all of a sudden'.

Whether privileged or not, a number of women embedded their feminism in a social justice framework. For Lea, feminism is 'a strand within social justice, but it's a significant strand. Because I'm a woman and it very much came from struggling with my own experiences and then sharing them with others'. Part of Lea's commitment to social justice has been expressed in empowering school students and adults in the community to make choices through education – 'it's about helping people have control over their lives'. Lea became the foundation principal of a re-entry school in the working-class community of Elizabeth in South Australia, many people describing the school as 'the spirit of Elizabeth coming through'.

Kerry's 'social justice bone' provoked sympathy ('or maybe it was empathy!' she later added) for a boy at school who was constantly picked on, and who 'even looked poorer than us'. Several women link their experiences of abuse and discrimination to 'the added disadvantage of being black' (Carol Hanlon in Hanlon and Stewart 1992:13); as Kerry says, 'try being both [Aboriginal and female] and strong, educated and wait for the fallout!' Some link their feminism with class inequalities (Johnson 1994:18; Rhiannon 1994:96–7; Rehfeldt 1994:167). As Joan, from a Catholic Laborite family, says: 'injustice comes into any of this doesn't it, whether it's racist, or sexist, or ageism, or whatever you like'.[1] Describing herself as a 'stickler for justice', Joan became a social worker in response to white people's 'demeaning' treatment of Indigenous Australians, 'particularly injustices to women and children': 'I don't think I've ever given it the label of feminist, because it was the kind of thinking I always had, if something was unjust it was unjust, no matter who it happened to'. In the United States such embedding of feminism within a social justice framework is less characteristic of younger generations of feminists. Women leaders in their forties and older tend to link their feminism, based on instances of personal discrimination, with 'injustices inflicted on other oppressed groups'. The youngest cohort was more likely to come to feminism through teaching women's studies, although a 'passion for justice and social change' is attributed to all three cohorts (Astin and Leland 1991:34–5,66,38).[2]

The point of much feminist scholarship and activism, however, is not only to say that women are disadvantaged because they are working-class or belong to ethnic minorities, but that they are also disadvantaged as women by structures which are just as concrete as the structures of class or ethnic inequality. Popular feminism seems to shy away from such a concept, not only because it appears to construct all men as the enemy and patriarchal structures as depressingly overwhelming, but also because we live in a society where liberalism is the hegemonic discourse. The success of liberal feminism reflects myopia, both among some feminists and the population at large, concerning the structures of inequality in society, whether they are based on class *or* gender. Thus, when women brand feminism as 'radical' it might not only mean they reject it as 'man-hating'. They also seem to refuse its understanding of women's structural inequalities based both on their gender and their class location. In a survey at Adelaide University those academics who were in favour of affirmative action saw discrimination as systemic, while those who saw the issue as individually based were much more opposed to interventions. More men and women in the humanities than the sciences understood systemic discrimination, although women in the sciences, as opposed to the men, were more willing to endorse 'special efforts' to attract female applicants to jobs (Mayer and Bacchi 1996). These results reveal the impact of theoretical discourses on world views as well as the impact of experience – the women in science – in questioning theoretical discourses. This underpins widespread discomfort with the Australian Labor Party's target of 35 per cent of winnable parliamentary seats to be contested by women by the year 2002 (Office of the Status of Women 1995a:55), which is seen as positive discrimination rather than an attempt to redress women's structural disadvantage.[3]

Agnes asserts that feminism means equal but not greater opportunities for women. Barbara cites a survey in the Queensland Labor Party, where 73 per cent of women said 'selection should be based on qualifications for the job rather than gender'. Barbara describes the 'best' person for the job as the most politically experienced, the one who has served their time in the Party, and the most capable. Thus, 'women's equality' is fine, but not these 'ruthless', 'radical feminists who want to put women on the top' and who take 'unfair advantage of the system', doing the things for which they condemned men. Barbara offers the example of a current affairs presenter who 'went all out to humiliate any male she interviewed and even made Wayne Goss lose his cool', thus deserving to be fired. Rita suggests the majority of so-called 'liberated' women do not analyse their own values before criticising those of others. While at a conference Rita and the other delegates went to a night club which had a male stripper. Rita thought: 'What are these women complaining about when they're doing the same thing to the men as what the men do to them?' Melinda, like Barbara, believes that some feminists want to be superior to men, so that men will have to argue for equal wages in fifty years time. Melinda gives as an example of reverse discrimination the disinclination of the Women's Investment Network to employ men. Melinda agrees that the company's goals included women being in charge of their finances, but suspects that the female managers did not want anyone in the organisation wearing pants and appearing 'dominant'.

However, while some of the women with whom I spoke were critical of quotas, they were also aware of feminist justifications for them, although they found these hard to articulate. Sue suggests: 'surely women can get in on their merits', but goes on to muse that without the quota: 'They still keep putting in men, don't you think?' Sue notes the structural barriers against women, the tension between family and career. Unlike Lea, Sue believes women have no choice but to start their political careers when young and so be accused either of neglecting their children or their political career. Melinda suspects quotas may possibly result in 'whacking in some woman who's useless in the job, where a guy might be better'. But she accepts that employers do discriminate on the basis of sex and sexuality. Melinda is searching for a path between what she calls 'the feminist view' and the 'sexist view'. In fact, she resorts to a very liberal strategy – free speech – to make this possible. Melinda twice comments: 'Everyone's a human and everyone has the right to be heard'. She has no qualms with a feminism or anti-racism which advocates equal speaking space. In this equal speaking space she hopes that the younger generation, her generation, will 'be a bit more, well, prepared to listen' and 'will be a bit more understanding' about issues that divide people. Thus, she desires a solution for women that does not necessitate accepting the reality of systemic disadvantage, that is, a solution based on free speech rather than apparently reverse discrimination. As she notes: 'maybe I believe in an ideal world'.

Without an understanding of the structural barriers which face women, quotas and other affirmative action measures seem 'unfair', seem to disadvantage men. While women from working-class backgrounds can understand how economic inequalities disadvantage poor women (and men), our policy-makers rarely frame any interventions in terms of overcoming those inequalities. Equality of opportunity, in a weak sense, is the best working-class people can hope for – a more or less free public education system, a welfare system that offers a minimum standard of living. Compensatory funds and programs in working-class schools are no longer the order of the day, as was proposed by the Whitlam government in the Karmel Report, for example. Similarly, quotas attempt to redress structural inequalities based on gender: different obligations for childcare, different evaluations by employers and political parties of men and women, different opportunities to accumulate the points by which candidates are judged. I have described women's responses to quotas as discomfort rather than opposition because, in Sue's and Melinda's cases at least, they can understand some of the structural reasons for quotas. Nevertheless, they cannot readily locate quotas within a rhetoric of 'fairness' or a fair go. Or not yet, anyway; this might come, just as equal pay for men and women is now almost universally taken for granted.

Thus, there is widespread support for women's equality of opportunity at work and in the home – at least in terms of domestic chores – in the rhetoric of most Australians. However, along with a reluctance to confront embedded disadvantage, an acceptance of women's bodily autonomy from men's desires has taken longer to crystallise. Indeed, backlash articles and opinions are beginning to emerge, for example, in the storm of debate around the sexual harassment case at Ormond College. In 1995 a judge suggested that where once women's allegations were treated as 'intrinsically unreliable', now they are 'effectively unchallengeable', especially in the case of remembered but long-past assaults (Justice David Ashley in Rachel Hawes, 'Judge fears sex allegations unchallengeable', *Weekend Australian*, 10–11 June 1995:3). This is not to suggest that all discussion in this area is of the backlash variety. See, for example, Camille Guy's (1996) article evaluating incidents like the Cleveland affair in England some years ago; its New Zealand equivalent in 1995 when young girls at Glenelg Children's Health Camp were genitally examined by a woman doctor without their parents' consent; adult daughters in therapy retrieving their repressed histories as incest victims; children who become pawns in custody battles through allegations of incest because of the appointment of workers with 'politically correct' beliefs; and the six young women who attacked lecturer and playwright, Mervyn Thompson, as a rapist and chained him to a tree in 1984. In terms of the 'sexual abuse recovery movement' Janice Haaken (1996) also provides a sympathetic analysis emphasising the widespread occurrence of sexual abuse, although she notes that trauma seems to create both 'intrusive remembering' (flashbacks) as well as 'amnesia for overwhelming events' and 'emotional numbing' so that one would normally expect a woman to have some traces in her memory of the abuse. She also suggests that in some cases abuse recovery may operate unconsciously as 'a socially sanctioned means of breaking free from familial entrapments' (Haaken 1996:1070, 1072).

Refuge advocates and workers have been called 'man-haters', 'lesbians' and 'sluts', while advocates of affirmative action are rarely so named. When the equal opportunity legislation was debated in federal parliament, a newspaper advertisement announced: 'Stop Ryan,

Australia's feminist dictator!' (Eisenstein 1985:113). The presumed rights of men to women's bodies strike deeper chords than the rights of women to an education and an income.

Victim Feminism and Sexuality Issues

> *Question:* Did women's studies mean that you saw the way you were treated before as unfair?
> *Answer:* Unfair? No, everything's unfair. At the time you think: 'This is a real shit', not: 'This is unfair'. Actually, it's interesting because later on when I identified as a feminist I did start seeing things in terms of being unfair. But that was useless. Looking back, it was quite a distraction, because it made me whinge and most of the time I couldn't afford to whinge, to sit down and go: 'Oh, this is so unfair'. Instead, I'd think: 'This is fucked, it's all fucked, it always was but how do I survive, because I have to'. Well, that's the way I see it. (Nadine)

Marilyn Lake (1995b:26) notes: 'A strange thing happened to feminism on its way into the 1990s'. From a definition within or against masculine political systems – liberal, socialist, radical – 'it has in recent times come to be represented as an expression of the alleged attributes of its proponents – hence "victim feminism", "puritan feminism" and now "punitive feminism"'. This third wave of 'feminism' focuses not on 'what is wrong with patriarchy so much as what is wrong with women (or more specifically, feminism)' (Kenny 1996:142). Thus, it is never oneself who is a victim feminist, although those that are have been differentiated from the writer in terms of either generation or privilege. In the quotation above, Nadine claims that the women who can afford to see things as 'unfair' 'whinge' – because they don't have to work out how to survive. Fotini Epanomitis (1996:180, 179) also suggests that 'the victim mentality in feminism is the territory of the privileged women'. Those with little power do not blame patriarchy, which is the 'flip-side of just blaming oneself' but negotiate with what precious little power they have. Again feminism, or at least a strand of it, is condemned for being either middle-class or individualistic, blind to the real structures of disadvantage in society.

Kathy Bail (1996:5) dissociates young women's feminism from victim feminism's dowdy asexual 'culture of complaint'. But for three older women, Alison, Phylis and Joan, it is younger women who adopt victim feminism. Alison suggests that before phrases like 'the glass ceiling' appeared: 'We expected the best, expected to be able to grow'. At art school in the early 1990s Alison and the other students were told: 'You're an *artist*, you're a *woman*. You'll always be *poor*. You've always got to expect to struggle'. While no doubt intended as a call to arms, it was actually 'a sort of negative feeling in feminism': 'struggle but you haven't a chance'. Like Nadine, Phylis as a young woman believed that discrimination was not her fault and focused on developing coping strategies. In the late 1980s in her women's studies course, Phylis 'didn't like the way we were more or less seen as victims'. Joan noted the sentiments in Doris Lessing's autobiography *Under My Skin*: 'when we looked forward to our lives as females, we were not full of fear and foreboding, we felt confident'. However, as she accumulated 'more and more evidence that women were ... treated hideously', Joan realised this attitude was at least partially born of ignorance. In retrospect, Joan was lucky not to have been 'raped over again' 'and, of course, women were raped, and it wasn't even known about'.

Most of the critics of victim feminism are equality feminists of one sort or another, focusing on women's rights to equal opportunities in education, work, domestic duties. Beatrice Faust's 'wimp' feminists are 'revolutionary' feminists, both Marxist and radical, who see either capitalism or men as the enemy. Good sensible reform feminists like herself go about empowering women (Faust 1994:51) and focus on 'basic' economic issues like women's poverty rather than issues like sexual harassment. Similarly, Christina Hoff Sommers (1994:24, 25) and Rene Denfeld (1995:5, 6, 9, 13) contrast the issues for 'truly' underprivileged women with issues of sexuality, vegetarianism and ethnic identity, Denfeld (1995:129–32, 10) adding 'goddess worship'. Sommers (1994:23, 25, 23) claims that 'privileged, middle-class protected women' in academia, women's organisations and bureaucracies are committed to initiating 'women into an appreciation of their subordinate situation in the patriarchy and the joys and comforts of group solidarity'. Daphne Patai and Naretta Koertge (1994:4–7) describe IDPOL, identity politics (which they note 'with satisfaction' could also stand for ideological policing), as a practice by which groups define themselves as disadvantaged or oppressed to 'seize their rightful share of power in the world'. Katie Roiphe (1993:35) criticises female students at Harvard University in 1986 who constructed themselves as helpless rape victims when, in fact, they were privileged and articulate future lawyers and journalists. Naomi Wolf, once located in the victim camp, has reneged from this position, both denying that *The Beauty Myth* was about 'the ways others try to victimize women' (Wolf 1993:140) and asserting a 'power feminism' in *Fire With Fire*.

In these formulations, the 'Noble Victim' (Dixson 1994:244-5) is attacked both for proclaiming her victimhood and for lying about her status, for being a wolf in sheep's clothing. Denfeld's and Sommers' attacks on academic feminism will no doubt be annoying and appear misguided to those of us who labour and learn therein. But it must be asked why younger feminists like Denfeld, Roiphe and Wolf, as well as older feminists like Sommers see the women's movement in the United States as increasingly apolitical in public spaces and non-objective (either too theoretical or too political) in university domains. There seem to be two recurring and inter-related themes which underlie the discontent. Firstly, Wolf and Denfeld see themselves as powerful and independent women rather than victims. Denfeld (1995:181, 250) is more inconsistent here, claiming both that soon the glass ceiling 'will shatter altogether' and that women of her generation, in contrast perhaps with luckier mothers, must 'balance our jobs and a devastating economic situation (roughly one in five members of my generation lives below the poverty line) with our desire to raise a family'.

Secondly, the term 'victim' disguises these women's discomfort with sexuality issues. Victim feminists are identified by their focus on issues like pornography and sexual harassment in which women are policed to refuse sexual relations with men (for example, see Denfeld 1995:93, 84). Equality feminists, by contrast, focus on issues like childcare, birth control, abortion rights, political parity, opposing censorship, dumping women's studies programs, and control of (real) sexual violence including rehabilitation (Denfeld 1995:266–79). Connected with this is a commitment to sexual libertarianism rather than an acceptance that heterosexual sex is almost inevitably an expression of power relations. Denfeld describes victim feminists as 'the New Victorians' because they want to 'create the very same morally pure yet helplessly martyred role that women suffered from a century ago'. This links these books with Australia's text, *The First Stone*, and helps explain the limited impact of Cassandra Pybus's book, *Seduction and Consent*.

Of the young women who 'went to the police' when they were sexually harassed by the master of Ormond College, Helen Garner claims that the feminism they represent is anti-erotic and disempowering: 'priggish, disingenuous, unforgiving' (Garner 1995:93) and a 'creation of a political position based on the virtue of helplessness' (Garner 1995:99). At one point, Garner (1995:163) makes a claim most feminists would reject: that 'sexual assault' is the price of 'the freedoms we demand', to live alone, be in public spaces. 'How can there be such a thing as *safety*? ... It is a woman's responsibility to protect herself against sexual assault.' But Garner retreats from such a claim in the face of 'the immense *weight* of men on women, the ubiquity of their attentions ... it seemed to me an illusion that women could learn to deal with this pressure briskly, forcefully, with humour and grace' (Garner 1995:171), although in a later lecture she deplores 'victimhood' and women's expectation that they can dress as they please and not invoke unwelcome responses (Trioli 1996:31). Thus, like Melinda, Garner wishes the world to be a certain way but fears it is not. The ambivalence in her text is an expression of this debate between desire and experience. Young feminists seem to express desire against experience: good feminism is 'unapologetically sexual; understands that good pleasures make good politics' (Wolf 1993:137); 'just as women of my generation believe in equality, so do the men' (Denfeld 1995:257).

Of course, the policing of women's bodily capacities and availability is the *sine qua non* of patriarchal oppression, as Trioli (1996:34) notes. This is the novel aspect of structural disadvantage which feminist theory has added to the disadvantages based on class and culture. Women who reject so-called 'victim' feminism are not only yearning for better behaved men, they are also refusing to acknowledge that we live in a patriarchal culture. This explains the apparent contradiction in Sommers' (1994:51) analysis, when she asserts that victim feminists are too radical, rather than too weak. She deplores their impatience 'with piecemeal liberal reformist solutions' for 'a more radical transformation of society'. Victim feminists are, in other parlance, radical feminists, women whose voices have lost some of their force since the 1970s; women who explored and condemned the sex-based oppressions built on the meanings of women's and men's bodies; women who still see individual-oriented solutions as inadequate to dislodging patriarchal structures. The analyses offered by Garner, Sommers or Denfeld are a variant of popular feminism, popular in their refusal to address the more intractable differences between men and women. Virginia Trioli (1996:63) captures this 'paradox' as 'an ideology of rampant individualism that travels alongside an assumed understanding of structural discrimination'.

Equal and Different

When women's liberationists shied away from a difference rhetoric in the 1970s it was partly because of the dominance of liberal discourses in western political culture. But it was also because difference had been understood in biological terms and translated as justification for women's limited options and inferiority. Although Lucinda has experienced an attempted rape, she believes women 'are asking to be raped by the way they dress'. Men have a 'basic instinct' which makes them find women 'physically' attractive. Gerda, an accomplished dressmaker, distinguishes between 'flattering', 'dignified' and 'feminine' fashions (including 'necklines that go right down to the waist at the back'), and 'sleazy fashions' like G-string bikinis. The latter tempt 'the poor man': 'they're still human, aren't they?' While Gerda contends that temptation is no excuse, 'still doesn't make it right', she does have some sympathy with men's difficulties. Both Lucinda and Gerda, along with almost all women, reject men's violence. Gerda condemns domestic violence as 'terrible' and 'disgusting', but suggests: 'it's probably because of drinking or some other problem, which has to be addressed as well. So, it's very hard, you still love the person but hate the sin'. Lucinda suggests that women sometimes bring violence on themselves: 'Pre-Germaine Greer days ladies didn't swear' and 'a man would stand up when a lady entered a room'. Instead of meeting abuse with abuse and violence with violence, women should 'try to defuse the situation'.

Lucinda and Gerda interpret feminist issues through a sociobiological lens which asserts the natural differences between men and women. Given this, these differences are challenged with grave consequences to the moral order. Lucinda suggests that women 'like to look appealing' because of the 'inbred' and 'natural process of hunting and looking for males'. Women's attempts to 'go against' their destiny as mothers, to proclaim their superiority at work or their masculinity by swearing, are counterproductive. Although there is a place for women at work, it has its biological limits. Where a female journalist might be entitled to equal pay, a woman carrying heavy burdens is likely 'to wake up with lowered insides' (meaning, perhaps, a fallen womb).

Gerda also draws a sharp distinction between economic equality and moral issues. Equal pay and equal opportunity 'were issues that really needed to be addressed'. But feminists are 'liberating men from responsibility' and thus undermine the dignity of women, as is indicated by men's failure to stand up for women on public transport. Contraception and abortion liberate men from sexual responsibility. The impact of feminist understandings is reflected in Gerda's difficulties in articulating her position. She is: 'not saying that, you have to be treated like, fragile objects, I don't mean that. Our dignity's gone down, as a woman, with who we really are, just through the freedom that's come with contraception and stuff like that'. Like Lucinda, Gerda is troubled by the blurring of gender roles which challenges 'our human nature' and undermines men's 'manhood' and the respect they give to women. Manhood is undermined by 'aggressive' 'strong women', causing men to become gay. Women must say: 'Look, you know, we want you to be men' and recapture some of their 'gentle femininity'. Gerda concludes: 'Maybe we need to look at where we were heading, maybe we've veered off a bit too strongly'.

Because of the demands made on them Rita notes that women need 'a certain aggression to survive'. However, like Gerda and Lucinda, Rita desires an expression of women's equality and not their dominance, through the 'very loving, caring, diplomatic way' women express their power in Italy. In fact, if Australian women had not 'lost the female tactic' of making 'a man look like he's in control', they would have done far more than 'crack the surface' of corporate life. Similarly, Barbara claims that women must 'use one great weapon that is forever at our disposal. Our femininity'. Rita would like to see 'a balance, an equality and a unity, everyone sort of respecting each other for where they're at'.

These women are yearning for a meaning of difference which is not about inequality and oppression but about mutual love and respect. This can be seen in the apparently trivial but pervasive example of 'the car door dilemma': 'If you want to be a bloody feminist, open the door for yourself' (Riley-Smith 1992:39). Yvonne complains that 'men are treating the women as men'. Instead of opening car doors for women: 'they're just as likely to stand outside and whistle and say "I'm here"'. Aquarius claims women have won their independence at the cost of 'first come first served for a seat on the bus and things like that'. Our society can understand the equality rhetoric in which feminists must expect no better treatment than that received by men. And we can understand the difference rhetoric, perhaps most widely voiced in terms of biologically innate different destinies and natures. Thus, opponents of sexual harassment legislation, like Helen Garner, claim that you cannot excise sex, the difference of women, from the workplace. Women like Gerda and Lucinda argue that equality for women in the public sphere affects relations in the private sphere, unmanning men and masculinising women.

But many women 'want equal opportunity, but we also want to be recognised as being different' (member of a focus group in Riley-Smith 1992:39). Liberal feminism's negotiation of this contradiction sends women off to work in suits or overalls to be treated as (well as) men, and to come home at night and share equally in housework or spending the family's budget. But popular feminism also demands that women cherish their difference and that men treat them with respect for being different, for being women. The concept which comes closest to negotiating 'equal but different' is the Kantian concept of equal worth, rendered popularly as 'humanism'. But this also poses dilemmas – for example, on what grounds can we justify when women and men are to be treated differently and when the same? How do we maintain a sense of women's difference as not inferiority? It is so easy to conclude that people come in a best sex, masculine, and a second sex, feminine.

However, it has been one of the great achievements of the women's movement, both here and elsewhere in the world, to convert apparent contradictions into unquestioned truths. To allow women to really become workers, it has been necessary to provide maternity leave and flexible working arrangements. To ensure these provisions do not discriminate against women they must be extended to and taken up by fathers. To reconstruct violence as something more than an expression of private domestic relations, feminists have calculated its economic costs and noted its impact on an efficient workforce. Being perhaps unduly optimistic in the face of global capitalism, economic rationalism, the persistence of patriarchal structures and the dominance of liberal discourses in the Australian environment, I do not think that the debates over quotas and sexual harassment are the end of the feminist chapter, but merely a paragraph in which new expanded notions of equity and femininity are being contested and constructed.

This book has sought to reveal the flow of feminism, the relationship between structure and agency as it is experienced, refused, seized, delayed in different ways by women with very different opportunities. Even so, the stories told by women across three generations reveal that the lessons are not completely different, even if they are not entirely the same. Every woman with whom I spoke could see some advantages from feminism, if not in her own life in the lives of others. In their actions, both small and large, the energies of the sixty women gathered between these covers have helped turn 'the wheel of time, to grind out a new era' (Louisa Lawson in 1889 quoted in Scutt 1991:xviii).

APPENDIX 1

Life Chances Data and Sources

Table A1.1 Life chances of three generations of Australian women

Characteristic			Grandmothers aged 65–75 %	Mothers aged 45–55 %	Daughters aged 25–35 %
Not completed secondary education		F	65	53	35
		M	47	35	30
Tertiary qualifications		F	3	6	13
		M	8	13	14
Remained single			5	11	20–25
Age at first marriage			21	22	25
Married by age 24			59	1971: 64	27
				1981: 46	
Family size			3	2	1.8
Remained childless			11	20	–
Median age first birth			–	23.7	26.1
Percentage of marriages ending in divorce			9–12	35–38	33–50
Labour force participation	1966		40	–	–
	1976		49	48	–
	1986		29	65	73
	projected			39	85
	male		77	88	93
Wages as % men's 1990s			80	71	90
Life expectancy			67	73	78

Sources: Australian Bureau of Statistics 1986:58,60; 1988b:16; 1992:168; 1993a:24, 29, 37, 120, 181; 1993c:44; Bureau of Immigration, Multicultural and Population Research 1996:34; Burns 1994:281, 283; Grimshaw et al. 1994:208; McDonald 1989; 1990:15–16; Peter McDonald, personal communication, September 1995; McGregor and Hopkins 1991:3; Office of the Status of Women 1992:10; Office of the Status of Women 1995a:20, Appendix 2.6, Appendix 2.8, Appendix 2.15.

APPENDIX 1

Table A1.2 Life chances of the sixty women in the study*

Socio-economic characteristic	Grandmothers (1914–32) %	Mothers (1935–55) %	Daughters (1956–72) %
Number in sample	12	34	14
Ethnic backgrounds:			
Anglo/Celtic	33 (72)[a,c]	50 (68)[a,c]	43 (85)[a,c]
First or second generation NESB	25	38	29
English	42	6	7
Indigenous Australian	0	6	21
Class of parents:[b]			
Working-class	50	59 (34)[c]	54 (23)[c]
Middle-class	50	41 (66)[c]	46 (77)[c]
Class of self:[b]			
Working-class	17 (34)[c]	9 (23)[c]	0
Middle-class	83 (66)[c]	91 (77)[c]	100
Education:			
Not completed high school	58 (65)	19 (53)	25 (35)
Post-secondary or high school certificate	25	31	25
Tertiary (enrolled or completed)	17 (3)[c,d]	50 (6)[c,d]	50 (13)[c,d]
Mature-age tertiary – enrolled or completed[g]	42	34	42
Marital status:			
Married or widowed	92	67	36
Divorced or separated	8	18	21
Single, lesbian partnership, etc.	0 (5)[c]	15 (11)[c]	42 (20–25)[c]
Geographical location:			
Now living non-urban	42	3	0
Born and early years non-urban	8	26	29
Lived at some time non-urban	8	3	7
Capital city	42	68 (84)[c,e]	64 (85)[c,e]
Status of daughters:			
Middle-class[b]	86	92	–
Tertiary enrolled or completed	43	56 (13)[c]	–
Average family size:			
Family of origin	4.1	3.4	4.4
Family of formation	3.3 (3.0)[c]	2.6[f] (2)[c]	1.4 (1.8)[c]

*Table A1.2 shows summary characteristics of the sixty women with whom I spoke compared with those of the population as a whole. The generations do not exactly match those of the cohorts discussed in the Introduction to this book, which has some influence on the results, but the major impact was the deliberate choice of theoretical sampling, to concentrate on women from lower socio-economic backgrounds, non-English speaking backgrounds, Indigenous Australian woman and women living outside the capital cities.

Notes to Table A1.2:

a In 1981, 72.4 per cent of women aged 55–59 were born in Australia, 68.1 per cent of women aged 35–44 were born in Australia and 84.9 per cent of women aged 15–19 were born in Australia (Australian Bureau of Statistics 1983:3).
b Based on occupation, so that those which generally require a degree (professional, managerial, etc.) as well as pink-collar workers such as sales and clerical were classified as middle-class, while casual work as well as unskilled and other blue-collar occupations were defined as working-class.
c Figures in parentheses are for the total Australian population where this data is available.
d The figures for the Australian population are for those who completed tertiary qualifications. The high level of tertiary completion rates in both the mothers and daughters is partly attributable to high educational levels among my sample of non-English speaking background women.
e Urban dwelling population, that is, living in centres of more than 1000 people (Australian Bureau of Statistics 1993b:9).
f 2.1 if Gerda's family of fourteen is excluded.
g Educational qualifications are more than 100 per cent if this figure is included.

Sources: Australian Bureau of Statistics 1986:58,60; 1988b:16; 1992:168; 1993a:24, 29, 37, 120, 181; 1993c:44, Bureau of Immigration, Multicultural and Population Research 1996:34; Burns 1994:281, 283; Grimshaw et al. 1994:208; McDonald 1989; 1990:15–16; Peter McDonald, personal communication, September 1995; McGregor and Hopkins 1991:3; Office of the Status of Women 1992:10, Office of the Status of Women 1995a:20, Appendix 2.6, Appendix 2.8, Appendix 2.15.

APPENDIX 2

Snowball and Other Strategies for Identifying Women Interviewed

The majority of the women who were interviewed were drawn from five 'samples'. Most of the women from non-English speaking backgrounds were part of a phenomenal network which Halina Netzel kindly shared with me. Further 'snowball' interviews were produced from this sample, for example, Agnes Whiten recommended two women whom I contacted through the Association of Non-English Speaking Women of Australia. Additionally, I contacted the President of the Vietnamese Women's Association who referred me to a founding mover of this Association. Griffith University allowed me to send a letter to all enrolled students over the age of 45, asking them to contact me if they were willing to be interviewed. I wrote to women in postcode areas which potentially indicated a lower socio-economic status (Rochedale, Acacia Ridge, Beaudesert, Oxley, Wilston, Inala, Daisy Hill). There was a 50 per cent response rate, although the majority of women who replied had some previous contact with me as a lecturer. To speak with women from rural and regional areas, I contacted the Queensland Country Women's Association, while Rosemary McBain of the Far North Queensland Family Resource Services kindly provided me with the names of women in Cairns from a variety of backgrounds. Fourthly, I interviewed three Indigenous Australian women I had met prior to the commencement of the project. One of these women, Aileen Moreton-Robinson, very kindly introduced me to a further three Indigenous Australian women. All these women were tertiary-educated, although born into what white Australia would probably consider economically deprived circumstances.

Possibly the most contentious 'sample' was my network of friends and acquaintances and their friends and acquaintances, from whom I drew three groups: women who had a moment of engagement with feminism, some of whom said their lives had been changed as a result; women in unusual occupations, ranging from police officer to former nun; women living as lesbians. Clearly, in a discipline which calls itself a social *science*, interviewing friends would be seen as lacking in objectivity and representation. My sample of women is not representative of each of their generations, as is shown above, even in crude statistical terms; nor was it meant to be. Furthermore, discussions with women in this fifth 'sample' produced, on the whole, a much more self-revealing engagement with the issues (some of which were extremely intimate), than did the interviews with the strangers in my group, who tended to adopt more of an 'official' life story as opposed to an interior self-questioning.

Notes

Introduction

1 Gisela Kaplan 1992:xx, who (Kaplan 1996:xiii) suggests a more pessimistic analysis of the Australian women's movement in her new book *The Meagre Harvest*; Marilyn French visiting from the United States, in Sawer and Groves 1994a:83; Hugh Mackay in Sawer and Groves 1994a:83; Steve Biddulph 1994:18.

2 In 1973–4 women earned incomes equal to half those of men; for those in full-time employment the rate was 65 per cent. By 1989–90 women who earned an income received 60 per cent of that earned by men; for full-time workers 75 per cent (Australian Bureau of Statistics 1993a:179). In the mid-1990s a woman who is single earns on average $79 less than the male $704 weekly earnings. Married women, however, earn $256 a week less (Trioli 1996:53).

3 There was a major increase in men's housework contributions between 1974 and 1987, but men born after 1957 do almost no extra housework over those born before 1957, apart from a little more time spent on cooking (Bittman 1995:12). In the late 1980s men with wives in paid employment spent about half as many hours on housework and childcare as their wives, who clocked up 43 to 56 hours per week (the former employed full-time and the latter part-time – Baxter and Gibson 1990:19, 22, 24). Recent data, however, suggests that full-time working wives have reduced their total paid and unpaid hours so that they only exceed those of their husbands by about 6 hours (Bryson 1996:214 citing Australian Bureau of Statistics data).

4 For example, contrast Sawer (1990), Franzway et al. (1989:133–55) and Yeatman (1990) on the effects of femocracy.

5 My definition of 'notable' is that of women as yet unpublished, although I have deliberately not interviewed 'famous' feminists, either as activists, femocrats or academics (Susan Magarey, Ann Curthoys and Marilyn Lake are writing a history of post-war feminism in Australia based, in part, on these women's reminiscences). However, as Heather Radi (1988a:xi) says in the introduction to the collected biographies of 200 women (at least half of whom were sufficiently well-known to appear in the *Australian Dictionary of Biography*), Eliza Pottie, inspired by her Christian beliefs to work for social

reform, was as well known in her time as Rose Scott but 'Scott is remembered; Pottie is forgotten. The preoccupations of later generations shape the recollection of the past' (Radi 1988a:xii).

6 In some of these collections, for example, see Susan Mitchell (1984, 1987, 1991), the focus is unashamedly on high-profile women. The 'Women's Voices, Women's Lives' series by Scutt (1995, 1994, 1993a, 1993b, 1992a, 1992b, 1987, 1985a, with several more in preparation) is described as 'more than a dozen volumes' which 'contain the stories of 350 women from all walks of life, written around themes of career and work, networks and influences, growing older, travelling and living in Australia and overseas, political activism and debate, life in the city and country, living alone and independently, women as mentors, women as mothers and daughters, women as sisters, young women as feminists, women joining the Women's Movement' (advertisement on inside back cover of *Australian Book Review* no. 173, August 1995, which goes on to list among the contributors women like Moira Rayner, Joan Kirner, Faith Bandler and Jean Arnot with their occupational designations). Thus, many voices gathered by Scutt are those of women whose names are familiar, at least in some circles.

7 The choice of these sites should cause no surprise and is supported by other research, for example, Christine Dann's (1985) survey of women's liberation in New Zealand contains chapters on politics, fertility, work, health, education 'Soul and Skin' (the peace movement, pornography, sexuality, the media), creativity and violence. Inger Agger (1994:16–17) addressed the personal lives of political refugees from the Middle East and South America through a list developed by New York Radical Feminists in the late 1960s which covered sexual development, sexual trauma, marriage, housework, pregnancies, births, motherhood, divorce and work.

8 Political refugees told Inger Agger (1994:16–17), a trained counsellor, amazingly intimate stories concerning their sexuality in Muslim or South American environments. However, a number of researchers speak of the felt lack of counselling skills in the face of intimate and painful stories in women's lives (for example, see Anderson in Anderson and Jack 1991:13).

9 There is some slippage in the definition of generations, both in this book and in general definitions. 'Baby boomers' were born between 1946 and 1960 and 'Generation X-ers' between 1961 and 1972 according to Safe and Whittaker (1994:10). Due to the vagaries associated with locating interviewees, the grandmothers in my study were actually aged between 63 and 80, the mothers were aged between 42 and 60 (the oldest because she had adopted a daughter when she was in her forties), and the daughters were aged between 23 and 40. Women on the cusp were allocated to either the daughters' or the mothers' generation on the basis of the stage of their life cycle. This adapts Karl Mannheim's suggestion that a political generation, as opposed to a biological one, experiences shared social conditions which contribute towards a shared culture and identity distinguishing it from previous generations (Whittier 1995:16).

10 From 43 per cent in 1984 to match the total female rate of 52 per cent in 1994 (Office of the Status of Women 1995a:43). Participation rates were lower for women of non-English speaking backgrounds (45.3 per cent – Women's Policy Unit 1994:2) and Indigenous Australian women. At the 1991 census 40 per cent of Aboriginal and Torres Strait Islander women were in the labour force, although 27.5 per cent were unemployed; the majority worked in the community service sector.

11 Between 1971 and 1981 the percentage of women married by the age of 24 fell from two-thirds to one-half, the rates being higher for Greek- and Italian-born women and lower for Asian-born women (Carmichael 1988:84).
12 I say 'arguably' because it has also been claimed that it was not young women in the universities in the 1960s who instigated women's liberation. Rather, it was their mothers who read Friedan and went back to college or work, sometimes spurred by divorce (Coontz 1992:164–6; see also Douglas 1994: 125). These women were later joined by the campus radicals outraged by their treatment in left politics.
13 In Australia baby boomers are a significant generation, comprising 30.5 per cent of the population in 1960, when they were all under 15 years old, and over half the Labor government's cabinet in 1994, although the entrepreneurial generation tends to be older, seven of the nine wealthiest entrepreneurs being born before 1945 (Safe and Whittaker 1994:11,16).
14 Bernadette Selfe (1995:244), also an Indigenous Australian, had a similar experience. The teacher never turned to her when her hand was up but would often select her when her hand was down, 'despite my indicating as clearly as could be that I did not know the answer'.

Part I Women's Lives Through A Feminist Lens

1 In 1894 South Australian women were the first women in the world to win the right to stand for parliament (Haines 1992a:51). They also won the vote more than fifty years after the first men won a limited franchise in an 1842 Act (Oldfield 1992:68), but New Zealand women had won it in 1893. There was a brief moment in 1864 when some women voted in Victoria under ratepayers' voting legislation (Haines 1992a:50).
2 In 1992 ranging between 6.1 per cent of the Members of the House of Representatives and 22.4 per cent of the Senate (Inquiry into Equal Opportunity and Equal Status for Women in Australia 1992:51, 59) and 15 (Western Australia) and 30 per cent (Northern Territory) of local government representatives (House of Representatives Standing Committee on Legal and Constitutional Affairs 1992:164). Marlene Goldsmith (1994:182, 183) remembers a day in 1991 when she was in the chair of the Legislative Council of New South Wales 'with a female minister leading for the government, a woman leading for the opposition, two female clerks and the only males being parliamentary attendants and a few backbenchers'.
3 There were still no women judges in the Supreme Courts of Tasmania, Western Australia, Victoria and Queensland in 1990 (Office of the Status of Women 1992:87; Rathus 1993:3). In the early 1990s there were seven women among the fifty-two Family Court judges, four among thirty-four Federal Court judges, and six among the 144 State and Territory Supreme Court judges, and around 8–15 per cent of magistrates although the Chief Magistrate in the Northern Territory was female; women represent less than 10 per cent of federal judicial officers (Law Reform Commission 1994:201; Office of the Status of Women 1992:87).
4 The first Australian Women's Charter Conference held in 1943 and organised by the United Associations of Women (Weeks 1994:16–17), represented ninety organisations and was larger than any feminist conferences previously held. The delegates, feminists mainly in their forties and fifties, demanded political and economic opportunities. In their refusal of 'vice' and 'seduction', they could not accommodate young women's 'female sexual desire' (Lake 1995a:72).

5 For example, see Eve Mahlab, who drafted WEL's Constitution, in Mitchell 1984:54.
6 The first women's advisor, Elizabeth Reid, was appointed in 1973 to assist the Prime Minister Gough Whitlam on women's issues. The first true femocrat, Sara Dowse, was appointed in 1974 to head the Women's Affairs section, renamed the Office of the Status of Women (OSW) in 1974 (Weeks 1994:18). Several hundred Australian feminists entered the bureaucracy in various States and federally in the following decade (Ryan 1990:83). In 1976 Labor governments were elected in Tasmania, South Australia and New South Wales; all appointed women's advisors and femocrat energy moved to the States. The Wran government in New South Wales appointed Carmel Niland as women's advisor in 1977, while women's advisors were appointed in the Northern Territory in 1982-3, in Western Australia in 1983-4 and in Queensland with the election of the Goss government in 1989.
7 For further references to the impact of the women's movement, see the edited collections by Broom (1984) and Baldock and Cass (1988) for welfare initiatives; a range of works which address women's working experiences, for example, Alford (1984), Mumford (1988) and O'Donnell and Hall (1988); Scutt (1990) and Graycar and Morgan (1990) for feminist interventions in the law.
8 The others are the recession, the reduced ability of first home buyers to buy a house, the spread of values which suggest marriage is not the only legitimate forum for sexual activity, the pressures put on marriage by the emphasis on individual satisfaction, and the fact that marriage became a less pivotal life cycle event in the face of emerging alternative options (Carmichael 1992:123-4; McDonald 1989:103; McDonald 1990:13, 14).

Chapter 1 Growing Up As Girls

1 Yasmin is referring to a different sense of touch from Young's sense. Young means the touch which appropriates, often in a sexual or condescending register (although it can also reflect greater intimacy between women). Yasmin means rough-house touching which is associated with sports and active play, and which can be perceived as more dangerous than it is until experienced.
2 See Grieve 1994:262-6, 170; Davies 1988:132-3. Anna notes that during play lunch at her son's kindergarten the latecomers were forced to sit at the mixed table once the boys' and girls' separate tables had filled up.
3 Three and a half hours compared with two hours a week (Bittman 1991:53). Johanna Wyn (1990:122) reports similar findings for girls from non-Anglo backgrounds in Melbourne in the mid-1980s, while in a rural Victorian town girls washed and ironed their brothers' clothes but boys did not do jobs for their sisters (Dempsey 1992:188-95).
4 Women's sport was less than 2 per cent of all media sports coverage in a 1990 survey (*Courier-Mail* 6/9/90:3). Netball is the sixth most popular game, with more registered players than rugby league. When netball recently achieved television coverage, players were asked to play in lycra body suits and were interviewed after the game without a trace of perspiration (Burroughs 1993:22-3).
5 Although Grace suggests that the secrecy might be about mystique rather than shame, women keeping 'a power base' through this '"woman" thing'.

6 R. W. Connell (1987:183) defines hegemonic masculinity as that which is most idealised and rewarded in patriarchal societies. In contrast, emphasised femininity is 'defined around compliance with this subordination [of women to men]', in contrast with forms of femininity based on strategies of resistance or non-compliance.

7 Studies suggest that sexual abuse of girls ranges between 5 per cent and 25 per cent and for boys is about 12 per cent. When sexual harassment was also included, Hite's latest report discovered that 31 per cent of young women had suffered sexual abuse from a male relative (Allen 1987:209; Allen 1989:237; Goldman and Goldman 1988:94-106; Hite 1994:215).

8 In 1992 Justice Bollen of the South Australian Supreme Court said that a husband was entitled to 'persuade' his wife to accept intercourse via 'a measure of rougher than usual handling' (Women's Health Policy Unit 1993b:34). In 1994 Justice Bland of the Victorian County Court repeated the often-stated claim that a woman who said 'no' to sexual advances often meant 'yes'. Both comments caused wide press coverage, expressing the 'outrage' of feminists, 'a barometer both of how much has changed – and what has not' (Summers 1994a:47).

Chapter 2 Training for Life

1 See Szirom 1991:130 for the influence of mothers on executive women. See Coate 1992:170; Scutt 1992:218; Maggie Tabberer in Mitchell 1984:113; Tom 1993:25; Spender 1992:51; Reynolds 1993:116 as women from Anglo-Celtic backgrounds. See Cafarella 1992:9; Ambikapathy 1992:222–4; Kaplan 1996:8 as immigrants to Australia.

2 OPAL (One People of Australia League) was founded in Brisbane in 1961 and has been criticised for being conservative and assimilationist. However, OPAL was one of the few Aboriginal organisations which existed before the election of the Whitlam government in 1972. Rita Huggins, director for twenty years, said OPAL allowed her to 'use my Aboriginality as a force, without being made to feel shame' (Rita Huggins in Huggins and Huggins 1994:101,87).

3 Women now make up 55 per cent of commencing university students, and still make up more than half if nursing is not counted in the figures (Office of the Status of Women 1992:10,109). While women are concentrated in the arts, humanities and nursing courses, they also make up at least 40 per cent of commencing students in medicine, business studies and veterinary science as well as higher degree courses. Only the male bastions of computing and engineering remain, women being only 12.5 per cent of engineering students (Geoff Maslen, 'Gender roles swapped', *Campus Review*, 30 March – 5 April 1995:1; Office of the Status of Women 1995a:16; Office of the Status of Women 1992:110–11). Of those aged 25 to 34 years old in 1989-90, 2.9 per cent of women and 30.9 per cent of men had trade certificates. In 1991 the enrolment of males in trades and other skills courses was almost twice that of females (Australian Bureau of Statistics 1993a:97). In the late 1980s participation of non-English speaking background people and Indigenous Australians was disproportionately low, but the rates for males and females was more equal (Pocock 1988:27, 33, 30, 31).

4 Lewis 1993:277-8; see also Lynne Spender 1992:51 for arts undergraduates; Rayner 1994:159 and Scutt 1992:219 for law students and staff in the mid-1960s and Clark 1990:39 for the late 1980s. In contrast, I found that the

gender-balanced law classes at the University of Queensland in the late 1980s responded with an uncomfortable silence to the classic sexist law 'jokes' (such as: 'bigamy is having two wives too many', or in an updated version, 'two mothers-in-law too many').

5 In contrast, Jan Carter found that for women born around the turn of the century, 'great-grandmothers' in the context of my study, 'early opportunities were shaped considerably by the occupation of the fathers', few women moving from their social origins (Carter 1981:4, 212). The level of education women received was strongly correlated with both father's class and their own occupations. Those from middle-class backgrounds became nurses and teachers, whereas those born into blue-collar families went into domestic service or became factory workers (Carter 1981:147, 163, 170, 204).

6 *The Women's Room* (1978), written by Marilyn French, charts the life of a woman who leaves an unsatisfactory marriage and finds herself through university studies, ultimately becoming an academic. As Teresa returned to university after the publication of French's novel, she is referring to women's changing expectations, as reflected in the book.

7 In 1990 only 10 per cent of Indigenous Australians over the age of 15 years held a post-secondary qualification compared with one-third of the total population (Senate Standing Committee on Employment, Education and Training 1990:16). The percentage of Indigenous Australian females who had a degree or higher in 1991 was 0.9 per cent (Office of the Status of Women 1995a:Appendix 2.9).

Chapter 3 Work

1 In 1992 women made up 42 per cent of employed persons; 32 per cent of those employed full-time and 75 per cent of those employed part-time. Women were twice as likely as men to be employed on a casual basis (Australia Bureau of Statistics 1993:123, 124).

2 Until quite recently even female-dominated occupations like nursing or clerical work were represented by male union leaders. Anna Booth became National Secretary of the then Clothing and Allied Trades Union of Australia in 1987 (Franzway 1994:41). In 1981 Jennie George of the New South Wales Teachers' Federation became the first woman to be elected to the ACTU executive, and is the first female vice-president and president (which she became in 1995).

3 See Sharp and Broomhill's (1988:130–58) sustained analysis of women's exclusion based on their part-time status, breaks from paid work, and disproportionate representation in occupational categories which do not have cover. Women still suffer from lack of access to superannuation funds, in 1991, 44 per cent of women in employment and 58 per cent of men in employment being covered by a scheme (House of Representatives Standing Committee on Legal and Constitutional Affairs 1992:97).

4 With the inclusion of overtime, women earned 78 per cent of what men earned per hour. Women's mean income in 1989–90 was about half of men's, $14 000 (Australian Bureau of Statistics 1993a:170); 70 per cent of Aboriginal and Torres Strait Islander women earned less than $16 000 (Women's Policy Unit 1994:3). Women's earnings are 77 per cent of men's for professionals and clerks, 70 per cent for managers and administrators, compared with 61 per cent for plant and machine operators and drivers (Australian Bureau of Statistics 1993a:183).

5 Union membership rates have fallen throughout the 1980s, so that in 1992 only 40 per cent of all wage and salary earners belonged to a union (for women the figure was 35 per cent) (Shute 1994:167–8; Booth and Rubenstein 1990:121). An ACTU survey in 1988 revealed that women expressed greater hostility towards unions, associating them with 'intimidation, thuggery and irresponsible strike action' (Shute 1994:169), results reproduced in a survey in South Australia in 1994, where women's distaste for unions increased with their length of association with them (study by Barbara Pocock reported in the *Weekend Australian*, 2–3 July 1994:10).

6 During 1991–2, of over 800 complaints under the Sex Discrimination Act, 46 per cent involved sexual harassment in employment (*OSWOMEN*, newsletter from Office of the Status of Women, 1992, no. 15 (December):4), complaints rising by another 50 per cent in Victoria the following year (*Age*, 4 October 1993). On Victorian figures, more than 2 per cent of working women make inquiries annually while about 0.05 per cent lay formal complaints (Trioli 1996:83–4).

7 *The First Stone* sold 30 000 copies in its first few weeks, generated a *Four Corners* program, feminist analyses (for example, see McDonald 1995; Curthoys 1995; Pybus 1995; Koval 1995) and other widespread media coverage, including *Who Weekly* (1 January 1996:70 who named Garner – 'the thrice-married feminist' – among the 'The 25 most intriguing people of 1995'). Garner's book is described as creating a 'backlash' in which critics 'howled that she'd betrayed the feminist cause' and Jenna Mead, Ormond College's former Committee for Equal Opportunity convenor, called it 'a shitty little book'. Garner retorted at the Sydney Institute 'black-tie dinner' against feminism's 'grimmer tribes' and 'perverse and idiotic' academics. Two publications by young feminists in 1996 explore the issues raised by *The First Stone*. See Bail (1996:9) who describes one of the complainants as now 'no victim ... she seemed more likely to want her feminism in a fun and feisty package' and Trioli (1996:8) who opens her book with a discussion of the issue, noting a harassing colleague who later rang, apologised and said it would never happen again – possibly a result of the legislation.

8 Katie Roiphe, a young woman, is just as critical as Garner of students (at Harvard University) who refused to face the fact that they wanted sexual attention and dressed to prove it (Roiphe 1993:125). Like Garner, she asserts: 'To find wanted sexual attention, you have to give and receive a certain amount of unwanted sexual attention' (Roiphe 1993:87). Prohibition of staff–student sexual relations in academia by removing the presumption that such relations are consensual is suggested with good reason, no more strange than the ethical rule that doctors should not have sexual relations with their patients (Bacchi 1994:55).

9 However, there are cases of its use by blue-collar workers. In *Najdovska v. Australian Iron and Steel* (1988), a group of women working for a subsidiary of Broken Hill Proprietary Company Limited successfully challenged the 'last on first off' dismissal policy for making retrenchments, as well as the use of 'protective' legislation which limited the weights women could lift (Booth and Rubenstein 1990:132). While the case has been accurately criticised as undermining a union victory against arbitrary dismissals by management (Thornton 1990:188), the union had failed to see the sex discriminatory effect of the 'last on first off' policy it had negotiated with management. In January 1994 a second group of 709 complainants achieved a settlement from AIS, this time based on waiting an average length of two years to be

offered a job when they applied between 1977 and 1981, while men waited two to three weeks (Anderson 1994:107).

10 Women's representation in management in 1994 was 60 per cent of what it would have been had it reflected women's representation in the workforce as a whole (Hede 1995:16); women make up about half as many senior executive service employees as would be the case if women and men with the same qualifications and length of service were promoted equally rapidly (House of Representatives Standing Committee on Legal and Constitutional Affairs 1992:51, 59); women remain severely under-represented as law firm partners (10 per cent of female solicitors compared with 41 per cent of male solicitors) in New South Wales (Pringle 1994:212).

11 Norman MacKenzie's appointment and work was described by Jean Arnot (1994:125) as 'a watershed in the recognition of women's treatment and status in Australia', receiving considerable media coverage. In 1962 his book, *Women in Australia*, described Australia as still more a man's country than other industrialised democracies, arguing for gender equality and closing the gap between women's potential and their achievement (for example, see Lees and Senyard (1987:84) among the commentators who cite Mackenzie as a significant and dissident voice in the early 1960s).

Chapter 4 Marriage and Motherhood

1 Among the mothers, those with higher degrees were twice as likely to be never married by the age of 35–39 compared with those with no qualifications. 12 per cent of professionally employed women aged 45-49 in 1981 were never married compared with 6 per cent of clerical workers and 3 per cent of service workers (Carmichael 1988:177, 178). A survey in 1983 revealed that younger women with higher levels of education were less likely to repartner, although the higher the occupational status and education of older men the more likely they were to repartner (McDonald 1986:60).

2 Support for childlessness was higher among the young, non-church goers and the university-educated, and lower among those born in Greece, Turkey, Italy and Malta (West 1987:41). In a 1989 survey 44 per cent disagreed that people who never have children lead empty lives (Evans 1992:36).

3 About one-third of women will have three or more children, a quarter will have one child, leaving about one-fifth who will have no children (McDonald 1995:45). Family sizes are slightly lower for women born in main English-speaking countries and slightly higher, and more often delayed until the woman is in her twenties, for women born in non-English speaking countries. Family sizes in Indigenous Australian families are about three children per woman, a decrease from about six children in the 1960s (Australian Bureau of Statistics 1994:24–6).

4 Right to Life associations formed from 1972 when Medicare combined with liberalised laws made abortion safe and cheap (Sawer and Simms 1993:238–9); press headlines condemned Leichhardt's abortion services which were so in demand that a free-standing abortion clinic, Preterm, was opened in 1974 (Broom 1991:4–5); an unsuccessful private member's Bill in 1989 attempted to stop Medicare refunds for abortions (Burgmann 1993: 109); the Goss government in Queensland, despite pressure from inside and outside the Labor Party, refused to decriminalise abortion in the early 1990s (Sawer and Simms 1993:166–7).

5 There may be as many as 100 000 Aboriginal adults in Australia who do not know their origins and cannot remember their families (Kaplan 1996:137). See also the biographies in Sykes, including Eva Leanne Johnson whose trauma is expressed in her playwriting career (Sykes 1993:49).
6 In one study the majority of white mothers who relinquished children for adoption reported it as the most stressful event in their lives, the sense of loss exacerbated where women felt they had no genuine control over the decision (Winkler and Keppel 1984:58–9, 61–9). Similar results were reported in a 1984 study of more than 300 surrogate mothers (Chesler 1988:117). The Human Rights and Equal Opportunity Commission National Inquiry into the Separation of Aboriginal and Torres Strait Islander Children from their Families in 1995 and 1996 attempted to 'reflect on the history of the relationship between Indigenous and non-Indigenous Australians and to reveal the impact of government policies on the lives of people who were removed from their families' (Human Rights Australia (1995) News Release 8 August). The commissioners heard tragic stories in all areas where they sat, although it was hoped the Inquiry would be a 'healing' process.
7 In 1981 among married couples where the wife was aged 25 to 34, the mean annual income of couples with children was two-thirds of the income of couples without children (McDonald 1989:103). In 1986 the median contribution of wives without children to the household income was 42 per cent, for married mothers it was 28 per cent (Gilding 1994:112).
8 Although generally described as very successful, in 1991 only 36 per cent of women received support from the fathers of their children (Women's Economic Think Tank 1991:3); a recent study questioned whether the scheme achieved the claimed collection rate of 73 per cent (Alexander 1995:8–9).
9 In the Australian Council of Women's consultations ('Australian Council of Women (ACW) Purple Post Card Campaign' 'Fourth United Nations World Conference on Women Beijing 4–15 September 1995: Infosheet No 4', August 1994:4).
10 See Ryan 1990:76, 80; Burgmann 1993:106–7. There has been an increase in government-funded childcare from 9.5 per cent of pre-school children in 1988 to an intention to meet 66 per cent of the demand in 1996 (Bryson 1994a:302), places increasing from 46 000 in 1983 to 269 000 in 1995, with a projected demand of 354 500 places by the turn of the century (Townsend 1995:5). Most of this demand is met by the cheaper option of home-based family day care and there is little community expectation that employers will provide work-based childcare, particularly for women in less skilled areas.
11 There are no correlations for socio-economic status. Women from non-English speaking backgrounds spend slightly more time on domestic duties; their husbands spend more time with children and less time on housework, although the totals are about the same as for English-speaking background men.
12 In national consultations in the 1990s, especially from women in the agricultural sector (Office of the Status of Women 1995a:53). Up until 1891, in official colonial statistics women working in the home were placed in the same table as those who did paid work. T. A. Coghlan, fuelled by the conviction that the quality of the workforce was improved when mothers were not in paid employment, introduced the contemporary distinction between breadwinners and dependants (Deacon 1989:137, 141).
13 By 1992 86 per cent of women who had to ask their husbands for help with housework said this changed their attitudes towards their partners, over half

of them either occasionally or seriously considering separation as a result (Gilding 1994:120). On the other hand, Janeen Baxter (forthcoming) suggests that women often report high levels of household work satisfaction, even when the allocation of tasks is unequal, suggesting that 'equity' still does not mean 'equality' in many households. Thus, Rita resists her husband's offers of household help, finding it hard to 'let go' of her desire to control the household.

14 Bittman (1995:12-15) suggests a little more time on cooking for men born after 1957), and on physical childcare and child minding for men born since the Second World War compared with the time they spent two decades ago. The ABS data reproduced by Bryson (1996:214) suggests, in comparison with Baxter's 1980s data, that full-time working wives had reduced their double shift from 80 to 70 hours a week by 1994, so that they only work six more hours than their husbands' double shift.

15 The process of shifting custody to women began in 1839 with Caroline Norton's activism and the Infant Custody Bill, which allowed a 'blameless' mother to apply for custody of children under 7 years of age. By the mid-1970s the 'deep genetic forces' linking mother and child jostled with comments on women in paid work (compare Glass J. A. in *Epperson* v. *Dampney* (1976) 10 ALR 227 at 241-2 and Stephen J. in *Raby* v. *Raby* [1976] FLC 90-104 at 75,486). A female Adelaide Family Court judge in 1987 refused custody to a mother unless she became pregnant and gave up work (*Swaney* v. *Ward* (1988) FLC 91-928 at 76,712), although the decision was reversed on appeal (76,714). A 1983 summary of several studies found that in contested cases between a third and two-thirds of awards were to the mother. Women without work were not preferred over working women but white-collar fathers were far more successful in gaining custody than were blue-collar fathers (Horwill and Bordow 1983:345).

16 An Australian Institute of Family Studies survey in 1986 showed that 56 per cent of the property (excluding superannuation) went to the wife, who was, however, the custodial parent in 83 per cent of cases (Scutt 1990:219).

17 In *The Second Stage* Friedan ([1981] 1983:41, 218–19) hopes for a further revolution which will enable women to '*choose* to have children' without giving up 'control of their lives', to have both feminism and the family, equality within and beyond the family.

Part II Present and Future Feminisms

1 See West and Blomberg (1990) for a discussion of the boundaries of 'women's movement'.

2 For example, women of the 'mothers' generation who note heroines and role models among previous generations include Manderson (1992:134-5), Irina Dunn (1992:99), Haines (1992b:70).

Chapter 5 Finding Feminism

1 Ruby Langford Gibini suggests that between 1986 and 1996 twenty-two Aboriginal women writers have written twenty-two books ('Aborigines reclaim identity through literature', *Australian*, 3 October 1996:4). For Indigenous Australian women's biographies, see Smith and Sykes 1981; Morgan 1987; Gaffney 1989; Langford 1988; Ward 1987; Ward 1991; Pring 1990; Sykes 1993. For women from non-English speaking backgrounds see D'Aprano

1977; Ciccotosto and Bosworth 1990; Kahan-Guidi and Weiss 1990; Walsh ed. 1993; Herne et al. eds 1992; and for a bibliography, Gunew et al. (eds) 1992.

2 The 'intelligent princess' rejects a prince who will not treat her as an equal during her quest for a husband (rather than the holy grail) (Gilbert 1989); Malu Kangka ('kangaroo girl') cannot grow into a woman and becomes her 'true self', a Malu, and she is 'happy for the rest of her life' (Davies 1993:47-8,186).

3 'If you think you are emancipated, you might consider the idea of tasting your menstrual blood – if it makes you sick, you've a long way to go, baby' (Greer 1971:51), who suggests the same test of 'repressed disgust' in relation to vaginal secretions (Greer 1971:259).

4 Dale Spender has analysed women's much lower use of a system designed largely by men, which offers sexually explicit virtual activities and allows anonymous sexual harassment through postings, and may require women to expose themselves to a locker-room atmosphere in computer laboratories (Spender 1995:168,194,182,220,214-15).

5 In 1989 Mark Thomas (1989:9) contrasted 'influential Australian thinkers' with 'stump jumpers, women authors, new boy networks'. Not surprisingly, then, there are no women included in his selection. In the same year, however, the *Bulletin*'s cover story (16 May 1989:48–55) dealing with six thinkers, 'considered by their peers to be among the best minds in the country' included one woman, the feminist philosopher, Elizabeth Grosz. In 1975 women occupied 64 per cent of junior academic positions, made up 20 per cent of associate professors and readers, and only 1 per cent of professors (Dixson 1994:40). By 1991 a higher percentage of women is found in the senior ranks, although women still comprise only one-third of all teaching and research positions (Australian Bureau of Statistics 1993a:108).

6 The first course was at Flinders University, the first program at the Australian National University in 1975, and the first department was at the University of Adelaide. There are only thirty tenured faculty positions designated as women's studies, with only two at the professorial level (Magarey et al. 1994:285, 288–9, 290; Ryan 1993:1; Gender Theory Group 1992:84; Davies 1986:8; Woodland 1989).

7 Catherine Armitage, 'Women's rights wronged', *Australian*, 10 October 1994:10; Trioli 1996:49–50.

8 However, Susan J. Douglas (1994:230) says of Greer and Gloria Steinem: 'precisely because they were tall, slim, and beautiful, they got away with saying things Friedan didn't dare utter'. Although Friedan was 'much more accommodating to men in her speeches and politics', she was 'cast as a man-hater'. In contrast, Steinem, described as 'the world's most beautiful byline', campaigned for Latin American farmworkers and shared platforms with African-American women when she espoused the feminist cause. Even so, because she was glamorous the press also represented Steinem as frivolous (Heilbrun 1995:100, 149).

9 Based on a ten-yearly survey of the *Courier-Mail* and *Sydney Morning Herald*, analysis of clippings file held in the Politics Department, Research School of Social Sciences, Australian National University. 'Accent', established in the Melbourne *Age* in 1966 to replace the formula of 'recipes, dressmaking and social chat' with 'fashion, home, food' and 'women who make the wheels go round in careers and society', went on to discuss abortion, women's contribution to the economy, rape and refuges (West 1987:5, 10, 19, 18, 51–2). In

like vein, between the 1950s and the 1990s the *Courier-Mail*'s 'Women's Page' became the 'Family' pages, 'For Women' and finally 'femail'.

10 Thus, in the discussion of the Family Law Bill in 1975 the commentary featured politicians' views: 'Bill will cause suffering and injustice – Killen'; 'Holy deadlock, not wedlock – Lamb'; 'attack on the homemakers' (John Howard) and 'marriage the only foundation of a decent society'. Women supporting the bill were confined to the letters to the editor or shown demonstrating in its favour (*Sydney Morning Herald*, 1 March 1975). In contrast, in 1983 opponents of the Sex Discrimination Bill, including Doug Anthony as leader of the National Party, are confined to the letters to the editor (*Australian*, 4 October 1983).

11 For example, see *Australian Financial Review*, 7 March 1995. Elisabeth Wynhausen, 'A nation of bullies' names the then Prime Minister Paul Keating, links bullying to sexual harassment, domestic violence and increasingly unequal incomes (*Australian* 'Weekend Review', 4–5 March 1995:1–2).

12 In both print and television media women's representation was greatest in human interest stories (37 per cent of the print media and 23 per cent of television), followed by politics (25 per cent) and crime (14 per cent of print and 20 per cent of television) and was less than 10 per cent of business and sports coverage. According to this survey, women were seldom asked for comment as experts. This may well be the general case, my content analysis focusing on 'women's issues' might suggest an apartheid in newspaper use of women's voices (Office of the Status of Women 1995a:73; Appendix 2.21).

13 In 1993 women made up at least 40 per cent of journalists, on-camera presenters, news editors and administrative officers in the Australian Broadcasting Corporation, but less than 25 per cent of overseas correspondents, executive producers or engineeering and technical personnel (3.3 per cent of the last group) (Office of the Status of Women 1995a:72).

14 Contrasting themselves with 'feminists', the focus group women of middle Australia said women 'need to' 'work together' with men and 'help each other', now that men were 'becoming a lot more emotional than they were 20 or 30 years ago' (Riley-Smith 1992:48). Agnes applauds assertiveness in the company of males but opposes separatism because 'we really have to help each other'. Many of the antifeminists whom Robyn Rowland (1984:229) interviewed took pride in their roles as mothers and wives, contrasting their experiences with the oppressive relations described by feminists. See also Anne Lewin (in Ford 1991:39), a lingerie and sleepwear manufacturer; Pat Lovell, film producer, who describes the women's movement as 'probably the most important thing that's happened to women all around the world' but who was put off by 'rampaging feminists who don't have a good thing to say about blokes' (in Mitchell 1984:143, 142).

15 In 1995 the then Governor-General, Bill Hayden, argued that because we do not discriminate against same-sex partnerships, we should logically allow contracts similar to marriage (Kaplan 1996:115).

16 Sluts and lesbians are aligned in 'queer theory' (Creed 1994) which rejects 'straight' sex as morally straightjacketed, for example, in its attacks on 'butch-fem' and 's/m' practices in gay relationships. Queer theory gathers up 'liminal' categories like bisexuals, transsexuals and prostitutes against the 'straight' community.

17 While Pat suggests that now 'the shelter is well supported in Cairns', Valerie remembers that when she joined the local women's centre, church people told her to 'have nothing to do with it at all, because they were radical. Not

very nice'. In the 1980s when the National Party State government 'repressed and discriminated against' gay men and women, Pat and her husband provided a facilitating front for services and advocacy for gay men and women.
18 See also Thelma Hunter 1994:207, and Caty Kyne 1995:25–6, who stresses she also 'had wonderful support from both lesbian and straight housemates and friends'.
19 For example, being refused custody as mothers, although the sexual preference of parents is no longer meant to be an issue (Graycar and Morgan 1990:253; Kaplan 1996:109). Kaplan (1996:116) reports that 160 pieces of legislation must be changed to provide legal equity for homosexuals, although some changes have been made in some jurisdictions, including laws against homosexual vilification and more flexible definitions of the family in relation to workplace conditions (Kaplan 1996:115, 111).
20 If Hanna joined the men 'they stopped talking. This type of thing is still happening'. Shirley, however, suggests that it was in Taiwanese society rather than Australian society that men discussed 'politics and the economy' and women 'their children and housekeeping'. Shirley preferred the men's conversations, claiming that this was how she 'learned' and came to 'know so much'.
21 Contrast Ridgeway 1986:43–4 and Roberta Sykes quoted in Jennett 1987:369 with Bell 1991:387; Bonner 1988:20 for the Ananga communities; Gaffney 1989:83–6, 132 for Torres Strait Island communities.
22 Louise Liddy-Corpus 1992:25; Tracey Moffatt in Sykes 1993:128–9; Marie Andrews 1992:91. After working on the *Women's Business* report, the first government report into the status of Indigenous Australian women in Australia, Aileen became aware of indigenous women's invisibility in the public sector, even though 'in my own community I knew women were strong'.

Chapter 6 Is Feminism a White Middle-Class Movement?

1 Domestic violence occurs in between a third and a quarter of cohabitations (Allen 1989:237; Matchett 1988). Each year in Australia about 100 women are killed and thousands injured as a result of criminal assaults by husbands and male partners (McGregor and Hopkins 1991:xix). Domestic violence offences account for at least one-fifth of police call-outs, while some calculations put the figure as high as 50 per cent of police time (McGregor and Hopkins 1991:76–7, 88–9). Male violence was the concern of 65 per cent of the submissions to *Equality Before the Law* (Law Reform Commission 1994:14) and nominated as their major concern by 20 per cent of women in the Australian Council for Women's 'purple postcard' campaign leading up to the World Conference of Women in Beijing in 1995 (Australian Council for Women 1995:12–13, 14).
2 Surveys in the 1980s suggested nearly 20 per cent of respondents believed violence by a man against his partner was acceptable in some circumstances and nearly a third believed it was a private matter between the couple (Graycar and Morgan 1990:280; McGregor and Hopkins 1991:41). A 1995 survey found that 93 per cent of respondents recognised domestic violence as a crime and 'a majority' do not accept alcohol or provocation as an excuse (Office of the Status of Women, 'Agenda', Issue 2, December 1995:2).
3 The first was established in 1974, with twenty-one refuges funded by the National Women's Refuge Program in 1975 (Burgmann 1993:95) and 163 in

1987. People escaping family violence take up a quarter of the accommodation within the Supported Accomodation Assistance Program (Office of the Status of Women 1995a:31).

4 Police, on the whole, respond more readily where a woman has such an order; in most States there are now more policewomen to deal with domestic violence, although they might, like Jennifer, consider that the protection order system is 'often' abused by women who want 'to get the other person in trouble'. She describes a wife who had 'only got her protection order that day, and she was back round at his place saying he's breached the order'.

5 In 1975 the Australian Migrant Women's Association was formed with International Women's Year funding (Sawer 1990:108). In 1981 the Migrant Women's Caucus emerged from the ACTU Conference. In 1985 following the Immigrant Women's Speakout at which both Matina and Gladys spoke, a number of migrant women's organisations were established, including an Immigrant Women's Resource Centre in New South Wales and the Association of Non-English Speaking Background Women in 1986, which was supported financially by the Office of the Status of Women. Matina was elected inaugural chair. Gladys became the assistant co-ordinator at the Migrant Resource Centre in Brisbane, fighting successfully to ensure that future co-ordinators were 'migrants': 'where migrants have the capability of doing it, if it's a migrant place, then migrants should run it'.

6 Police have not only failed to respond to Indigenous Australian rape complainants, but sometimes perpetuate their own rapes on complainants (Fesl 1993:61).

7 Similar sentiments are expressed by Jacqualine Hobbs (1995:256) who sees work in Aboriginal organisations as 'more important than Women's Movement activities as such', but notes that 'Women are becoming more powerful through the Women's Movement and making changes'.

8 Aboriginal people are nine times as likely to be victims of homicide as white people and thirteen times as likely to be offenders; in about one-fifth of recorded cases the relationship was spousal (Office of the Status of Women 1995a:31).

9 Studies reveal that women fight equally as often as men although they suffer more severe physical consequences (Johnston 1991b:100; Burbank 1994:97–8).

10 O'Shane 1993:75 for South Australia in 1976; Johnston 1991a:192, 194 for Australia in 1988; Cunneen 1992b:10–11 for imprisonment for drunkenness, disorderly conduct and assault in Western Australia. In terms of police cell custody rates, 25.4 per cent of men taken into custody in August 1988 were Aboriginal but 48.9 per cent of women taken into custody were Aboriginal, where Indigenous Australians make up 1.1 per cent of the Australian population (Johnston 1991a:192,194,221).

11 In 1984 forty-five women trained as regional broadcasters in the Community Employment Program and produced a series of programs called 'Outback and Outspoken' (Rigg and Copeland 1985:165).

12 Between 1978 and 1992 the percentage of farm employers who were women rose from about one-third to over a half, the percentage of self-employed farmers who were women from a tenth to over one-third and as salary earners from one-quarter to one-third (Sheridan 1994:20–1).

13 Farms are rarely split if this means the loss of a viable production unit, usually depriving the wife of the matrimonial home (Teather and Franklin 1994:6; Alston 1994:27).

14 Only 12.5 per cent of Alston's (1995:127) sample reported active involvement in agripolitics. Heather Mitchell has been president of the Victorian Farmers' Federation and a vice president of the National Farmers' Federation. The Cattlemen's Union has had several women on its council (Rick Farley (1995) 'Rural women and the National Farmers' Federation (NFF)', *Country Web*, No. 8:9).

15 The CWA's current membership in New South Wales of 15 500 is about half the 1950s' membership, while the majority of members appear to be over 60 years old (Teather 1994:135). Yvonne suggests younger women are either uninterested in voluntary groups, or are drawn to school and preschool parents and citizens associations, while Elizabeth Teather (1994:135–7) suggests that the 'maternalism' of the CWA disinclines younger women from joining.

16 Women in Agriculture, emerging from the first national conference for 'country women' held in 1979, has placed pressure on government departments to be more responsive to women's needs (Hogan 1994:32–3, 35) and 'the more traditional farmer organisations [to become] aware of some of their inequalities and barriers' (McGowan 1995:19).

17 Thus, a letter from the CWA (Narrandera) called on the ABC not to televise the Sydney Gay and Lesbian Mardi Gras in 1995 (Marsh 1995:550). According to Berenice, the women who branded Jessie 'as a real women's libber' are members of the CWA.

Chapter 7 Beating The Backlash

1 Office of the Status of Women (1992:105); although Dale Spender (1995: 179) suggests that teachers often fail to guarantee this access. In the face of the continued failure of these initiatives, Western Australian schools have made a basic set of subjects compulsory to all students, boys and girls (Parker and Offer 1989).

2 Boys were more frequently criticised for lack of neatness and girls for the intellectual aspects of their work (Kenway and Willis 1990:25). At university such an evaluation possibly affected two famous feminists, Beatrice Faust and Germaine Greer, who were awarded 2A honours degrees which limited their future academic choices (Faust in Mitchell 1984:17–18).

3 This is not to say that harassment does not occur between girls, whose early verbal sophistication outmatches young boys' 'cave-like tandem play' in which they perform the same activities alongside each other (Anna). Rumour-mongering, sexual name-calling (most often 'lesbian') (Cameron 1995:11), 'bitchy' gossip (Melinda) and taunting are used to divide and recombine girls' friendship groups. Melinda suggests this is because girls 'don't have much in their life' in comparison with boys, who she admits 'can't be honest about their feelings'. Both boys and girls taunted Jennifer about her breasts; girls would 'walk along and shove their chest out and say, "Guess who I am"'. Later, she realised she should have replied, 'Jealous' – and to the boys 'It's only because you can't get your hands on them'.

4 When I addressed the North Queensland Peninsula Branch of the Association of Women Educators on 27 July 1995, although I did not mention the backlash in education, a spontaneous discussion broke out. They expressed a concern I have heard since: that while boys clearly need attention especially in relation to behaviour problems affecting their (and the girls') learning, there is a fear resources will be directed away from girls' learning needs. Recent federal and New South Wales government inquiries propose

strategies by which boys can excel at other than computers and sports, overcome 'behavioural and learning difficulties', 'aggressive behaviour' including 'sexual harassment' in primary school, low self-esteem and lack of communication skills (Carolyn Jones, 'Boy burn-out: the affirmative action dilemma', *Australian*, 27 July 1995).

5 Such policies sometimes attempt to recruit and place females in groups so they do not face discrimination alone ('Building a big future', *Women & Work*, Women's Bureau, DEET 1993 14(3):9–10). Sexual harassment and an unyielding masculinist work culture have also been reported for Argyle Diamond mine's employment of sixty women (women being two in a hundred of labourers in mining and construction), the New South Wales Fire Brigade and the Australian Maritime School in Tasmania where, despite most female enrolments in the top 10 per cent of the intake, none have stayed the course to graduation (Inquiry into Equal Opportunity and Equal Status for Women in Australia 1992:38–9).

6 See Koppelman (1993:50–3) and Koppelman's (1985) collection of short stories about mothers and daughters. Suzanna Walters (1992:35–40, 75, 128, 181) contrasts popular representations of the 'evil mother incarnate' – cause of all her daughter's problems – in films like *Mommie Dearest* with late 1980s scripts like Amy Tan's *The Joy Luck Club*. Relationships between mothers and daughters can still be full of 'bitterness and misunderstanding', but the reader/viewer is given access to the mothers' 'understanding of their daughters'.

7 In an A. G. McNair-Anderson young person's poll (reported in the ABC's 'Attitude' program on Feminism on 16 June 1994), while 70 per cent of female respondents said feminism had made a positive difference to their lives and 33 per cent felt comfortable calling themselves feminists, 65 per cent disagreed that being feminist means giving up being feminine.

8 The content analysis of the 1951, 1971 and 1991 editions of *Seventeen*, a magazine in the United States, reveals that discussion of women's issues – particularly those which questioned fashion, romantic love and traditional roles – peaked in 1971, as did anti-establishment issues. On the other hand, attention to minority issues, especially violence and discrimination against minorities, and environmental issues rose dramatically over the four decades (Budgeon and Currie 1995:178).

9 See also Roz Sutton's letter to the *Courier-Mail* (22 December 1995:14) contesting Geraldine Doogue's 'patronising' account of debutante balls and quoting academic, Johanna Wyn, who noted that 'misguided older feminists forgot about the fun things'.

10 Like Freud, the object-relations theorists are interested in how children develop sexual object choice or aim and thus focus on the child's relationship with each of its parents in its sexual development. Feminist object relations theorists like Nancy Chodorow and Jessica Benjamin are equally interested in how children develop *social* relations with others.

11 Thus, when Yvonne married Mervyn he asked whether her sons were 'boys or pansies'. By 'pansies', Mervyn meant 'wimps' rather than affectionate nurturing boys. Mervyn 'took them in hand', preparing the path to manhood through discipline.

12 Perhaps it is not surprising then, that sons (as well as daughters), are living longer with their parents. In 1992, 55 per cent of males and 40 per cent of females aged 20–24 were living at home, a rise since 1979 of 10 per cent for males and 15 per cent for females (McDonald 1995:28).

13 The few well-known artists of the grandmothers' generation like Ola Cohn, Ailsa O'Connor and Margaret Preston, did not receive 'career benefits' such as a more professional context of tuition, arts administrators and more commercial galleries which became routine from the 1960s (Peers 1993:122). Both Janine Burke (1990:1) dealing with art in general and Catriona Moore (1991:xiii, 5) for photography suggest that the women's movement nurtured the resurgence of women's art in the 1970s.

Conclusion: Feminist Futures?

1 Of disability, Rebecca Maxwell (1992:200, 201) suggests that in the 1980s women's movement, prior to the International Year of Disabled Persons, her 'disability made a large gap' with other self-styled feminist women (see also Hall 1992:102).
2 See also Rowland (1984:229) for Australian feminists. Indeed, women's notion of social justice may often be more personal and intimate than men's, women thinking of colleagues and families, men of targeted populations (Davidson 1992:40); a distinction Carol Gilligan (1982) calls the 'ethic of care' as opposed to the 'ethic of justice'.
3 Feminists may have reduced their chances of success in achieving popular understanding of men's structural advantage because of the reluctance of femocrats to discuss any reductions in privilege men will suffer as a result of feminism. Thus, it has not been the politics of (men's) advantage which has shaped femocrat policies but the politics of (women's) disadvantage (Eveline 1994:141–2). As Marian Sawer notes: 'The first rule of democratic politics is never to be seen to be taking anything away from anyone' (Sawer in Eveline 1994:141).

Bibliography

Agger, Inger 1994. *The Blue Room: Trauma and Testimony Among Refugee Women. A Psycho-Social Exploration* London: Zed.
Agnew, Russell et al. 1993. 'Equality before the law: discussion paper 54', Sydney: Australian Law Reform Commission.
Alcorso, Caroline 1993a. ' "And I'd like to thank my wife . . . ": gender dynamics and the ethnic "family business"' *Australian Feminist Studies* 17:93–108.
Alcorso, Caroline 1993b. 'Economic stocktake: trends and issues for non-English speaking background women' *Australian Feminist Studies* 18:49–66.
Aldunte, Raquel and Revelo, Gladys 1987. 'Latin American community' *Papers from the seminar 'Domestic Violence – A Cross Cultural Perspective'* Canberra: Department of Immigration, Local Government and Ethnic Affairs.
Alexander, Liz 1995. 'Australia's child support scheme: much promised, little delivered?' *Family Matters* 42:6–11.
Alford, Katrina 1984. *Production or Reproduction? An Economic History of Women in Australia 1788–1850* Melbourne: Oxford University Press.
Allen, Judith 1990. *Sex and Secrets: Crimes Involving Australian Women Since 1880* Melbourne: Oxford University Press.
Allen, Judith 1989. 'From women's history to a history of the sexes' in James Walter (ed.) *Australian Studies: A Survey* Melbourne: Oxford University Press.
Allen, Judith 1987. 'Policing since 1880: some questions of sex' in Mark Finnane (ed.) *Policing in Australia: Historical Perspectives* Kensington: New South Wales University Press.
Allen, Judith 1982. 'Octavius Beale reconsidered: infanticide, babyfarming and abortion in NSW 1880–1939' in Sydney Labour History Group *What Rough Beast? The State and Social Order in Australian History* Sydney: George Allen and Unwin.
Alston, Margaret 1995. *Women on the Land: The Hidden Heart of Rural Australia* Kensington: University of New South Wales Press.
Alston, Margaret 1994. 'Feminism and farm women' in Margaret-Ann Franklin, Leonie M. Short and Elizabeth K. Tether (eds) *Country Women at the Crossroads: Perspectives on the Lives of Rural Australian Women in the 1990s* Armidale: University of New England Press.
Alvarez, Amaya Jane 1993. 'Invisible workers and invisible barriers: women at the

CSIR in the 1930s and the 1940s' in Farley Kelly (ed.) *On the Edge of Discovery* Melbourne: Text Publishing Company.
Ambikapathy, Patmalar 1992. 'Contradictions' in Jocelynne A. Scutt (ed.) *As A Woman: Writing Women's Lives* Melbourne: Artemis.
Anderson, Jill 1994. 'Iron & steel' *Alternative Law Journal* 19(3):107–10.
Anderson, Kathryn and Jack, Dana C. 1991. 'Learning to listen: interview techniques and analyses' in Sherna Berger Gluck and Daphne Patai (eds) *Women's Words: The Female Practice of Oral History* New York: Routledge.
Andrews, Marie 1992. 'For my people' in Jocelynne A. Scutt (ed.) *As A Woman: Writing Women's Lives* Melbourne: Artemis.
Armstead, Cathleen 1995. 'Writing contradictions: feminist research and feminist writing' *Women's Studies International Forum* 18(5/6):627–36.
Arnold, Jennifer M. 1991. 'Women in transition: a feminist analysis' Honours thesis submitted to the Department of Anthropology and Sociology, University of Queensland.
Arnot, Jean F. 1994. 'Embedded in the soul' in Jocelynne A. Scutt (ed.) *Taking a Stand: Women in Politics and Society* Melbourne: Artemis.
Astin, Helen S. and Leland, Carole 1991. *Women of Influence, Women of Vision: A Cross-Generational Study of Leaders and Social Change* San Francisco: Jossey-Bass.
Atkinson, Judy 1990. 'Violence against Aboriginal women: reconstitution of community law – the way forward' *Aboriginal Law Bulletin* 2(46):6–9.
Atkinson, Paul 1978. 'Fitness, feminism and schooling' in Sara Delamont and Lorna Duffin (eds) *The Nineteenth Century Woman* Croom Helm: London.
Australian Bureau of Statistics 1994. *Australian Women's Year Book 1994* Canberra: Australian Government Publishing Service.
Australian Bureau of Statistics 1993a. *Women in Australia* Canberra: Australian Bureau of Statistics.
Australian Bureau of Statistics 1993b. *Population Growth and Distribution in Australia* Canberra: Australian Bureau of Statistics.
Australian Bureau of Statistics 1989. *Census of Population and Housing 30 June 1986: Cross-Classified Characteristics of Persons and Dwellings – Australia* Canberra: Australian Bureau of Statistics.
Australian Bureau of Statistics 1988. *Overseas-Born Australians 1988: A Statistical Profile* Canberra: Commonwealth of Australia.
Australian Bureau of Statistics 1983. *Cross-Classified Characteristics of Persons and Dwellings: 1981 Census of Population and Housing* Canberra: Australian Bureau of Statistics.
Australian Council for Women 1995. 'Report on consultations with non-government organisations and Australian women, February to September 1994' Canberra: Office of the Status of Women, Department of Prime Minister and Cabinet.
Bacchi, Carol 1994. ' "Consent or "coercion"? Removing conflict of interest from staff-student relations' *Australian Universities' Review* 37(2):55–61.
Bacchi, Carol 1990. *Same Difference* Sydney: Allen and Unwin.
Bacchi, Carol and Jose, Jim 1994. 'Historicising sexual harassment' *Women's History Review* 3(2):263–70 .
Bail, Kathy 1996. 'Introduction' in Kathy Bail (ed.) *DIY Feminism* St Leonards: Allen and Unwin.
Baldini, Gwen 1995. 'A whole world of difference' in Jocelynne Scutt (ed.) *City Women Country Women: Crossing the Boundaries* Melbourne: Artemis.
Baldock, Cora V. 1993. 'Irene Greenwood' *Australian Feminist Studies* 17:1–4.

Baldock, Cora and Cass, Bettina (eds) 1988. *Women, Social Welfare and the State* Sydney: Allen and Unwin.

Balfour, Kath 1993. 'Reclaiming power' in Jocelynne A. Scutt (ed.) *Glorious Age* Melbourne: Artemis.

Bandler, Faith 1992. 'A good innings' in Jocelynne A. Scutt (ed.) *As A Woman: Writing Women's Lives* Melbourne: Artemis.

Barwick, Diane E. 1970. '"And the lubras are ladies now": Victorian Aboriginal women on mission stations 1860–1886' in Faye Gale (ed.) *Women's Position in Aboriginal Society* Canberra: Australian Institute of Aboriginal Studies.

Bates, Frank 1989. 'Of beating and bondage – sex, shame, and similar facts in recent law' *Criminal Law Journal* 13:117–32.

Baxter, Janeen and Gibson, Diane with Lynch-Blosse, Mark 1990. *Double Take: The Links Between Paid and Unpaid Work* Canberra: Australian Government Publishing Service.

Baxter, Janine, 'Moving toward equality? Questions of change and equality in household work patterns' in Moira Gatens and Alison Mackinnon (eds) *Designing Women: Sexuality, Work and Policy* forthcoming, Cambridge University Press.

Baxter, Janeen and Kane, Emily W. 1995. 'Dependence and independence: a cross-national analysis of gender inequality and gender attitudes' *Gender & Society* 9(2):193–215.

Bell, Diane 1991. 'Intraracial rape revisited: on forging a feminist future beyond factions and frightening politics' *Women's Studies International Forum* 14(5):385–412.

Bellear, Lisa 1992. 'Keep fighting, keep speaking out' in Jocelynne A. Scutt (ed.) *Breaking Through: Women, Work and Careers* North Melbourne: Artemis.

Benjamin, Jessica 1990. *The Bonds of Love: Psycho Analysis, Feminism and the Problem of Domination* London: Virago.

Bennett, Roberta S., Whitaker, K. Gail, Woolley Smith, Nina Jo, Sablove, Anne 1987. 'Changing the rules of the game: reflections toward a feminist analysis of sport' *Women's Studies International Forum* 10(4):369–80.

Bernard, Jessie 1972. *The Future of Marriage* London: Souvenir Press.

Biddulph, Steve 1994. *Manhood: A Book About Setting Men Free* Sydney: Finch Publishing.

Billson, Janet Mancini 1991. 'The progressive verification method: toward a feminist methodology for studying women cross-culturally' *Women's Studies International Forum* 14(3):201–15.

Bin-Sallik, Mary Ann 1993. 'Harvard: a Djaru woman's perspective' in Jocelynne A. Scutt (ed.) *No Fear of Flying: Women at Home and Abroad* Melbourne: Artemis.

Bittman, Michael 1995. 'Changes at the heart of family households' *Family Matters* 40:10–15.

Bittman, Michael 1991. *Juggling Time: How Australian Families Use Time* Canberra: Office of the Status of Women, Department of Prime Minister and Cabinet.

Bittman, Michael and Lovejoy, Frances 1993. 'Domestic power: negotiating an unequal division of labour within a framework of equality' *Australian and New Zealand Journal of Sociology* 29(3):302–21.

Black, Ollie and Whitehorn, Jill 1992. 'Vitalstatistix Theatre Company' in Christine Hyde et al. *Facts and Femininity: Factors that Affect Girls Learning* Canberra: Department of Employment, Education and Training.

Bland, Lucy 1987. 'The married woman, the "new woman" and the feminist: sexual politics of the 1890s' in Jane Rendall (ed.) *Equal or Different: Women's Politics 1800–1914* Oxford: Basil Blackwell.
Bonner, N. T. 1988. *Always Anangu: A Review of the Pitjantjatjara and Yankunjatjara Aboriginal Communities of Central Australia* Canberra: Department of Aboriginal Affairs.
Booth, Anna and Rubenstein, Linda 1990. 'Women in trade unions in Australia' in Sophie Watson (ed.) *Playing the State: Australian Feminist Interventions* Sydney: Allen and Unwin.
Borland, Katherine 1991. '"That's Not What I Said": interpretive conflict in oral narrative research' in Sherna Berger Gluck and Daphne Patai (eds) *Women's Words: The Female Practice of Oral History* New York: Routledge.
Brady, Veronica 1995. 'Forty fathoms out' in Jocelynne Scutt (ed.) *Singular Women: Reclaiming Spinsterhood* Melbourne: Artemis.
Brockett, Linda and Murray, Alison 1994. 'Thai sex workers in Sydney' in Roberta Perkins, Garry Prestage, Rachel Sharpe and Frances Lovejoy (eds) *Sex Work and Sex Workers in Australia* Sydney: University of New South Wales Press.
Broom, Dorothy H. 1991. *Damned If We Do: Contradictions in Women's Health Care* North Sydney: Allen and Unwin.
Broom, Dorothy H. (ed.) 1984. *Unfinished Business: Social Justice for Women in Australia* Sydney: Allen and Unwin.
Brownmiller, Susan 1975. *Against Our Will: Men, Women and Rape* New York: Simon and Schuster.
Bryson, Lois 1996. 'Revaluing the household economy' *Women's Studies International Forum* 19(3):207–19.
Bryson, Lois 1994a. 'The welfare state and economic adjustment' in Stephen Bell and Brian Head (eds) *State, Economy and Public Policy in Australia* Melbourne: Oxford University Press.
Bryson, Lois 1994b. 'Women, paid work and social policy' in Norma Grieve and Ailsa Burns (eds) *Australian Women: Contemporary Feminist Thought* Melbourne: Oxford University Press.
Bryson, Lois 1987. 'Sport and the maintenance of masculine hegemony' *Women's Studies International Forum* 10(4):349–60.
Budgeon, Shelley and Currie, Dawn H. 1995. 'From feminism to postfeminism: women's liberation in fashion magazines' *Women's Studies International Forum* 18(2):173–86.
Bunkle, Phillida 1980. 'The origins of the women's movement in New Zealand: the Women's Christian Temperance Union 1885–1895' in Phillida Bunkle and Beryl Hughes (eds) *Women in New Zealand Society* Auckland: George Allen and Unwin.
Burbank, Victoria Katherine 1994. *Fighting Women: Anger and Aggression in Aboriginal Australia* Berkeley, Los Angeles: University of California Press.
Bureau of Immigration, Multicultural and Population Research 1996a. 'Births, deaths, marriages and migration', *Bureau of Immigration, Multicultural and Population Research Bulletin* 17:58–9.
Bureau of Immigration, Multicultural and Population Research 1996b. 'Greeks and Italians produce smaller families' *Bureau of Immigration, Multicultural and Population Research Bulletin* 17:34.
Burgmann, Verity 1993. *Power and Protest: Movements for Change in Australian Society* St Leonards: Allen and Unwin.

Burke, Janine 1990. *Field of Vision: A Decade of Change: Women's Art in the Seventies* Ringwood: Penguin.

Burke, Janine 1976. 'Australian women artists' in Kiffy Carter et al. (eds) *Australian Women Artists One Hundred Years: 1840–1940* Melbourne: Ewing and George Paton Galleries and Melbourne University Union.

Burns, Ailsa 1994. 'Why do women put up with the double load?' in Norma Grieve and Ailsa Burns (eds) *Australian Women: Contemporary Feminist Thought* Melbourne: Oxford University Press.

Burns, Ailsa 1986. 'Why do women continue to marry?' in Norma Grieve and Ailsa Burns (eds) *Australian Women: New Feminist Perspectives* Melbourne: Oxford University Press.

Burroughs, Angela 1993. 'Doing a netball' *Black Cockatoo* 1(1):22–3.

Buswell, Val 1993. 'Eighty–eight's fair enough' in Jocelynne A. Scutt (ed.) *Glorious Age* Melbourne: Artemis.

Caine, Barbara 1995. 'Women's studies, feminist traditions and the problem of history' in Barbara Caine and Rosemary Pringle (eds) *Transitions: New Australian Feminisms* St Leonards: Allen and Unwin.

Cafarella, Jane 1992. 'Something of my own' in Jocelynne A. Scutt (ed.) *Breaking Through: Women, Work and Careers* North Melbourne: Artemis.

Caine, Barbara 1992. *Victorian Feminists* Oxford: Oxford University Press.

Cameron, Susan 1995. 'Girls and boys in Australian schools' *Women's Studies Resource Centre Newsletter* 21(2):9–12.

Campbell, Beatrix 1987. *The Iron Ladies: Why Do Women Vote Tory?* London: Virago.

Carey, Gabrielle and Lette, Kathy 1979. *Puberty Blues* Ringwood: McPhee Gribble/Penguin.

Carmichael, Gordon A. 1992. 'So many children: colonial and post-colonial demographic patterns' in Kay Saunders and Raymond Evans (eds) *Gender Relations in Australia* Sydney: Harcourt Brace Jovanovich.

Carmichael, Gordon A. 1988. *With This Ring. First Marriage Patterns, Trends and Prospects in Australia* Canberra: Department of Demography, Australian National University and Australian Institute of Family Studies.

Carter, Betty et al. 1987. 'Borning: pmere laltyeke anwerne ampe mpwaretyeke – Congress Alukura by the Grandmother's law' *Australian Aboriginal Studies* 1:2–33.

Carter, David 1992. 'Manning Clark's hat: public and national intellectuals' in Tony Bennett et al. (eds) *Celebrating the Nation: A Critical Study of Australia's Bicentenary* St Leonards: Allen and Unwin.

Carter, Jan 1981. *Nothing to Spare: Recollections of Australian Pioneering Women* Ringwood: Penguin.

Cass, Bettina 1986. *The Social Security Review Issues Paper No. 1: Income Support for Families and Children* Canberra: Australian Government Publishing Service.

Castles, Alex C. and Harris, Michael C. 1987. *Lawmakers and Wayward Whigs: Government and Law in South Australia 1836–1986* Adelaide: Wakefield Press.

Cavuoto, Diana 1993. 'Who needs a passport?' in Barbara Walsh (ed.) *Growing Up Italian in Australia: Eleven Young Australian Women Talk About Their Childhood* Sydney: State Library of New South Wales.

Charlesworth, Hilary and Ingleby, Richard 1988. 'The sexual division of labour and family property law' *Law in Context* 6(1):29–47.

Chesler, Phyllis 1988. *Sacred Bond: The Legacy of Baby M* New York: Times Books (Random House).

Chesterman, Colleen 1993. 'Refractory Girl and the arts' in Refractory Girl (ed.) *Refractory Voices: Feminist Perspectives from Refractory Girl* Sydney: Refractory Girl Feminist Journal.
Chisholm, Richard 1985. 'Destined children: Aboriginal child welfare in Australia: directions of change in law and policy, part 1' *Australian Law Bulletin* 14:6–8.
Chodorow, Nancy 1978. *The Reproduction of Mothering: Psychoanalysis and the Sociology of Gender* Berkeley: University of California Press.
Ciccotosto, Emma and Bosworth, Michael 1990. *Emma: A Translated Life* Fremantle: Fremantle Arts Centre Press.
Clague, Joyce 1993. 'Staying to the end' in Jocelynne A. Scutt (ed.) *Glorious Age* Melbourne: Artemis.
Clark, Margaret Louden 1990. 'Women in law' *Legal Service Bulletin* 15(1):38–9.
Coate, Jennifer 1992. 'Slipping through the net' in Jocelynne A. Scutt (ed.) *Breaking Through: Women, Work and Careers* North Melbourne: Artemis.
Cockburn, Cynthia 1991. *In the Way of Women: Men's Resistance to Sex Equality in Organization* New York: ILR Press.
Connell, R. W. 1995. *Masculinities* St Leonards: Allen and Unwin.
Connell, R. W. 1992. 'A very straight gay: masculinity, homosexual experience, and the dynamics of gender' *American Sociological Review* 57(6):735–51.
Connell, Robert W. 1990. 'A whole new world: remaking masculinity in the context of the environmental movement' *Gender and Society* 4(4):452–78.
Connell, R. W. 1987. *Gender and Power: Society, the Person and Sexual Politics* Stanford: Stanford University Press.
Connell, R. W., Ashenden, D. J., Kessler, S., and Dowsett, G. W. 1982. *Making the Difference: Schools, Families and Social Division* Sydney: George Allen and Unwin.
Cook, Judith A. and Fonow, Mary Margaret 1986. 'Knowledge and women's interests: issues of epistemology and methodology in feminist sociological research' *Sociological Inquiry* 56(1):2–29.
Coolwell, Wayne 1993. *My Kind of People: Achievement, Identity and Aboriginality* St Lucia: University of Queensland Press.
Coontz, Stephanie 1992. *The Way We Never Were: American Families and the Nostalgia Trap* New York: HarperCollins.
Cox, Eva 1993. 'Policy contest: immigrant women on a flat playing field' *Australian Feminist Studies* 18:25–48.
Coxsedge, Joan 1993. 'Busy stirring' in Jocelynne A. Scutt (ed.) *Glorious Age* Melbourne: Artemis.
Cranny-Francis, Anne 1992. *Engendered Fictions* Kensington: New South Wales University Press.
Creed, Barbara 1994. 'Queer theory and its discontents: queer desires, queer cinema' in Norma Grieve and Ailsa Burns (eds) *Australian Women: Contemporary Feminist Thought* Melbourne: Oxford University Press.
Crosby, Heather 1993. 'The becoming of a sceptical optimist' in Jocelynne A. Scutt (ed.) *Glorious Age* Melbourne: Artemis.
Crouch, Mira and Manderson, Lenore 1993. *New Motherhood: Cultural and Personal Transitions in the 1980s* Y-Parc Yverdon, Switzerland: Gordon and Breach.
Culley, Margo et al. 1985. 'Anger and authority in the introductory women's studies classroom' in Margo Culley and Catherine Portuges (eds) *Gendered Subjects: The Dynamics of Feminist Teaching* Boston: Routledge and Kegan Paul.

Cung, Hoang Quoc 1995. 'Vietnamese family: the foundation of society and nation – spirit of responsibility, obligation and gratitude', *Integration*, 3(7):48–9.
Cunneen, Chris 1992. 'Judicial racism' *Aboriginal Law Bulletin* 2(58):9–11.
Curthoys, Ann 1995. 'Helen Garner's *The First Stone*' *Australian Feminist Studies* 21:203–11.
Curthoys, Ann 1993. 'Feminism, citizenship and national identity' *Feminist Review* 44:19–38.
Curthoys, Ann 1992. 'Doing it for themselves: the women's movement since 1970' in Kay Saunders and Raymond Evans (eds) *Gender Relations in Australia* Sydney: Harcourt Brace Jovanovich.
Curthoys, Ann and Muecke, Stephen 1993. 'Australia, for example' in Wayne Hudson and David Carter (eds) *The Republicanism Debate* Kensington: University of New South Wales Press.
Cusack, Dymphna and James, Florence 1988. *Come in Spinner* North Ryde: Angus and Robertson, first published 1951.
Dann, Christine 1985. *Up From Under: Women's Liberation in New Zealand 1970–1985* Wellington: Allen and Unwin New Zealand in association with Port Nicholson Press.
D'Aprano, Zelda 1977. *Zelda: The Becoming of a Woman* Melbourne: self-published.
Davey, Kath 1995. 'Up and out of the kitchen sink' in Jocelynne Scutt (ed.) *City Women, Country Women: Crossing the Boundaries* Melbourne: Artemis.
Davidson, Gay 1992. 'Running free – then confronting the barriers' in Jocelynne A. Scutt (ed.) *Breaking Through: Women, Work and Careers* North Melbourne: Artemis.
Davies, Bronwyn 1993. *Shards of Glass: Children Reading and Writing Beyond Gendered Identities* St Leonards: Allen and Unwin.
Davies, Bronwyn 1989. *Frogs and Snails and Feminist Tales* Sydney: Allen and Unwin.
Davis, Kathy 1995. *Reshaping the Female Body: The Dilemma of Cosmetic Surgery* New York and London: Routledge.
Daylight, Phyllis and Johnstone, Mary 1986. *Women's Business: Report of Aboriginal Women's Task Force* Canberra: Office of Status of Women, Department of Prime Minister and Cabinet.
de Beauvoir, Simone 1953. *The Second Sex* translated and edited by H. M. Pashley, London: Cape.
de Beauvoir, Simone 1974. *Memoirs of a Dutiful Daughter* translated by James Kirkup, New York: Harper Colophon, first published 1958.
de Lepervanche, Marie 1989. 'Women, nation and the state in Australia' in Nira Yuval-Davis and Floya Anthias (eds) *Woman-Nation-State* Houndmills, Basingstoke: Macmillan.
Deacon, Desley 1989. *Managing Gender: The State, the New Middle Class and Women Workers 1830-1930* Melbourne: Oxford University Press.
Dell'oso, Anna Maria 1993. 'The sewing machine' in Barbara Walsh (ed.) *Growing Up Italian in Australia: Eleven Young Australian Women Talk About Their Childhood* Sydney: State Library of New South Wales.
Dempsey, Ken 1992. *A Man's Town: Inequality Between Women and Men in Rural Australia* Melbourne: Melbourne University Press.
Denfeld, Rene 1995. *The New Victorians: A Young Woman's Challenge to the Old Feminist Order* St Leonards: Allen and Unwin.

Densmore, Dana 1973. 'Independence from the sexual revolution' in Anne Koedt, Ellen Levine and Anita Rapone (eds) *Radical Feminism* New York: Quadrangle Books.
Department of Employment, Education and Training 1991. *Australia's Workforce in the Year 2001* Canberra: Australian Government Publishing Service.
Department of Sport, Recreation and Tourism 1986. 'Recreation participation survey May 1986', Canberra: Department of Sport, Recreation and Tourism.
Despoja, Shirley Stott 1992. 'Fighting for fair shares' in Jocelynne A. Scutt (ed.) *Breaking Through: Women, Work and Careers* North Melbourne: Artemis.
Dinesen, Isak 1957. *Last Tales* London: University of Chicago Press.
Dinnerstein, Dorothy 1977. *The Mermaid and the Minatour* New York: Harper and Row.
Ditton, Pamela 1992. 'From periphery to centre' in Jocelynne A. Scutt (ed.) *As A Woman: Writing Women's Lives* Melbourne: Artemis.
Dixson, Miriam 1994. *The Real Matilda, Woman and Identity in Australia, 1788 to the Present* Ringwood: Penguin, 3rd edn, 1st edn 1976.
Donaldson, Tamsin 1991. 'Australian tales of mystery and miscegenation' *Meanjin* 50(2/3):341–52.
Douglas, Susan J. 1994. *Where the Girls Are: Growing Up Female with the Mass Media* London: Penguin.
Doyle, Margaret 1995. 'Of restaurants, singularity, and the general joys of living' in Jocelynne A. Scutt (ed.) *Singular Women: Reclaiming Spinsterhood* Melbourne: Artemis.
Dudgeon, Pat, Lazaroo, Simone and Pickett, Harry 1990. 'Aboriginal girls: self-esteem or self-determination?' in Jane Kenway and Sue Willis (eds) *Hearts and Minds: Self-esteem and the Schooling of Girls* London: Falmer Press.
Dunn, Irina 1992. 'Careering through life' in Jocelynne A. Scutt (ed.) *Breaking Through: Women, Work and Careers* North Melbourne: Artemis.
Durham, Helen 1995. 'Self-portrait with crayons' *Australian Feminist Law Journal* 4 (March):113–32.
Edgar, Don 1989. 'The social cost of poverty' in Don Edgar et al. (eds) *Child Poverty* Sydney: Australian Institute of Family Studies and Allen and Unwin.
Edwards, Coral and Read, Peter 1989. *The Lost Children* Sydney: Doubleday.
Edwards, Meredith 1981. *Financial Arrangements Within Families Part 1* Canberra: National Women's Advisory Council.
Eisenstein, Hester 1996. *Inside Agitators: Australian Femocrats and the State* St Leonards: Allen and Unwin.
Eisenstein, Hester 1991. *Gender Shock: Practising Feminism on Two Continents* North Sydney: Allen and Unwin.
Eisenstein, Hester 1985. 'The gender of bureaucracy: reflections on feminism and the state' in J. Goodnow and C. Pateman (eds) *Women, Social Science and Public Policy* Sydney: Allen and Unwin.
Elder, Catriona 1993. '"The question of the unmarried": some meanings of being single in Australia in the 1920s and 1930s' *Australian Feminist Studies* 18:151–73.
Epanomitis, Fotini 1996. 'Double lives: nothing but a bit of blood and gristle' in Kathy Bail (ed.) *DIY Feminism* St Leonards: Allen and Unwin.
Erika, Sabina 1994. 'Together, we can do anything' in Jocelynne A. Scutt (ed.) *Taking a Stand: Women in Politics and Society* Melbourne: Artemis.

Evans, Raymond 1992. 'A gun in the oven: masculinism and gendered violence' in Kay Saunders and Raymond Evans (eds) *Gender Relations in Australia* Sydney: Harcourt Brace Jovanovich.

Eveline, Joan 1995. 'Surviving the belt shop blues: women miners and critical acts' *Australian Journal of Political Science* 30(1):91–107.

Eveline, Joan 1994. 'The politics of advantage' *Australian Feminist Studies* 19:129–54.

Ewington, Julie 1995. 'Number magic: the trouble with women, art and representation' in Barbara Caine and Rosemary Pringle (eds) *Transitions: New Australian Feminisms* St Leonards: Allen and Unwin.

Expert Panel of the National Health and Medical Research Council 1995. *Services for the Termination of Pregnancy in Australia: A Review – Draft Consultation Document – September 1995* Canberra: National Health and Medical Research Council.

Faludi, Susan 1991. *Backlash* New York: Crown.

Faust, Beatrice 1994. *Backlash? Balderdash! Where Feminism is Going Right* Kensington: University of New South Wales Press.

Ferres, Kay 1993. 'Introduction: in the shadow of the nineties: women writing in Australia, 1890–1930' in Kay Ferres (ed.) *The Time to Write: Australian Women Writers 1890–1930* Ringwood: Penguin.

Fesl, Eve Mumewa D. 1993. *Conned!* St Lucia: University of Queensland Press.

Fesl, Eve Mumewa D. 1989. 'Race and racism: white manoeuvres and Koori oppression' *Social Justice* 16(3):30–4.

Finch, Lynette 1993. *The Classing Gaze: Sexuality, Class and Surveillance* St Leonards: Allen and Unwin.

Fingleton, Diane 1992. 'Why am I doing this?' in Jocelynne A. Scutt (ed.) *Breaking Through: Women, Work and Careers* North Melbourne: Artemis.

Finlay, Carol 1994. ' "I'm not a feminist but.. " : women firefighters', paper presented to the Australian Sociological Association, Deakin University, Geelong, December 1994.

Finlayson, Lara 1995. 'Keeping my options open' in Jocelynne Scutt (ed.) *City Women, Country Women: Crossing the Boundaries* Melbourne: Artemis.

Ford, Carolyn 1991. *Women Mean Business: Interviews with Top Australian Business Women* Melbourne: Mandarin.

Fox-Genovese, Elizabeth 1988. 'My statue, myself: autobiographical writings of Afro-American women' in Benstock Shari (ed.) *The Private Self: Theory and Practice of Women's Autobiographical Writings* London: Routledge.

Frances, Raelene 1994. 'The history of female prostitution in Australia' in Roberta Perkins, Garry Prestage, Rachel Sharpe and Frances Lovejoy (eds) *Sex Work and Sex Workers in Australia* Sydney: University of New South Wales Press.

Franzway, Suzanne 1994. 'On women joining unions: Anna Booth, activism and altruism' *Hecate* 20(1):40–57.

Franzway, Suzanne, Court, Dianne, Connell, R. W. 1989. *Staking a Claim: Feminism, Bureaucracy and the State* Sydney: Allen and Unwin.

French, Marilyn 1992. *The War Against Women* London: Hamish Hamilton.

French, Marilyn 1978. *The Women's Room* London: Deutsch, first published 1978.

Friedan, Betty 1983. *The Second Stage* London: Abacus, first published in 1981.

Friedan, Betty 1965. *The Feminine Mystique* Harmondsworth: Penguin, first published in 1963.

Funder, Kathleen 1986. 'Work and marriage partnership' in Peter McDonald (ed.) *Settling Up: Property and Income Distribution on Divorce in Australia* Melbourne: Australian Institute of Family Studies/Prentice-Hall.

Gaffney, Ellie 1993. 'The women's time has arrived' in Jocelynne A. Scutt (ed.) *Glorious Age* Melbourne: Artemis.
Gaffney, Ellie 1989. *Somebody Now: The Autobiography of Ellie Gaffney, a Woman of Torres Strait* Canberra: Aboriginal Studies Press.
Gale, Faye (ed.) 1983. *We are Bosses Ourselves: The Status and Role of Aboriginal Women Today* Canberra: Australian Institute of Aboriginal Studies.
Garner, Helen 1995. *The First Stone: Some Questions About Sex and Power* Sydney: Pan Macmillan.
Geiger, Susan 1992. 'What's so feminist about doing women's oral history?' in Cheryl Johnson-Odim and Margaret Strobel (eds) *Expanding the Boundaries of Women's History* Bloomington and Indianapolis: Indiana University Press.
Gelb, Joyce 1989. *Feminism and Politics: A Comparative Perspective* Berkeley and Los Angeles: University of California Press.
Gender Theory Group 1992. *Women's Studies in Australian Universities: A Directory* Perth: Gender Theory Group, Curtin University of Technology.
Gibbs, Anna 1995. 'Writing/eroticism/transgression: Gertrude Stein and the experience of the other' in Barbara Caine and Rosemary Pringle (eds) *Transitions: New Australian Feminisms* St Leonards: Allen and Unwin.
Gilbert, Pam 1989. 'Stoning the romance: girls as resistant readers and writers' in Ros Thorpe et al. (eds) *Women in Isolation: Collected Papers, Women's Studies Section ANZAAS Congress*, 1987 Townsville: Department of Behavioural Sciences, James Cook University of North Queensland.
Gilbert, Pam and Taylor, Sandra 1991. *Fashioning the Feminine: Girls, Popular Culture and Schooling* Sydney: Allen and Unwin.
Gilding, Michael 1994. 'Gender roles in contemporary Australia' in Kate Pritchard Hughes (ed.) *Contemporary Australian Feminism* Melbourne: Longman Cheshire.
Gilding, Michael 1991. *The Making and Breaking of the Australian Family* North Sydney: Allen and Unwin.
Gilligan, Carol 1982. *In a Different Voice* Cambridge, Massachusetts: Harvard University Press.
Giuffré, Giulia 1992. 'Who do you think you are?' in Karen Herne, Joanne Travaglia and Elizabeth Weiss (eds) *Who Do You Think You Are? Second Generation Immigrant Women in Australia* Broadway: Women's Redress Press.
Glezer, Helen 1988. *Maternity Leave in Australia: Employee and Employer Experiences. Report of a Survey* Melbourne: Australian Institute of Family Studies.
Glickman, Rose L. 1993. *Daughters of Feminists: Young Feminist Mothers Talk About Their Lives* New York: St Martins Press.
Glucksmann, Miriam 1994. 'The work of knowledge and the knowledge of women's work' in Mary Maynard and June Purvis (eds) *Researching Women's Lives from a Feminist Perspective* London: Taylor and Francis.
Glynn, Sean 1970. *Urbanization in Australian History 1788–1900* Melbourne: Nelson.
Goodall, Heather 1990. ' "Saving the children": gender and the colonization of Aboriginal children in NSW, 1788 to 1990' *Aboriginal Law Bulletin* 2(44):6–9.
Goodall, Heather and Huggins, Jackie 1992. 'Aboriginal women are everywhere: contemporary struggles' in Kay Saunders and Raymond Evans (eds) *Gender Relations in Australia* Sydney: Harcourt Brace Jovanovich.
Goldman, R. J. and Goldman, J. D. C. 1988. 'The prevalence and nature of child sexual abuse in Australia' *Australian Journal of Sex, Marriage and the Family* 9(2):94–106.

Goldsmith, Marlene 1994. 'Stranger in a strange pond' in Jocelynne A. Scutt (ed.) *Taking a Stand: Women in Politics and Society* Melbourne: Artemis.
Goode, Christine 1992. 'Deputy secretary, Department of Transport and Communcations' *Six Careers: Women Managers in the Australian Public Service* Barton: Public Service Commission.
Grant, Judith 1994. *Fundamental Feminism: Contesting the Core Concepts of Feminist Theory* New York: Routledge.
Graycar, Regina 1995. 'The gender of judgements: an introduction' in Margaret Thornton (ed.) *Public and Private: Feminist Legal Debates* Melbourne: Oxford University Press.
Graycar, Regina 1990. 'Equality begins at home' in Regina Graycar (ed.) *Dissenting Opinions: Feminist Explorations in Law and Society* Sydney: Allen and Unwin.
Graycar, Regina and Morgan, Jenny 1990. *The Hidden Gender of Law* Leichhardt: Federation Press.
Greenwood, Irene 1992. 'Chronicle of change' in Jocelynne A. Scutt (ed.) *As A Woman: Writing Women's Lives* Melbourne: Artemis.
Greer, Germaine 1971. *The Female Eunuch* London: Granada, first published 1970.
Grieve, Norma 1994. 'Can a boy be a girlfriend? The legacy of gender segregation in childhood play' in Norma Grieve and Ailsa Burns (eds) *Australian Women: Contemporary Feminist Thought* Melbourne: Oxford University Press.
Griffiths, Vivienne 1988. 'Stepping out: the importance of dancing for young women' in Erica Wimbush and Margaret Talbot (eds) *Relative Freedoms: Women and Leisure* Milton Keynes: Open University Press.
Grimshaw, Patricia 1993. 'The "equals and comrades of men"?: *Tocsin* and "the woman question"' in Susan Magarey et al. (eds) *Debutante Nation: Feminism Contests the 1890s* North Sydney: Allen and Unwin.
Grimshaw, Patricia, Lake, Marilyn, McGrath, Ann, and Quartly, Marian 1994. *Creating a Nation* Melbourne: McPhee Gribble.
Grosz, Elizabeth 1989. *Sexual Subversions* Sydney: Allen and Unwin.
Gunew, Sneja et al. (eds) 1992. *A Bibliography of Australian Multicultural Writers* Geelong: Centre for Studies in Literary Education, Deakin University.
Guy, Camille 1996. 'Feminism and sexual abuse: troubled thoughts on some New Zealand issues' *Feminist Review* 52:154–68.
Haaken, Janice 1996. 'The recovery of memory, fantasy, and desire: feminist approaches to sexual abuse and psychic trauma' *Signs* 21(4):1069–94.
Haines, Janine 1992a. *Suffrage to Sufferance: 100 Years of Women in Politics* St Leonards: Allen and Unwin.
Haines, Janine 1992b. 'A sort of crusade' in Jocelynne A. Scutt (ed.) *Breaking Through: Women, Work and Careers* North Melbourne: Artemis.
Hanlon, Carol and Stewart, Terry 1992. 'Aboriginal girls and education' in Christine Hyde et al. (eds) *Facts and Femininity: Factors that Affect Girls Learning* Canberra: Department of Employment, Education and Training.
Hatty, Suzanne E. 1992. 'The desired object: prostitution in Canada, United States and Australia' in Sally-Anne Gerull and Boronia Halstead (eds) *Sex Industry and Public Policy* Canberra: Australian Institute of Criminology.
Healthsharing Women 1994. 'Women, health and the rural decline in Victoria' in Margaret-Ann Franklin, Leonie M. Short and Elizabeth K. Tether (eds) *Country Women at the Crossroads: Perspectives on the Lives of Rural Australian Women in the 1990s* Armidale: University of New England Press.

Hede, Andrew 1995. 'Managerial inequality in the Australian workforce: a longitudinal analysis' *International Review of Women and Leadership* 1(1):11–21.
Heilbrun, Carolyn G. 1995. *The Education of a Woman: The Life of Gloria Steinem* New York: Dial Press.
Henry, Margaret 1993. 'Learning to please myself' in Jocelynne A. Scutt (ed.) *Glorious Age* Melbourne: Artemis.
Henry, Kristin and Derlet, Marlene 1993. *Talking Up a Storm: Nine Women and Consciousness-Raising* Marrickville: Hale and Iremonger.
Hermes, Joke 1992. 'Sexuality in lesbian romance fiction' *Feminist Review* 24:49–66.
Herne, Karen, Travaglia, Joanne and Weiss, Elizabeth (eds) 1992. *Who Do You Think You Are? Second Generation Immigrant Women in Australia* Broadway: Women's Redress Press.
Hernes, Helga Maria 1988. 'The welfare state citizenship of Scandinavian women' in Kathleen B. Jones and Anna G. Jónasdóttir (eds) *The Political Interests of Gender* London: Sage.
Hewett, Peg 1994. 'Peggy's story' in Jocelynne A. Scutt (ed.) *Taking a Stand: Women in Politics and Society* Melbourne: Artemis.
Hindhaugh, Christina 1992. *For Better, For Worse And For Lunch* Sydney: Angus and Robertson.
Hite, Shere 1994. *The Hite Report on the Family: Growing Up Under Patriarchy* London: Bloomsbury.
Ho, Thuy Ai 1995. 'Vietnamese Women's Association in NSW Inc Annual Report 1994–95' Sydney: Vietnamese Women's Association in NSW Inc.
Hobbs, Jacqualine 1995. 'Another country' in Jocelynne A. Scutt (ed.) *City Women, Country Women: Crossing the Boundaries* Melbourne: Artemis.
Hodge, Bob and Mishra, Vijay 1991. *Dark Side of the Dream: Australian Literature and the Postcolonial Mind* North Sydney: Allen and Unwin.
Hoff, Joan 1994. 'Gender as a postmodern category of paralysis' *Women's Studies International Forum* 17(4):443–7.
Hogan, Elizabeth 1994. 'Making women visible: reflections on working with women in agriculture in Victoria' in Margaret–Ann Franklin, Leonie M. Short and Elizabeth K. Tether (eds) *Country Women at the Crossroads: Perspectives on the Lives of Rural Australian Women in the 1990s* Armidale: University of New England Press.
Hooton, Joy 1990. *Stories of Herself When Young: Autobiographies of Childhood By Australian Women* Melbourne: Oxford University Press.
Horwill, Frank M. and Bordow, Sophy 1983. *The Outcome of Defended Custody Cases in the Family Court of Australia* Sydney: Family Court of Australia.
House of Representatives Standing Committee on Legal and Constitutional Affairs, 1992. *Half Way to Equal: Inquiry into Equal Opportunity and Equal Status for Women in Australia* Canberra: Australian Government Publishing Service.
Huata, Donna Awatere 1993. 'Walking on eggs' in Sue Kedgley and Mary Varnham (eds) *Heading Nowhere in a Navy Blue Suit and Other Tales from the Feminist Revolution* Wellington: Daphne Brasel Associates Press.
Huggins, Jackie 1994. 'A contemporary view of Aboriginal women's relationship to the white women's movement' in Norma Grieve and Ailsa Burns (eds) *Australian Women: Contemporary Feminist Thought* Melbourne: Oxford University Press.

Huggins, Jackie 1992. 'But you couldn't possibly . . . !' in Jocelynne A. Scutt (ed.) *Breaking Through: Women, Work and Careers* North Melbourne: Artemis.

Huggins, Rita and Huggins, Jackie 1994. *Auntie Rita* Canberra: Aboriginal Studies Press, Australian Institute of Aboriginal Studies.

Hughes, Paul 1987. *Aboriginal Culture and Learning Styles – A Challenge for Academics in Higher Education Institutions* Armidale: University of New England.

Hunter, Thelma 1994. 'Travails of a liberal feminist: an autobiographical essay' *Australian Feminist Studies* 20:203–15.

Hutchinson, Carrie 1993. 'Young hot and feminist' *Refractory Girl* 46:9–13.

Hutchison, Noel 1976. 'Australian women sculptors 1840–1940' in Kiffy Carter et al. (eds) *Australian Women Artists, One Hundred Years: 1840–1940* Melbourne: Ewing and George Paton Galleries and Melbourne University Union.

Jackson, Donna 1994. 'A twinkle in my eye' in Jocelynne A. Scutt (ed.) *Taking a Stand: Women in Politics and Society* Melbourne: Artemis.

Jackson, Judy 1994. 'Getting out and doing something' in Jocelynne A. Scutt (ed.) *Taking a Stand: Women in Politics and Society* Melbourne: Artemis.

Jacobs, Jane M. 1994. 'Earth honouring: western desires and indigenous knowledges' *Meanjin* 53(2):305–14.

Jaggar, Alison M. 1994a. 'Introduction' to 'The personal as political' in Alison M. Jaggar (ed.) *Living with Contradictions: Controversies in Feminist Social Ethics* Boulder: Westview Press.

Jaggar, Alison M. 1994b. 'Introduction' to 'Marketing femininity' in Alison M. Jaggar (ed.) *Living with Contradictions: Controversies in Feminist Social Ethics* Boulder: Westview Press.

James, Stanlie M. 1992. 'Mothering: a possible black feminist link to social transformation?' in Stanlie M. James and Abena P. A. Busia (eds) *Theorizing Black Feminisms: The Visionary Pragmatism of Black Women* New York: Routledge.

Jean, Carole 1994. 'Costs of children update' *Family Matters*, August 1994, 38:16.

Jeffreys, Sheila 1994. 'Setting the agenda' in Jocelynne A. Scutt (ed.) *Taking a Stand: Women in Politics and Society* Melbourne: Artemis.

Jennett, Christine 1987. 'The feminist enterprise' in Christine Jennett and Randall G. Stewart (eds) *Three Worlds of Inequality: Race, Class and Gender* Melbourne: Macmillan.

Johnson, Lesley 1993. *The Modern Girl: Girlhood and Growing Up* Sydney: Allen and Unwin.

Johnson, Eva 1994. 'A question of difference' in Jocelynne A. Scutt (ed.) *Taking a Stand: Women in Politics and Society* Melbourne: Artemis.

Johnson, Rhondda 1994. 'Tess of the western suburbs' in Jocelynne A. Scutt (ed.) *Taking a Stand: Women in Politics and Society* Melbourne: Artemis.

Johnston, Elliott 1991a. *Royal Commission into Aboriginal Deaths in Custody: National Report Volume 1* Canberra: Australian Government Publishing Service.

Johnston, Elliott 1991b. *Royal Commission into Aboriginal Deaths in Custody: National Report Volume 2* Canberra: Australian Government Publishing Service.

Jones, F. L. 1991. *Ancestry Groups in Australia: A Descriptive Overview* Wollongong: Centre for Multicultural Studies.

Jones, Fiorenza and Diack, Elena 1987. 'Italian community' in *Papers from the Seminar 'Domestic Violence – A Cross Cultural Perspective'* Canberra: Department of Immigration, Local Government and Ethnic Affairs.

Kahan-Guidi, Anna Maria and Weiss, Elizabeth (eds) 1990. *Forza e Coraggio/ Give Me Strength: Italian Australian Women Speak* Sydney: Women's Redress Press.

Kalantzis, Mary 1990. 'Ethnicity meets gender meets class in Australia' in Sophie Watson (ed.) *Playing the State: Australian Feminist Interventions* Sydney: Allen and Unwin.

Kaplan, Gisela 1996. *The Meagre Harvest: The Australian Women's Movement 1950s–1990s* St Leonards: Allen and Unwin.

Kaplan, Gisela 1992. *Contemporary Western European Feminism* North Sydney: Allen and Unwin.

Kenny, Kath 1996. 'Sex and harassment: live from the mouths of babes' in Kathy Bail (ed.) *DIY Feminism* St Leonards: Allen and Unwin.

Kenway, Jane 1990. 'Privileged girls, private schools and the culture of "success"' in Jane Kenway and Sue Willis (eds) *Hearts and Minds: Self-esteem and the Schooling of Girls* London: Falmer Press.

Kilmartin, Christine 1995. 'National Aboriginal and Torres Strait Islander survey 1994' *Family Matters* 40:40–3.

King, Catherine 1992. 'Making things mean: cultural representations in objects' in Frances Bonner et al. (eds) *Imagining Women* Cambridge: Polity Press and Open University.

Kishwar, Madhu 1995. 'A code for self-monitoring: some thoughts on action' *Manushi* 85:5–10,12,14–17.

Knapman, Claudia 1993. 'Reconstructing mothering: feminism and the Early Childhood Centre' *Australian Feminist Studies* 18:111–31.

Knibiehler, Yvonne 1992. 'Chronology and women's history' in Michelle Perrot (ed.) *Writing Women's History*, translated by Felicia Pheasant, Oxford: Blackwell.

Koedt, Anne 1973. 'The myth of the vaginal orgasm' in Anne Koedt, Ellen Levine and Anita Rapone (eds) *Radical Feminism* New York: Quadrangle Books.

Koppelman, Susan 1993. 'Between mothers and daughters: stories across a generation: the personal is political in life and literature' *Women's Studies International Forum* 16(1):47–56.

Koppelman, Susan 1985. *Between Mothers and Daughters: Stories Across a Generation* New York: Feminist Press.

Koval, Romana 1995. 'Romana Koval talks to Helen Garner and Cassandra Pybus' *Australian Book Review* 170:9–12.

Kuh, Debbie 1995. 'Singular: verb' in Jocelynne A. Scutt (ed.) *Singular Women: Reclaiming Spinsterhood* Melbourne: Artemis.

Küppers, Gaby 1994. *Companeras: Voices from the Latin American Women's Movement* London: Latin American Bureau.

Kyne, Caty 1995. 'Going it alone' in Jocelynne A. Scutt (ed.) *Singular Women: Reclaiming Spinsterhood* Melbourne: Artemis.

La Marchesina, Concetta 1994. 'Working with women in the workplace: the story of WICH' in Wendy Weeks (ed.) *Women Working Together: Lessons from Feminist Women's Services* Melbourne: Longman Cheshire.

Lake, Marilyn 1995a. 'Female desires: the meaning of World War II' in Joy Damousi and Marilyn Lake (eds) *Gender and War: Australians at War in the Twentieth Century* Cambridge: Cambridge University Press.

Lake Marilyn 1995b. 'Three perspectives on Helen Garner's *The First Stone*' *Australian Book Review* 174 (September):26–7.

Lake, Marilyn 1994. 'Between Old World "Barbarism" and Stone Age "Primitivism": the double difference of the white Australian feminist' in

Norma Grieve and Ailsa Burns (eds) *Australian Women: Contemporary Feminist Thought* Melbourne: Oxford University Press.

Lake, Marilyn 1992. 'Mission Impossible: how men gave birth to the Australian nation – nationalism, gender and other seminal acts' *Gender and History* 4(3):305–22.

Lake, Marilyn 1986. 'The politics of respectability: identifying the masculinist context' *Historical Studies* 22(86):116–31.

Langford, Ruby 1988. *Don't Take Your Love to Town* Ringwood: Penguin.

Langton, Marcia et al. 1991. '"Too much sorry business" – the report of the Aboriginal Issues Unit of the Northern Territory' in Elliott Johnston, *Royal Commission into Aboriginal Deaths in Custody: National Report Volume 5*, Canberra: Australian Government Publishing Service.

Law Reform Commission 1994. *Equality Before the Law: Women's Equality* Sydney: Commonwealth of Australia.

Lawrence, Carmen 1994. 'Personal comment' *Australian Feminist Studies* 19:9–15.

Law, Sylvia A. 1984. 'Rethinking sex and the Constitution' *University of Pennsylvania Law Review* 132(4):955–1034.

Lee, Gloria 1993. 'Sitting out in the hills in China' in Jocelynne A. Scutt (ed.) *No Fear of Flying: Women at Home and Abroad* Melbourne: Artemis.

Lees, Stella and Senyard, June 1987. *The 1950s and How Australians Became a Modern Society and Everyone Got a Home and Car* South Yarra, Hyland House.

Lessing, Doris 1994. *Under My Skin* London: HarperCollins.

Levine, Philippa 1990. *Feminist Lives in Victorian England: Private Roles and Public Commitment* Oxford: Basil Blackwell.

Lewis, Barbara 1994. 'Politics in the blood' in Jocelynne A. Scutt (ed.) *Taking a Stand: Women in Politics and Society* Melbourne: Artemis.

Lewis, Helen 1989. *Part-time Work: Trends and Issues* Canberra: Department of Employment, Education and Training, Australian Government Publishing Service.

Lewis, Sue 1993. 'Lessons to learn: gender and science education' in Farley Kelly (ed.) *On the Edge of Discovery* Melbourne: Text Publishing Company.

Liddy-Corpus, Louise 1992. 'Taking control now' in Jocelynne A. Scutt (ed.) *Breaking Through: Women, Work and Careers* North Melbourne: Artemis.

Lopez, Ofelia 1993. 'Becoming a walking book' in Jocelynne A. Scutt (ed.) *No Fear of Flying: Women at Home and Abroad* Melbourne: Artemis.

Loro, Adriana 1992. 'Working with girls of Italian background' in Christine Hyde et al. (eds) *Facts and Femininity: Factors that Affect Girls Learning* Canberra; Department of Employment, Education and Training.

Lucashenko, Melissa 1994. 'No other truth?: Aboriginal women and Australian feminism' *Social Alternatives* 12(4):21–4.

Lucashenko, Melissa and Best, Odette 1995. 'Women bashing: an Aboriginal perspective' *Social Alternatives* 14(1):19–22.

Luke, Allan 1995. 'Getting our hands dirty: provisional politics in postmodern conditions' in Richard Smith and Philip Wexler (eds) *After Postmodernism: Education, Politics and Identity* London: Falmer Press.

Lupton, Gillian, Short, Patricia M. and Whip, Rosemary 1992. *Society and Gender: An Introduction to Sociology* South Melbourne: Macmillan.

Lyons, Gregory 1984. 'Aboriginal Legal Services' in Peter Hanks and Bryan Keon-Cohen (eds) *Aborigines and the Law* Sydney: George Allen and Unwin.

Lyons-Lee, Lenore and Collins, Janine 1995. 'Interviews: do feminists need a "How To" manual?', presentation in the Faculty of Humanities, Griffith University, Nathan.

McBain, Rosemary 1994. 'Housing affordability' *The Far Northern Bush Telegraph* 8 (April):4–5.

McCreadie, Sue and Nightingale, Martina 1994. 'Challenges for women trade unionists' *Social Alternatives* 12(4):39–42.

McDonald, Kevin 1995. 'Leeching the meanings of human experience' *Arena Magazine* 17:44–8.

McDonald, Peter 1995. *Families in Australia: A Socio-Demographic Perspective* Australian Institute of Family Studies: Melbourne.

McDonald, Peter 1990. 'The 1980s: social and economic change affecting families' *Family Matters* 26:13–18.

McDonald, Peter 1989. 'Can the family survive?' in Tom Jagtenberg and Phillip D'Alton (eds) *Four Dimensional Space* Sydney: Harper and Row.

McDonald, Peter 1986. 'Family reformation' in Peter McDonald (ed.) *Settling Up: Property and Income Distribution on Divorce in Australia* Melbourne: Australian Institute of Family Studies/Prentice-Hall.

McFerrin, Ludo 1993. 'Domestic violence – stories, scandals and serious analyses' in Refractory Girl (ed.) *Refractory Voices: Feminist Perspectives from Refractory Girl* Sydney: Refractory Girl Feminist Journal.

McFerren, Ludo 1990. 'Interpretation of a frontline state: Australian women's refuges and the state' in Sophie Watson (ed.) *Playing the State: Australian Feminist Interventions* Sydney: Allen and Unwin.

McGowan, Cathy 1995. 'Australian women in agriculture' *Country Web* 8:19.

McGregor, Heather and Hopkins, Andrew 1991. *Working for Change: The Movement Against Domestic Violence* North Sydney: Allen and Unwin.

Mackinnon, Alison 1993. 'The state as an agent of demographic change? The higher education of women and fertility decline 1880–1930' in Renate Howe (ed.) *Women and the State: Australian Perspectives* special edn of *Journal of Australian Studies*, Bundoora: La Trobe University Press in association with the Centre for Australian Studies, Deakin University, and the Ideas for Australia Program.

MacKinnon, Catharine A. 1987. *Feminism Unmodified: Discourses on Life and Law* Cambridge: Harvard University Press.

McNeill, Edith 1994. 'Trust and the innermost pain of the soul' in Jocelynne A. Scutt (ed.) *Taking a Stand: Women in Politics and Society* Melbourne: Artemis.

McRobbie, Angela 1984. 'Dance and social fantasy' in Angela McRobbie and Mica Nava (eds) *Gender and Generation* Basingstoke: Macmillan.

Magarey, Susan, Ryan, Lyndall and Sheridan, Susan 1994. 'Women's studies in Australia' in Norma Grieve and Ailsa Burns (eds) *Australian Women: Contemporary Feminist Thought* Melbourne: Oxford University Press.

Manderson, Lenore 1992. 'Patterns of shadows' in Jocelynne A. Scutt (ed.) *As A Woman: Writing Women's Lives* Melbourne: Artemis.

Marcus, Sharon 1992. 'Fighting bodies, fighting words: a theory and politics of rape prevention' in Judith Butler and Joan W. Scott (eds) *Feminists Theorize the Political* New York: Routledge.

Marginson, Melba 1992. 'Not for the money' in Jocelynne A. Scutt (ed.) *Breaking Through: Women, Work and Careers* North Melbourne: Artemis.

Marginson, Simon 1993. *Education and Public Policy in Australia* Cambridge: Cambridge University Press.

Marsh, Ian 1995. 'The 1994 Mardi Gras telecast: conflicting minorities and the judgement of public interests' *Australian Journal of Political Science* 30(3):545–60.

Mason, Carolyn 1994. 'Women's policy in Queensland' *Social Alternatives* 12(4):13–16.

Maroske, Sara 1993. '"The whole great continent as a present": nineteenth-century Australian women workers in science' in Farley Kelly (ed.) *On the Edge of Discovery* Melbourne: Text Publishing Company.

Martin, Jeannie 1991. 'Multiculturalism and feminism' in Gill Bottomley et al. (eds) *Intersexions: Gender/Class/Culture/Ethnicity* North Sydney: Allen and Unwin.

Matchett, Ruth 1988. *Beyond These Walls: Report of the Queensland Domestic Violence Task Force* Brisbane: Queensland Government.

Mayer, Peter and Bacchi, Carol 1996. 'The two cultures of equal opportunity', unpublished paper, Politics Department, University of Adelaide.

Mayers, Naomi 1992. 'Growing to meet the work's demands' in Nan Gallagher (ed.) *A Story to Tell: The Working Lives of Ten Aboriginal Australians* Cambridge: Cambridge University Press.

Mayle, Peter 1975. *Where Did I Come From?: The Facts of Life Without Any Nonsense and With Illustrations* Melbourne: Sun Books.

Maynard, Mary 1994. 'Methods, practice and epistemology: the debate about feminism and research' in Mary Maynard and June Purvis (eds) *Researching Women's Lives from a Feminist Perspective* London: Taylor and Francis.

Maynard, Mary and Purvis, June 1994. 'Doing feminist research' in Mary Maynard and June Purvis (eds) *Researching Women's Lives from a Feminist Perspective* London: Taylor and Francis.

Meadows, Geoff 1994. 'Community involvement in planning: becoming a reality in Far North Queensland' *Far Northern Bush Telegraph* 5 (July):8–9.

Mendelsohn, Thea 1993. 'A leafy path' in Jocelynne A. Scutt (ed.) *Glorious Age* Melbourne: Artemis.

Middleton, Sue 1993. *Educating Feminists: Life Histories and Pedagogies* New York and London: Teachers College Press.

Millan, Marianne 1993. 'Education' in Refractory Girl (ed.) *Refractory Voices: Feminist Perspectives from Refractory Girl* Sydney: Refractory Girl Feminist Journal.

Miller, Lydia 1993. 'The women's movement and Aboriginal women' in Refractory Girl (ed.) *Refractory Voices: Feminist Perspectives from Refractory Girl* Sydney: Refractory Girl Feminist Journal.

Mills, Ros and Duffield, Rob 1994. 'Rape crisis services in Queensland' in Gail Reekie (ed.) *On the Edge: Women's Experiences of Queensland* St Lucia: University of Queensland Press.

Mitchell, Jenni 1994. 'Grass roots and government initiative: Victoria's rural women's network' in Margaret-Ann Franklin, Leonie M. Short and Elizabeth K. Tether (eds) *Country Women at the Crossroads: Perspectives on the Lives of Rural Australian Women in the 1990s* Armidale: University of New England Press.

Mitchell, Susan 1991. *Tall Poppies Too* Ringwood: Penguin.

Mitchell, Susan 1987. *The Matriarchs: Twelve Australian Women Talk About Their Lives to Susan Mitchell* Ringwood: Penguin.

Mitchell, Susan 1984. *Tall Poppies* Ringwood: Penguin.

Mitchell, Susan and Dyer, Ken 1985. *Winning Women: Challenging the Norms in Australian Sport* Ringwood: Penguin.

Moi, Toril 1994. *Simone de Beauvoir: The Making of an Intellectual Woman* Oxford UK and Cambridge USA: Blackwell.

Momot, Chris 1994. 'Looking back, smiling' in Jocelynne A. Scutt (ed.) *Taking a Stand: Women in Politics and Society* Melbourne: Artemis.

Moore, Catriona 1991. *Indecent Exposures: Twenty Years of Australian Feminist Photography* St Leonards: Allen and Unwin in association with Power Institute of Fine Arts.
Moreton-Robinson, Aileen 1992. 'Masking gender and exalting race: indigenous women and Commonwealth employment policies' *Australian Feminist Studies* 15:5–24.
Morgan, Jenny 1995. 'Sexual harassment in the public/private dichotomy: equality, morality and morals' in Margaret Thornton (ed.) *Public and Private: Feminist Legal Debates* Melbourne: Oxford University Press.
Morgan, Sally 1987. *My Place* Fremantle: Fremantle Arts Centre Press.
Moyal, Ann 1995. *Breakfast With Beaverbrook: Memoirs of an Independent Woman* Sydney: Hale and Iremonger.
Mumford, Karen 1989. *Women Working: Economics and Reality* Sydney: Allen and Unwin.
Naffine, Ngaire 1990. *Law and the Sexes: Explorations in Feminist Jurisprudence* Sydney: Allen and Unwin.
Nathan, Pam. 1987. 'Borning: the Congress Alukura by the Grandmother's law' *Arena* 79:44–7.
Nathan, Pam 1980. *A Home Away From Home: A Study of the Aboriginal Health Service in Fitzroy* Bundoora, Victoria: Preston Institute of Technology.
Neave, Marcia 1994. 'Prostitution laws in Australia: past history and current trends' in Roberta Perkins, Garry Prestage, Rachel Sharpe and Frances Lovejoy (eds) *Sex Work and Sex Workers in Australia* Sydney: University of New South Wales Press.
Neave, Marcia 1992. 'From difference to sameness – law and women's work' *Melbourne University Law Review* 18(4):768–807.
Newton, Stella Mary 1974. *Health, Art and Reason: Dress Reformers of the Nineteenth Century* London: John Murray.
Nicholson, Victoria 1993. 'Summers of our discontent' *Refractory Girl* 46:17–19.
Noonuccal, Oodgeroo 1989. 'Towards a global village in the southern hemisphere' Nathan: Institute for Cultural Policy Studies, Division of Humanities, Griffith University.
Oakley, Ann 1981. 'Interviewing women: a contradiction in terms' in Helen Roberts (ed.) *Doing Feminist Research* London: Routledge and Kegan Paul.
O'Donovan, Katherine 1985. *Sexual Divisions in Law* London: Weidenfeld and Nicolson.
O'Loughlin, Iris 1994. 'The production of Australian women's plays' *Australian Women's Book Review* 6(2):26–7.
O'Neill, John 1995. 'Women who've won' *Independent Monthly* February:26–32.
O'Shane, Pat 1994. 'Launch of the Australian Feminist Law Journal, August 29 1993 the University of Melbourne' *Australian Feminist Law Journal* 2 (March):3–12.
O'Shane, Pat 1993. 'Aboriginal women and the women's movement' in Refractory Girl (ed.) *Refractory Voices: Feminist Perspectives from Refractory Girl* Sydney: Refractory Girl Feminist Journal.
Office of the Status of Women, Department of the Prime Minister and Cabinet 1995a. *Australian National Report to the United Nations Fourth World Conference on Women* Canberra: Commonwealth of Australia.
Office of the Status of Women, Department of Prime Minister and Cabinet, 1995b. 'Fourth United Nations World Conference on Women Beijing 4–15 September 1995' Infosheet Number 8:4.

Office of the Status of Women, Department of the Prime Minister and Cabinet 1992. *Women in Australia: Australia's Second Progress Report on Implementing the United Nations Convention on the Elimination of All Forms of Discrimination Against Women* Canberra: Commonwealth of Australia.
Oldfield, Audrey 1992. *Woman Suffrage in Australia: A Gift or a Struggle?* Cambridge: Cambridge University Press.
Parella, Lucia 1993. 'Participation in government structures: progress or co-option?' *Australian Feminist Studies* 18:67–79.
Parker, Lesley H. and Offer, Jenny A. 1989. 'In favour of compulsory science' in Gilah C. Leder and Shirley N. Sampson (eds) *Educating Girls* Sydney: Allen and Unwin.
Patai, Daphne and Koertge, Noretta 1994. *Professing Feminism: Cautionary Tales from the Strange World of Women's Studies* New York: Basic Books.
Pavan, Carmelle 1994. 'The fighting spirit' in Jocelynne A. Scutt (ed.) *Taking a Stand: Women in Politics and Society* Melbourne: Artemis.
Peers, Juliet 1993. *More Than Just Gumtrees: A Personal, Social and Artistic History of the Melbourne Society of Women Painters and Sculptors* Melbourne: Melbourne Society of Women Painters and Sculptors in association with Dawn Revival Press.
Pellizzari, Monica 1993. 'A woman, a wog and a westie' in Barbara Walsh (ed.) *Growing Up Italian in Australia: Eleven Young Australian Women Talk About Their Childhood* Sydney: State Library of New South Wales.
Perkins, Roberta 1994. 'Female prostitution' in Roberta Perkins, Garry Prestage, Rachel Sharpe and Frances Lovejoy (eds) *Sex Work and Sex Workers in Australia* Sydney: University of New South Wales Press.
Perkins, Roberta 1989. *Working Girls: Prostitutes, Their Life and Social Control* Canberra: Australian Institute of Criminology.
Petrovic, Daniella, Kokokiris, Maria and Kalinowska, Monica 1994. *Livin' Large* Sydney: Pan Macmillan.
Pittman, Elizabeth and Sugimoto, Yoshio 1978. 'The Melbourne *Herald*'s description of women's roles, 1947–1976' *Australian and New Zealand Journal of Sociology* 14(2):200–4.
Pixley, Jocelyn 1992. 'Citizen, worker or client? State, class and welfare' in Michael Muetzelfeldt (ed.) *Society, State and Politics in Australia* Leichhardt: Pluto Press.
Pocock, Barbara 1988. *Demanding Skill* Sydney: Allen and Unwin.
Poole, Marilyn 1986. *Idols and Ideals* Melbourne: AE Press.
Poole, Millicent J. 1986. 'Choices and constraints: the education of girls' in Norma Grieve and Ailsa Burns (eds) *Australian Women: New Feminist Perspectives* Melbourne: Oxford University Press.
Poole, Millicent E. and Beswick, David G. 1989. 'Girls' expectations' in Gilah C. Leder and Shirley N. Sampson (eds) *Educating Girls: Practice and Research* Sydney: Allen and Unwin.
Prestage, Garrett and Perkins, Roberta 1994. 'Introduction' in Roberta Perkins, Garry Prestage, Rachel Sharpe and Frances Lovejoy (eds) *Sex Work and Sex Workers in Australia* Sydney: University of New South Wales Press.
Pring, Adele (ed.) 1990. *Women of the Centre* Apollo Bay; Pascoe Publishing.
Pringle, Rosemary 1996. 'Women doctors – making some difference?', professorial lecture, Griffith University, 10 October 1996.
Pringle, Rosemary 1995. 'Destablising patriarchy' in Barbara Caine and Rosemary Pringle (eds) *Transitions: New Australian Feminisms* St Leonards: Allen and Unwin.

Pringle, Rosemary 1994. 'Ladies to women: women and the professions' in Norma Grieve and Ailsa Burns (eds) *Australian Women: Contemporary Feminist Thought* Melbourne: Oxford University Press.
Pringle, Rosemary 1988. *Secretaries Talk: Sexuality, Power and Work* Sydney: Allen and Unwin.
Pringle, Rosemary and Watson, Sophie 1992. ' "Women's interests and the post-structuralist state' in Michelle Barrett and Anne Phillips (eds) *Destabilizing Theory: Contemporary Feminist Debates* Cambridge: Polity.
Probert, Belinda 1989. *Working Life* Melbourne: McPhee Gribble.
Quadrio, Carolyn and Quadrio, Lisa 1994. 'Sta thika sou (And here's to yours)' in Dale Spender (ed.) *Weddings and Wives* Melbourne: Penguin.
Pusey, Michael 1991. *Economic Rationalism in Canberra: A Nation Building State Changes its Mind* Cambridge: Cambridge University Press.
Pybus, Cassandra 1995. 'Cassandra Pybus reviews Helen Garner's *The First Stone*' *Australian Book Review* 170:6–8.
Radi, Heather 1988. 'Margaret Catchpole' in Heather Radi (ed.) *200 Australian Women* Broadway: Women's Redress Press.
Radway, Janice 1984. *Reading The Romance: Women, Patriarchy and Popular Literature* Chapel Hill: University of North Carolina Press.
Rathus, Zoe 1993. *Rougher Than Usual Handling: Women and The Criminal Justice System* West End, Brisbane: Women's Legal Service.
Rayner, Moira 1994. 'Middle aged ways' *Australian Feminist Law* Journal 3 (August):157–72.
Rayner, Moira 1992. 'Confessions of a femme sole' in Jocelynne A. Scutt (ed.) *As A Woman: Writing Women's Lives* Melbourne: Artemis.
Refractory Girl (ed.) 1993. *Refractory Voices: Feminist Perspectives from Refractory Girl* Sydney: Refractory Girl Feminist Journal.
Rehfeldt, Nancy 1994. 'Like my mother' in Jocelynne A. Scutt (ed.) *Taking a Stand: Women in Politics and Society* Melbourne: Artemis.
Reiger, Kerreen M. 1985. *The Disenchantment of the Home: Modernizing the Australian Family 1880–1940* Melbourne: Oxford University Press.
Reinharz, Shulamit 1992. *Feminist Methods in Social Research* New York: Oxford University Press.
Rendall, Jane 1987. 'Introduction' in Jane Rendall (ed.) *Equal or Different: Women's Politics 1800–1914* Oxford: Basil Blackwell.
Reynolds, Margaret 1996. 'Towards a republic and women's equal participation in parliament' in Jeannette Hoorn and David Goodman (eds) *Vox Republica: Feminism and the Republic, special edn of the Journal of Australian Studies* 47, Bundoora: La Trobe University Press.
Reynolds, Margaret 1993. 'Growing older – like a good wine' in Jocelynne A. Scutt (ed.) *Glorious Age* Melbourne: Artemis.
Rhiannon, Lee 1994. ' "Old sisters" and the new future' in Jocelynne A. Scutt (ed.) *Taking a Stand: Women in Politics and Society* Melbourne: Artemis.
Rich, Adrienne 1983. 'Compulsory heterosexuality and lesbian existence' in Ann Snitow et al. (eds) *Desire: The Politics of Sexuality* London: Virago.
Rich, Adrienne 1977. *Of Woman Born: Motherhood as an Experience and Institution* London: Virago.
Richards, Janeece 1995. 'Demanding a voice' in Jocelynne A. Scutt (ed.) *City Women, Country Women: Crossing the Boundaries* Melbourne: Artemis.
Ridgeway, Beverley 1986. 'Domestic violence: Aboriginal women's viewpoint' in Suzanne E. Hatty (ed.) *National Conference on Domestic Violence: Proceedings* Volume 1, Canberra: Australian Institute of Criminology.

Rigg, Julie and Copeland, Julie (eds) 1985. *Coming Out! Women's Voices, Women's Lives: A Selection From ABC Radio's Coming Out Show* Melbourne: Nelson in association with Australian Broadcasting Corporation.
Riley-Smith, Barbara 1992. 'The women's view: market research study on women's perceptions of themselves and government programs and policies' Canberra: Office of the Status of Women, Department of Prime Minister and Cabinet.
Roberts, Bev 1995. 'Urban consciousness and the extravagance of nature' in Jocelynne A. Scutt (ed.) *City Women, Country Women: Crossing the Boundaries* Melbourne: Artemis.
Rogers, Victoria, Baldock, Cora V. and Milligan, Denise 1993. *What Difference Does it Make? A Pilot Study of Women in the Performing and Visual Arts in Western Australia* Redfern: Australian Council for the Arts.
Roiphe, Katie 1993. *The Morning After: Sex, Fear, and Feminism* London: Hamish Hamilton.
Ronalds, Chris 1987. *Affirmative Action and Sex Discrimination: A Handbook of Legal Rights for Women* Sydney: Pluto Press.
Rosener, Judy B. 1995. *America's Competitive Secret: Utilizing Women as a Management Strategy* New York: Oxford University Press.
Rossi, Lucy 1990. 'Lucy Rossi' in Anna Maria Kahan-Guidi and Elizabeth Weiss (eds) *Forza e Coraggio/Give Me Strength: Italian Australian Women Speak* Sydney: Women's Redress Press.
Rowan, Dawn 1992. 'Beware, oh take care' in Jocelynne A. Scutt (ed.) *Breaking Through: Women, Work and Careers* North Melbourne: Artemis.
Rowbotham, Sheila 1992. *Women in Movement: Feminism and Social Action* London: Routledge.
Rowe, Mary 1981. 'The minutiae of discrimination: the need for support' in Barbara L. Forisha and Barbara H. Goldman (eds) *Outsiders on the Inside: Women and Organizations* Englewood Cliffs: Prentice-Hall.
Rowland, Robyn 1992. *Living Laboratories: Women and Reproductive Technologies* South Melbourne: Sun Books.
Rowland, Robyn 1984. (ed. and introducer) *Women Who Do and Women Who Don't Join the Women's Movement* London: Routledge and Kegan Paul.
Rowlands, Shane and Henderson, Margaret 1996. 'Damned bores and slick sisters: the selling of blockbuster feminism in Australia' *Australian Feminist Studies* 11(23):9–16.
Ryan, Barbara B. 1992. *Feminism and the Women's Movement: Dynamics of Change in Social Movement, Ideology and Activism* New York: Routledge.
Ryan, Lyndall 1993. 'Women's studies in the university seminar' *Australian Women's Studies Association Newsletter* 8(2):1–2,5–6.
Ryan, Lyndall 1990. 'Feminism and the federal bureaucracy 1972–1983' in Sophie Watson (ed.) *Playing the State: Australian Feminist Interventions* Sydney: Allen and Unwin.
Safe, Mike and Whittaker, Mark 1994. 'The baby boomers of 1994: changing their ways but still wanting power' *Australian Magazine* 26–27 February 1994:10–22.
Salamone, Giovanna 1993. 'Transitions' in Jocelynne A. Scutt (ed.) *Glorious Age* Melbourne: Artemis.
Sampson, Shirley 1993. 'The Australian *Women's Weekly* today: education and the aspirations of girls' in Refractory Girl (ed.) *Refractory Voices: Feminist Perspectives from Refractory Girl* Sydney: Refractory Girl Feminist Journal.

Sawer, Marian 1993. 'Reclaiming social liberalism: the women's movement and the state' in Renate Howe (ed.) *Women and the State: Australian Perspectives, special edn of Journal of Australian Studies*, Bundoora: La Trobe University Press in association with the Centre for Australian Studies, Deakin University, and the Ideas for Australia Program .

Sawer, Marian 1989. 'Monitoring social justice' in 'Social Justice in Australia' *Supplement to Australian Society* (December 1988/January 1989):18–20.

Sawer, Marian 1990. *Sisters in Suits: Women and Public Policy in Australia* Sydney: Allen and Unwin.

Sawer, Marion and Groves, Abigail 1994a. *Working From the Inside: Twenty Years of the Office of the Status of Women* Canberra: Department of the Prime Minister and Cabinet, Australian Government Publishing Service.

Sawer, Marian and Groves, Abigail 1994b. '"The women's lobby": networks, coalition building and the women of middle Australia' *Australian Journal of Political Science* 29(3):435–59.

Sawer, Marian and Simms, Marian 1993. *A Woman's Place: Women and Politics in Australia* North Sydney: Allen and Unwin, 2nd edn; first published 1984.

Schultz, Julianne 1993. 'Women and the media – the struggle for space' in Refractory Girl (ed.) *Refractory Voices: Feminist Perspectives from Refractory Girl* Sydney: Refractory Girl Feminist Journal.

Scutt, Jocelynne A. (ed.) 1995. *City Women, Country Women: Crossing the Boundaries* Melbourne: Artemis.

Scutt, Jocelynne A. (ed.) 1994. *Taking a Stand: Women in Politics and Society* Melbourne: Artemis.

Scutt, Jocelynne A. (ed.) 1993a. *Glorious Age* Melbourne: Artemis.

Scutt, Jocelynne A. (ed.) 1993b. *No Fear of Flying: Women at Home and Abroad* Melbourne: Artemis.

Scutt, Jocelynne A. (ed.) 1992a. *Breaking Through: Women, Work and Careers* Artemis Press.

Scutt, Jocelynne A. (ed.) 1992b. *As A Woman: Writing Women's Lives* Melbourne: Artemis.

Scutt, Jocelynne 1991. 'Foreword' in Heather McGregor and Andrew Hopkins *Working For Change: The Movement Against Domestic Violence* North Sydney: Allen and Unwin.

Scutt, Jocelynne 1990. *Women and the Law: Commentary and Materials* Sydney: Law Book Company.

Scutt, Jocelynne A. 1985a. *Growing Up Feminist: The New Generation of Australian Women* North Ryde: Angus and Robertson.

Scutt, Jocelynne A. 1985b. 'In pursuit of equality: women and legal thought 1788–1984' in J. Goodnow and C. Pateman (eds) *Women, Social Science and Public Policy* Sydney: Allen and Unwin.

Schmolke, Sue 1992. 'Genesis – Tennant Creek' in Jocelynne A. Scutt (ed.) *Breaking Through: Women, Work and Careers* North Melbourne: Artemis.

Schubert, Misha 1994. 'Inventive, gutsy, determined women' in Jocelynne A. Scutt (ed.) *Taking a Stand: Women in Politics and Society* Melbourne: Artemis.

Sedgwick, Eve Kosofsky 1990. *Epistemology of the Closet* Berkeley and Los Angeles: University of California Press.

Segal, Lyn 1994. *Straight Sex: Rethinking the Politics of Pleasure* Berkeley and Los Angeles: University of California Press.

Selby, Wendy 1994. ' "Raising an interrogatory eyebrow": women's responses to the Infant Welfare Movement in Queensland, 1918–1939' in Gail Reekie

(ed.) *On the Edge: Women's Experiences of Queensland* St Lucia: University of Queensland Press.
Selfe, Bernadette 1995. 'Believing in myself' in Jocelynne A. Scutt (ed.) 1995. *Singular Women: Reclaiming Spinsterhood* Melbourne: Artemis.
Senate Standing Committee on Employment, Education and Training 1990. *Priorities for Reform in Higher Education*, chaired by Terry Aulich, Canberra: Australian Government Publishing Service.
Setches, Kay 1992. 'No circuses, no unreal promises' in Jocelynne A. Scutt (ed.) *As A Woman: Writing Women's Lives* Melbourne: Artemis.
Sex Discrimination Commissioner 1992. *Report on Review of Permanent Exemptions Under the Sex Discrimination Act 1984* Canberra: Australian Government Publishing Service.
Shannon, Moira 1994. 'As long as I draw breath' in Jocelynne A. Scutt (ed.) *Taking a Stand: Women in Politics and Society* Melbourne: Artemis.
Shapcott, David 1988. *The Face of the Rapist* Auckland: Penguin.
Sharp, Rhonda and Broomhill, Ray 1988. *Short-changed: Women and Economic Policies* Sydney: Allen and Unwin.
Shaw, Bruce 1989. ' "For remember": some Aboriginal and white reactions to life histories recently published' *Oral History Association of Australia Journal* 11:87–105.
Sheridan, Alison 1994. 'Women in agriculture – where are they?' in Margaret-Ann Franklin, Leonie M. Short and Elizabeth K. Tether (eds) *Country Women at the Crossroads: Perspectives on the Lives of Rural Australian Women in the 1990s* Armidale: University of New England Press.
Sheridan, Susan 1995. 'Reading the *Women's Weekly*: feminism, femininity and popular culture' in Barbara Caine and Rosemary Pringle (eds) *Transitions: New Australian Feminisms* St Leonards: Allen and Unwin.
Sheridan, Susan 1993a. 'The Woman's Voice on Sexuality' in Susan Magarey et al. (eds) *Debutante Nation: Feminism Contests the 1890s* North Sydney: Allen and Unwin.
Sheridan, Susan 1993b. 'Women's studies' in Refractory Girl (ed.) *Refractory Voices: Feminist Perspectives from Refractory Girl* Sydney: Refractory Girl Feminist Journal.
Shortlander, Sandra 1992. 'The canary down the mine' in Jocelynne A. Scutt (ed.) *As A Woman: Writing Women's Lives* Melbourne: Artemis.
Shreve, Anita 1989. *Women Together, Women Alone: The Legacy of the Consciousness-Raising Movement* New York: Viking Penguin.
Shute, Carmel 1994. 'Unequal partners: women, power and the trade union movement' in Norma Grieve and Ailsa Burns (eds) *Australian Women: Contemporary Feminist Thought* Melbourne: Oxford University Press.
Sievers, Sharon 1992. 'Six (or more) feminists in search of a historian' in Cheryl Johnson-Odim and Margaret Strobel (eds) *Expanding the Boundaries of Women's History* Bloomington and Indianapolis: Indiana University Press.
Simms, Marian 1994. 'Women, the state and public policy' in Stephen Bell and Brian Head (eds) *State, Economy and Public Policy in Australia* Melbourne: Oxford University Press.
Skeggs, Beverley 1995. 'Women's studies in Britain in the 1990s: entitlement cultures and institutional constraints' *Women's Studies International Forum* 18(4):475–85.
Skrapec, Candice 1993. 'The female serial killer: an evolving criminality' in Helen Birch (ed.) *Moving Targets, Women Murder and Representation* London: Virago.

Slattery, Phil 1993. 'The beauty of a rock' in Jocelynne A. Scutt (ed.) *Glorious Age* Melbourne: Artemis.
Smallwood, Gracelyn 1992. 'Demanding more than a great vocabulary' in Jocelynne A. Scutt (ed.) *Breaking Through: Women, Work and Careers* North Melbourne: Artemis.
Smart, Carol 1984. 'Marriage, divorce and women's economic dependency: a discussion of the politics of private maintenance' in Michael D. A. Freeman (ed.) *The State, the Law, and the Family* London: Tavistock.
Smith, Babette 1995. *Mothers and Sons: The Truth About Mother-Son Relationships* St Leonards: Allen and Unwin.
Smith, Shirley and Sykes, Bobbi 1981. *MumShirl* Richmond: Heinemann.
Smith, Sidonie 1993. *Subjectivity, Identity and the Body: Women's Autobiographical Practices in the Twentieth Century* Bloomington and Indianapolis: Indiana University Press.
Smith-Rosenberg, Carroll 1983. 'The female world of love and ritual: relations between women in nineteenth-century America' in Elizabeth Abel and Emily K. Abel (eds) *The Signs Reader: Women, Gender and Scholarship* Chicago: University of Chicago Press.
Snowden, Collette 1981. 'Women's consciousness of their role-structure', thesis presented in partial fulfilment of BA Honours degree in Politics, University of Adelaide.
Sommers, Christina Hoff 1994. *Who Stole Feminism? How Women Have Betrayed Women* New York: Simon and Schuster.
Spearitt, Katie 1994. 'The sexual economics of colonial marriage' in Gail Reekie (ed.) *On the Edge: Women's Experiences of Queensland* St Lucia: University of Queensland Press.
Spender, Dale 1995. *Nattering on the Net: Women, Power and Cyberspace* North Melbourne: Spinifex Press.
Spender, Dale 1990. *Heroines: A Contemporary Anthology of Australian Women Writers* Ringwood: Penguin.
Spender, Dale 1982. *Women of Ideas And What Men Have Done to Them: From Aphra Behn to Adrienne Rich* London: Routledge and Kegan Paul.
Spender, Lynne 1992. 'You can really grow – or simply grow older' in Jocelynne A. Scutt (ed.) *As A Woman: Writing Women's Lives* Melbourne: Artemis.
Spongberg, Mary 1993. 'If she's so great, how come so many pigs dig her? Germaine Greer and the mainstream press' *Women's History Review* 2(3):407–19.
Stacey, Judith 1991. 'Can there be a feminist ethnography?' in Sherna Berger Gluck and Daphne Patai (eds) *Women's Words: The Female Practice of Oral History* New York: Routledge.
Stacey, Judith 1990. *Brave New Families: Stories of Domestic Upheaval in Late Twentieth Century America* New York: Basic Books HarperCollins.
Stainsby, Mary 1995. 'Hearing it from the women themselves' in Jocelynne A. Scutt (ed.) *Singular Women: Reclaiming Spinsterhood* Melbourne: Artemis.
Stevens, Joyce 1993. 'A reasonable exchange' in Jocelynne A. Scutt (ed.) *Glorious Age* Melbourne: Artemis.
Steinem, Gloria 1983. *Outrageous Acts and Everyday Rebellions* New York: New American Library.
Still, Leonie 1991. *Enterprising Women: Australian Women Managers and Entrepreneurs* North Sydney: Allen and Unwin.
Stuart, Andrea 1990. 'Feminism: dead or alive?' in John Rutherford (ed.) *Identity: Community, Culture, Difference* London: Lawrence and Wishart.

Sullivan, Barbara 1994. 'Feminism and female prostitution' in Roberta Perkins, Garry Prestage, Rachel Sharpe and Frances Lovejoy (eds) *Sex Work and Sex Workers in Australia* Sydney: University of New South Wales Press.
Summers, Anne 1994a. *Damned Whores and God's Police* Ringwood: Penguin, 2nd edn, first published in 1975.
Summers, Anne 1994b. Keynote address at the Australian Women's Studies Association 1994 Conference: Women and the Politics of Change, Australian Women's Research Centre, Deakin University, Geelong, 4–6 December.
Summers, Anne 1993. 'The future of feminism – a letter to the next generation' in Refractory Girl (ed.) *Refractory Voices: Feminist Perspectives from Refractory Girl* Sydney: Refractory Girl Feminist Journal.
Summers, Anne 1986. 'Mandarins or missionaries: women in the federal bureaucracy' in Norma Grieve and Ailsa Burns (eds) *Australian Women: New Feminist Perspectives* Melbourne: Oxford University Press.
Summers, Anne 1970. 'Women's consciousness of their role-structure', thesis presented in partial fulfilment of BA Honours degree in Politics, University of Adelaide.
Sweeney, Desmond 1995. 'Aboriginal child welfare: thanks for the apology, but what about real change?' *Aboriginal Law Bulletin* 3(76):4–9.
Sykes, Roberta 1993. *Murawina: Australian Women of High Achievement* Sydney: Doubleday.
Szaszy, Dame Mira 1993. 'Opening my mouth' in Sue Kedgley and Mary Varnham (eds) *Heading Nowhere in a Navy Blue Suit and Other Tales from the Feminist Revolution* Wellington: Daphne Brasel Associates Press.
Szirom, Tricia 1991. *Striking Success: Australian Women Talk About Success* North Sydney: Allen and Unwin.
Tan, Amy 1990. *The Joy Luck Club* London: Minerva (Octopus).
Te Awekotuku, Ngahuia 1991. 'Mana wahine: seeking meanings for ourselves' in Maud Cahill and Christine Dann (eds) *Changing Our Lives: Women Working in the Women's Liberation Movement 1970–1990* Wellington: Bridget Williams Books.
Teather, Elizabeth K. 1994. 'CWA at the Crossroads' in Margaret-Ann Franklin, Leonie M. Short and Elizabeth K. Tether (eds) *Country Women at the Crossroads: Perspectives on the Lives of Rural Australian Women in the 1990s* Armidale: University of New England Press.
Teather, Elizabeth K. and Franklin, Margaret-Ann 1994. 'Signposts for rural women in the 1990s' in Margaret-Ann Franklin, Leonie M. Short and Elizabeth K. Tether (eds) *Country Women at the Crossroads: Perspectives on the Lives of Rural Australia Women in the 1990s* Armidale: University of New England Press.
Temkin, Jennifer 1987. *Rape and the Legal Process* London: Sweet and Maxwell.
Thomas, Lyn 1995. 'In love with Inspector Morse: feminist subculture and quality television' *Feminist Review* 51:1–25.
Thomas, Mark 1989. *Australia in Mind: Thirteen Influential Australian Thinkers* Sydney: Hale and Iremonger.
Thompson, Sharon 1995. *Going All the Way: Teenage Girls' Tales of Sex, Romance and Pregnancy* New York: Hill and Wang.
Thornton, Margaret 1990. *The Liberal Promise: Anti-Discrimination Legislation in Australia* Melbourne: Oxford University Press.
Timaepatua, Monica 1992. 'Nginingawila ngirramini kapi parlingarri purumowu ngawa-ampi ngawa-maniguwi' in Nan Gallagher (ed.) *A Story to Tell: The*

Working Lives of Ten Aboriginal Australians Cambridge: Cambridge University Press.
Tom, Jean 1993. 'Finding the pattern in a rich life' in Jocelynne A. Scutt (ed.) *Glorious Age* Melbourne: Artemis.
Tompsett, Joan 1993. 'Women can do anything' in Jocelynne A. Scutt (ed.) *Glorious Age* Melbourne: Artemis.
Tonkinson, Myrna 1988. 'Sisterhood or Aboriginal servitude? Black women and white women on the Australian frontier' *Aboriginal History* 12(1):27–39.
Townsend, Kathleen 1995. 'Women and labour' *Australian Feminist Studies* 22:1–8.
Trioli, Virginia 1996. *Generation f: Sex, Power and the Young Feminist* Port Melbourne: Minerva.
Vallesi, Mariella 1993. 'Seasons' in Barbara Walsh (ed.) *Growing Up Italian in Australia: Eleven Young Australian Women Talk About Their Childhood* Sydney: State Library of New South Wales.
Vasta, Ellie 1993. 'Immigrant women and the politics of resistance' *Australian Feminist Studies* 18:5–23.
Vasta, Ellie 1992. 'The second generation' in Stephen Castles et al. (eds) *Australia's Italians: Culture and Community in a Changing Society* St Leonards: Allen and Unwin.
Vasta, Ellie 1991. 'Gender, class and ethnic relations: the domestic and work experiences of Italian migrant women in Australia' in Gill Bottomley et al. (eds) *Intersexions: Gender/Class/Culture/Ethnicity* North Sydney: Allen and Unwin.
Vasta, Ellie, Rando, Gaetano, Castles, Stephen and Alcorso, Caroline 1992. 'The Italo-Australian community on the Pacific Rim' in Stephen Castles et al. (eds) *Australia's Italians: Culture and Community in a Changing Society* St Leonards: Allen and Unwin.
Walby, Sylvia 1990. *Theorizing Patriarchy* Oxford: Basil Blackwell.
Walden, Inara 1995. ' "To send her to service": Aboriginal domestic servants' *Aboriginal Law Bulletin* 3(76):12–14.
Walker, Viv 1991. 'A working-class woman meets feminism' in Maud Cahill and Christine Dann (eds) *Changing Our Lives: Women Working in the Women's Liberation Movement 1970–1990* Wellington: Bridget Williams Books.
Walters, Suzanna Danuta 1992. *Lives Together/Worlds Apart: Mothers and Daughters in Popular Culture* Berkeley, Los Angeles and Oxford: University of California Press.
Walwicz, Ania 1990. 'Australia' in Ken Goodwin and Alan Lawson (eds) *The Macmillan Anthology of Australian Literature* Melbourne: Macmillan.
Ward, Glenyse 1991. *Unna You Fullas* Broome: Magabala.
Ward, Glenyse 1987. *Wandering Girl* Broome: Magabala.
Ware, Susan 1993. *Still Missing: Amelia Earhart and the Search for Modern Feminism* New York: W. W. Norton and Company.
Warner, Lesley 1994. 'Educational needs and opportunites for rural women: the Queensland experience' in Margaret-Ann Franklin, Leonie M. Short and Elizabeth K. Tether (eds) *Country Women at the Crossroads: Perspectives on the Lives of Rural Australian Women in the 1990s* Armidale: University of New England Press.
Watson, Sophie 1990. 'Feminist cultural production: the Tampax mafia, an interview with Chris Westwood of the Belvoir Street Theatre' in Sophie Watson (ed.) *Playing the State: Australian Feminist Interventions* Sydney: Allen and Unwin.

Watson, Ian 1994. 'Class memory: an alternative approach to class identity' *Labour History* 67:23–41.
Watson, Irene 1992. 'Surviving as a people' in Jocelynne A. Scutt (ed.) *Breaking Through: Women, Work and Careers* North Melbourne: Artemis.
Watson, Lilla 1994. 'Keynote address', Australian Women's Studies Association 1994 Conference: Women and the Politics of Change, Australian Women's Research Centre, Deakin University, Geelong, 4–6 December.
Watson, Lilla 1987. 'Sister, black is the colour of my soul' in Jocelynne A. Scutt (ed.) *Different Lives: Reflections on the Women's Movement and Visions of its Future* Ringwood: Penguin.
Watson, Sophie (ed.) 1990. *Playing the State: Australian Feminist Interventions* Sydney: Allen and Unwin.
Watts, Carolyn 1992. 'No well lit path' in Jocelynne A. Scutt (ed.) *Breaking Through: Women, Work and Careers* North Melbourne: Artemis.
Wearing, Betsy 1984. *The Ideology of Motherhood* Sydney: George Allen and Unwin.
Weeks, Wendy 1994. 'Introduction' in Wendy Weeks (ed.) *Women Working Together: Lessons from Feminist Women's Services* Melbourne: Longman Cheshire.
West, Guida and Blomberg, Rhoda Lois 1990. 'Reconstructing social protest from a feminist perspective' in Guida West and Rhoda Lois Blomberg (eds) *Women and Social Protest* New York: Oxford University Press.
West, Rosemary (ed.) 1987. *The Changing Role of Women: 21 Years of Accent* Melbourne: Age Education Unit.
Whitbread, Anne 1988. 'Female teachers are women first: sexual harassment at work' in Dale Spender and Elizabeth Sarah (eds) *Learning to Lose: Sexism in Education* London: Women's Press.
Whiting, Pat 1972. 'Female sexuality: its political implications' in Michelene Wandor (compiler) *The Body Politic: Women's Liberation in Britain* London: Stage.
Whittier, Nancy 1995. *Feminist Generations: The Persistence of the Radical Women's Movement* Philadelphia: Temple University Press.
Wigmore, John 1970. *On Evidence* Boston: Little Brown.
Williams, Elizabeth 1987. 'Aboriginal first, woman second' in Jocelynne A. Scutt (ed.) *Different Lives: Reflections on the Women's Movement and Visions of its Future* Ringwood: Penguin.
Williams, Sue 1995. 'We are feminists but . . . ' *Australian Weekend Magazine* 28–29 January 1995:19–27.
Winkler, Robin and van Keppel, Margaret 1984. *Relinquishing Mothers in Adoption* Melbourne: Institute of Family Studies.
Winship, Janice 1985. ' "A girl needs to get street-wise": magazines for the 1980s' *Feminist Review* 21:25–46.
Wolf, Naomi 1993. *Fire with Fire* New York: Random House.
Wolf, Naomi 1990. *The Beauty Myth* London: Chatto and Windus.
Women's Economic Think Tank 1991. *Sole Parents* Oyster Bay, Sydney: Sole Parents' Union.
Women's Health Policy Unit, Queensland Health 1993a. *Towards a Queensland Women's Health Policy – Social Justice for Women – Green Paper* Brisbane: Queensland Health.
Women's Health Policy Unit, Queensland Health 1993b. *Draft Protocols for Working with Women Who Have Been Raped and/or Sexually Assaulted* Brisbane: Queensland Health.

Women's Policy Unit, 1994. 'A profile of women in Queensland', leaflet accompanying the *Women's Budget Statement 1994–95* Brisbane: Women's Policy Unit, Office of the Cabinet, Queensland.

Women's Policy Unit 1992a. *Women's Experience of Crimes of Personal Violence: A Gender Analysis of the 1991 Queensland Crime Victims Survey* Brisbane: Women's Policy Unit, Office of the Cabinet, Queensland.

Women's Policy Unit 1992b. *Stop Violence Against Women: Queensland Government Statement of Achievements* Brisbane: Women's Policy Unit, Office of the Cabinet, Queensland.

Woodland, Jacqui 1989. 'Women's studies at Australian universities – looking towards the nineties', paper presented at the Australian Women's Studies Association First National Conference, Adelaide, 6–8 August.

Wyn, Johanna 1990. 'Working-class girls and educational outcomes: is self-esteem an issue?' in Jane Kenway and Sue Willis (eds) *Hearts and Minds: Self-esteem and the Schooling of Girls* London: Falmer Press.

Yeatman, Anna 1990. *Bureaucrats, Technocrats, Femocrats: Essays on the Contemporary Australian State* North Sydney: Allen and Unwin.

Young, Iris Marion 1990. *Throwing Like a Girl and Other Essays in Feminist Philosophy and Social Theory* Bloomington and Indianapolis: Indiana University Press.

Index

abortion, ix, 15, 23, 25, 104–6, 238 n.4,
affirmative action, *see* equal opportunities and legislation
agency, 2–3, 8, 9, 12, 13–17, 66–7, 128, 130–1, 134, 135, 139, 141, 183–4, 211, 225; *see also* life histories
anti-discrimination legislation, 71–2, 76, 81, 82, 237 n.9; *see also* Sex Discrimination Act
architecture, 79–80
Arnot, Jea, 93, 126
assault, domestic, 15, 16, 43–4, 67, 103, 118–19, 120, 141, 142, 159–61, 199, 222–3, 243 n.1, 243 n.2, 243–4 n.3, 244 n.4, 244 n.8
assault, sexual, ix, 5, 14–15, 20, 32, 34, 42–3, 102, 118–19, 166–7, 168, 218, 221–2, 235 n.7; *see also* harassment, sexual

baby boomers, *see* generations of women
backlash against feminism, 4, 182–3, 186, 204, 218
Bandler, Faith, 170
Beauvoir, Simone de, 133–4, 137
biography, 1–2, 8, 10, 240–1 n.1
bra-burning, 144, 146–7, 163
breast-feeding, 101–2

Campaign Against Moral Persecution, 151

career counselling at school, 53–4
careers, *see* work
childbirth, 11, 98, 101, 103
childcare, *see* housework and childcare
childcare policies, 22, 109, 239 n.10
choice, women's, *see* agency
church, women in, 178–80
class and feminism, *see* feminism as white middle-class movement, feminism and structural disadvantage
cohabitation, 11, 23, 193
consciousness-raising, 13, 36, 129
Country Women's Association, 21, 171, 174–7, 203, 245 n.15
courtship, 112
Cusack, Dymphna, 134
custody of children, 117, 240 n.15

discrimination
 in education, 49, 53, 54–6, 59–60, 61, 63, 185, 191; against boys, 186, 245–6 n.4
 in employment and work, 63, 66, 72–3, 76–7, 78, 80–1, 238 n.10, 189–90, 217
 by parents, 50
Dinesen, Isak, 1
divorce, 11, 65, 96, 116–20
divorce, economic effects of, 117–18, 240 n.16
domestic violence, *see* assault, domestic

276

INDEX

Dowse, Sara, 234 n.5
economic rationalism, 5–6, 213
education, 11, 27, 54, 184–8
  experiences of, 16–17, 25, 32, 55, 137–40, 180, 185, 187–8
  feminist impact on, 184–6
  mature-age entry and experiences, 25, 58, 60–7
  mature age entry and husbands' support, 64–5
educational aspirations
  for daughters, 24–5, 29, 47–8, 51, 186–7
  in daughters, 25, 46, 48, 49–50, 52–3, 62–3
  suggested by schools, 53–6, 57
  see also TAFE, universities, schools, single sex schools and classrooms
engineering, women in, 58, 88, 90
equal opportunities initiatives and legislation, 57–8, 71–2, 75, 80–1, 85, 188, 224, 243 n.19, 246 n.5
equal pay, 21, 73–5; *see also* work
equality of women, support for, 69, 95, 144, 182, 222
ethnic communities
  significance of, 157–61
  and different responses to domestic violence, 160–1
ethnicity and feminism, *see* feminism as white middle-class movement, feminism, Indigenous, feminism, Non-English Speaking Background women's, feminism and structural disadvantage

factory work, experiences of, 85–6
fairness, popular senses of, 29, 50, 67–8, 73, 74–5, 76, 87, 130
family planning, *see* reproductive choices
family experiences, 30, 67, 157
family formation and structure, 11, 30, 246 n.12
family wage, 73
farm women, 78–9, 171–7, 244 n.12, 244 n.13, 245 n.14
  and feminism, 156
fashion, 39–42, 147, 148, 197, 202
fashion and workplace requirements, 40–2, 92–3
Faust, Beatrice, 4

Female Eunuch, The, x, 2, 133, 135–7, 214; *see also* Greer, Germaine
femininity, 1, 26–7, 28, 40, 83, 183, 192, 223–4, 246 n.7
  and assault, 34, 44
  emphasised, 235 n.6
  and sports, 33
  and women's use of their bodies, 26
femocrats, femocracy, 22–3, 231 n.4, 234 n.6
feminism
  coined as a term, xi
  and changing expectations, self-evaluations, 63, 76, 77, 121–2, 128–43, 183, 192–3, 211
  and the church, 178–80
  criticisms of, 3–5, 144
  daughters', 196–9, 213
  and farm women, 176–7, 245 n.16
  Indigenous Australian, 154–5, 167, 170
  nineteenth-century, 19–21
  Non-English Speaking Background women's, 161–3, 213–14, 244 n.5
  popular, 3, 143–7, 182, 196, 211–12, 216, 222
  radical, man-hating, 147, 148, 192, 199, 216, 221, 223, 242 n.14
  and social justice, 215–16, 247 n.2
  and structural disadvantage, 212–19
  success of, 3–5, 144; *see also* equality of women, support for
  victim, 219–22
  as white middle-class movement, x, 6, 123–4, 133, 138, 146, 152, 154–5, 156–7, 159, 161–71, 213–5, 219, 220
  and women's issues, representation in the media, 145–6, 198, 241–2 n.9, 242 n.10, 242 n.12, 244 n.11, 246 n.8
  see also women's liberation movement, women's movement
feminist, women's self-definitions as, 143, 212–15
feminist literature
  children's, 133, 241 n.2
  impact of 132–7, 176–7
fertility, 11, 20, 99, 205–6, 238 n.3; *see also* abortion, reproductive choices

First Stone, The, see Garner, Helen
French, Marilyn, 63, 121, 134
friends, female, 65, 154

Garner, Helen, 3, 85, 201–2, 224, 237 n.7
generations of women, ix, 3, 10–12, 22, 34–5, 46–7, 226–8, 232 n.9, 233 n.13
  and different expectations, 182, 183–4, 195, 205–9
  and education, 186–8
  and feminist disputes between, 126–7, 194, 195–6, 246 n.6
  and marriage and family expectations, 96, 201–2, 238 n.1
  and occupational expectations, 71, 94, 188–9
  and sexuality, 38–9
  and tertiary study, 61–2, 65–6
glass ceiling, 5, 88
Greenwood, Irene, 126, 146
Greer, Germaine, 2, 36, 95, 126, 132, 135–6, 138, 140, 144–5, 177, 245 n.2

harassment, sexual, 4, 16, 78, 81–4, 88, 89, 186, 242 n.11, 245 n.3, 246 n.5; *see also* Garner, Helen
housewives, perceived status of, 111, 113, 114, 139
housework and childcare, 5, 27, 30, 69, 107–10, 113–16, 231 n.3
  husbands' and wives' compared, 114–16, 130, 173, 202–3, 208, 239 n.11, 239 n.13, 240 n.14
housework, daughters' and sons' compared, 28–30, 234 n.3

Indigenous women and white women, mutual support, 170
Indigenous women's political issues, 165–6, 168–9
internet, 241 n.4
interviews, 8, 9; *see also* methodology

Lawrence, Carmen, 3, 21, 22, 24, 56
legal profession, 20, 233 n.3
leisure pursuits, 28, 69; *see also* sports
lesbianism
  and feminism, 139, 144, 147–9, 152–3, 163, 242 n.14

and parental reactions, 152
and realisation of sexual orientation, 150–1
lesbians, lesbianism, 39, 60, 72, 136, 147–53,
Lessing, Doris, 137, 220
life histories, life history method, 6–8, 14
life plan, daughters' 206–9
Livin' Large, 35–6

management, women in, 87–90, 238 n.10; *see also* workforce, sex segregation of
marriage, 11, 21, 23, 96, 110–12, 233 n.11
marriage bar, ix, 72–4
marriage, motherhood and work, assumed conflict between, 44–5, 50, 53, 93–4, 109, 192
marriage rates, 11, 23, 96, 234 n.8
masculinity, 5, 7, 20, 28, 35, 146, 162, 182–3, 200–5, 245–6 n.4
masculinity, hegemonic, 235 n.6
mature-age entry, *see* education, mature-age entry
media, representation of feminism and women's issues, *see* feminism and women's issues, representation in the media
menstruation, 31, 37
methodology, 6–9, 229–30; *see also* interviews, sampling methods
Mitchell, Dame Roma, 20
modelling, 40–2, 197
motherhood, 21, 25, 61, 97–104, 106–21, 206, 207
  state support for, 108–9
mothering and feminism, assumed conflict between, 92, 104, 119–20, 121, 139, 177, 242 n.14
mothers' relationships
  with daughters, 94–5
  with sons, 200–4

non-traditional occupations, 148, 189–91
Niland, Carmel, 56, 234 n.6

object relations theory, 200–1, 246 n.10
occupational segregation, *see* workforce, sex segregation

INDEX

Office of the Status of Women, 23
Oodgeroo Noonuccual, 170
O'Shane, Pat, 165, 167, 170

policing, women in, 84, 190–1
politics, political participation, 20, 22, 89–90, 233 n.2
property settlement, *see* divorce
prostitution, *see* sex workers
Puberty Blues, 34–5
public hotel bars, women's access to, 131–2

queer theory, 242 n.16
quotas for women, 4, 216–18

racism, 66, 158, 159, 165–7, 169, 187–8, 202
  in women's movement, 162, 167
rape, date rape, *see* assault, sexual
refuges, *see* assault, domestic
Reid, Elizabeth, 23, 234 n.6
relationships with men, young women's, 192–3
reproductive choices, 36–7, 99–101; *see also* abortion
Reynolds, Margaret, 141, 170
romance fiction, 31–2, 97, 112, 133
Ryan, Edna, 36, 126

sampling methods, 10, 12, 229–30
secretarial work, 82, 83, 86, 88
Sex Discrimination Act, 178, 237 n.6; *see also* anti-discrimination legislation
sex education, *see* reproductive choices
sex workers, 7–8, 91–3
sexual assault, *see* assault, sexual
sexual experiences of sex, 31, 36, 37–8
sexual revolution, 36
sexuality, beliefs and prescriptions concerning, 20, 21, 32, 34, 35, 37–9, 83
single sex schools and classrooms, x, 56–7, 184–5
socially theorised life history, *see* life histories
sports, 27, 28, 32–4, 35, 234 n.4
Street, Jessie, 36, 126
structures, 114, 131, 141, 197
  and feminism, 23–4, 125, 210–11, 216–19, 220, 222, 225; *see also* agency

suffrage, 19, 233 n.1
Summers, Anne, ix, 2, 126, 138
superannuation, 236 n.3

TAFE educational experiences, 57–8, 235 n.3
teaching, women in, 40–1, 74–5, 75–6, 79, 89, 187–8

Union of Australian Women, 21, 22, 74
unions, unionism, 70, 73, 74, 77, 82, 236 n.2, 237 n.5, 237 n.9
universities as white middle-class environments, 60
university education, 58–67, 235 n.3; *see also* education

violence, *see* assault

wages, women's, ix, 4, 231 n.2, 236 n.4; *see also* equal pay
women's biography, *see* biography
Women's Electoral Lobby, 22, 140–1
women's liberation movement, 2, 12, 19, 22, 140, 233 n.12
women's movement, 2, 231 n.5, 234 n.7
  definition, 124–5
women's organisations and groups, 59, 140–3
Women's Room, The, *see* French, Marilyn
women's studies, 137–40, 220–1, 241 n.6
Woolf, Virginia, 134
work
  and dress codes, *see* fashion and workplace requirements
  expectations concerning, 44–5, 48–9, 90, 188–9
  and family, tensions between, 69, 73, 75–6, 101, 203, 205–9
  paid, 4, 11, 15, 189–92, 232 n.10, 236 n.1
  unpaid, *see* housework and childcare
workforce, sex segregation in, 69–71, 172, 178, 189, 241 n.5, 242, n.13
workplace cultures, 78–81, 88–90